THE ROLE OF SPEECH PERCEPTION IN PHONOLOGY

The Role of Speech Perception in Phonology

Edited by

Elizabeth Hume and Keith Johnson

Department of Linguistics
The Ohio State University
Columbus, Ohio

Academic Press

San Diego   New York   Boston
London   Sydney   Tokyo   Toronto

Academic Press
a Harcourt Science and Technology Company
525 B Street, Suite 1900, San Diego, California 92101-4495
http://www.academicpress.com

Academic Press Limited
Harcourt Place, 32 Jamestown Road, London NW1 7BY, UK
http://www.academicpress.com

Library of Congress Catalog Card Number: 00-111385

International Standard Book Number: 0-12-361351-5

PRINTED IN UNITED STATES OF AMERICA
01   02   03   04   05   06   SB   9   8   7   6   5   4   3   2   1

Contents

Foreword   vii
Björn Lindblom

Contributors   xiii

Preface   xv

Section I

The Interplay of Speech Perception and Phonology

Chapter 1
A Model of the Interplay of Speech Perception and Phonology
Elizabeth Hume and Keith Johnson   3

Chapter 2
The Interplay of Phonology and Perception Considered from the
Perspective of Perceptual Organization
Robert E. Remez   27

Section II

The Perceptual Basis of Phonological Systems

Chapter 3
Patterns of Perceptual Compensation and Their Phonological
Consequences
Patrice Speeter Beddor, Rena Arens Krakow, and
Stephanie Lindemann   55

Chapter 4
Markedness and Consonant Confusion Asymmetries
Steve S. Chang, Madelaine C. Plauché, and John J. Ohala   79

Chapter 5
Effects of Vowel Context on Consonant Place Identification:
Implications for a Theory of Phonologization
Jennifer Cole and Khalil Iskarous 103

Chapter 6
Adaptive Design of Sound Systems: Some Auditory Considerations
Randy L. Diehl, Michelle R. Molis, and Wendy A. Castleman 123

Chapter 7
The Limits of Phonetic Determinism in Phonology:
*NC Revisited
Larry M. Hyman 141

Chapter 8
Contrast Dispersion and Russian Palatalization
Jaye Padgett 187

Chapter 9
Directional Asymmetries in Place Assimilation:
A Perceptual Account
Donca Steriade 219

Chapter 10
Perceptual Cues in Contrast Maintenance
Richard Wright. 251

Index 279

Foreword

Numerous recent developments show that phonologists are making serious efforts to explicitly link their descriptions of sound patterns more tightly to the production and perception of speech than was previously the case. This movement now seems to be gaining momentum on the international scene.

The present volume is an important contribution to this paradigm. The common theme of the papers is the role of perception in phonology. This topic is illuminated by a number of studies dealing with, for instance, how speech percepts change when contextual information is present or lost, and what the consequences of such effects are for phonology; how listener misperceptions shed light on why sound changes often tend to be asymmetrical; how back vowel harmony patterns can facilitate the perception of consonant place; how the need for auditory distinctiveness tends to mold phonological systems; patterns of Russian palatalization analyzed in terms of a criterion of adaptive dispersion; the finding that the formant transitions of CV syllables offer the listener more robust place cues than VC sequences. Attempts are also made to formally represent and model the interaction between perceptual processes and phonology.

This theme serves as a reminder of the broader context in which the present book should be read, viz., the longstanding, but so far unresolved, controversy between, for want of better terms, the "formalist" and "functionalist" camps.

In this book a meeting of the minds takes place. Experimentalists and phonologists of a formalist background join forces to show why phonology is perceptual. That by itself is significant and sends a clear message to the field.

Most scientists would undoubtedly endorse the idea that, when they cannot make direct observations of the mechanisms responsible for the phenomena they are describing, they are forced to postulate (invent without *independent* empirical motivation) an abstract formal model to account for the data. In the absence of direct experimental data on the underlying mechanisms, this model is their theory of the phenomena. That is indeed how science works, although not the only way (more anon).

By analogy, when linguists cannot make direct observations of the mechanisms responsible for the phenomena they are describing — for the sake of argument, let us say they cannot "get inside the mind" (see below) — they are forced to postulate (invent without *independent* empirical motivation) an abstract formal model to account for the data. Under the conditions mentioned, this process is the (perfectly respectable) origin of "formalist" descriptions in linguistics.

But would it be correct to say that scientists would stop as soon as they had a descriptively adequate abstract formal model and not proceed to ask if its underlying structure is physically real or not? No, such an account would be incomplete and would therefore misrepresent general science in a significant way.

Assume that two different mathematical descriptions of the same phenomena have been proposed. They are equally accurate in their numerical predictions. One of them is a kind of black box whose contents do not matter as long as it describes the data satisfactorily. The other is derived from facts and principles established in empirical research on different, but related, topics. Which one would be preferred? The answer is straightforward: the one deduced from the "realities" already independently established.

Normal science is conducted on the basis of a systematic interaction between predictive theory construction and checks against observed facts. The "physical reality" criterion comes in at two levels: in evaluating the predictions against the data, and in constraining the choice of the theory's most basic assumptions.

Quantitative descriptions that have minimal empirical constraints on their fundamental premises and inner structure are essentially "*curve-fitting*" exercises. They are totally in the hands of the surface data, their formal structures having no other motivation than that of making the right predictions. At the other end of the continuum are "*first-principles*" accounts, that is, frameworks that aim at maximizing their reliance on independent knowledge and that can move their "axioms" deeper as more and more is being learned. This second part of theory construction is a crucial part of the dynamics of general science and an activity that linguistic inquiry cannot ignore with impunity.

Examples of the dramatic interplay between theory and experiment are numerous in the history of science. For instance, consider the grand quest for a "final theory" of physics (Weinberg, 1992). This is a theory whose goal is to unify previous successful and comprehensive, but nonetheless, less complete theories, for example, Newtonian gravity, thermodynamics, and the electromagnetic wave theory of light.

While science can be said to distinguish between theories that are explanatory and non-explanatory, it is important to note that, among the former, there are no absolute explanations, only a continuum of deeper and deeper accounts. Hence, the success of a theory is, among other things, to be measured relative to the depth at which we find its axioms. The choice of axioms in a theory is constantly being challenged by an eternal search for ever more profound and accurate descriptions. The physicist's "dream of a final theory" is an instance of this.

By analogy, "Is it psychologically real?" is always going to be a legitimate question in the behavioral sciences. Raising it should not be seen as an irrational and non-professional refusal to "go abstract" or to acknowledge the important and legitimate role of formal models in science. It is simply an expression of a methodologically respectable stance that helps minimize the problem of producing epiphenomenal descriptions inherent in exclusively data-driven theorizing.

This volume provides a great deal of compelling evidence that perception plays an important role in shaping sound patterns and that it should therefore be accorded an explanatory role in linguistic theory. If the human mind is partly shaped by the channels through which we access the world, then the prospects of getting experimental access to it would seem rather favorable.

An experience from my student years comes to mind as I consider these issues. By my supervisor, Gunnar Fant, I had been asked to make some short-term spectra of synthetic vowels. When I showed him what I had produced on the lab spectrograph, he dismissed it and told me that I had obviously overloaded the machine. I was at first a bit shocked. What did he know about that? He had not been there. So I persisted, believing that I had done all I could not to distort the signal. He would not listen and talked about "spurious" formants. What I did not know was that the signal went to the spectrograph's VU-meter by way of a preamplifier. That meant that an acceptable reading on the VU-meter was no guarantee for a clean signal. Finally, I saw that I had collected some pretty bad data.

Later I also realized that it had been Fant's superior theoretical understanding that enabled him to spot the spurious spectral peaks and valleys and draw the conclusion about the overloading. Knowing acoustic theory, he had a very clear idea of what a "possible formant-pattern" ought to look like for a vowel. He was therefore able to correctly reject the data, whereas with my very limited understanding of acoustic theory I was all too eager to measure the frequency of any spectral maximum and be led astray by what I naively thought was a set of carefully collected "facts."

I learned at least two things from this experience. A good theory based on independently established knowledge — in this case, the acoustic theory of speech production — is a valuable tool and a desirable prerequisite when one tries to distinguish between experimental fact and artifact. The question "Are these phenomena physically real?" does in fact arise routinely in physics and other experimental disciplines. It is a real issue.

The second lesson taught was that, while it is true that the acoustic theory of speech production is a formal mathematical theory, there was no way that this theory could have been developed according to the formalist strategy advocated for research in linguistics. In other words, it could not have been put together as a result of observing a large number of speech spectra, looking for regularities and then systematizing them and proposing a formal model with underlying abstract constructs such as formants. The more I studied acoustic phonetics, the more vividly a different story unfolded. It became evident that historically this theory has been derived from "physical realities" independently established such as the experimentally observed properties of elastic media and the speed of sound, and the principle of conservation of mass. In other words, it had not been postulated/invented from large amounts of spectral display data but derived deductively from independently known facts and principles.

The debate triggered by Jackendoff (1989) and Anderson's (1989) review of Johnson-Laird (1988) should also be mentioned here. G. A. Miller (1990) made the following concluding remarks about it:

> [M]y own view is that linguists and psychologists subscribe to different theories of explanation. Linguists tend to accept simplifications as explanations. For example, a grammarian who can replace language-specific rewriting rules with X-bar theory and lexicalization feels that he has explained something: the work formerly done by a vast array of specific rules can now be done with a simple schema. For a psychologist, on the other hand, an explanation is something phrased in terms of cause and effect, antecedent and subsequent, stimulus and response. *To an experimental psychologist, X-bar theory is not an explanation: rather, if it is true, it is something to be explained.*
>
> [. . .] until simplification can be seen as a clear step toward causal laws — a halfway house, so to speak, on the road to causal explanation — the average psychologist, like the average layperson, will remain skeptical of the grammarian's claims of scientific progress. (Miller, 1990, p. 321, italics mine)

My aim here has been to suggest that a purely formalist approach conforms *only in part* with how good science is done in other disciplines. It is correct to assume that, when direct observations of the underlying mechanisms cannot be made, an abstract formal model has to be invented/postulated to account for the data. But it is not the highest ranking approach. The most highly valued description is the "first-principles" account, the quest for which is an ever ongoing process. Given that observation, we realize that, over the long term, physics and the natural sciences are solidly "functionalist."

To clarify, rejecting a purely formalist approach does not mean saying no to formal models. Nor does it mean rejecting the possibility (brought up by Hyman in this volume) of grammars having a residue of idiosyncratic (functionally inexplicable) properties. However, it *does* imply a more bullish market for functionalism in linguistics.

Where does all this leave the idea that there is a limit to what can be explained with the aid of phonetics and external factors? What formal residual properties of grammar will they leave unexplained? In my opinion, that is an empirical question. Whether we assume that this "formal residue" will be large or small, our strategy for finding out will be the same: formulating and testing theories that make maximum use of phonetic and other constraints. Let us be open-minded about the explanatory scope of external vs. formal factors. Let us follow the example set by the present contributors for perception and try to follow it up also in other domains such as production and development. Let us moreover explore the possibility of modeling "formal" attributes of sound structures as *emergent* processes (Lindblom, 2000).

I would like to conclude these remarks by reviewing some neuro-developmental work with major positive implications for the perceptual approach taken in this book.

A few decades ago, in Nobel Prize-winning work, Hubel & Wiesel showed that the visual cortex of cats has a complex anatomical structure. It is organized in columns whose cells have certain specialized "feature detecting" properties. Some have an "orientation preference" responding best to edges at some particular angle. Others show "ocular dominance," responding preferentially to inputs from one eye or the other. This organization is distributed across the visual cortex in so-called orientation columns and ocular dominance columns.

It might be assumed that anything so specialized must be mostly genetically determined, but it turns out that animals are not born with these complex columnar structures in place. To develop normally they presuppose visual experience. That has been inferred from experiments with newborn kittens who were kept in total darkness for several weeks and were then found to be permanently blind, though their eyes and brain were normal in all other respects.

Similar results were recently reported for ferrets (Sharma *et al.*, 2000) whose visual systems were manipulated after birth by rerouting visual nerve fibers to the auditory cortex, a region whose neuroanatomy differs from that of the visual cortex. Subsequent examination of the ferrets' auditory areas revealed the existence of orientation modules, that is, a columnar organization similar to that of the normal visual cortex.

What these findings suggest is that the ocular dominance and orientation columns are not innate in the strong sense of being entirely prespecified in the genes. Rather, they are *emergent* structures formed in a self-organizing way through the interaction of visual input and genetic factors. The implications for phonology and linguistics are numerous.

First, note the striking contrast between the above findings and the description of the "language organ" prespecified in our genetic endowment and postulated by proponents of Universal Grammar. Chomsky would no doubt tell us that it would be wrongheaded to ask "Is UG biologically real?" But if we do so anyway, the non-biological qualities of UG are rather dramatically exposed by the neuro-biological facts just reported.

A further implication is this: what may look absolutely idiosyncratic and at first blush impossible to relate to "external factors" could perhaps after all be explained in terms of perceptual experience (Johnson & Mullenix, 1987) and as products of emergent development.

REFERENCES

Anderson, S. R. (1981). Why phonology isn't "natural." *Linguistic Inquiry, 12,* 493–539.

Anderson, S. R. (1989). P. N. Johnson-Laird, *The computer and the mind* (1988). *Language, 65*(4), 800–811.

Jackendoff, R. S. (1988). Why are they saying these things about us? *Natural Language and Linguistic Theory 6,* 435–442.

Johnson, K., & Mullenix, J. (1997). Complex representations used in speech processing: Overview of the book. In K. Johnson & J. Mullenix (Eds.), *Talker variability in speech processing* (pp. 1–8). San Diego: Academic Press.

Johnson-Laird, P. N. (1988). *The computer and the mind.* Cambridge: Harvard University Press.

Lindblom, B. (2000). Developmental origins of adult phonology: The interplay between phonetic emergents and evolutionary adaptations. In K. Kohler, R. Diehl, O. Engstrand, & J. Kingston (Eds.), *Speech communication and language development: Adaptation and emergence.* Special issue of *Phonetica.*

Miller, G. A. (1990). Linguists, psychologists, and the cognitive sciences. *Language, 66*(2), 317–322.

Sharma, J., Angelucci, A., & Mriganka, S. (2000). Induction of visual orientation modules in auditory cortex. *Nature, 404,* 841–847.

Weinberg, S. (1992). *Dreams of a final theory.* New York: Pantheon.

Björn Lindblom
Stockholm University
University of Texas, Austin

Contributors

Numbers in parentheses indicate the pages on which the authors' contributions begin.

Patrice Speeter Beddor (55). Department of Linguistics, University of Michigan, Ann Arbor <beddor@umich.edu>

Wendy A. Castleman (123). Interaction Technology Laboratory, Motorola PCS, Piscataway, New Jersey <wendy.castleman@motorola.com> (formerly Department of Psychology, University of Texas, Austin)

Steve S. Chang (79). Department of Linguistics, University of California, Berkeley <changs@socrates.berkeley.edu>

Jennifer Cole (103). Department of Linguistics, University of Illinois, Urbana-Champaign <j-cole5@uiuc.edu>

Randy L. Diehl (123). Department of Psychology, University of Texas, Austin <diehl@psy.utexas.edu>

Elizabeth Hume (3). Department of Linguistics, The Ohio State University, Columbus <ehume@ling.ohio-state.edu>

Larry M. Hyman (141). Department of Linguistics, University of California, Berkeley <hyman@socrates.berkeley.edu>

Khalil Iskarous (103). Haskins Laboratories, New Haven, Connecticut <iskarous@alvin.haskins.yale.edu> (formerly Department of Linguistics, University of Illinois, Urbana-Champaign)

Keith Johnson (3). Department of Linguistics, The Ohio State University, Columbus <kjohnson@ling.ohio-state.edu>

Rena Arens Krakow (55). Department of Communication Sciences, Temple University, Philadelphia, Pennsylvania <rkrakow@unix.temple.edu>

Björn Lindblom (xi). Department of Linguistics, University of Texas, Austin <blindblom@mail.utexas.edu>

Stephanie Lindemann (55). Department of Linguistics, University of Michigan, Ann Arbor <lindeman@umich.edu>

Michelle R. Molis (123). Department of Psychology, University of Texas, Austin <molis@mail.utexas.edu>

John J. Ohala (79). Department of Linguistics, University of California, Berkeley <ohala@socrates.berkeley.edu>

Jaye Padgett (187). Department of Linguistics, Stevenson College, University of California, Santa Cruz <padgett@cats.ucsc.edu>

Madelaine C. Plauché (79). Department of Linguistics, University of California, Berkeley <mcp@socrates.berkeley.edu>

Robert E. Remez (27). Department of Psychology, Barnard College, New York <remez@columbia.edu>

Donca Steriade (219). Department of Linguistics, University of California, Los Angeles <steriade@humnet.ucla.edu>

Richard Wright (251). Department of Linguistics, University of Washington, Seattle <rawright@u.washington.edu>

Preface

The articulatory foundations of language sound patterns have been explored for centuries and serve as a solid base for concepts in modern phonological theory both regarding the representation of phonological units and the motivation of phonological processes. An early attempt to rationalize phonology in terms of a combined articulatory/auditory model (e.g., Jakobson *et al.*, 1951/1976) was spurred by technological advances in instrumental phonetics — particularly the development of the sound spectrograph — but was not widely adopted because the intellectual base needed for correct evaluation of acoustic phonetic cues was not sufficiently well developed. The intervening years have seen further advances in technology and a dramatic expansion of the base of knowledge regarding processes of speech perception. These developments lead naturally to a reappraisal and reconsideration of the role of perceptual phenomena in phonology, which is currently flourishing in several research centers throughout the world.

Concurrent with these developments in speech perception research are developments in phonological theory that open the way to incorporate insights from speech perception research into formal models of phonology. In particular, the trend to adopt constraint-based models of phonology has led to increased focus on the articulatory and perceptual bases of constraints in these models. As a result, there is a renewed interest in exploring the role of perceptual phenomena as a source of explanation for crosslinguistic sounds patterns.

These developments in speech perception and phonology provide a solid foundation for significant progress in elucidating the sound structures of language. This volume is intended as a contribution to this growing field of enquiry. By presenting this collection of interdisciplinary studies, we also hope to encourage effective future interactions among speech perception researchers and phonologists as a means of coming to a more comprehensive understanding of language sound structures.

The chapters in this volume are based on talks presented at the satellite meeting "The Role of Perceptual Phenomena in Phonology" held in conjunction with the XIVth International Congress of Phonetic Sciences. The goal of this satellite meeting was to provide a forum for interaction among speech perception researchers and phonology researchers, and consisted of invited and contributed papers by researchers in each of these fields. The specific goals of the meeting were to identify classes of perceptual mechanisms that may offer promising insights into phonological patterns, and classes of phonological models that can capture language-universal and language-specific auditory/perceptual generalizations.

The satellite meeting would not have been the success that it was without the contributions of many people. It is perhaps most fitting to begin our acknowledgments by thanking John Ohala, the director of ICPhS99, for encouraging us to organize the satellite meeting and for participating in it despite his hectic schedule at ICPhS. For assistance with the organization of the meeting, we are grateful to Lily Liaw, Misun Seo, Stephen Winters, and especially, Jeff Mielke. We would also like to express our gratitude to each of the invited speakers: Patrice Beddor, Jennifer Cole, Randy Diehl, Edward Flemming, Larry Hyman, John Ohala, Jaye Padgett, Robert Remez, Donca Steriade, and Richard Wright. The fact that each one enthusiastically committed to participate in the workshop was not only encouraging for us; it underscored our belief that researchers in the areas of phonology and speech perception are eager for meaningful and productive interactions. The day-long event was further enriched by a poster session. We would like to thank the following researchers for presenting posters at the satellite meeting: J. Fraser Bennett, Paul Boersma, Heidi Fleischhacker, Alexei Kochetov, Tivoli Majors, Betsy McCall, Kyoko Nagao, Olena Ovcharova, Thomas Sawallis, and Stephen Winters. (The list of talks and posters given at the workshop appears at the end of the preface.) Naturally, we would also like to extend our appreciation to the more than 100 participants from around the world who attended the meeting. Funding for the meeting was generously provided by an award from the National Science Foundation (#BCS-9905819) and from The Ohio State University Center for Cognitive Science.

We also owe thanks to a number of people who helped us produce this book. Robert Remez generously advocated on our behalf with Mark Zadrozny at Academic Press. John Kingston kindly served as a reviewer, as did the participants of a seminar that we co-taught in Fall 1999: Tim Face, Tsan Huang, Scott Kiesling, Matt Makashay, Jeff Mielke, Amanda Miller-Ockhuizen, Jennifer Muller, Misun Seo, Georgios Tserdanelis, Steve Winters and Peggy Wong. The contributions that these PhD students and researchers made to this book is extraordinary. We are also grateful to Björn Lindblom, who graciously agreed to write the foreword for this volume. The highest order of thanks goes, of course, to the authors who were good natured and (for the most part) prompt throughout the process of submitting and revising the chapters.

The Role of Speech Perception
Phenomena in Phonology

A Satellite Meeting of the International Congress
of Phonetic Sciences — San Francisco, CA 1999

Talks

Patrice Speeter Beddor (University of Michigan): "Conditions on perception and their consequences for phonology"

Jennifer Cole and Khalil Iskarous (University of Illinois): "Contextual effects of consonant place identification: Implications for a theory of phonologization"

Randy Diehl (University of Texas): "Discovering phonological universals in the perception of speech analogs"

Edward Flemming (Stanford): "How to formalize constraints on perceptual distinctiveness"

Elizabeth Hume and Keith Johnson (Ohio State University): "The role of speech perception in phonology"

Larry Hyman (University of California, Berkeley): "Perception and the state/process distinction in phonology"

John Ohala, Madelaine Plauché, Steve Chang, and Julie Lewis (University of California, Berkeley): "Auditory factors in asymmetry of direction of some sound changes"

Jaye Padgett (University of California, Santa Cruz): "Contrast dispersion and Russian palatalization"

Robert Remez (Barnard College): "The multimodal nature of speech"

Donca Steriade (UCLA): "Perceptual factors in place assimilation"

Richard Wright (University of Washington): "Perceptual cues in contrast maintenance"

Posters

J. Fraser Bennett (SIL and University of Texas, Arlington): "Glottal epenthesis in Thai as a perceptually motivated displaced contrast"

Paul Boersma (University of Amsterdam): "Why a separate perception grammar?"

Heidi Fleischhacker (UCLA): "The prothesis–epenthesis pattern: a perceptual account"

Alexei Kochetov (University of Toronto): "What makes a coda contrastive?"

Tivoli Majors (University of Texas, Austin, and University of Missouri, St. Louis): "Perceptually motivated phonology: The case of stress-dependent harmony"

Betsy McCall and Kyoko Nagao (Indiana University and Konan University): "A perception-based account of mimetic palatalization in Japanese"

Olena Ovcharova (Ohio State University): "A perception-based study of consonant deletion in Turkish"

Thomas Sawallis (Florida Gulf Coast): "A valid method for cross-language comparison of acoustic cues weights"

Stephen Winters (Ohio State University): "Testing the relative salience of audio and visual cues for stop place of articulation"

SECTION

THE INTERPLAY OF SPEECH PERCEPTION AND PHONOLOGY

CHAPTER

A Model of the Interplay of Speech Perception and Phonology

Elizabeth Hume
Keith Johnson

Department of Linguistics
The Ohio State University
Columbus, Ohio 43210

I. Introduction
II. The Interplay of Speech Perception and Phonology
   A. The Influence of Phonological Systems on Speech Perception
   B. The Influence of Speech Perception on Phonological Systems
III. The Interaction of External Forces and Phonology
IV. Implementation
   A. Interactions of External Forces
   B. Language Specificity
V. Conclusions
   Acknowledgments
   Notes
   References

I. INTRODUCTION

It has proven practical over a long history of research on language sound systems to rationalize phonological units and processes in terms of speech articulation. The Sanskrit grammarians, for example, focused on vocal anatomy and articulatory processes to the exclusion of descriptions of acoustic or auditory impressions produced by speech sounds (Allen, 1953). Similarly, the nineteenth century linguists Bell (1867), Sweet (1877), Sievers (1881), Passy (1890), and Rousselot (1897–1901) all focused primarily on speech articulation to explain sound change, and describe similarities and differences across languages and in language teaching. For example, the Sweet/Bell system of vowel classification (still widely used in phonological description) and their iconic phonetic alphabets were based on speech articulation. This tradition of articulatory phonetics also formed the basis for the structuralists' approach to phonetics and phonology (Pike, 1943).

It is arguably the case that this early and prolonged emphasis on the articulatory foundations of sound systems was due to the fact that the articulators are open to observation. The linguist can observe the movements of the lips, jaw, and (with a little more ingenuity) the tongue, and the availability of such observations provided an important point of reference for theories of phonology by making available a set of explanatory mechanisms that can be applied to phonological patterns.

Rationalization of language sound systems from the point of view of the listener has, however, had a more spotted history. Some of the more obvious auditory properties have been noted (e.g., sonority, Sievers, 1881), but it was only recently — after the development of the sound spectrograph — that a comprehensive approach to language sound structure in terms of acoustic/auditory properties was attempted (Jakobson, Fant, & Halle, 1951). However, JFH's attempt was impeded by the newness of the available technology and the relative paucity of perceptual data (which at the time was limited to basic psychoacoustic measures of pitch, loudness, and duration together with the earliest works on speech intelligibility for voice transmission over telephone lines). In his book on acoustic phonetics, Joos (1948) suggested that linguists would not readily accept auditory/acoustic foundations in the rationalization of language sound systems. Concerning Jespersen's (1904) chapter "Akustisch oder Genetisch," Joos said,

> [Jespersen] showed that, however desirable it might seem to base phonetic categories upon acoustic characteristics, it was then impossible to make any progress in that direction because of the incapacity of the known instruments to furnish adequate data. Making a virtue of necessity, phoneticians have developed phonetic theory entirely upon the articulatory ("genetisch") basis, and developed it to the point where inadequacy is seldom if ever noticed. Nothing happened to shake

Jespersen's conclusion for nearly half a century. During this time the technicians produced no instrument which could deal with the central problem, and phonetic doctrine crystallized in the tradition that articulation can alone support linguistically useful phonetic categories. (Joos, 1948, p. 7)

Joos's comments foreshadowed theoretical developments in the years following JFH in which linguists returned to the more established knowledge-base provided by the phonetic study of speech articulation (Chomsky & Halle, 1968). One change in attitude that has persisted, however, is that after JFH it is often assumed that phonological features have dual definitions both in terms of audition/acoustics and articulation (see, e.g., Hume, 1994 regarding [coronal]). Yet, despite this acknowledged role for auditory aspects of speech, perceptual effects and auditory properties of sound have less commonly played a role in linguists' speculations on the role of phonetics in phonological patterns (though see, e.g., Bladon, 1986; Donegan, 1978; Liljencrants & Björn, 1972; Lindblom, 1990; Martinet, 1955; Ohala, 1990, 1993).

It is significant, therefore, that the role of speech perception in language sound systems has recently seen a revival of interest among phonologists. This increasing interest appears to be driven by two factors. First, rapid technological advances over the last 10 to 15 years have made it feasible to collect a wide range of perceptual data both in the laboratory and in the field (e.g., Wright, 1996). This in turn has made it possible for researchers to work out some general properties of speech perception that appear to be relevant in stating phonological patterns. Second, the development of Optimality Theory (Prince & Smolensky, 1993; McCarthy & Prince, 1993) has allowed for the statement of perceptually grounded constraints that interact dynamically with constraints motivated by other general principles. As a result, there has been a new and growing interest in exploring the role of perceptual phenomena in accounting for crosslinguistic sound patterns (e.g., Boersma, 1998; Côté, 1997; Flemming, 1995; Hume, 1998; Jun, 1995; Hayes, 1999; Ovcharova, 1999; Silverman, 1995; Steriade, 1995, 1997). For instance, building on insights from, for example, Kingston (1985) and Ohala (1981), in addition to the notion of phonetically grounded constraints (e.g., Archangeli & Pulleyblank, 1994), Steriade's (1995, 1997) pioneering work in this area explores the extent to which phonological constraints grounded in perceptual cues account for crosslinguistic patterns of laryngeal neutralization and retroflexion. Regarding the former, Steriade argues that loss of laryngeal contrast occurs in contexts in which the perceptual cues to the specific contrast are relatively weak. Conversely, contrasts are maintained in positions that are high on the scale of perceptual salience.

These developments in speech perception and phonological research provide a solid foundation for continued and significant progress in understanding language sound systems. The time then seems ripe to consider the interplay of speech perception and phonology more closely. In this regard, there are at least three key research questions that we see as important starting points for this endeavor. First, to what extent does speech perception influence phonological systems? Second, to what extent does the phonological structure of language influence speech perception? Third, where do speech perception phenomena belong in relation to a formal description of the sound structure of language? In the following sections we address each of these questions, first, by focusing on the interplay of phonology and speech perception, and then by laying out a general model for the study of the interaction of phonology with external forces such as speech perception.

II. THE INTERPLAY OF SPEECH PERCEPTION AND PHONOLOGY

In this section, we present a range of evidence, including new work from our lab, pointing to the influence of language sound structure on speech perception, as well as the influence of speech perception on phonological systems.

A. The Influence of Phonological Systems on Speech Perception

That phonological systems have an influence on speech perception is suggested by a variety of evidence. For example, studies in second-language learning (e.g., Best *et al.*, 1988; Polka & Werker, 1994) have found that listeners are more adept at perceiving sounds of their native language than those of a second language acquired later in life. Furthermore, first-language acquisition research (e.g., Kuhl *et al.*, 1992) shows that perceptual learning occurs as babies' perceptual systems become tuned to language-specific phonetic patterns, such as typical vowel formant ranges. Additionally, model studies (Guenther & Gjaja, 1996; Makashay & Johnson, 1998) have explored auditory neural map formation mechanisms that may be involved in phonetic acquisition. Adaptive neural network models of perceptual learning show human-like patterns of phonetic tuning using idealized pseudo-phonetic data (Guenther & Gjaja, 1996) and using real phonetic data (Makashay & Johnson, 1998).

Phonological systems of contrast may also influence perception (e.g., Dupoux *et al.*, 1997; Lee *et al.*, 1996). For example, experimental results from Hume, Johnson, Seo, Tserdanelis, & Winters (1999) indicate that, for both Korean and American English listeners, transition stimuli have a greater amount of consonant place information than burst stimuli. However, it is interesting that for Korean listeners this difference between bursts and transitions was greater than it was for American English listeners. In other words, Korean listeners were better able to identify a consonant's place of articulation from the transition stimuli alone than were American listeners. One explanation for this finding relates to differences in the system of phonological contrasts in each language. Unlike English, Korean includes the set of phonological contrasts among tense, lax, and aspirated stops, which is cued in part by the amplitude of aspiration. The presence of these phonological contrasts may lead Korean listeners to focus greater attention on the interval of time following the stop release burst, that is, on the transitions.

B. The Influence of Speech Perception on Phonological Systems

Speech perception plays at least three distinct roles in shaping language sound systems: (a) failure to perceptually compensate for articulatory effects; (b) avoidance of weakly perceptible contrasts; and (c) avoidance of noticeable alternations.

Ohala's (1981) account of the listener as a source of sound change is one of the most explicit accounts of a point of contact between speech perception and language sound structure. In this account, listeners may fail to perceptually compensate for coarticulation and come to use different articulatory targets in their own speech by misapprehending speech produced by others (see also Beddor *et al.*, 2001, this volume). This is illustrated in (1), where a speaker in uttering /xy/[1] produces [wy] because of coarticulation between [x] and [y]. The listener fails to compensate for the coarticulation and so presumes that the first speaker intended to say /wy/:

(1)   /xy/ → [wy] → /wy/

The common process of palatalization (or rather, coronalization, see, e.g., Hume, 1994) may also have its roots in misperception. Chang *et al.* (2001, this volume) and Clements (1999) suggest that the common manner change of a velar stop to a palato-alveolar affricate before a front vowel is due to the listener's reinterpretation of the velar's aspiration as the frication noise of a strident consonant. Thus, synchronic variability or diachronic change in sound patterns may be due to the listener's misperceptions, that is, a phonetics/phonology mismatch.

The second area in which speech perception exerts influence on phonological systems derives from the fact that contrasts of weak perceptibility tend to be avoided in language. For example, sound differences that are relatively imperceptible tend not to be used contrastively in language. In the extreme case this can be an absolute prohibition. Illustrations of such imperceptible contrasts include inter-dental [θ] versus dental [θ], concave versus convex tongue shape for lax vowels, etc. These are all pronounceable, but low salience, contrasts that are not used in language.

Contrast is relevant from both paradigmatic and syntagmatic perspectives, and weak contrast along either dimension may be avoided by enhancing, or optimizing, the contrast, on the one hand, or sacrificing it, on the other. This can be achieved by means of a variety of repair strategies, including epenthesis, metathesis, dissimilation, assimilation, and deletion. Among these strategies, epenthesis, dissimilation, and metathesis tend to optimize contrast, while with assimilation and deletion contrast is sacrificed.

To illustrate, **epenthesis** in Maltese can be seen as strengthening a length contrast among consonants. In this process, the vowel [i] is epenthesized before a word-initial geminate consonant, created by the concatenation of the imperfective morpheme /t/ and a stem-initial coronal obstruent, for example, /t+dierek/ [id-dierek] 'to rise early, 3rd p. imperf' (Aquilina, 1959; Hume, 1996). Since the perceptual cues to word-initial geminates, stops especially, are relatively weak (see, e.g., Abramson, 1987; Muller, in preparation), insertion of a vowel before the geminate enhances the perceptibility of consonant length and, hence, the identity of the imperfective morpheme. Contrast optimization also occurs in English plural noun formation where a vowel precedes the plural morpheme just in case the noun stem ends in a sibilant consonant, e.g., dishes, judges, cf. modems, cats. Since the plural morpheme is itself a sibilant, the appearance of a vowel between the two consonants renders the distinction between the segments more perceptible. This is all the more important given that the second sibilant alone carries the meaning of the plural morpheme. That contrast is strengthened in this manner follows from the view that large modulations in the speech signal serve to increase the salience of cues in the portion of the signal where the modulation takes place (Ohala, 1993; Kawasaki, 1982). It makes sense that modulation would enhance the perceptibility of fricative sequences because otherwise auditory masking would obscure place information in adjacent fricatives (Bladon, 1986).

Many cases of **dissimilation** receive the same account. In Greek, for in-stance, consonant clusters comprised of two stops or two fricatives optionally dissimilate, resulting in variation among, for example, [pt] ~ [ft] (epta ~ efta 'seven'); and [fθ] ~ [ft] (fθinos ~ ftinos 'cheap' (masc. nom.) (Newton, 1972; Tserdanelis, 2001). Dissimilation effects a difference in manner of the two seg-ments, enhancing syntagmatic contrast by increasing the modulation between adjacent segments.

Perceptibility can also be a trigger for **metathesis**. To cite but one example, in Faroese, the sequence /sk/ metathesizes just in case a stop consonant follows, e.g., /baisk + t/ [baikst] *[baiskt] 'bitter, neut.sg.' (Jacobsen & Matras, 1961;

Lockwood, 1955; Rischel, 1972; Seo & Hume, 2001). Hume (1998, 2001) argues that consonant/consonant metathesis in Faroese, as in many other languages, serves to enhance both paradigmatic and syntagmatic contrast.[2] The problem with the unmetathesized sequence stems from the fact that a stop consonant would be sandwiched between two consonants, a context of poor perceptibility for the stop, in particular. To repair the sequence, the consonants switch order so that the weaker stop consonant is positioned in a more robust context. Thus, the perceptibility gain in the output is achieved by shifting the stop to postvocalic position, a context with more robust stop place cues. The fricative consonant, with stronger internal place cues, fares better in interconsonantal position. Winters (2001) also found evidence of a perceptibility gain for patterns of stop/stop metathesis observed crosslinguistically in VCCV sequences (see also Steriade, 2001, this volume).

Contrary to the repair strategies above in which the avoidance of a weak contrast is achieved by perceptual optimization, in cases of total segment **assimilation** and **deletion**, contrast is instead sacrificed. For example, in Korean the sequences /n+l/, /l+n/ are realized as [ll], e.g., /non-li/ [nolli] 'logic', /səl-nal/ [səllal] 'New Year's day' (see, e.g., Davis & Shin, 1999; Seo, 2001). In Seo's (2001) discussion of the role of perception in Korean assimilation, she notes that the syntagmatic contrast of the nasal/lateral sequence is of low salience, given the acoustic/auditory similarity of the two segment types. The articulatory effort required to maintain a perceptually salient contrast between the two segments is outweighed by, what we speculate to be, the articulatory forces driving assimilation. The consequence is a loss of nasal–oral contrast in this context. For further discussion on the possible link between perception and assimilation, see Hura *et al.* (1992), Jun (1995), Ohala (1990), Steriade (2001, this volume), and Winters (2001).

The ultimate sacrifice in contrast occurs with segment deletion, such as Turkish /h/ deletion. Experimental evidence supports the perceptual basis of this type of deletion. As Mielke (2001) and Ovcharova (1999) show, /h/ optionally deletes in contexts in which it is relatively imperceptible, such as after an aspirated stop but not before ([ethem] ~ [etem] 'proper name'; [kahpe] *[ka:pe] 'harlot'), word-finally but not word-initially ([timsah][3] ~ [timsa:] 'crocodile'; [hava] *[ava] 'air'), and adjacent to a fricative ([safha] ~ [safa] 'sleep'; [tahsil] ~ [ta:sil] 'education').

The third area in which speech perception exerts influence on phonological systems concerns the avoidance of noticeable alternations. In this function, perception is seen as a type of filter on sound change. For example, Kohler (1990) states that changes are "only accepted (1) if they bear an auditory similarity to their points of departure, and (2) if the situational context does not force the speaker to rate the cost of a misunderstanding or a breakdown of communication very high" (p. 89). Note that the filter has two aspects, the first purely in terms of perceptual salience and the second in terms of the communicative context. Drawing on evidence from assimilation, Steriade (1999) interprets the communicative aspect of the filter in a more sociolinguistic manner: "innovation is channeled [. . .] in the direction that is least likely to yield blatant departures from the [established pronunciation] norm."

Huang's (2001) study of tone sandhi in Mandarin Chinese illustrates this effect. Mandarin has four lexical tones: level-high (55), mid-rising (35), low-falling-rising (214), and high-falling (51). (Numbers in parentheses indicate the pitch values of the tones on a five-level scale.) The phonological process under study concerns the well-known tone sandhi in which a low-falling-rising tone is simplified to mid-rising just in case it is followed by another low-falling-rising tone, that is, /214 214/ → [35 214]. Huang argues that this process is a case of perceptually tolerated articulatory simplification (Hura *et al.*, 1992; Kohler, 1990; Steriade, 2001, this volume). In other words, the contour tone 214 is simplified to 35, rather than to 55 or 51, one of the other two "simpler" tones in the language, because 214 is more similar to 35 than it is to either of the other tones. The phonological change is, therefore, less noticeable. To test this hypothesis, native speakers of American English and Mandarin Chinese discriminated pairs of the four Mandarin Chinese tones. The results support Huang's hypothesis: listeners from both languages had the greatest difficulty distinguishing between 35 and 214, as shown in Figure 1.1. It is interesting to note that this tendency was much more pronounced for Mandarin Chinese listeners, suggesting a further effect of phonology on perception (see §IV.B for related discussion).

While the preceding studies focus on the perceptual/communicative aspects of the filter, we interpret it more broadly, as including at least four external forces: perception, production, generalization, and conformity. This can be illustrated in general terms in the context of the five phonological repair strategies noted above. As shown in Figure 1.2, for every sound or sound sequence that is ripe for change (for perceptual, articulatory or other reasons), there are a variety of potential ways in which a sequence can be modified. For example, to repair a given sequence "*xy*", any of the five repair strategies given below could be used, that is, a segment could be epenthesized between "*x*" and "*y*," the order of the two segments could be reversed, one of the segments could be deleted, and so on. There can also be more than one possible output for a given repair strategy. With respect to epenthesis, for example, the sequence "*xy*" could be repaired by inserting a segment between the two sounds, before the entire sequence, or after it. All three patterns are observed crosslinguistically (see Broselow, 1981, and Kenstowicz, 1994, for related discussion). The selection of the output is determined by filters, of which perception is one. How this filtering is implemented constitutes the focus of section IV.

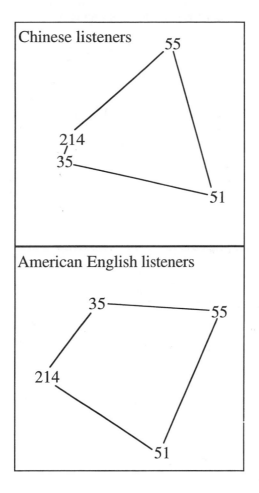

Figure 1.1. The four tones of Mandarin Chinese in perceptual space for Mandarin Chinese listeners and American English listeners. Multidimensional scaling data from Huang (2000).

III. THE INTERACTION OF EXTERNAL FORCES AND PHONOLOGY

To study the role of speech perception in phonology it is necessary to conceive of ways that realities in the domain of speech perception interface with the cognitive symbolic representation of language sound structure. Realities in speech perception are tied up with physical acoustic descriptions of speech sounds and the

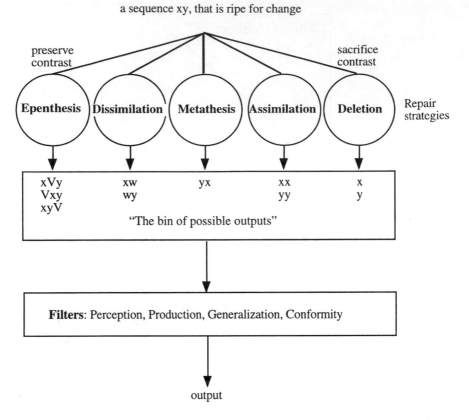

Figure 1.2. Characterization of phonological repair strategies, and the role of filters in selecting among possible outputs.

auditory transduction of speech sounds in the auditory periphery. Phonological systems, on the other hand, are symbolic in nature, dissociated from any particular physical event in the world. Indeed, such is the independence of phonology from the physical world that it can be said that two people share the same symbolic phonological system, speak the same language, even though their experience of physical events in the world does not overlap at all. Prior to mass communication this may have been the rule.

The problem is thus a classic one in the study of language sound systems, namely, the relationship between phonetics and phonology. The phonetics/phonology interface problem is an instance also of the classic philosophical problem on the relationship between the mind and the body. Our strategy may or may not be relevant for other instances of the mind/body problem (whether in other domains in linguistics, or in more remote areas of cognitive science). But, as practicing scientists, we need an approach that will make it possible to pursue scientific study at this one particular point of mind/body contact. For this, we propose the model shown in Figure 1.3.

In the study of language sound systems, we work with two symbolic domains: the one cognitive, the other formal. The cognitive symbolic representation of a language's sound system, characterized as *p* in Figure 1.3, is embodied in an individual's brain. We may assume that *p* is a component of *l*, the cognitive symbolic representation of a language. The linguistic sound system of a community of speakers/listeners can thus be defined as a collection of *p*'s. The formal

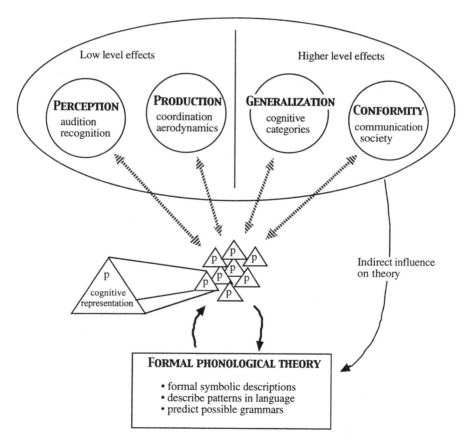

Figure 1.3.   A general model of the interplay of external forces and phonology, broadly defined.

symbolic domain defines the inventory of symbols and the procedures for symbol manipulation found in formal linguistic descriptions. The theory describes sound patterns observed in language; hence, the arrow pointing from *p* to *Formal Phonological Theory* in Figure 1.3. It is these sound patterns that constitute the data that the theory is based on. The arrow pointing from *Formal Phonological Theory* to *p* reflects the goal of phonological theory to predict possible grammars. A formal symbolic description is not the same as a cognitive symbolic representation. Nonetheless, formal descriptions that remain consistent with what is known about cognitive representation provide insight into the cognitive representation by providing a language for discussing the intricacies of the mind.

The relationship between external factors and the two symbolic domains is also illustrated in Figure 1.3. Two familiar low-level effects in the model, *perception* and *production*, have been discussed for decades in functional accounts of sound patterns. The role of "ease of perception" and "ease of production" are widely cited, though specific proposals as to how they may influence language are rare. Notice that, in our view, perceptual and productive abilities can both influence the sound system of language as well as be influenced by one's language, hence the bidirectional arrows in the diagram between these effects and *p*. Examples of these influences are provided in section IV (see also §II regarding perception). Also included in the model are two higher level effects, *generalization* and *conformity*. Generalization refers to the tendency to simplify cognitive representations relative to the sensory reality experienced. This tendency for generalization underlies category formation in cognitive systems generally, and we see it as related to linguistic processes such as paradigm leveling and analogy. Conformity relates to the social and communicative factors that play an important role in shaping language sound structure. From a social perspective, the need to conform to a linguistic norm, for example, can exert influence over an individual's cognitive language sound patterns. The need in a communicative system to use forms that others will identify and accept also influences sound systems. Further discussion of the bidirectional influence of the two higher level factors appears in section IV below.[4]

In our view, cognitive language sound patterns (*p*) are directly influenced by these external forces. However, the connection between formal phonological theory and the external forces is indirect (for an alternative view see, e.g., Flemming, 1995; Steriade, 2001, this volume). The formal theory describes patterns found in individual languages, and from these derives crosslinguistic generalizations about those patterns. To the extent that language sound patterns are caused by external factors such as speech perception, these factors are reflected in the formal phonological theory. Yet, to incorporate them directly into phonological theory erroneously implies that they are exclusive to language. On the contrary, the cognitive factor, generalization, for example, relates not only to linguistic category formation, but to category formation in general. Similarly, speech perception uses perceptual abilities that are also relevant to general auditory and visual perception (Fowler, 1986). We refer the reader to Hale & Reiss (2000) for related discussion.

We view the model outlined in Figure 1.3 as a starting point for the study of the interplay of external forces and phonology, broadly defined. Each aspect of the model constitutes an important area of research which, together, will lead to a more comprehensive understanding of language sound structures.

IV. IMPLEMENTATION

Section II provided evidence that speech perception influences phonology and vice versa, and section III outlined a rather abstract model of how external forces interact with phonology. This section explores in more detail how to implement this model.

The interplay of perception and phonology occurs in time because speech perception is a process that occurs in time — the process of word recognition has a measurable onset and offset. Similarly, speech production is also a process that occurs in time. The higher-level functions, generalization and conformity, are also tied to events in time; generalization to the process of language acquisition and perhaps also aspects of continuing language use, and conformity to events of personal interaction involving language use. Therefore, because these external forces operate on events in time, our model of the interplay of perception and phonology is implemented over time. That is, perception exerts influence on an individual's cognitive domain at a particular point in time, resulting in a modified representation of the sound system in question. In more formal terms, we suggest that the interplay of speech perception and phonology is implemented as the mapping from p to p', where p is a cognitive symbolic sound system at some particular time t, and p' is a cognitive symbolic sound system at some later time $t+\delta$. The mapping $p > p'$ (Figure 1.4) is made up of a set of parallel filters or transduction functions comprised of the external forces introduced in section II.

To understand how perception filters p, suppose that p requires the perception of a distinction that is somewhat hard to hear. In some instances, the difficult distinction required by p will be missed, simply misheard, so p will undergo a change to p'. This is very much in the spirit of Ohala's (1981) account of the listener as a source of sound change. The filtering action imposed by production takes a similar form. The cognitive symbolic representation p requires that the

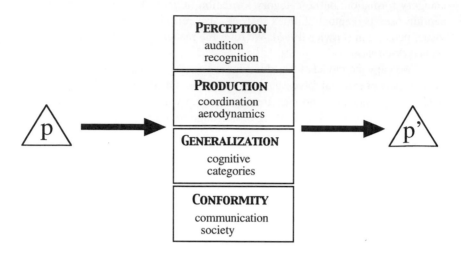

Figure 1.4. The mapping of *p* onto *p'* can be decomposed into a set of filters. Each component of the mapping process independently influences the relationship between *p* and *p'* and, hence, the structure of *p'*.

speaker make a sound that is hard to say. In some instances the speaker will fail to produce the sound and say something else, and in this way contribute to a change in *p*. The filtering action of generalization is a little different from these. Here *p* appears to have a regular pattern that the cognitive system captures by reorganizing *p*. The cognitive category formation mechanism that we envision forms generalizations at the lowest level of acoustic/phonetic categories up to abstract morphophonemic patterns. Finally, conformity tends to bring *p* into line with the linguistic norms of the community whenever *p* differs from those norms.

      This model raises two important implementation issues. First, it is necessary to give an account of interactions among external forces in this model. How is the perceptual filter modulated by the production filter? How can conformity prevent changes that are motivated by perceptual or productive ease? Second, the language specificity of the external phonological forces (the upward-going arrows in Figure 1.3) needs to be addressed. How are external forces dependent on or shaped by the cognitive symbolic representation of language sound systems? We treat interactions among forces as a problem of understanding the time scale of phonetic mutation, and we treat language specificity by referring to *p* in the definition of the forces.

A. Interactions of External Forces

The four filters in Figure 1.4 (the external phonological forces) can be treated as completely independent of one another. Interactions of opposing tendencies in this model occur in cycling $p > p'$ ($> p$ ...), where the interval between cycles is very short. A change that reduces cost on one function may produce increased cost on another function and so be quickly reversed. For example, the sound pattern [nt] may be changed to [nd] in order to achieve lower articulatory cost (avoiding the modulation of voicing). In the next cycle, [nd] may be changed back to [nt] because [nd] conflicts with conformity (e.g., [nd] diverges too much from the socially accepted pronunciation norm).

This view is consistent with Joseph & Janda's (1988) view that sound change occurs in synchrony, that is, in the present:

> Diachrony is best viewed as the set of transitions between successive synchronic states, so that language change is necessarily something that always takes place in the present and is therefore governed in every instance by constraints on synchronic grammars. (Joseph & Janda, 1988, p. 194)

While it is traditional in diachronic linguistics to think of sound change over hundreds or thousands of years, there is no principled reason to restrict ourselves to such long time spans. Indeed, the study of sound change in progress (Labov, 1994) sheds light on changes seen over long time spans by exploring changes with a finer-grained time scale. This is because the same principles that apply over centuries are at work in daily language use as well.

Thus, unlike a view of sound change that uses a coarse-grained time scale, our model handles interactions among forces by adopting a fine-grained scale, as illustrated in Figure 1.5. The function $p(t)$, which shows the development of sound p over time, has local noise overlaying global stability. Through the sequential interaction of forces, it is a self-organizing system that is nonetheless in constant flux.

B. Language Specificity

The model in Figure 1.3 has bidirectional arrows between the cognitive symbolic representations p and each of the external forces. We saw in section 2 that there is some evidence that speech perception processes are language specific, influenced, for example, by the system of contrasts in a language. Further evidence of the language specificity of speech perception can be seen in Mielke's (2001) study of /h/ perception in English, French, Turkish, and Arabic. Figure 1.6 shows average

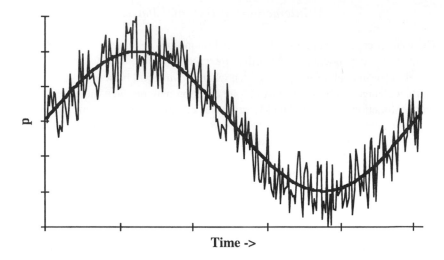

Figure 1.5. A coarse-grained time scale shows general tendencies, illustrated by the slowly changing line, while a fine-grained time scale shows rapidly fluctuating change. Time in this illustration is on the horizontal axis, and the vertical axis is meant to show, in an abstract one-dimensional projection, the location p of a language in the space of possible languages.

sensitivity to /h/ in a variety of segmental contexts in Mielke's study. (Sensitivity was estimated using the signal detection measure d'.) Two aspects of these data are relevant in the current discussion. First, the crosslinguistic differences are striking. The two languages with limited /h/ distributions, English and French, show low /h/ salience, while the two languages with extensive /h/ distributions, Turkish and Arabic, show high /h/ salience. Second, despite these crosslinguistic differences, all four of the languages show similar patterns of salience as a function of different segmental environments.

   With these data in mind, we could say that the perceptual influence on phonology is static because the pattern of perceptual salience in segmental context remains relatively constant across languages, but the perceptual influence on phonology is also dynamic because overall /h/ salience differs from language to language. The influence of perception on p includes both the universal static aspect of perception and the language-specific dynamic aspect. The upward pointing part of the bidirectional arrow from p to perception is meant to depict the fact that language sound systems shape perception.

   There is also evidence that language sound systems can influence speech production, linguistic generalization, and social conformity. The language-universal aspect of production has been a focus of research for over a century. However,

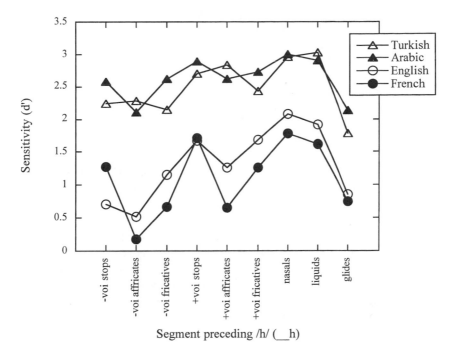

Figure 1.6.   Perceptual sensitivity to /h/ in different segmental contexts by listeners of American English, Turkish, Arabic, and French. Data from Mielke (2000).

it seems undeniable that any definition of easy or hard sounds or sound sequences must make reference to the native language(s) of the speaker. A post-alveolar click with velar accompaniment [!x] may be very hard for a person who doesn't speak !Xóõ, while it is perfectly natural to the native speaker. But as with perception, ease of production is both language universal and language specific. We expect that within-language gradients of productive ease will be similar across comparable languages. For example, the tendency for consonant clusters to be homorganic seems evident in most languages that allow consonant clusters.

The higher-level functions, generalization and conformity, also show both language-universal and language-specific aspects. For example, generalization appears to use language-universal natural categories for speech sounds, as codified in distinctive feature theory. This is analogous to the tendency for there to be crossculturally ubiquitous natural semantic categories for objects in the natural world such as birds or trees. However, just as cultures may vary as to whether a bat is a bird, or a bush is a tree, so the extension of distinctive features may be language specific for some sounds. For example, /l/ operates as a continuant in some languages of Australia, e.g., Djapu and Gurindji, and as a noncontinuant in other languages, e.g., Cypriot Greek (Hume & Odden, 1996).

Similarly, conformity as an external force on language sound systems is both language universal and language specific. One language-universal aspect of conformity derives from a general tendency for accommodation in human interactions (linguistic or not; Giles, 1973; Doise *et al.*, 1976). Of course, the particular linguistic norms of a speech community are language specific. For example, in one dialect 'cat' may be pronounced [kæt], while in another it is [kæʔ]. So, cognitive symbolic representations define norms, and conformity derives expectations based on those norms. But in addition to this, the drive for accommodation itself may be altered by p. It seems logical that, if a community has a fairly diverse makeup such that people are exposed to a large range of linguistic variation, then the tendency for accommodation, and hence conformity, may be lessened.

To summarize, there is evidence that p influences each of the four external phonological forces. This justifies the bidirectional arrows in Figure 1.3. However, in our sketch of the implementation (Figure 1.4) there is no explicit account of bidirectionality.

We could implement language specificity as a type of cyclic filtering, where the external forces are altered (filtered) by p as schematized in (2). (2a) shows the idea that was presented earlier in Figure 1.4. (2b) extends this notion to suggest that p also serves as a kind of function on the set of external forces.

(2) (a) $p \rightarrow$ filter $\rightarrow p'$ (a') $f(p) = p'$
     (b) filter $\rightarrow p \rightarrow$ filter' (b') $p(f) = f'$

However, notice that the language specificity of the external forces derives from the fact that we define each of them in terms of p. That is, /h/ is perceptually salient in languages that have extensive /h/ distributions. /!x/ is pronounceable in languages that have /!x/ in their system of phonological contrasts. Similarly, generalization and conformity are both operations over the contents of p. So, by defining the external forces in terms of the cognitive symbolic representation of language sound structure (a system of contrasts and a lexicon of word forms that make use of those contrasts) we have built language specificity into them.

V. CONCLUSIONS

The model outlined above is presented as a starting point for the study of the interplay of speech perception and phonology, defined to include the cognitive and formal representations of phonological systems. The aim of this chapter has been to situate the study of the interplay of these two domains in a broader context, taking into account other factors such as speech production, linguistic cognition, and social influence. While we recognize that this venture is necessarily program-matic, we see each aspect of the model as constituting an important area of research, which, together, will lead to a more comprehensive understanding of language sound structures.

ACKNOWLEGMENTS

We would like to thank the members of our phonetics/phonology seminars for their very valuable and thoughtful input on this research. Thanks to Tim Face, Tsan Huang, Scott Kiesling, Matt Makashay, Jeff Mielke, Amanda Miller-Ockhuizen, Jennifer Muller, Misun Seo, Georgios Tserdanelis, Steve Winters, and Peggy Wong. We are also grateful to Jose Ignacio Hualde, Brian Joseph, Jaye Padgett, and the members of the audiences at the University of Chicago and at the 1999 ICPhS Satellite Meeting, "The Role of Perception in Phonology," for their helpful comments. The authors' names are listed alphabetically.

NOTES

1. In this discussion, x, y, and w are used as variables over phonetic symbols.
2. See Blevins & Garrett (1998) for discussion of the role of perception in conso-nant/vowel metathesis.
3. Deletion of /h/ word-finally seems to be categorical for at least some speakers.
4. We do not rule out the possibility of other external factors. For example, Karen Landahl has suggested to us that ecological factors may have an influence on language sound systems. We leave this topic open for future consideration. We also considered whether to add learnability to the inventory, but decided that this is subsumed under the other factors.

REFERENCES

Abramson, A. (1987). Word-initial consonant length in Pattani Malay. *ICPhS 11*, 68–70.

Allen, W. S. (1953). *Phonetics in ancient India*. London: Oxford University Press.

Aquilina, J. (1959). *The structure of Maltese*. Valletta, Malta: Progress Press.

Archangeli, D., & Pulleyblank, D. (1994). *Grounded phonology*. Cambridge: MIT Press.

Bell, A. M. (1867). *Visible speech*. London: Simpkin, Marshall & Co.

Beddor, P., Krakow, R. A., & Lindemann, S. (2001). Patterns of perceptual compensation and their phonological consequences. In E. Hume & K. Johnson (Eds.), *The role of speech perception in phonology* (pp. 55–78). New York: Academic Press.

Best, C. T., McRoberts, G., & Sithole, N. (1988). Examination of perceptual reorganization for nonnative speech contrasts: Zulu click discrimination by English-speaking adults and infants. *Journal of Experimental Psychology: Human Perception and Performance, 14*, 345–360.

Bladon, A. (1986). Phonetics for hearers. In G. McGregor (Ed.), *Language for hearers* (pp. 1–24). Oxford: Pergamon.

Blevins, J., & Garrett, A. (1998). The origins of consonant/vowel metathesis. *Language, 74*, 508–553.

Boersma, P. (1998). *Functional phonology*. Unpublished doctoral dissertation. University of Amsterdam.

Broselow, E. (1981). On predicting the interaction of stress and epenthesis. *Glossa, 16*, 115–132.

Chang, S., Plauché, M., & Ohala, J. (2001). Markedness and consonant confusion asymmetries. In E. Hume & K. Johnson (Eds.), *The role of speech perception in phonology* (pp. 79–101). New York: Academic Press.

Chomsky, N., & Halle, M. (1968). *The sound pattern of English*. New York: Harper & Row.

Clements, G. N. (1999). Affricates as non-contoured stops. In O. Fujimura, B. Joseph, & B. Palek (Eds.), *Proceedings of LP'98: Item order in language and speech* (pp. 271–299). Prague: Karolinum Press.

Côté, M.-H. (1997). Phonetic salience and consonant cluster simplification. In B. Bruening, Y. Kang, & M. McGinnis (Eds.), *MITWPL 30* (pp. 229–262). Cambridge: MIT Press.

Davis, S., & Shin, S.-H. (1999). The syllable contact constraint in Korean: An optimality-theoretic analysis. *Journal of East Asian Linguistics, 8*, 285–312.

Donegan, P. (1978). *The natural phonology of vowels*. Doctoral dissertation, Ohio State University. New York: Garland Press, 1985.

Doise, W., Sinclair, A., & Bourhis, R. (1976). Evaluation of accent convergence and divergence in cooperative and competitive intergroup situations. *British Journal of Social and Clinical Psychology, 15*, 247–252.

Dupoux, E., Pallier, C., Sebastian, N., & Mehler, J. (1997). A distressing "deafness" in French? *Journal of Memory and Language, 36*, 406–421.

Flemming, E. S. (1995). *Auditory representations in phonology*. Unpublished doctoral dissertation, University of California at Los Angeles.

Fowler, C. A. (1986). An event approach to the study of speech perception. *Journal of Phonetics, 14*, 3–28.

Giles, H. (1973). Accent mobility: A model and some data. *Anthropological Linguistics*, *15*, 87–105.

Guenther, F., & Gjaja, M. (1996). The perceptual magnet effect as an emergent property of neural map formation. *Journal of the Acoustical Society of America*, *100*, 1111–1121.

Hale, M., & Reiss, C. (2000). "Substance abuse" and "dysfunctionalism": Current trends in phonology. *Linguistic Inquiry*, *31*, 157–169.

Hayes, B. (1999). Phonetically driven phonology: The role of optimality theory and inductive grounding. In M. Donnell, E. Moraucsik, F. Newmeyer, M. Noonan, & K. Wheatley (Eds.), *Functionalism and Formalism in Linguistics*. Studies in Language Companion Series 41 (Vol. 1, pp. 243–285). Amsterdam: Benjamins.

Huang, T. (2001). Tone perception by speakers of Mandarin Chinese and American English. *The Interplay of Speech Perception and Phonology, OSUWPL, 55*.

Hume, E. (1994). *Front vowels, coronal consonants and their interaction in nonlinear phonology*. Doctoral dissertation, Cornell University. New York: Garland.

Hume, E. (1996). Coronal consonant, front vowel parallels in Maltese. *Natural Language and Linguistic Theory*, *14*, 163–203.

Hume, E. (1997). *Towards an explanation of consonant/consonant metathesis*. Unpublished manuscript, Ohio State University.

Hume, E. (1998). The role of perceptibility in consonant/consonant metathesis. *Proceedings of the West Coast Conference on Formal Linguistics*, *17*, 293–307.

Hume, E. (2001). Metathesis: Formal and functional considerations. In E. Hume, N. Smith, & J. van de Weijer (Eds.), *Surface syllable structure and segment sequencing*. Leiden: Holland Institute of Linguistics.

Hume, E., & Odden, D. (1996). Reconsidering [consonantal]. *Phonology 13*, 345–376.

Hume, E., Johnson, K., Seo, M., Tserdanelis, G., & Winters, S. (1999). A cross-linguistic study of stop place perception. *Proceedings of the XIVth International Congress of Phonetic Sciences*, pp. 2069–2072.

Hume, E., Smith, N., & van de Weijer, J. (Eds.) (2000). *Surface syllable structure and segment sequencing*. Leiden: Holland Institute of Linguistics.

Hura, S. L., Lindblom, B., & Diehl, R. L. (1992). On the role of perception in shaping phonological assimilation rules. *Language & Speech*, *35*(1,2), 59–72.

Jacobsen, M. A., & Matras, C. (1961). *Førosysk-Donsk Ordabók*. Tørshavn: Føroya Fródskaparfelag.

Jakobson, R., Fant, G., & Halle, M. (1951). *Preliminaries to speech analysis*. Cambridge: MIT Press.

Jespersen, O. (1904). *Phonetische grundfragen*. Leipzig: B. G. Tuebner.

Joos, M. (1948). Acoustic phonetics. *Language*, *24*(Suppl.), 1–137.

Joseph, B., & Janda, R. (1988). The how and why of diachronic morphologization and demorphologization. In M. Hammond & M. Noonan (Eds.), *Theoretical morphology*. New York: Academic Press.

Jun, J. (1995). Place assimilation as the result of conflicting perceptual and articulatory constraints. *Proceedings of WCCFL 14*, pp. 221–237.

Kawasaki, H. (1982). *An acoustic basis for universal constraints on sound sequences.* Unpublished doctoral dissertation, University of California at Berkeley.

Kenstowicz, M. (1994). Syllabification in Chukchee: A constraints-based analysis. In A. Davison *et al.* (Eds.), *Proceedings of the 4th Annual Meeting of the Formal Linguistics Society of Midamerica* (pp. 160–181). Iowa City: University of Iowa.

Kingston, J. (1985). *The phonetics and phonology of the timing of oral and glottal events.* Unpublished doctoral dissertation, University of California at Berkeley.

Kohler, K. (1990). Segmental reduction in connected speech: Phonological facts and phonetic explanations. In W. J. Hardcastle & A. Marchal (Eds.), *Speech production and speech modeling* (pp. 69–92). Dordrecht: Kluwer Academic Publishers.

Kuhl, P. K., Williams, K. A., Lacerda, F., Stevens, K. N., & Lindblom, B. (1992). Linguistic experience alters phonetic perception in infants by 6 months of age. *Science*, *255*, 606–608.

Labov, W. (1994). *Principles of linguistic change: Internal factors.* Oxford: Blackwell.

Lee, Y.-S., Vakoch, D., & Wurm, L. (1996). Tone perception in Cantonese and Mandarin: A cross-linguistic comparison. *Journal of Psycholinguistic Research*, *25*, 527–542.

Liljencrants, J., & Björn, L. (1972). Numerical simulation of vowel quality systems: The role of perceptual contrast. *Language*, *48*(4), 839–862.

Lindblom, B. (1990). Explaining phonetic variation: A sketch of the H&H theory. In W. J. Hardcastle & A. Marchal (Eds.), *Speech production and speech modeling* (pp. 403–440). Dordrecht: Kluwer Academic Publishers.

Lockwood, W. B. (1955). *An introduction to modern Faroese.* Copenhagen: Ejnar Munksgaard.

Makashay, M., & Johnson, K. (1998). Surveying auditory space using vowel formant data. *The sound of the future: A global view of acoustics in the 21st century: Proceedings of the 16th International Congress on Acoustics and 135th Meeting of the Acoustical Society of America*, pp. 2037–2038.

Martinet, André. (1955). *Economie des changements phonétiques.* Berne: Éditions A. Francke AG Verlag.

McCarthy, J., & Prince, A. (1993). *Prosodic morphology.* Unpublished manuscript, University of Massachusetts, Amherst.

Mielke, J. (2001). A perceptual account of Turkish h-deletion. *The Interplay of Speech Perception and Phonology, OSUWPL, 55.*

Muller, J. (in preparation). *The phonetics and phonology of initial geminates.* Unpublished doctoral dissertation, Ohio State University.

Newton, B. (1972). *The generative interpretation of dialect: A study of modern Greek phonology.* Cambridge: Cambridge University Press.

Ohala, J. (1981). The listener as a source of sound change. In C. S. Masek, R. A. Hendrik, & M. F. Miller (Eds.), *Papers from the parasession on language and behavior: Chicago Linguistics Society* (pp. 178–203). Chicago: Chicago Linguistics Society.

Ohala, J. (1990). The phonetics and phonology of aspects of assimilation. In J. Kingston & M. Beckman (Eds.), *Papers in laboratory phonology*, Vol. 1: *Between the grammar and the physics of speech* (pp. 258–275). Cambridge: Cambridge University Press.

Ohala, J. (1993). The perceptual basis of some sound patterns. In D. A. Connell & A. Arvaniti (Eds.), *Papers in laboratory phonology*, Vol. 4: *Phonology and phonetic evidence* (pp. 87–94). Cambridge: Cambridge University Press.

Ovcharova, O. (1999). *A perception-based study of consonant deletion in Turkish.* Poster presented at the ICPhS Satellite Meeting, "The Role of Perception in Phonology," San Francisco. July.

Passy, P. (1890). *Étude sur les changements phonétiques et leur caractères généraux.* Paris: Librairie Firmin-Didot.

Pike, K. (1943). *Phonetics.* Ann Arbor: University of Michigan Press.

Polka, L., & Werker, J. (1994). Developmental changes in perception of nonnative vowel contrasts. *Journal of Experimental Psychology: Human Perception and Performance, 20,* 421–435.

Prince, A., & Smolensky, P. (1993). *Optimality theory: Constraint interaction in generative grammar.* Unpublished manuscript, Rutgers University, New Brunswick, NJ, and the University of Colorado, Boulder.

Rischel, J. (1972). Consonant reduction in Faroese noncompound wordforms. In E. S. Firchow, K. Grimstad, N. Hasselmo & W. O'Neil (Eds.), *Studies for Einar Haugen.* The Hague: Mouton.

Rousselot, L'Abbe P. J. (1897–1901). *Principes de phonétique expérimentale*, 2 vols. Paris: H. Welter.

Seo, M. (2001). The realization of l/n sequences in Korean. *The Interplay of Speech Perception and Phonology, OSUWPL, 55.*

Seo, M., & Hume, E. (2001). A comparative account of metathesis in Faroese and Lithuanian. In E. Hume, N. Smith, & J. van de Weijer (Eds.), *Surface syllable structure and segment sequencing.* Leiden: Holland Institute of Linguistics.

Sievers, E. (1881). *Grundzüge der Phonetik.* Leipzig: Breitkopf & Hartel.

Silverman, D. (1995). *Phasing and recoverability.* Doctoral dissertation, University of California at Los Angeles. New York: Garland Press.

Steriade, D. (1995). *Licensing retroflexion.* Unpublished manuscript, University of California at Los Angeles.

Steriade, D. (1997). *Phonetics in phonology: The case of laryngeal neutralization.* Unpublished manuscript, University of California at Los Angeles.

Steriade, D. (1999). *Perceptual factors in place assimilation.* Paper presented at "The role of speech perception phenomena in phonology," a satellite meeting of ICPhS '99, San Francisco, CA.

Steriade, D. (2001). Directional asymmetries in assimilation: A directional account. In E. Hume & K. Johnson (Eds.), *The role of speech perception in phonology* (pp. 219–250). New York: Academic Press.

Sweet, H. (1877). *A handbook of phonetics.* Oxford: Clarendon Press.

Tserdanelis, G. (2001). Manner dissimilation directionality in Greek. *The interplay of speech perception and phonology, OSUWPL, 55.*

Winters, S. (2001). VCCV perception: Putting place in its place. In E. Hume, N. Smith, & J. van de Weijer (Eds.), *Surface syllable structure and segment sequencing.* Leiden: Holland Institute of Linguistics.

Wright, R. A. (1996). *Consonant clusters and cue preservation in Tsou.* Unpublished doctoral dissertation, University of California at Los Angeles.

CHAPTER

The Interplay of Phonology and Perception Considered from the Perspective of Perceptual Organization

Robert E. Remez

Department of Psychology
Barnard College
New York, New York 10027-6598

  I. Perceptual Organization of Speech
 II. Unimodal Auditory Perceptual Organization of Speech
     A. Sinewave Replication of Utterances
     B. Quantized Noise–Band Signals
     C. A Unimodal, Preliminary Conclusion
III. Multimodal Perceptual Organization of Speech
     A. Multimodal Perception of Speech and Other Events
     B. The Role of Familiarity in Multimodal Perceptual Organization
 IV. Several Conclusions
     Acknowledgments
     References

> It is the dichotomous scale of distinctive features, in particular, and the whole patterning of the linguistic code, in general, that to a large extent determines our perception of the speech sounds. We perceive them not as mere sounds but specifically as speech components. More than this, the way we perceive them is determined by the phonemic pattern most familiar to us. [. . .] If on the aural level, too, speech analysis were to be conducted in terms of the binary phonemic oppositions, the task would be substantially facilitated and could supply the most instructive correlates of the distinctive features. [. . .] In short, for the study of speech sounds on any level whatsoever their linguistic function is decisive.
>
> *Jakobson, Fant, & Halle, 1951/1976, pp. 10–11*

The voice in the headphones declared, "The wrong shot led the farm." This sentence was one of many used to assess a perceiver's sensitivity to the linguistic form of speech in exclusion of its sense (Nye & Gaitenby, 1974). In this regard, the emphasis was well placed, for the capacity of utterances to assert or to promise or to demand depends as much on the intelligibility of linguistic form as on the lucidity of the message. But, as decades of study have shown, a close consideration of linguistic form exposes a deep empirical and theoretical problem. Within a language, words are composed from a finite and small inventory of phonemic contrasts. English, according to this analysis, uses three dozen consonants and vowels, give or take a few, and when theoretical disputes have occurred about this stratum of linguistic description, the outcomes recast the phoneme roster only slightly. Were utterances to express the phonemic constituents of words in a straightforward acoustic semaphore, the program of speech perception would be a simple one: (1) sense each acoustic constituent; and, (2) match it to its phoneme. Yet we have known since *Preliminaries to Speech Analysis* (Jakobson *et al.*, 1951/1976) that the phonetic expression of phoneme contrasts is graded in continuous and indefinitely vast physical variation. The problem solved by a perceiver identifying an instance of a phoneme is far from simple: (1) identify its acoustic correlates despite the continuity of variation that obscures the beginning and end of its portion of the physical signal, and (2) assess its acoustic essence despite an indefinitely large set of acoustic manifestations. How, then, does a listener identify phonemes given incommensurate phonetic forms on which to rely?

In the formulation of the problem given in *Preliminaries*, there appeared to be hope for a solution by means of perception. Specifically, it was conceivable that a sensory system registers graded physical variation discontinuously, exaggerating some sensory aspects and minimizing others. In this conceptualization, a sensory faculty hypothetically promotes the categorization of sounds along the dimensions of its inherent distortion. This prominent possibility has been considered when asking about the influence of perception on phonology. If a raw auditory system can be likened to a collection of locks, and the sound inventory of a language to a set of keys, then perceptual standards for consonants and vowels imaginably take a rather specific sensory form, as is sometimes proposed (Diehl *et al.*, 1991; Kuhl, 1992) or disputed (Fowler, 1991; Liberman & Cooper, 1972; Remez & Rubin, 1983). This contest is brought to mind by appeals to the qualitative impressions of speech — *psychoacoustics*, most prominently — in describing or explaining synchronic and diachronic phonological form.

The thesis of this essay is that a psychoacoustic setting is self-evidently natural but insufficient to create an account of phonetic perception. This is so because the detailed sensory constituents of speech responsible for psychoacoustic impressions seem to matter far less in phonetic perception than the orderly progression of sensory variation stemming from the talker's utterance. This premise is fatal to any definition of phonemic or phonetic types by means of short-term sensory properties, whether psychoacoustic or other. It seems that a talker is understood because of the transparency of articulatory, physical, and sensory media to phonetic attributes, which themselves are symbolic objects. In the spirit of *Preliminaries*, we might say that phonology governs perception, and not vice versa. By reviewing some of the key findings in the perceptual organization of speech, we can appreciate the significance of this perceptual characteristic of linguistic communication, thereby guiding our enduring search for the cognitive principles of segmental perception.

I. PERCEPTUAL ORGANIZATION OF SPEECH

Describing the nature of spoken communication, Jakobson *et al.* (1951/1976) offered a brief quotation from Norbert Wiener (1950): "In the problem of decoding, the most important information we can possess is the knowledge that the message we are reading is not gibberish." For the perceiver, this knowledge is equivalent to a state of organized perception, in which perceptual analysis can ensue because the contents of sensory domains to be analyzed are well defined. Most narrowly, perceptual organization occurs once a perceiver has aggregated the sensory manifestations of a talker's utterance. In the terms defined by Bregman & Pinker (1978), the sensory effects of a perceptual object are parsed from other concurrent sensory activity and can be analyzed for phonetic attributes.

A general description of perceptual organization pertinent to speech is given in Figure 2.1. Four sensory systems are impressionable to attributes of a talker and a message. When a talker reflects light, produces sound, is in direct physical contact with a perceiver, or is a source of odorant molecules (on the stream of expired air, or perhaps from perfume), each sensory system registers aspects of the message or

Perceptual Organization of Speech

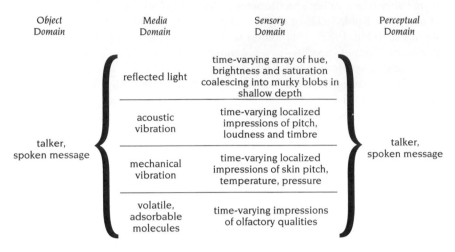

| | Object
Domain | Media
Domain | Sensory
Domain | Perceptual
Domain |

talker, spoken message	reflected light	time-varying array of hue, brightness and saturation coalescing into murky blobs in shallow depth	talker, spoken message
acoustic vibration	time-varying localized impressions of pitch, loudness and timbre
mechanical vibration	time-varying localized impressions of skin pitch, temperature, pressure
volatile, adsorbable molecules	time-varying impressions of olfactory qualities

Figure 2.1. A conceptualization of the perceptual organization and analysis of speech.

talker conveyed in patterned physical media. These sensory attributes are combined in a perceptual impression of a talker and a spoken message. The most familiar example of perceptual organization of speech is given in Cherry's (1953) cocktail party phenomenon, in which the perceiver isolates the sensory elements originating in the speech of a specific talker from all others, as well as from the sensory attributes of nonvocal events of the gathering. When organization is defective, either because of omission of elements that are part of the target speech stream or because of an intrusion of sensory elements that do not belong to the attended speech, analysis of the phonetic properties is harmed. In such circumstances, the linguistic form of the message may be perceptually indeterminate, or may be perceived erroneously, or may be guessed by the perceiver.

II. UNIMODAL AUDITORY PERCEPTUAL ORGANIZATION OF SPEECH

In considering unimodal auditory perceptual organization of speech, we find an opportunity to estimate the interchange of phonology and perception. This possibility is due to the maturity of the dominant account of auditory perceptual organization, which derives from gestalt demonstrations (Wertheimer, 1923), and is buttressed by a volume of recent psychoacoustic and computational modeling

Auditory Scene Analysis

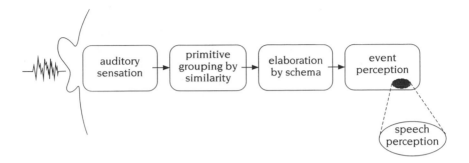

Figure 2.2.   Auditory Scene Analysis. After Bregman (1990).

(Bregman, 1990; Brown & Cooke, 1994; Ellis, 1996). This general account, Auditory Scene Analysis, proposes a two-stage model of perceptual organization and analysis. First, as Figure 2.2 shows, grouping of auditory sensory elements into sets of like items occurs by automatic application of primitive principles indifferent to acoustic phonetics: coincident onset, common modulation, similarity in frequency or in change in frequency, similarity in short-term spectrum, closure of brief gaps, and continuity in change. The formation of a perceptual stream segregates its elementary constituents from those composing other streams, and an index of the establishment of organized groups is the perceptual impossibility of assessing the intercalation order of elements across streams. Second, an organized stream is evaluated in comparison to schematically represented knowledge of the likely sensory effects created by experience of familiar objects and events. Within this familiar set is speech, and although messages are typically original, the linguistic form of a message is familiar and representable with other types of familiar sound structure (Bregman, 1990).

    The premises of this general perceptual model are clear, and permit a definitive test of its adequacy for organizing a speech signal. This is due to an assertion that similarity is the sole standard for primitive grouping, and to an assertion that knowledge of typical auditory form provides relief when the grouping by primitive mechanisms is indeterminate, incomplete, or prone to error. If auditory perceptual organization has constrained the production of sound in language, then the sensory properties of speech must conform to the model's standard for elements common to a perceptual stream. Similarly, a perceiver's success with a speech signal must be predictable from the likelihood that sensory details reflect prior encounters with speech.

In a review of this general auditory account (Remez *et al.*, 1994), my colleagues and I considered its plausibility with respect to the acoustic heterogeneity of speech, and the evidence of perceptual tolerance for departure of speech signals from familiar sensory manifestations. Specifically, we asked whether the constituents of a speech signal issuing from a single talker in a quiet environment (a more intimate cocktail party than imagined by Cherry) conceivably cohere into a perceptual stream by virtue of their collective similarity and continuity. Figure 2.3 shows a spectrogram of an utterance that we marked according to the gestalt-derived grouping component of Auditory Scene Analysis, and counted ten separate perceptual streams that would be composed from the constituents of this prosaic sentence. On the principle of spectral similarity, and in the absence of physical continuity to bind the dissimilar elements, one stream forms of the frictions associated with the production of [ð]; a second from the friction of instances of [s]; a third from the release bursts of the [d]; a fourth from the friction of the [z]; a fifth from the aspirate releases of the [p]; a sixth from the friction of the [č]; a seventh from the intermittent formants associated with [n]; and one for each of the three lowest-frequency oral formants that onset and rise or fall in frequency asynchronously, and are therefore split despite the weak promotion of grouping by harmonic relatedness and common amplitude modulation (cf. Breg-

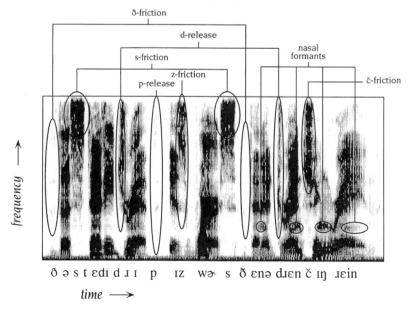

Figure 2.3. The acoustic diversity of the constituents of a speech signal. Reprinted with permission from the author and the American Psychological Association.

man *et al.*, 1985). To draw the obvious conclusion, without a supplementary contrivance to block or to reverse the application of the similarity criteria, the auditory organizing principles fracture speech into streams. In contrast, the grouping principles of the general auditory account are ideal for the signal constituents of a hypothetical language consisting solely of slowly changing vowels phonated with a glottal mode that minimizes the production of noise-bands in the spectrum (see Klatt & Klatt, 1990; Stevens, 1999) or, for a phonology consisting of reduplicated homorganic fricatives. If phonology were governed by the constraints of auditory perception, insofar as they are described in Auditory Scene Analysis, we would observe rather different phoneme inventories than we see, for example, in English.

A second stage is available within Auditory Scene Analysis, though it fares no better than the first when challenged to organize a speech signal veridically. The model describes the application of schematically represented knowledge when the sensory form to be organized is familiar, and it is proposed (Bregman, 1990) as a potential means by which to recover from erroneous parsing of an auditory sensory pattern. This cognitive device is an instance of a knowledge-driven process (Bobrow & Norman, 1975). By relying on knowledge of familiar occurrences, the sensory pattern organized into a stream by gestalt-derived principles is weighed against a schematic representation of the event that gave rise to the sensory pattern in the first place. The perceiver's knowledge supplements the sensory information, and gaps or intrusions in the grouped but as yet unidentified sensory pattern can be readily revised from memory. This faculty of perception is quite powerful, yet we faulted it as a contributor to perceptual organization of speech on four counts; these points are presented in great detail in our review (Remez *et al.*, 1994). First, resort to knowledge is implausible in the organization of speech, which must occur rather urgently, surely within the first 90–100 ms after transduction while the rapidly fading auditory trace remains available. This urgency constraint does not characterize engineering solutions to organization (Klatt, 1989), which can hold a sensory trace of speech indefinitely, and surely throughout a leisurely interrogation of long-term memory. Second, competence in the auditory perceptual organization of speech appears rather early in development, in the first few months of life (Eimas & Miller, 1992; Newman & Jusczyk, 1995); the principles governing perceptual organization seem to antedate rather than derive from knowledge of the form of spoken language. Third, resort to knowledge is too weak to undo the effects of primary auditory grouping, for no evidence exists that practice releases a perceiver from the effects of primitive grouping mechanisms.

Fourth, a reliance on normative knowledge of phonetic sensory qualities is the heart of the schematic component. In this conceptualization, auditory grouping can produce a defective internal representation of a speech signal due to the segregation of one or another of its auditory constituents; the second stage of Auditory Scene Analysis can repair it by resort to knowledge of the typical distribution of sensory effects of utterances. However, this premise is contradicted by the great variety of physical and sensory manifestations of speech, occasioned by anatomical differences among talkers and a wide range of natural and artifactual means by which spoken exchanges occur. To a first approximation, it seems that a perceiver follows the coherent time-varying pattern of a speech signal instead of accruing familiar auditory elements piecemeal.

A. Sinewave Replication of Utterances

We tested for such sensitivity to speechlike patterns independent of speechlike elements, using sinewave replicas of utterances. In this sort of synthetic acoustic pattern, the gross shape of the spectral variation of speech is preserved, but the naturally occurring acoustic vocal products are exchanged for sinusoids; we have used three and sometimes four digital oscillators to create a sinewave utterance replica. Figure 2.4 illustrates the spectral differences between natural and replicated speech, in this instance, a syllable, [dʒɑ].

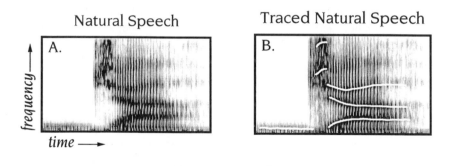

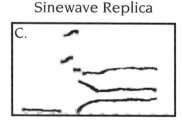

Figure 2.4. Replication of the time-varying pattern of a speech signal by three sinusoids, shown in spectrograms: (**A**) natural speech; (**B**) pattern of spectral prominences marked by traces; (**C**) sinewave pattern resulting from use of the spectral peak analysis to control digital oscillators.

Tone analogs of speech have a dual effect on a perceiver, for they are intelligible phonetically while evoking an impression of contrapuntal tones varying in pitch and loudness. In other words, the tones are split into separate streams just as the gestalt-derived principles require, but they are also phonetically coherent, in exception to the gestalt-derived grouping principles, and despite the absence of acoustic ingredients that typify speech (Remez *et al.*, in press). Of course, the tones in a sinewave replica usually issue from a single spatial location, and similarity in location has figured in some discussions of grouping (Darwin & Hukin, 1999). To provide an ultimate test of the persistence of perceptual organization of speech, we imposed the conditions of (1) dissimilarity in the location of its elements, (2) violation of the primitive principles of grouping, and (3) absence of familiar auditory forms. The test is diagrammed in Figure 2.5.

Using three sinewaves in place of the oral formants and a fourth in place of the fricative formant, we replicated a set of English sentences exhibiting the full variety of phone classes. In a test of intelligibility, we presented all of the tones except the analog of the second formant to one ear of a listener, and the isolated second formant analog to the other ear. In some conditions, a supernumerary tone was also presented in the frequency band of the second formant tone analog. This extra tone was delivered to the ear receiving the sinusoidal sentence replica lacking only a second formant tone analog, which was presented to the opposite ear, as Figure 2.5 shows. The listener's task here was straightforward: to understand the sentence, a perceiver must integrate sinusoidal elements across the ears, despite spatial dissimilarity, violation of other gestalt grouping criteria, and lack

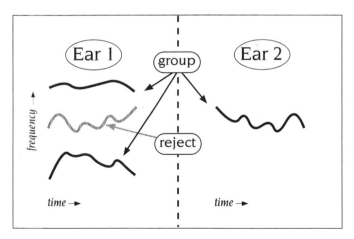

Figure 2.5. A dichotic test of perceptual organization in the absence of familiar sensory ingredients.

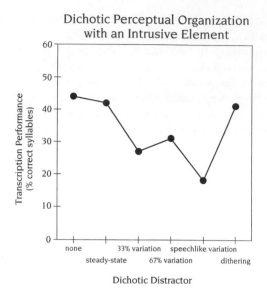

Figure 2.6. Findings in a test of dichotic perceptual organization of speech with an intrusive element. The transcriptions were scored conservatively for the percent of available syllables that were correctly transcribed.

of familiarity of these acoustic elements as components of speech signals. In conditions with an intrusive element, the listener must ignore the foil and attend to the tones that gel.

Figure 2.6 shows the group performance on tests of intelligibility, in which naive participants simply wrote the sentence that the tones conveyed. The condition in which the task simply required integration of spatially disparate tone components is labeled "none," indicating that there was no intrusive element, and performance here is at its best. Perceptual organization persists contrary to general perceptual principles even when the last aspect of similarity exhibited by the sinusoidal components — location — is eliminated.

Performance was also unperturbed by the presence of an intrusive tone if it did not exhibit speechlike frequency variation. This is shown in the conditions in which an intrusive constant frequency tone was presented at the average frequency of the true second formant analog, the "steady-state" condition in Figure 2.6, and in which an intrusive time-varying tone oscillated regularly between frequencies 10% above and 10% below the average frequency of the true second formant tone analog, labeled "dithering" in Figure 2.6. However, speechlike frequency variation impaired dichotic perceptual organization, as seen in the condition labeled "speechlike variation." In this condition the intrusive tone was derived by temporally inverting the true second formant analog. This time-reversed second formant analog exhibited the same range and rate of frequency excursion as the temporally veridical tone did, and impaired the organization of the true second formant analog in the opposite ear. We also tested variants of the intrusive tone that we graded to exhibit 33 and 67% of the speechlike frequency variation of the time-reversed second formant tone. This was accomplished by straining the frequency parameters in the sinewave synthesizer to depart from the average value of the second formant by 33 or 67% of the actual value. These tones interfered with dichotic perceptual organization more than the constant or dithering tones had, though less than the speechlike tone.

This assessment of the prevailing general model of auditory perceptual organization allows a clear conclusion: the diversity of the components of the speech signal and its time-varying complexity fall well beyond the range encompassed by the simple grouping criteria and reliance on schematic representations of familiar sensory attributes. Evidently, the listener who organizes an auditory sensory pattern as a speech stream is attuned to the pattern of speechlike acoustic variation of a phonetic expression, and exhibits this susceptibility in defining a sensory domain of elements fit to analyze perceptually. In the most general terms, the satisfaction of this standard of speechlike variation across a pattern of acoustic elements qualifies any one of them as a speech cue.

B. Quantized Noise-Band Signals

If the only unimodal evidence opposing a general auditory account were the tests using sinewave analogs, we might hesitate to claim so plainly that the perceptual organization of speech occurs by virtue of principles distinct from those of the auditory sense. However, the studies of quantized noise-band signals (Shannon *et al.*, 1995) offer an equally persuasive assay of the general auditory principles of perceptual organization and the apparent exclusion from their effects that speech enjoys. While the sinewave replication technique eliminates the fine spectral grain of speech and concentrates the signal at the amplitude maxima, the quantized noise-band transform creates a complementary effect. With sinewave replicas, the spectrum is reduced to frequency variation across a set of nonharmonically related tones. With noise-band signals, the spectrotemporal properties of natural speech are reduced to amplitude variation across a small set of noise-bands of stationary frequency. Figure 2.7 portrays the relation between natural speech and two transformed signals, both of which are intelligible. To see why this kind of signal also poses a problem for the standard auditory account, consider how it is created.

As we observed when surveying the diverse acoustic components of speech, the spectrum is densely patterned. The transformation of the natural spectrum into

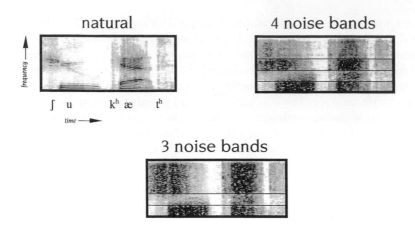

Figure 2.7. A spectrographic portrait of the quantized noise-band transformation of a speech spectrum (redrawn from Shannon *et al.*, 1995). The left panel shows a narrow-band spectrogram of a natural utterance. The center panel shows the effect of composing the signal as four constant frequency noise-bands, the right panel shows the effect of composing the signal as three constant frequency noise-bands. Both quantized signals are intelligible.

quantized noise-bands eliminates the pattern in detail, first by dividing the full spectrum into a small set of broad bands and integrating the energy within each. These instantaneous measures of the energy integrated within several nonoverlapping frequency regions are then fed to an acoustic emitter, which modulates the amplitude of several band-limited noise sources, each of which matches the band of one of the analyzers. For instance, the signal composed by analyzing natural speech into four frequency bands and adding the four matching noise sources together mimics the speech signal in very coarse detail. The center panel of Figure 2.7 shows the effect of transforming a natural speech signal into a noise-band pattern comprising four elements: one noise source spans upper and lower cuts of 0–800 Hz, the next spans 801–1600 Hz, the third 1601 Hz–4 kHz, and the last from 4 to 8 kHz.

How well does a general auditory account fare in explaining the perceptual organization of phonetically coherent noise-bands? The challenge to the auditory theory in this instance is to accommodate a listener's readiness to bind four concurrent noises into a coherent stream, thereby to comprehend the phonetic form of their variation. Once again, the general account of auditory organization requires similarity among elements to cast them into a single perceptual stream; but, the great frequency differences between noise-bands opposes grouping by similarity, whether of frequency or of timbre. Likewise, the asynchronous changes in acoustic power of the noise-bands render them dissimilar, an impediment to grouping by gestalt means. The primary automatic grouping mechanism is likely to segregate the auditory correlates of the four noise-bands in different perceptual streams. In the absence of similarity among elements, the general auditory account allows a knowledge-driven secondary process to intercede, though our review of auditory organization judged it an implausible stage in the perception of speech, for it is too slow, too weak, and warrants a false description of the infant human listener. It is also significant that, in detail, a quantized noise-band rendition of a speech signal does not resemble the acoustic form of speech. Even whispering, which evokes qualitative impressions remotely akin to noise-band signals, typically exhibits a strong harmonic component that the noise-band signals lack (Catford, 1988); and, of course, whispered speech exhibits a nonstationary spectrum due to frequency variation in its resonance bands, in marked contrast to the stationary spectrum of each of the noise sources in quantized noise-band signals. A knowledge-driven perceptual process that knows only the typical sensory manifestations of speech sounds should decline to categorize noise-band spectra as speechlike. The proof of this discovery by Shannon *et al.* (1995) is that it is possible to satisfy the abstract spectrotemporal criteria for phonetic perceptual organization with a signal that simply lacks narrow-band amplitude peaks. Our ultimate characterization of the unimodal grouping principle must acknowledge that a speech signal can be peaked (as in the case of natural speech, synthetic speech, or sinewave replicas of utterances) or not.

C. A Unimodal, Preliminary Conclusion

The function of perceptual organization is selective, identifying the sensory effects proper to a specific object or event. In the unimodal auditory instances that we have investigated, we gauged the relation of perception and phonology by considering an account that defines auditory perceptual organization generally, according to psychoacoustic criteria. Having exposed the nature of perceptual organization in reference to psychoacoustics, we then calibrated the usefulness of the general auditory account for the acoustic and auditory properties of speech. This comparison of the general auditory model with the circumstances of speech perception exposed inadequacies in the auditory account in both of its key processes. Empirical tests of the critical premises of the auditory model exposed cases in which phonetic perceptual organization persisted despite violation of the gestalt-derived primitive grouping stage and despite the atypical spectra perceived as speech.

In retrospect, these inadequacies seem due to a crucial misstep in describing the relation between the mechanical events that produce acoustic effects and a listener's perceptual discovery of them. Specifically, the model asserts that a primitive analysis tantamount to a classification of acoustic elements is sufficient to identify sensory effects of a single cause. This cannot be the right method for devising a theory satisfactory for speech, though. The exploitation of the vocal tract for expressing phoneme contrasts produces an array of hisses, buzzes, clicks, whistles, and hums, and to sort them into streams of like elements disrupts the continuity of speech. More realistically, the organizational function detects the sensory effects of an ongoing modulation of a complex articulatory resource, and collects the sensory effects that conform to grammatically governed sound production. In the general auditory account, an emphasis on psychoacoustics to the detriment of acoustic mechanics has produced a description of auditory perceptual organization that fails to explain the organization of natural speech and of its derivatives, sinewave replicas, and quantized noise-band transforms. For the wider objective of perceptual theory, it remains to be determined whether auditory organization of speech is a special case of unimodal auditory organization, or whether the evidence of speech brought against the claims of the gestalt-derived auditory model falsifies it. But, before the focus of this essay turns to an even more general multimodal case, it is useful to note the verdict that the dominant theory of auditory perceptual organization based on psychoacoustics has so little to offer in explaining the auditory perceptual organization of speech.

III. Multimodal Perceptual Organization of Speech

Because the problem of auditory organization is to select sensory constituents originating in a specific sound source, there is at least some prospect that a general auditory account based on psychoacoustics is pertinent. But, does a general auditory account of perceptual organization apply to a multimodal instance? In this situation, the function of perceptual organization is to select sensory constituents of an event that is seen and heard. No auditory sensory element is ever similar, formally, to a visual element, and a premise other than exact similarity must be motivated for integrating sound and sight. In fact, one debate in recent research on multimodal speech perception has concerned the moment during the act of perceiving when a common metric is applied to evaluate sound and sight. If the moment of sensory integration occurs early in perceptual organization, as some have claimed (Green & Miller, 1985), then the perceptual organization of speech does in fact encompass unanalyzed sensory forms grouped into a perceptual stream across modalities. If integration occurs late, as others have argued (Massaro & Stork, 1998), then perceptual organization does not occur multimodally, and the senses combine only after perceptual analysis has transpired. This contention is prominent in ongoing research about speech, and the empirical mist has not yet cleared to expose a continuous landscape of evidence. Because two completely different empirical methods are in use, there appear to be genuine instances in the technical literature of early and of late integration.

In one method, a perceiver is asked to attend to a multimodal display of speech in which neither the visual component nor the auditory component is sufficient to evoke phonetic impressions in isolation from the other. An important example of this was reported by Rosen *et al.* (1981), whose test subjects viewed a fluent talker while listening to an amplified electroglottograph output. The linguistic content of the speech was ordinary but unpredictable in detail, and neither the sight of the face nor the sound of the glottal pulsing was adequate to evoke phonetic perception. In combination, though, the audiovisual presentation was impressively intelligible. In this sort of situation, organization cannot proceed unimodally, with phonetic analysis occurring separately in visual and auditory modalities, and with multimodal integration occurring as the concluding step in perception. There would be nothing phonetic to combine at the end of unimodal analysis. Instead, it seems reasonable to presume that this kind of phenomenon requires an account of early integration of the senses preliminary to analysis, in which the talker's message becomes perceptible because an aggregate of visual and auditory sensory activity yields a pattern sufficient to analyze. Such a finding obliges the theorist to describe multimodal organization in the same terms as unimodal organization.

In a second empirical method, the visual pattern of an articulating face and the auditory pattern of speech are each effective independently in evoking phonetic perception. Perhaps the perceiver ineluctably combines visual and auditory sensory activity before phonetic analysis even though each modality alone is sufficient to conclude in a well-formed phonetic impression. In that case, perception might differ nonetheless from the impressions that derive from either sensory mode alone. There is an alternative conceptualization of this circumstance in which the perceiver is portrayed as an agent who adjudicates an intersensory conflict. Accordingly, intersensory combination is thought to occur after phonetic attributes are determined independently in each modality (Massaro & Stork, 1998). Incomplete blending of the registered attributes is common, yielding a multisensory outcome that also differs from either modality alone. Each method appears to warrant a different account of multimodal perceptual organization.

In late audiovisual combination, each modality hastens along independently of the other, and, accordingly, the motivating question of this essay has already been answered for this version of multimodal organization. Because the principles deriving from psychoacoustics do not describe the auditory perceptual coherence of speech signals, we can answer that multimodal perception does not constrain phonology unless those pressures are primarily visual. We ought not dismiss this possibility as absurd without discussion of the potentially converging sources of sensory constraint that might apply to phonology. After all, the language learner proceeds multimodally (Guenther, 1995; Locke, 1993). Perception is *auditory* when listening to the speech of others, *auditory-reafferent* when listening to self-produced speech, *visual* when watching the speech production of another, *visual-reafferent* when watching self-produced speech in a mirror, *orofacial tactile* when feeling the surfaces of the articulators in contact with each other, or feeling them vibrate during speech production, and *thoracically* and *orofacially haptic* when feeling the sense of effort, placement, and configuration of the airway and articulators. Indeed, the sensory projections of phoneme contrasts are multidimensional, and we assume at our peril that the auditory perceptual constraints alone determine phonology within the convergence of limits.

In early combination of sensory ingredients, modalities mingle to define a multisensory domain of perceptual analysis despite dissimilarity among the elements of each modality (see Figure 2.1). A general account of sensory combination in perceptual organization is yet to be devised to explain the principles of intersensory binding, although there are notable elaborations of dimensional correspondence in vision and hearing (e.g., Marks, 1975, 1987), and physiological investigations of functional convergence along the neuraxis (Stein *et al.*, 1995). Without a unified account, right or wrong, any test of the interchange of phonology and perception in a multisensory circumstance must be less well resolved; the clinical impact of this problem is discussed by Watson *et al.*, (1996). In order to estimate the likelihood that a general perceptual account of multimodal correspondence describes speech, we compare the benchmarks for intersensory combination when the events are spoken or not. And, in order to estimate the role of familiarity with the sensory manifestations of speech, we consider several experiments that posed this question directly.

A. Multimodal Perception of Speech and Other Events

An opportunity to assess the interchange of phonology and perception multimodally is afforded by research on the registration of sensory alignment. One form of coincidence is temporal, and the sensitivity of a perceiver to temporal agreement in visual and auditory experience is straightforward to assess. In a project reported by Hirsh & Sherrick (1961), observers were able to detect a departure from simultaneity at discrepancies briefer than 20 ms. Two recent projects studied audiovisual speech perception and calibrated the temporal constraints on intermodal integration, and found that this standard for resolving sensory coincidence poorly predicts the characteristics of intersensory coherence for speech.

In one study (Munhall *et al.*, 1996), a perceiver was asked to watch a video display of a face articulating either [ɑgɑ] or [igi] on each trial paired with an acoustic signal of a voice articulating [ɑbɑ]. When auditory and visual streams were temporally coincident, the perceiver reported the consonant as [d], an instance of the phenomenon of auditory–visual phonetic blending first described by McGurk & McDonald (1976). The procedure used by Munhall *et al.* imposed discrepancies in the temporal alignment of visual and acoustic displays by presenting the acoustic signal either leading the visual display or lagging it in increments of 60 ms; the range of values extended to ±360 ms. Of course, at the extreme instances of temporal discrepancy, intermodal blending was not observed and the test subjects reported the consonant as [b]. But, at intervals of acoustic lead and lag as great as 180 ms, at which discrepancies between sight and sound are noticeable, subjects continued to report the syllable as [d]. In other words, the criteria for intersensory combination in this study did not match the detection threshold measures for intersensory temporal discrepancy.

A confirming finding is reported by Bertelson *et al.* (1997), who combined temporal desynchronization with spatial dislocation of the visual display and the acoustic signal. In a project that compared event perception and phonetic perception, subjects sat in an enclosure depicted schematically in Figure 2.8. To appraise the relation of audiovisual event perception to audiovisual

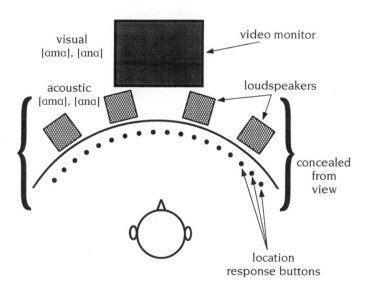

Figure 2.8. A schematic depiction of the test enclosure used by Bertelson *et al.* (1997). A subject viewed an articulating or stationary face on the video monitor while listening to an acoustic speech signal played through one of four concealed loudspeakers. The acoustic signal led or lagged the visual display. At the end of each trial, a subject reported (1) the apparent location of the sound by pressing a concealed button easily within reach, and (2) reported the identity of the consonant.

phonetic perception, Bertelson *et al.* asked subjects to report a consonant on each trial, and also measured *ventriloquism*, the extent to which the apparent location of a sound source is influenced by the concurrent appearance of a visual event. Therefore, this test permits a contrast between two kinds of multimodal perceptual organization of the same sensory ingredients: (1) the perceptual organization of the event (a person at a specific location, talking), and (2) the phonetic organization of the spoken message (resulting in the perception of a series of phonetic segments).

The acoustic signal was the sound of a voice articulating either [ɑmɑ] or [ɑnɑ], and was presented on each trial by one of four concealed loudspeakers flanking a centrally placed video monitor. The concurrently visible face also articulated [ɑmɑ] or [ɑnɑ], or in control conditions was still. A subject indicated the apparent location of the hidden sound source by pressing one of the concealed buttons that spanned the enclosure, and reported the consonant as [m] or [n]. Ventriloquism and audiovisual speech perception were measured both when the acoustic and visual presentations were synchronized, and when the acoustic signal led or lagged the visual, in parallel to the conditions used by Munhall *et al.*; both instances of intersensory combination, the location of the sound source and the identity of the intervocalic consonant, were standardized relative to the effect on perception of the acoustic signal presented with a motionless face.

The result of this experiment provides evidence about the relation between general perceptual resources of audiovisual integration and of the perceptual organization of speech. The finding is consistent with the general pattern described here. Visual presentation of an articulating face lured the perceived location of the sound of speech toward the center of the enclosure. The spatial effect was greatest when the visual and auditory signals were discrepant, the face articulated [ɑmɑ], the acoustic signal was [ɑnɑ], and the acoustic signal lagged the visual signal by 150 ms. Taking spatial organization of the multimodal event as a standard, the sensory combination of visual and auditory sources should have reprised the outcome of the ventriloquism test. Instead, the phonetic effect of the visual presentation was greatest when the face articulated [ɑnɑ], the acoustic signal was [ɑmɑ]; and, provocatively, this audiovisual phonetic interaction occurred over a wide range of temporal discrepancies, from an acoustic lead as great at 150 ms, to lags as great as 300 ms.

While confirming the tolerance for temporal discrepancy in phonetic perceptual organization reported by Munhall *et al.*, Bertelson *et al.* (1997) also provide a crucial index of this perceptual characteristic relative to organization of events, and report that the standards differ. It seems unlikely, for instance, that these findings are produced by a single organizing mechanism common to spatial event perception and phonetic perceptual purposes. Instead, it seems as though the perception of speech exerts a constraint on perceptual organization whether this transpires unimodally or multimodally.

B. The Role of Familiarity in Multimodal Perceptual Organization

One way that we assessed the role of familiarity in the multimodal perceptual organization of speech was to study the audiovisual integration of vision and audition when the auditory constituents were partial sinewave replicas of utterances. In this test (Remez *et al.*, 1998) we captured video and audio samples of the speech of a talker simultaneously, and then replicated the acoustic spectra according to the method described in Figure 2.4. We then composed a set of test materials in which the realistic view of the face was combined with individual tone components, none of which was a familiar constituent of acoustic speech signals, and none of which evoked familiar qualitative impressions of speech. In transcription tests with these sentence-length items, we found that the only single tone formant analog that combined effectively with the visual presentation of the articulating face was the analog of the second formant (cf. Bernstein *et al.*, 1992). Other tones, including a single tone replicating the pattern of the fundamental frequency, failed to bind to the visual presentation of the face as indicated by a measure of transcription performance (cf. McGrath & Summerfield, 1985; Rosen *et al.*, 1981). In some respects, this outcome was a surprise, inasmuch as the second formant of speech is often described as an acoustic correlate of the placement of the tongue. If the visual presentation of the face already provides information about the place of articulation for anteriorly articulated segments, we might have expected acoustic correlates of the manner and voicing of speech segments available in the tone analogs of the first formant or of the fundamental frequency of phonation to promote organization, at least according to the form of teleology that parsimony prescribes. Instead, the sensory combination of visual and auditory constituents occurred when they were consistent, not when they were complementary.

A profound clue about the operating dynamic of perceptual organization is revealed in a study of the role of familiarity in multimodal speech perception. In a test of consonant perception, Fowler & Dekle (1991) devised a method that separately assessed the effects of familiarity and *lawful specification*, in their term. If specification indicates the implication of a distal event by a proximal sensory pattern, then lawful specification asserts a necessary relation between the transformations of objects and events and the forms of sensory flux to which they correspond. A perceiver who is responsive to lawful specification is able to transcend the lack of familiarity of sensory properties in order to attend to a familiar mechanical system although inexperienced in the form of sensory contact. The evidence is easy to understand, and includes the conditions described in Figure 2.9.

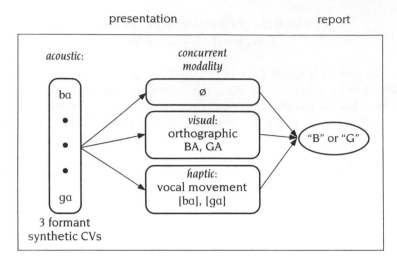

Figure 2.9. Design of a test of multimodal phonetic organization by Fowler & Dekle (1991).

A series of synthetic three-formant consonant–vowel syllables ranging from [bɑ] to [gɑ] were composed by varying the onset frequency and frequency excursion of the resonance peak of the second formant. These acoustic items were categorized in isolation by a set of listeners. Then, each listener was asked to report the phonetic properties of the items from the acoustic test set while attending to a concurrent event. In a condition that was both visual and familiar, listeners saw the orthographic form representing the consonant; in a condition that was both haptic and unfamiliar, listeners felt the articulating face of one of the experimenters producing a consonant–vowel syllable in synchrony with the presentation of each of the acoustic items. In describing these test conditions, Fowler & Dekle argue that an orthographic form evokes an impression of a phonetic form by virtue of familiarity, while the haptic experience of an articulating face, while unfamiliar to participants in the study, provides sensory experience that is lawfully related to a subject's knowledge of the production of phonological structure. The results, shown in Figure 2.10, corroborate this argument. The left panel shows the identification function for acoustic presentations accompanied by orthographic images, the right panel shows the identification function for acoustic presentations accompanied by haptic impressions. Only in the haptic conditions was speech perception organized multimodally, despite the long experience of test subjects (college students, after all) with printed forms of language. The abstractness of the perceiver's unprecedented knowledge and attention to sensory forms in this haptic case parallels the unimodal and multimodal findings with sinewave signals, in

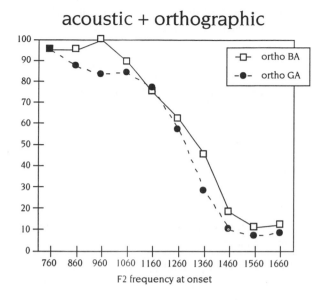

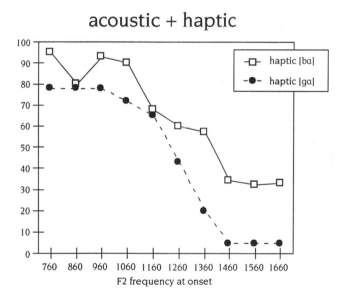

Figure 2.10.   Identification of consonant place of articulation under concurrent influence of (left panel) orthographic and (right panel) haptic perception. Redrawn from Fowler & Dekle (1991).

which the novelty and strangeness of the experience of language proved to be only a slight impediment to phonetic perceptual organization.

IV. SEVERAL CONCLUSIONS

A few conclusions are conservatively warranted by the cases of unimodal and multimodal perceptual organization that we have considered here:

> Multimodal perceptual organization is susceptible to time-varying properties of the sensory effects of speech.
>
> Sensitivity to time-varying sensory properties can be tolerant of unfamiliar and unnatural elements composing a spectrotemporal pattern.
>
> Reliance on spectrotemporal pattern in lieu of familiar elements requires a lawful relation between linguistic phonological intentions in speech production and the sensory consequences of phonetic expression.

And, on the topic of the interchange of phonology and perception, a few conclusions can also be ventured without abandoning caution:

> Fundamental perceptual functions detect and maintain the coherent continuity of a speech signal despite the sensory heterogeneity of natural vocal production.
>
> The disposition to organize perceptual streams across the senses is uninstructed and ineluctable.
>
> It is unlikely that phonological contrasts require a perceiver to detect subtle details of sensation close to the limits of auditory or visual sensory resolution.

Our studies and those of our colleagues show that speech perception remains robust under conditions never entertained in *Preliminaries*. Jakobson *et al.* quote S. S. Stevens, "the fact of redundancy increases the reliability of speech communication, and makes it resistant to many types of distortion. By limiting the number of discriminations required of the listener and by assisting his choice through the redundant coding of information, we make talking to one another a reasonably satisfactory business" (p. 8).

The redundancy they were contemplating was attributable to allophonic variation in production, or to multiple acoustic effects of a single articulation; or to similarity in auditory effect of several physically distinct signals. These are normative notions, and they make an implicit appeal to a kind of phenomenal essentialism: the recognition of phonemic types is brought about by a luxuriously redundant set of sensory correlates of each feature. At times, too, the distribution of the feature alternations are correlated, though this allophonic property is a perceived attribute of speech rather than a means to perceive speech. In this vein, the research that composed the details of my argument here extends this notion of redundancy, though not by adding attributes of the same type as gestures, acoustic cues, or auditory attributes. Instead, this work has elaborated the susceptibility of a competent perceiver to sensory variation that is related in quite an abstract way to the typical visual or auditory pattern of speakers and speech. This abstractness is evidence of a specific kind of perceptual function at work in speech perception, one which is relatively impervious to the physical distortions that lend such experiences — of sinewave replicas and quantized noise-band transforms — an anomalous quality. The perceiver, in my view, is thereby relieved of devotion to the principles of similarity and familiarity in evaluating novel sensory forms. Put simply, the sinewave replicas are intelligible because they satisfy an abstract description of the sensory variation that issues from grammatically governed vocal sound production, not because they are similar to vocal sound in detail, nor because they are familiar. It is a great puzzle that the perceiver comes to apply such an abstract and perhaps imaginative capacity for transforming the sensory realm.

ACKNOWLEDGMENTS

I am grateful to the editors of this volume for the provocation to make this case; and to my generous multimodal colleagues for their intellectual patience and counsel: Eric Bateson, Christian Benoît, Lynne Bernstein, Paul Bertelson, Carol Fowler, David Pisoni, and Philip Rubin. This research was supported by an award to Barnard College from The National Institute on Deafness and Other Communicative Disorders (DC00308).

REFERENCES

Bernstein, L. E., Coulter, D. C., O'Connell, M. P., Eberhardt, S. P., & Demorest, M. E. (1992). *Vibrotactile and haptic speech codes.* Paper presented at the Second International Conference on Tactile Aids, Hearing Aids, & Cochlear Implants, Royal Institute of Technology, Stockholm, Sweden, 9–11 June 1992.

Bertelson, P., Vroomen, J., & de Gelder, B. (1997). Auditory–visual interaction in voice localization and in bimodal speech recognition: The effects of desynchronization. In C. Benoît & R. Campbell (Eds.), *Proceedings of the workshop on audio-visual speech processing: Cognitive and computational approaches* (pp. 97–100). Rhodes: ESCA.

Bobrow, D. G., & Norman, D. A. (1975). Some principles of memory schemata. In D. C. Bobrow & A. M. Collins (Eds.), *Representation and understanding* (pp. 131–149). New York: Academic Press.

Bregman, A. S. (1990). *Auditory scene analysis.* Cambridge: MIT Press.

Bregman, A. S., & Pinker, S. (1978). Auditory streaming and the building of timbre. *Canadian Journal of Psychology, 32,* 19–31.

Bregman, A. S., Abramson, J., Doehring, P., & Darwin, C. J. (1985). Spectral integration based on common amplitude modulation. *Perception & Psychophysics, 37,* 483–493.

Brown, G. J., & Cooke, M. (1994). Computational auditory scene analysis. *Computer Speech and Language, 8,* 297–336.

Catford, J. C. (1988). *A practical introduction to phonetics.* Oxford: Oxford University Press.

Cherry, E. C. (1953). Some experiments on the recognition of speech, with one and two ears. *Journal of the Acoustical Society of America, 25,* 975–979.

Darwin, C. J., & Hukin, R. W. (1999). Auditory objects of attention: The role of interaural time-differences. *Journal of Experimental Psychology: Human Perception and Performance, 25,* 617–629.

Diehl, R. L., Kluender, K. R., Walsh, M. A., & Parker, E. M. (1991). Auditory enhancement in speech perception and phonology. In R. R. Hoffman & D. S. Palermo (Eds.), *Cognition and the symbolic processes: Applied and ecological perspectives* (pp. 59–76). Hillsdale, NJ: Lawrence Erlbaum.

Eimas, P. D., & Miller, J. L. (1992). Organization in the perception of speech by young infants. *Psychological Science, 3,* 340–345.

Ellis, D. P. W. (1996). *Prediction-driven computational auditory scene analysis.* Unpublished doctoral dissertation, Department of Electrical Engineering and Computer Science, Massachusetts Institute of Technology.

Fowler, C. A. (1991). Auditory perception is not special: We see the world, we feel the world, we hear the world. *Journal of the Acoustical Society of America, 89,* 2910–2915.

Fowler, C. A., & Dekle, D. J. (1991). Listening with eye and hand: Cross-modal contributions to speech perception. *Journal of Experimental Psychology: Human Perception and Performance, 17,* 816–828.

Green, K. P., & Miller, J. L. (1985). On the role of visual rate information in phonetic perception. *Perception & Psychophysics, 38,* 269–276.

Guenther, F. H. (1995). Speech sound acquisition, coarticulation, and rate effects in a neural network model of speech production. *Psychological Review, 102,* 594–621.

Hirsh, I. J., & Sherrick, C. E. (1961). Perceived order in different sense modalities. *Journal of Experimental Psychology, 62,* 423–432.

Howell, P. (1987). Delayed auditory feedback with delayed sounds varying in duration. *Perception & Psychophysics*, *42*, 166–172.

Jakobson, R., Fant, G., & Halle, M. (1976). *Preliminaries to speech analysis*. Cambridge: MIT Press. (Original work published 1951.)

Klatt, D. H. (1989). Review of selected models of speech perception. In W. Marslen-Wilson (Ed.), *Lexical representation and process* (pp. 169–226). Cambridge: MIT Press.

Klatt, D. H., & Klatt, L. C. (1990). Analysis, synthesis, and perception of voice quality variations among female and male talkers. *Journal of the Acoustical Society of America*, *87*, 820–857.

Kuhl, P. K. (1992). Psychoacoustics and speech perception: Internal standards, perceptual anchors, and prototypes. In L. A. Werner & E. W. Rubel (Eds.), *Developmental psychoacoustics* (pp. 293–332). Washington, DC: American Psychological Association.

Liberman, A. M., & Cooper, F. S. (1972). In search of the acoustic cues. In A. Valdman (Ed.), *Papers in linguistics and phonetics to the memory of Pierre Delattre* (pp. 329–338). The Hague: Mouton.

Locke, J. L. (1993). The role of the face in vocal learning and the development of spoken language. In B. de Boysson-Bardies, S. de Schonen, P. Jusczyk, P. MacNeilage, & J. Morton (Eds.), *Developmental neurocognition: Speech and face processing in the first year of life* (pp. 317–328). Dordrecht: Kluwer Academic.

Marks, L. E. (1975). On colored-hearing synesthesia: Cross-modal translations of sensory dimensions. *Psychological Bulletin, 82*, 303–331.

Marks, L. E. (1987). On cross-modal similarity: Auditory-visual interactions in speeded discrimination. *Journal of Experimental Psychology: Human Perception and Performance, 13*, 384–394.

Massaro, D. W., & Stork, D. G. (1998). Speech recognition and sensory integration. *American Scientist, 86*, 236–244.

McGrath, M., & Summerfield, Q. (1985). Intermodal timing relations and audio-visual speech recognition by normal-hearing adults. *Journal of the Acoustical Society of America, 77*, 678–685.

McGurk, H., & MacDonald, J. (1976). Hearing lips and seeing voices. *Nature, 264*, 746–748.

Munhall, K. G., Gribble, P., Sacco, L., & Ward, M. (1996). Temporal constraints on the McGurk effect. *Perception & Psychophysics, 58*, 351–362.

Newman, R. S., & Jusczyk, P. W. (1995). The cocktail party effect in infants. *Perception & Psychophysics, 58*, 1145–1156.

Nye, P. W., & Gaitenby, J. (1974). The intelligibility of synthetic monosyllable words in short syntactically normal sentences. *Haskins Laboratories Status Report on Speech Research, SR-37/38*, 169–190.

Remez, R. E., & Rubin, P. E. (1983). The stream of speech. *Scandinavian Journal of Psychology, 24*, 63–66.

Remez, R. E., Rubin, P. E., Berns, S. M., Pardo, J. S., & Lang, J. M. (1994). On the perceptual organization of speech. *Psychological Review*, *101*, 129–156.

Remez, R. E., Fellowes, J. M., Pisoni, D. B., Goh, W. D., & Rubin, P. E. (1998). Multimodal perceptual organization of speech: Evidence from tone analogs of spoken utterances. *Speech Communication*, *26*, 65–73.

Remez, R. E., Pardo, J. S., Piorkowski, R. L., & Rubin, P. E. (in press). On the bistability of sinusoidal replicas of speech. *Psychological Science*.

Rosen, S. M., Fourcin, A. J., & Moore, B. C. J. (1981). Voice pitch as an aid to lipreading. *Nature*, *291*, 150–152.

Shannon, R. V., Zeng, F.-G., Kamath, V., Wygonski, J., & Ekelid, M. (1995). Speech recognition with primarily temporal cues. *Science*, *270*, 303–304.

Stein, B. E., Wallace, M. T., & Meredith, A. M. (1995). Neural mechanisms mediating attention and orientation to multisensory cues. In M. S. Gazzaniga (Ed.), *The cognitive neurosciences* (pp. 683–702). Cambridge: MIT Press.

Stevens, K. N. (1999). *Acoustic phonetics*. Cambridge: MIT Press.

Watson, C. S., Qiu, W. W., Chamberlain, M. M., & Li, S. (1996). Auditory and visual speech perception: Confirmation of a modality-independent source of individual differences in speech recognition. *Journal of the Acoustical Society of America*, *100*, 1153–1162.

Wertheimer, M. (1923). Unsuchungen zur Lehre von der Gestalt, II. *Psychologische Forschung*, *4*, 301–350. [Translated as "Laws of organization in perceptual forms," in W. D. Ellis (Ed.), *A sourcebook of Gestalt psychology* (pp. 71–88). London: Routledge & Kegan Paul, 1938.]

Wiener, N. (1950). *The human use of human beings: Cybernetics and society*. Boston: Houghton Mifflin.

SECTION

THE PERCEPTUAL BASIS OF
PHONOLOGICAL SYSTEMS

CHAPTER

Patterns of Perceptual Compensation and Their Phonological Consequences

Patrice Speeter Beddor

Department of Linguistics
University of Michigan
Ann Arbor, Michigan 48109

Rena Arens Krakow

Department of Communication Sciences
Temple University
Philadelphia, Pennsylvania 19122

Stephanie Lindemann

Department of Linguistics
University of Michigan
Ann Arbor, Michigan 48109

I. Introduction
II. Vowel-to-Vowel Coarticulation
  A. Perception of Vowel-to-Vowel Coarticulatory Effects
  B. Linking Perception of Vowel-to-Vowel Coarticulation to Vowel Harmony Systems
III. Nasal Coarticulation
  A. Perception of Coarticulatory Vowel Nasalization
  B. Linking Perception of Nasal Coarticulation to Phonological Patterns
IV. Concluding Remarks
Acknowledgments
Notes
References

55

The Role of Speech Perception in Phonology
Copyright © 2001 by Academic Press. All rights of reproduction in any form reserved.

I. INTRODUCTION

This chapter takes as its starting point the well-attested notion that perceptual factors play an important role in shaping phonological systems. Other chapters in this book provide strong evidence of the pervasiveness of perceptual influences. The focus of our investigation is *how* perceptual phenomena become part of, or are incorporated into, phonological systems, and whether the results of experimental work in speech perception might help us identify specific conditions that facilitate such incorporation.

Experimental data delineate the types of information that listeners extract from the acoustic signal, and the conditions under which listeners are better or worse at extracting and using this information. One type of information to which listeners are particularly sensitive is coarticulatory variation. Listeners use coarticulatory variation as information about sounds that are further up or down the speech stream. A strong measure of listeners' use of coarticulatory variation is that, in some instances, this variation is sufficient for listeners to recover deleted portions of an acoustic signal. For example, Alfonso & Baer (1982) and van Heuven & Dupuis (1991) found that listeners, presented with the initial V_1C from original V_1CV_2 sequences, could identify the deleted second vowel on the basis of coarticulatory information in the first vowel. Listeners apparently attributed some aspect(s) of the acoustic signal of a target segment to the coarticulatory influence of an upcoming segment, which helped them identify that (experimentally deleted) segment. Other studies have shown that coarticulatory information speeds listeners' reaction times in identifying other portions of the signal, or in word recognition. In these studies, listeners responded faster, and often with fewer errors, when identifying stimuli containing coarticulatorily appropriate information than when identifying stimuli lacking this information (e.g., Martin & Bunnell, 1982; Fowler, 1984; Whalen, 1984; Manuel, 1987; Nguyen & Hawkins, 1999).

If listeners more accurately and more rapidly identify an influencing segment when given information about its coarticulatory influence on a target segment, then we might expect that listeners would also compensate for the acoustic effects of coarticulation on a target segment when judging the nature of that segment. Indeed, experimental evidence shows response patterns indicating that listeners attribute the acoustic effects of a coarticulatory context on a target sound not to the target but rather to the context. Consider, for example, evidence from the nasal coarticulation literature. Kawasaki (1986) applied varying degrees of attenuation to the nasal consonants of [mĩm], [mãm], and [mõm] and showed that English-speaking listeners heard the nasal vowels as relatively oral when the nasal consonants were clearly audible, but as increasingly nasal with decreasing intensity of the nasal consonants. Krakow *et al.* (1988) found that listeners (again, English-speaking) misjudged the height of nasal vowels when they were in an oral consonant context ([bɛd]), but not when the same vowels were in a coarticulatorily appropriate nasal consonant context ([bɛnd]). Manuel (1995) investigated carry-over nasalization of /n/ on /ð/ (in sequences such as *win those*) and obtained perceptual responses consistent with the view that listeners heard contextual nasalization of /ð/ as due to the flanking nasal consonant. In all three cases, listeners used the nasal consonant context in making judgments about a segment that was modified by that context, and their response patterns indicated that listeners ascribed the acoustic consequences of coarticulation to their source (but cf. Kingston & Macmillan, 1995). Such response patterns have been found for a range of segmental and prosodic properties (e.g., Kunisaki & Fujisaki, 1977; Mann, 1980; Mann & Repp, 1980; Fowler, 1981, 1984; Whalen, 1981, 1989; Petersen, 1986; Silverman, 1987; Fowler *et al.*, 1990; Xu, 1994; Pardo & Fowler, 1997; Fowler *et al.*, 1999).

What might be the consequences of listeners' perception of the acoustic effects of coarticulation for phonological systems? Ohala (1981, 1986, 1993) has proposed that, if listeners fail to detect the source of coarticulatory variation (or if, for example, learners are relatively inexperienced in dealing with contextual variation), they might perceive the variation as intrinsic to the target segment. Systematic misperceptions along these lines could lead to phonologization of the variation (e.g., failure to detect the nasal consonant in [ṼN] could result in the well-attested change VN → Ṽ). In other words, this account suggests that percep-tual compensation should, under most circumstances, minimize the phonological consequences of coarticulation because, in attributing the variation to its source, the listener correctly identifies the intended utterance. But if the conditioning environment is not clearly detected for some reason, or not associated with the coarticulatory effects, perceptual compensation is effectively ruled out.

The position we take here regarding perception of coarticulatory variation assigns yet a more prominent role to the listener, one in which coarticulatory variation might have phonological consequences even in the context of a detected coarticulatory source. This position is based on our investigation of two types of coarticulation: vowel-to-vowel coarticulation and nasal coarticulation. For both types of coarticulation, coarticulatory context was manipulated in order to inves-tigate the conditions under which listeners were more and less successful at attributing the acoustic effects of coarticulation to their coarticulatory source. The general experimental approach involved the use of naturally produced utterances to which we applied excising and cross-splicing techniques that placed vowels into coarticulatorily inappropriate as well as appropriate contexts, allowing us to test listeners' sensitivity to the presence versus absence of appropriate coarticulatory information. We intentionally chose coarticulatory effects known to have conse-quences for phonology; hence we studied vowel-to-vowel coarticulation because of its relation to vowel harmony, and nasal coarticulation because of its relation to distinctive vowel nasalization and nasal harmony.

We will show that the results contribute to the literature on how speech perception patterns help to shape phonological systems in two ways. First, the general pattern of results that emerges from the experimental data is that coarticulatory compensation is not "perfect." Listeners do compensate for the acoustic effects of coarticulation, indicating that they associate (at least some portion of) these effects with their coarticulatory source. However, even in the context of a clearly audible coarticulatory source, listeners do not fully compensate for the acoustic consequences of coarticulation. It is this partial compensation for coarticulatory variation that leads us to assign a relatively prominent role to the listener in terms of potential consequences for phonology. Partial compensation means that perceptual association of coarticulatory effects with their source may not fully disambiguate the nature of an intended target segment. The second contribution to the literature on the role of perception in phonology will be to show that the detailed patterns of partial compensation for coarticulation correspond to patterns of change and patterns of contrast in phonological systems.

II. VOWEL-TO-VOWEL COARTICULATION

A. Perception of Vowel-to-Vowel Coarticulatory Effects

We investigated listeners' use of vowel-to-vowel coarticulatory effects using a discrimination paradigm similar to that used by Fowler (1981). The original stimuli, produced by a female speaker of American English, were two-syllable utterances of the form ['bV$_1$bV$_2$], where the vowels were [i e a o u]; multiple repetitions of all possible combinations of the five vowels (e.g., ['biba], ['bube], ['baba]) were recorded. Acoustic measures of this speaker's disyllables showed extensive carryover effects of V$_1$ on V$_2$. (See Beddor *et al.*, 2000, for a full-scale presentation of the experimental methods.)

To explore listeners' sensitivity to the carryover effects, we selected the disyllables with the most salient effects, based on a combination of formant measures and pilot perceptual assessment of second syllables excised from their original context. (The excised syllables consisted of V$_2$ plus the preceding [b], including stop closure and any burst.) In creating the test stimuli, the excised [bV$_2$]s selected on the basis of pilot testing were cross-spliced into either another token of the original context (so that all test stimuli underwent splicing) or into a different [bV$_1$_] context. The cross-splicing was constrained such that the original and 'replaced' V$_2$s were phonologically the same (e.g., /a/s always replaced /a/s, /i/s replaced /i/s, and so on). Figure 3.1 gives sample original and cross-spliced utterances. The subscript notation indicates the original vowel context in which the cross-spliced vowel was produced (i.e., [$_i$a] = /a/ from original [biba] and [$_a$a] = /a/ from original [baba]).

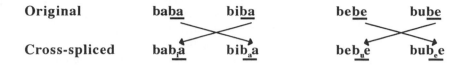

Figure 3.1. Examples of cross-splicing for vowel-to-vowel carryover coarticulation.

We paired the manipulated stimuli using a 4IAX discrimination task in which each trial consisted of two pairs of stimuli. In all trials, the V_2s of one pair were acoustically different (due to different coarticulatory effects) and the V_2s of the other pair were acoustically identical; all V_2s in a trial were phonologically the same. In the *control* trials, only [bV_2] was manipulated and the context was held constant. For example, in control trial [bib$_i$a–bib$_i$a]/[bib$_i$a–bib$_a$a], all V_2s occur in the V_1 context [i]. The control trials were included to verify that listeners could detect the V_2 differences (e.g., [$_i$a] versus [$_a$a]).

For each *test* trial, the V_2s of one pair were acoustically different (due to the coarticulatory influences of V_1), and both were in coarticulatorily appropriate contexts; the V_2s of the other pair were acoustically identical, but one was in a coarticulatorily *in*appropriate context. Two test trial types are illustrated in Table 3.1. Notice that for each pairing of acoustically different vowels in appropriate contexts (left side of table) there are two possible pairings of identical vowels (right): one in which V_2 comes from a disyllable in which V_1 and V_2 were

TABLE 3.1

Sample Discrimination Test Trials for the Vowel-to-Vowel
Coarticulation Experiment

		Acoustically different V_2s		Acoustically identical V_2s
$V_1 = $ /i/, $V_2 = $ /a/	Prototypical		/	bib$_a$**a**–bab$_a$a
	Non-prototypical	bib$_i$a–bab$_a$a	/	bib$_i$a–bab$_i$**a**
$V_1 = $ /u/, $V_2 = $ /e/	Prototypical	bub$_u$e–beb$_e$e	/	bub$_e$**e**–beb$_e$e
	Non-prototypical		/	bub$_u$e–beb$_u$**e**

Bold vowels are coarticulatorily inappropriate; all others are appropriate to their context.

(phonologically) identical (i.e., V_2 was produced in the context of itself; $[_aa]$ or $[_ee]$ in the top row of each section), and the other in which V_2 comes from a disyllable in which V_1 and V_2 were phonologically distinct (i.e., V_2 was produced in the context of a different vowel; $[_ia]$ or $[_ue]$ in the bottom row of each section). Our acoustic measures suggest that vowels produced in the context of themselves are more prototypical or canonical versions of these vowels (closer, for example, in formant values to the less coarticulated V_1 versions); we propose below that a theory of coarticulatory compensation predicts that listeners will respond differently to the prototypical, as compared to the non-prototypical, pairings.

The test design shown in Table 3.1 was applied to nine different V_1–V_2 pairings: *i–a, i–o, e–a, e–o, a–o, o–a, o–e, u–a*, and *u–e*. There were three different tokens of each pairing. As indicated above, corresponding to each test pairing was a control trial in which context was held constant. For all trials, listeners were asked to choose the pair in which the second vowels sounded *more different*. (Therefore the correct responses in Table 3.1 would always be the left pair, although the order of pair presentation was of course balanced in the actual test.) The listeners were 16 native speakers of American English.

Before turning to the results, we consider the predictions of a theory of compensation for coarticulation. The theory predicts that listeners will consistently choose the wrong pair member for the test trials. This is because listeners should hear acoustically different vowels that are both in coarticulatorily appropriate contexts as similar: the coarticulatory variation that distinguishes the vowels is attributed to the vowel context. For example, in the pair $[bib_ia–bab_aa]$, if listeners (correctly) hear the fronted and raised $[_ia]$ as due to the preceding /i/, then $[_ia]$ should sound similar to (unfronted and unraised) $[_aa]$ in the /a/ context. In addition, listeners should hear acoustically identical vowels, one of which is in an *in*appropriate context, as different because listeners would compensate for coarticulatory effects only for the vowel in the appropriate context. For example, in the pair $[bib_ia–bab_ia]$, the fronted and raised quality of $[_ia]$ would be attributed to context only in the first pair member, and the two (identical) $[_ia]$s would sound different.

A second prediction is that listeners should compensate more — which in this experimental paradigm means that they would make more mistakes — on trials with non-prototypical effects than on trials with prototypical effects. Compare two representative trials from Table 3.1:

Prototypical:	$bib_ia–bab_a\mathbf{a}$ / $bib_a\mathbf{a}–bab_aa$
Non-prototypical:	$bib_ia–bab_a\mathbf{a}$ / $bib_ia–bab_i\mathbf{a}$

As we have just seen, compensatory responses in part involve hearing identical vowels, one of which is in an inappropriate context (i.e., the vowel in bold in each trial), as different. An inappropriate non-prototypical effect should be easy for listeners to detect: such acoustic patterns normally occur only as the result of coarticulation; they are highly unexpected (and sound unusual) when removed from their original context. Consequently, although [ᵢa] in [bibᵢa] sounds natural, [ᵢa] in [babᵢa] does not, resulting in an identical vowel pairing which is likely to mislead listeners. In comparison, inappropriate prototypical effects — such as [ₐa] in [bibₐa] — should be more difficult for listeners to detect because these effects are roughly equivalent to lack of coarticulation. This situation should be close to careful productions that might occur in natural speech situations. In this prototypical case, then, the identical vowels will sound relatively natural in both contexts; hence listeners will be less likely to incorrectly select this pair as more different. The resulting order of difficulty predicted by a theory of compensation for coarticulation is control (least difficult), then prototypical, then non-prototypical (most difficult) trials.

The percentage correct responses to the discrimination test for vowel-to-vowel coarticulation are given in Figure 3.2, pooling across the responses of the 16 American English listeners. The abscissa indicates the nine types of vowel pairings. Four pairings tested sensitivity to carryover coarticulatory effects of front vowels

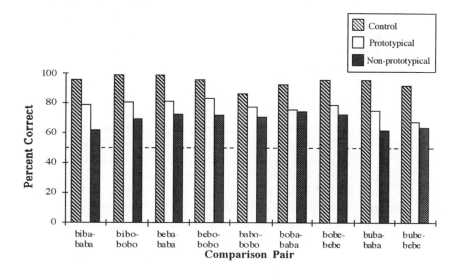

Figure 3.2. Pooled percentage correct responses of 16 listeners to the discrimination test for vowel-to-vowel coarticulation, according to type of V_1–V_2 pairing. Bar type indicates the trial type for each pairing: hatched = control, open = prototypical, and solid = non-prototypical. For example, for the left-most *i–a* pairing:

hatched = bibᵢa–bibₐa / bibᵢa–bibᵢa

open = bibᵢa–babₐa / bibₐa–babₐa

solid = bibᵢa–babₐa / bibᵢa–babᵢa

(Recall that listeners chose the pair in which the *second* vowels sounded more different.) The dashed horizontal line indicates chance (50%) performance.

on non-front vowels (*i–a, i–o, e–a, e–o*), two tested the effects of non-front vowels on front vowels (*o–e, u–e*), and three looked at non-front vowel pairings (*a–o, o–a, u–a*). The three trial types for each pairing — control trial, prototypical trial, and non-prototypical trial — are represented by the different bar types.

The vowel pairings in Figure 3.2 all show similar patterns of results. In all cases, listeners were able to accurately identify the "different" pair in the control trials (as high as 99% for the *i–o* and *e–a* pairings); only in one case did control trial performance fall below 90% (86% for *a–o*). Performance accuracy dropped by an average of 17% from the control to the corresponding prototypical trial (range 8–25%). This drop was significant for all but the *a–o* pairing. In addition, for all pairings, the non-prototypical trials yielded the poorest performance of all trial types, with an average decrease of 9% from the prototypical trials (range 2–18%). The overall decrease in accuracy from the prototypical to the corresponding non-prototypical trials was highly significant; statistical comparisons for the individual pairings showed the decrease to be significant for the majority, but not all, of the nine vowel pairings (decreases of 9% or more were significant). Note, however, that performance was above chance (50%) for all vowel pairings and trial types.

These results are consistent with expectations: the predicted order of difficulty — control, then prototypical, then non-prototypical — was obtained for all vowel pairings. The prototypical/non-prototypical difference indicates that listeners were more often misled by identical vowel pairings when one of the vowels was in a highly unexpected coarticulatory context, which we take as evidence that listeners' responses exhibited *coarticulatory* influences rather than purely auditory contrast effects (cf. Lotto *et al.*, 1997; Lotto & Kluender, 1998).

That performance on even the non-prototypical trials remained above chance means that, although listeners often gave responses consistent with coarticulatory compensation (in that coarticulatory appropriateness of vowel differences often overrode acoustic vowel identity), they did not *consistently* select the (incorrect) compensatory response. Such incomplete or partial compensation is also consistent with previous investigations along these lines. Aspects of this experiment were modeled after Fowler's (1981) study of perception of anticipatory and carryover effects of flanking vowels on unstressed /ə/. In that early study of compensation, Fowler's emphasis was on whether compensation would occur, rather than on whether it was complete. For trials similar to our non-prototypical trials, Fowler found that, although compensation did occur, listeners often did not select the compensatory response.[1]

B. Linking Perception of Vowel-to-Vowel Coarticulation to Vowel Harmony Systems

What are the implications of these findings for natural communicative interactions? The compensatory perceptual responses that are errors in this experimental paradigm would not be errors in real-life interactions: attributing coarticulatory variation to the source of the variation facilitates perception and hence should reduce the chances of such variation becoming phonologized, as noted by Ohala (1981). On the other hand, partial compensation for coarticulation — here, attributing some but not all of the acoustic effects of V_1 on V_2 to V_1 — means that there is a detectable coarticulatory "residue" on V_2 that the listener does not attribute to context. As a result, the relevant acoustic properties are divided between the context and the target sound. We have suggested elsewhere (Beddor & Krakow, 1998) that such an outcome is not unexpected within an approach to perception which recognizes that contextual information is only one of many types of information available to listeners in making perceptual decisions (e.g., Hawkins, 1995), and an approach to coarticulation, which recognizes the considerable variability in extent of coarticulation across speakers, rate, and prosodic and segmental contexts.

A likely phonological consequence of hearing the effects of vowel-to-vowel coarticulation as belonging to both the source of coarticulation and the target vowel is vowel harmony. In languages exhibiting vowel harmony, only a restricted set of vowels sharing one or more features (e.g., degree of rounding, backness, or height) can co-occur within a specified domain, usually a word. For example, in harmony systems in which the harmonic feature is backness, vowels within a word are usually either front or non-front, with most front–back combinations being disallowed.

Ideally, in assigning the listener a role in the development of vowel harmony systems, we seek to relate patterns in the perceptual results to specific patterns observed in vowel harmony systems. For example, in stress-dependent harmony systems, harmony is triggered by the stressed vowel of a word. Majors (1998, 1999) explored the possible phonetic basis for such systems, showing that (English) stressed vowels exert greater coarticulatory influences on unstressed vowels than vice versa, and that these effects on unstressed vowels were sufficiently large for listeners to detect. (The effects on unstressed vowels were presumably easier to detect than the weaker effects on stressed vowels, although this was not tested.)

A pattern in vowel harmony systems that is potentially relevant to our perceptual data concerns neutral vowels, that is, vowels in a harmonic domain that neither harmonize nor spread their own harmony. In backness harmony systems, high front [i] and, to a lesser extent, mid front [e] are often neutral to harmony, as is the case in many Uralic and Altaic languages (Goldsmith, 1985; van der Hulst & Smith, 1986; Farkas & Beddor, 1987; Harms, 1987; van der Hulst & van de Weijer, 1995). Table 3.2 provides illustrative examples from Hungarian. Most native roots in Hungarian obey backness harmony, and suffix vowels are either front or back depending on root vowel backness, as in Table 3.2a. However, Hungarian long and short /i(:)/ and /e(:)/ are neutral. As shown in Table 3.2b, the backness of suffix vowels, such as dative [nak]/[nek], is unaffected by a preceding

TABLE 3.2

Hungarian Vowel Harmony

		root + dative	gloss
a. Harmonic roots	back	va:ros + nak	'city (dative)'
	front	örom + nek	'joy (dative)'
b. Roots with neutral vowels	back-neutral	papi:r + nak	'paper (dative)'
	front-neutral	rövid + nek	'short (dative)'

high (or mid) unrounded front vowel. If vowel-to-vowel coarticulation is the phonetic source of vowel harmony, neutral vowel behavior leads us to expect relatively weak coarticulatory effects of back vowels on [i] and [e]. Because weaker coarticulatory effects should be less perceptible than stronger ones, listeners should be relatively insensitive to the carryover acoustic effects of V_1 on V_2 when V_2 is [i] or [e].

The experimental results given in Figure 3.2, combined with the results of the pilot testing leading up to this experiment, suggest possible links between perception of the effects of vowel-to-vowel coarticulation and neutral vowels in backness harmony systems. With regard to pilot testing, recall that, in designing stimulus materials that would explore listeners' sensitivity to the acoustic effects of coarticulation in different vowel contexts, we selected effects large enough to be reliably detected in the control trials (where context was held constant). Although the original recorded stimuli involved all possible pairings of [i], [e], [a], [o], and [u], pilot testing showed that none of the pairings with [i] in V_2 position (*a–i*, *o–i*, *e–i*, and *u–i*) yielded sufficiently large carryover effects; the same result held for two of the pairings with [e] in V_2 position (*a–e* and *i–e*).[2] Thus, our pilot tests indicated that listeners were insensitive to the coarticulatory effects of a preceding vowel on [i], and to a lesser extent [e], which parallels the phonological situation with neutral vowels. (Acoustic studies of vowel-to-vowel coarticulation have also noted that [i] is particularly resistant to coarticulation; Magen, 1984; Recasens, 1987, 1989; Farnetani, 1990; Beddor & Yavuz, 1995.)

Our main perceptual test results in Figure 3.2 provide further evidence along these lines. The two pairings with [e] in V_2 position that were included in the test design were among the pairings for which listeners were least sensitive to contextual effects (i.e., the differences between listener responses to the prototypical and non-prototypical trials were not significant for *u–e* or *o–e*). Consequently, we would argue that listener inability to systematically detect the small effects of vowel-to-vowel coarticulation on [i] and [e] plays a role in backness harmony systems.[3] More generally, our across-the-board finding of partial compensation for vowel-to-vowel coarticulation, coupled with the systematic differences between prototypical and non-prototypical pairings, suggest that there is a coarticulatory residue that listeners attribute to the target. It is reasonable to speculate that this residue, if phonologized, could result in vowel harmony.

III. Nasal Coarticulation

A. Perception of Coarticulatory Vowel Nasalization

In studying nasal coarticulation, we used a discrimination paradigm similar to that for vowel-to-vowel coarticulation. However, in this case, we systematically manipulated the consonantal, rather than the vocalic, context in which the vowels occurred. In addition, whereas we focused in the other experiment on carryover effects, here we examined bidirectional effects on vowels from preceding and following nasal consonants. (A detailed report of this experiment is provided in Beddor & Krakow, 1999.)

The original stimuli for this experiment were produced by a male speaker of American English and included oral vowels in oral consonant contexts and nasal vowels in nasal consonant contexts, specifically *bode*, *moan*, *bed*, and *men*. The oral and nasal vowels were cross-spliced into either a different token of the original context or into the context having the "opposite" nasality. Thus, with respect to the latter manipulation, nasal [õ] from *moan* was spliced into the oral context [b_d] from original *bode* and oral [o] from *bode* was spliced into the nasal context [m_n] from original *moan*. The vowels from *bed* and *men* were cross-spliced in the same fashion. In addition, we included vowels excised from their original contexts to be played to listeners in isolation. Isolated vowel conditions were investigated because we aimed to test listener sensitivity to vowel nasality under a variety of contextual conditions, and a pilot study had indicated that American English listeners might be more sensitive to nasal vowels in isolation than in an oral consonant context. Examples of both cross-spliced and excised stimulus types are shown in Figure 3.3 for the /o/ stimuli.

Our main interest was in determining listeners' sensitivity to vowel nasality in and out of a nasalizing context. As in the previous experiment, we tested sensitivity using a 4IAX discrimination paradigm in which trials had one pair with acoustically different vowels — here, one oral and the other nasal — and another pair with identical vowels, either both oral or both nasal. In the control trials, context was held constant and only vowel nasality varied (e.g., [bod–bõd]/[bod–bod]; [mon–mõn]/[mõn–mõn]).

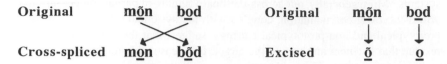

Figure 3.3. Examples of excising and cross-splicing for nasal coarticulation.

The design for the test trials, in which both context and vowel nasality were manipulated, is given in Table 3.3. Four test trial types paired vowels in an oral consonant context with an isolated vowel (top two sections); four additional trial types paired vowels in a nasal consonant context with an isolated vowel (third and fourth sections); and two trial types paired vowels in oral and nasal consonant contexts (bottom section). For the last trial types (bottom section), we used the same design as for the earlier study: in the pair with identical vowels, one vowel was in a coarticulatorily inappropriate context; in the pair with different vowels, both were in appropriate contexts. (This aspect of the experimental design was not possible for isolated nasal vowels, which are coarticulatorily inappropriate in English.) Similar to the first study, the nasal vowels in oral contexts might be

TABLE 3.3

Sample Discrimination Test Trials for the Nasal Coarticulation Experiment

		Acoustically different Vs			Acoustically identical Vs
Oral context–isolation	Oral	bod–õ	/		bod–o
	Nasal		/		bõd–õ
	Oral	bõd–o	/		bod–o
	Nasal		/		bõd–õ
Nasal context–isolation	Oral	mõn–o	/		mon–o
	Nasal		/		mõn–õ
	Oral	mon–õ	/		mon–o
	Nasal		/		mõn–õ
Oral context–nasal context	Oral	bod–mõn	/		bod–mon
	Nasal		/		bõd–mõn

The same design was also applied to the /e/ stimuli.

viewed as non-prototypical effects, and oral vowels in nasal contexts as prototypical effects. However, unlike vowel-to-vowel coarticulation where, for example, [bib$_a$a] would be close to a careful production, [mon] is not possible in American English, making the prototypical/non-prototypical distinction not entirely parallel.

The test design in Table 3.3 was applied not only to the stimuli created from original *bode* and *moan*, but also from original *bed* and *men* (using two tokens of each original word). In each trial, listeners were asked to identify the pair in which the vowels sounded "more different." Listeners were 16 native speakers of American English, none of whom had participated in the first experiment.

The predictions of a compensation hypothesis correspond to those we described for the stimuli investigating vowel-to-vowel coarticulation. Performance on control trials should be accurate. For test trials with a nasal vowel in a nasal consonant context, compensation predicts that listeners will systematically make the wrong choice. For example, if listeners hear the nasalization in [mõn] as belonging to the nasal consonants, then the nasal [õ] in [mõn] should sound similar to the non-nasal [o] in [bod]. In contrast, listeners should be accurate on trials *not* involving the nasal consonant context because there would be no context that would trigger compensation. Compensation does not make clear predictions about accuracy for oral vowels in a nasal consonant context ([mon]); whether listeners compensate for expected, but missing, coarticulatory nasalization is an open question.

We report the results for the combined data obtained on the /ɛ/ and /o/ stimulus sets, which overall showed highly similar patterns. The control data showed that listeners were highly accurate at identifying the pair with the "more different" vowels, with performance ranging narrowly from 95 to 98%. In contrast, the test pairings resulted in a range of performance from near chance to well above. The results for the test pairs are shown in Figure 3.4. Performance on each non-identical (oral–nasal) vowel pair is plotted along the abscissa as a function of the corresponding identical vowel pair, either two oral or two nasal vowels (shown by bar type). Each pair of bars in Figure 3.4 corresponds to one cell in Table 3.3.

The test trial results show that several factors influence listeners' sensitivity to the acoustic differences between oral and nasal vowels. First, the presence of a nasal consonant context significantly reduces the accuracy of judgments of oral–nasal vowel differences. Discrimination is highly accurate (around 90%) when the pairings do not include a vowel in a nasal consonant context (two left sets of bars) and performance drops by 7–11% when the oral vowels are placed in a nasal consonant context (NVN–Ṽ pairings). Second, accuracy is again significantly reduced (by another 13%) when the vowel in the nasal consonant context is a coarticulatorily appropriate nasal vowel (NṼN–V pairings). Third, as predicted, performance is worst (significantly so; at or somewhat below chance) when the nasal vowel in the nasal consonant context is paired with an oral vowel in an oral consonant context (NṼN–CVC pairings). Finally, for all comparisons, accuracy

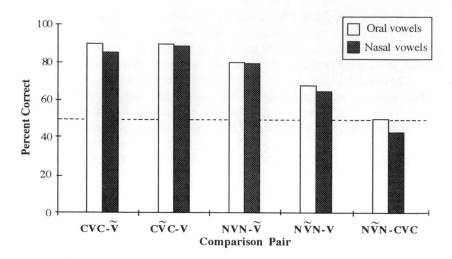

Figure 3.4. Pooled percentage correct responses of 16 listeners to the discrimination test for nasal coarticulation, according to context and type of oral–nasal (i.e., different) vowel pairing. Bar type indicates the identical vowel pairing: both oral or both nasal. Each pair of bars corresponds to a cell in Table 3.3. For example, for the left-most CVC-Ṽ pairing: open = CVC–Ṽ/CVC–V; solid = CVC–Ṽ/CṼ–Ṽ.

was somewhat (although in most cases only marginally and not significantly) reduced when the matched vowels were nasal than when they were oral (compare filled bars to unfilled bars). Whether this difference is an effect of the phonological status of vowel nasalization in American English or an effect of acoustic/auditory properties is unclear.

This pattern of performance provides insights concerning listeners' ability to disentangle (or compensate for) coarticulatory effects of adjacent segments on a target sound. A compensation hypothesis predicts that the listener will attribute vowel nasality in English to an audible nasal consonant context. That nasal vowels in nasal consonant contexts are the hardest to discriminate and most likely to lead to errors (i.e., compensatory responses) is consistent with this claim. Importantly, however, the data show that compensation for coarticulatory nasalization is *partial* rather than complete. Listeners respond as though they are aware of the presence of some nasality on the vowel; they do not provide a pattern of responses indicating that they hear the contextually nasalized vowel as fully "oral." Neither do they respond as though it sounds fully "nasal."

The evidence for partial compensation for coarticulatory nasalization is thus consistent with that for vowel-to-vowel coarticulation. However, it does appear that, in this study, listeners compensated more for nasal coarticulation than for vowel-to-vowel coarticulation, because performance dropped to chance only in the nasal study (albeit only on the NṼN–CVC comparisons). One possible explanation is that the coarticulatory effects in the nasalization study were greater than those in the vowel-to-vowel experiment; greater effects should be more perceptible and, as a result, should more consistently lead to compensation. Another possibility is that listeners compensated more in the nasal study because we selected a context that provided listeners with two influencing segments (N_N) to which to attribute the coarticulatory effects. Our experimental design does not allow us to tease apart these accounts.

B. Linking Perception of Nasal Coarticulation to Phonological Patterns

The results obtained for the nasal coarticulation data also provide insights into the relation between patterns of partial compensation on the one hand, and the historical development of distinctive nasal vowels and phonological constraints on oral–nasal vowel contrasts on the other. One of the most robust patterns in the perceptual data is listeners' difficulty in determining the nasality of vowels in a nasal consonant context: nasal vowels in nasal consonant contexts do not sound fully oral or nasal. Interpreted in terms of its possible phonological consequences, this experimental finding suggests that distinctive nasal vowels might emerge in contexts in which they were previously contextually nasalized, and this is, in fact, the most common historical source of distinctive nasal vowels in the world's languages (Entenman, 1977; Hajek, 1997; among others).[4]

That nasal vowels in a nasalizing context sound neither fully nasal nor oral, combined with the finding that oral vowels in a nasal consonant context are also not heard as fully oral, indicates that it would be difficult to maintain a phonological contrast between oral and nasal vowels in a nasal consonant context. The phonological evidence shows that languages rarely preserve such contrasts *before* a nasal consonant; in this regard, note the frequent historical loss of a following nasal consonant with distinctive vowel nasalization (Ohala, 1993). Although less common, some languages do not preserve the oral–nasal vowel contrast *after* a nasal consonant (Kawasaki, 1986), a situation that is also linked in some languages to the historical evolution of nasal vowels. For example, Hyman (1972) argued that distinctive nasal vowels in the Kwa languages evolved from earlier /NV/ sequences. Neutralization of the oral–nasal vowel distinction in nasal consonant contexts can also result from nasal harmony, as in Gokana, where nasal consonants trigger both rightward spreading of nasality through vowels (and consonants if the nasal consonant is initial; Hyman, 1982; see also Piggott, 1988). Furthermore, languages that contrast /V/ and /Ṽ/ may (partially) denasalize nasal consonants

70 PATRICE BEDDOR, RENA KRAKOW, and STEPHANIE LINDEMANN

next to an oral vowel, or partially nasalize oral stops next to a nasal vowel (as in Apinaye; Hyman, 1975; Kawasaki, 1986). Such phonological patterns support the experimentally based notion that the contrast between a nasal and an oral vowel is difficult to maintain in a nasal consonant context.

Although the experiment reported here does not directly speak to this issue, as we have just noted, oral–nasal vowel distinctions are more likely to be lost before rather than after a nasal consonant, and we believe that production and perception data on coarticulation provide some insight into this difference. In comparing our data on nasal coarticulation with both our data and Fowler's (1981) on vowel-to-vowel coarticulation, we argued that one interpretation of the three studies taken together was that, the more robust the coarticulatory effects in production, the more robust the compensatory responses of listeners. We argued this on the basis of greater compensation for bidirectional than unidirectional coarticulatory effects. However, in addition to differences between bi- versus unidirectional effects, effects can be stronger in one direction than the other. For example, Fowler (1981) found stronger carryover than anticipatory vowel-to-vowel effects in English and relatedly greater compensation for carryover than anticipatory coarticulation. Although we did not compare here compensation for anticipatory versus carryover coarticulation, we would expect greater compensation for anticipatory effects of nasalization since syllable-final nasal consonants are associated with lower positions of the velum and longer durations of low positioning (Krakow, 1999).[5] This would suggest that listeners are likely to have more problems maintaining a distinction between oral and nasal vowels before than after a nasal consonant, which is consistent with the phonological evidence.

Another aspect of the timing of the low velum position for nasalization — and, we would argue, listeners' perception of these coarticulatory effects — may be associated with yet another set of phonological patterns involving nasality. As pointed out by Hajek (1997), in some languages, including Northern Italian dialects, distinctive nasal vowels evolved in VNC contexts (VNC > ṽC) before they evolved in VN# contexts. In addition, synchronically, some languages with distinctive nasal vowels contrast /ṽ/ and /VN/ (which may be phonetically [ṼN]) word-finally, but neutralize this distinction when N is followed by an oral C, as in French (e.g., /pɛ̃/ 'bread,' /pɛn/ 'pain,' /pɛ̃s/ 'pinch,' but */pɛns/). The articulatory evidence suggests that vowels in CVNC sequences might be more nasal than vowels in CVN sequences. Kent and colleagues (1974), for example, showed that, when a nasal consonant is followed immediately by an oral consonant, the requirement of the high velum in such close proximity to a nasal segment requires a very early onset for the velum raising gesture. This appears to have the effect of an earlier onset for the low velum position. If listeners only partially compensate for coarticulatory effects, such early lowering may lead to yet greater difficulty in maintaining a perceptual contrast between oral and nasal vowels in a nasal consonant context.

IV. CONCLUDING REMARKS

The most robust finding in our perceptual investigation of vowel-to-vowel and nasal coarticulation is that, when judging the nature of a target segment, listeners partially compensated for the acoustic effects of a nearby segment on the target. Compensation was measured by the extent to which coarticulatory appropriateness of vowel differences overrode acoustic identity in listeners' judgments of vowel similarity. In both experiments, listeners chose the coarticulatorily appropriate — that is, the compensatory — response often, although not consistently. That listeners are sensitive to coarticulatory variation, and its contextual appropriateness, is consistent with a growing body of perceptual evidence indicating that coarticulatory variation can facilitate listeners' recovery of speakers' intended utterances. At the same time, listeners are far from perfect compensators: apparently, the acoustic signal (at least in these laboratory conditions) does not always provide sufficient information for listeners to correctly attribute all the acoustic consequences of coarticulation to their source. A coarticulatory environment may be unambiguously present; however, the extent to which it influences the target segment may remain unclear to the listener. Factors influencing the extent of compensation include the particular context in which the coarticulated target sound is embedded and the particular contrast with which the listener is faced (e.g., note in Figure 3.4 the increasing compensation from left to right as vocalic contexts and contrasts change).[6]

The parallel patterns of partial compensation for vowel-to-vowel and nasal coarticulation are especially noteworthy as the two kinds of coarticulation involve the influences of different articulators: the relevant articulators for vowel-to-vowel patterns are the tongue, jaw, and lips, whereas for nasal coarticulation the articulator is the velum. Furthermore, taken together, study of these coarticulatory patterns examined effects of consonants on vowels (nasal coarticulation) and of vowels on vowels (vowel-to-vowel coarticulation), as well as the effects of anticipatory coarticulation (for nasal coarticulation) and carryover coarticulation (for vowel-to-vowel and nasal coarticulation).

We have suggested that the finding that listeners compensate for coarticulation, but not perfectly so, is in many respects not surprising once we recognize how variable coarticulation is. For example, in vowel-to-vowel coarticulation, speaker-to-speaker differences are an important source of differing patterns of coarticulation. For the American English speaker whose data were manipulated here, as well as for the productions of the speakers studied by Fowler (1981), carryover effects exceeded anticipatory effects. However, this pattern does not hold for all the speakers whose productions have been examined in our laboratory. Magen (1997) also reports variability among American English speakers in vowel-to vowel coarticulation, and across-speaker variability has been reported for other languages as well (e.g., Italian; Vayra *et al.*, 1987). The vowel-to-vowel coarticulation literature also provides substantial evidence of variability due to speaking rate, and segmental and prosodic factors (see Farnetani, 1990, for a review; also, Magen, 1997; Majors, 1998). Similarly, sources of variation in nasal coarticulation include segmental structure (Bell-Berti, 1993), as well as such nonsegmental factors as speaking rate and style, in addition to clause, word, and syllable position (for reviews, see Krakow, 1993, 1999). Speaker-to-speaker differences in nasal coarticulation include dialect (Kavanagh *et al.*, 1994) and gender-based (Litzaw & Dalston, 1992) influences. Listeners' considerable experience with native-language coarticulatory structures may well lead them to expect certain general coarticulatory patterns, but the variability in the production of these structures is in keeping with the perceptual finding that there is often a coarticulatory "residue" that listeners do not attribute to context.

Listeners' partial compensation for coarticulatory effects provides a mechanism for the incorporation of perceptually based phenomena into phonological systems. In describing this mechanism, we build on Ohala's insight that listeners' failure to "normalize the variable speech signal" (1993, p. 162) could lead to phonologization of coarticulatory effects. But partial compensation broadens the scope of the conditions under which coarticulatory variation might become phonological patterns over time. If the experimental evidence reflects usual listening conditions, partial compensation may be the norm rather the exception — keeping in mind, of course, that in natural communicative settings listeners have access to other types of information in arriving at perceptual decisions.

Support for our argument that partial compensation for coarticulation plays a role in shaping phonological structure was provided by comparing the detailed patterns of partial compensation with phonological patterns in vowel systems. Compensation for nasal coarticulation, as compared to vowel-to-vowel coarticulation, yielded more variable performance across vowel contexts and paired vowel contrasts, thereby offering more opportunity to explore perceptual–phonological links. However, possible links between perception of vowel-to-vowel coarticulation and vowel harmony systems were also drawn. In addition, for both types of coarticulation, we posited a close relationship between the spatial and temporal extent of speakers' patterns of coarticulation and listeners' patterns of compensation. This relationship means that the relative contributions of the speaker and the listener to the phonology of vowel systems are not always readily disentangled. In the case of vowel-to-vowel coarticulation, this is especially true for /i/ and /e/ — that is, the neutral vowels in many backness harmony systems. As noted, acoustic studies of vowel-to-vowel coarticulation have shown that these vowels, especially /i/, exhibit relatively small coarticulatory effects. This may be due to relatively tight articulatory constraints on the range of palatal constrictions that give rise to an acceptable /i/ (e.g., Fowler, 1993). Alternatively, it may be that palatal constrictions for /i/ are *acoustically* stable, with small changes in front–back constriction having a negligible effect on formant frequencies (Goldstein, 1983; Stevens, 1989); the listener would play a more prominent role in this latter case. A third alternative is that both articulatory and acoustic–perceptual factors are involved. Regardless, it is listeners' inability to systematically detect these small variations that renders these vowels phonologically neutral. More generally, it is the listener who mediates which aspects of coarticulatory variation become part of phonology, and an important component of this mediation process is compensation. In our view, compensation that is partial, and consistently more extensive under some context and contrast conditions than others, is particularly conducive to phonologization of coarticulatory variation. The close parallels between patterns of partial compensation and the phonological data strengthen this claim.

ACKNOWLEDGMENTS

The research reported here was supported in part by NSF Grant SBR 9319597 to Patrice Beddor, NIH Grant NS-131617 to Haskins Laboratories, and a University of Michigan Department of Linguistics/Rackham Graduate School Research Partnership to Stephanie Lindemann and Patrice Beddor. We thank James Harnsberger for assistance in data collection and numerous discussions. Oral versions of this paper benefitted from the comments of the University of Michigan phonetics–phonology discussion group and participants in the ICPhS satellite meeting. An earlier written version also benefitted from the editors' helpful comments.

NOTES

1. In Fowler's (1981) study, unlike the current study, overall performance fell somewhat below chance. We expect that the greater tendency of listeners in that study to judge vowel similarity on the basis of coarticulatory appropriateness rather than acoustic similarity is linked to stimulus differences between the two studies. Fowler's stimuli were trisyllables, with most pairings involving acoustic differences due to both anticipatory and carryover effects. Indeed, Fowler found that the error rate was higher (i.e., more compensatory responses) for pairings involving bidirectional (anticipatory and carryover) influences than those involving unidirectional influences.

2. The only other original vowel pairings that did not yield reliably detectable effects of V_1 on V_2 involved [u] in the V_2 position. We attribute this to the centralized /u/ articulations of this speaker, regardless of vowel context.

3. See Ohala (1994) for a perceptual account of the failure of neutral vowels to trigger their own harmony. See also Harms (1987) for an alternative phonetic account to ours concerning the failure of neutral vowels to harmonize.

4. At first glance, it might seem as though the relatively high rate of compensation for pairings with NṼN would lead to the prediction of a negligible effect on phonological systems since, as argued in section I, more compensation should mean greater ability to disentangle the contribution of the nasal consonant to vowel nasality. Indeed, this should hold if listeners consistently compensated for nasality in NṼN utterances. However, we would argue that, when listeners' performance is close to *chance* (e.g., the NṼN–CVC pairings), the disentanglement remains difficult.

5. The lower position of the velum in VN than NV sequences may be subject to dialectal and cross-language variation. See Chafcouloff & Marchal (1999) for a review of anticipatory compared to carryover effects of nasalization.

6. Theoretically, given variability in coarticulation, the same factors that lead to partial or under-compensation for coarticulatory effects might be expected to lead to over-compensation if listeners' expectations concerning the extent of coarticulation in particular contexts are not met. However, the present experiments were not designed to investigate this possibility.

REFERENCES

Alfonso, P. J., & Baer, T. (1982). Dynamics of vowel articulation. *Language and Speech, 25*, 151–173.

Beddor, P. S., & Krakow, R. A. (1998). Perceptual confusions and phonological change: How confused is the listener? In B. K. Bergen, M. C. Plauché, & A. C. Bailey (Eds.), *Proceedings of the 24th Annual Meeting of the Berkeley Linguistics Society* (pp. 320–334). Berkeley: Berkeley Linguistics Society.

Beddor, P. S., & Krakow, R. A. (1999). Perception of coarticulatory nasalization by speakers of English and Thai: Evidence for partial compensation. *Journal of the Acoustical Society of America, 106*, 2868–2887.

Beddor, P. S., & Yavuz, H. K. (1995). The relation between vowel-to-vowel coarticulation and vowel harmony in Turkish. In K. Elenius & P. Branderud (Eds.), *Proceedings of the 13th International Congress of Phonetic Sciences* (Vol. 2, pp. 44–51). Stockholm: KTH and Stockholm University.

Beddor, P. S., Harnsberger, J., & Lindemann, S. (2000). *Language-specific patterns of vowel-to-vowel coarticulation: Acoustic structures and their perceptual correlates.* Unpublished manuscript.

Bell-Berti, F. (1993). Understanding velic motor control: Studies of segmental context. In M. K. Huffman & R. A. Krakow (Eds.), *Nasals, nasalization, and the velum* (pp. 63–85). New York: Academic Press.

Chafcouloff, M., & Marchal, A. (1999). Velopharyngeal coarticulation. In W. J. Hardcastle & N. Hewlett (Eds.), *Coarticulation: Theory, data and techniques* (pp. 69–79). Cambridge: Cambridge University Press.

Entenman, G. (1977). *The development of nasal vowels.* Unpublished doctoral dissertation, University of Texas, Austin.

Farkas, D. F., & Beddor, P. S. (1987). Privative and equipollent backness in Hungarian. In A. Bosch, B. Need, & E. Schiller (Eds.), *Parasession on autosegmental and metrical phonology* (pp. 90–105). Chicago: Chicago Linguistic Society.

Farnetani, E. (1990). V–C–V lingual coarticulation and its spatiotemporal domain. In W. J. Hardcastle & A. Marchal (Eds.), *Speech production and speech modeling* (pp. 93–130). Dordrecht: Kluwer Academic.

Fowler, C. A. (1981). Production and perception of coarticulation among stressed and unstressed vowels. *Journal of Speech and Hearing Research, 46,* 127–139.

Fowler, C. A. (1984). Segmentation of coarticulated speech in perception. *Perception and Psychophysics, 36,* 359–368.

Fowler, C. A. (1993). Phonological and articulatory characteristics of spoken language. In G. Blanken, J. Dittmann, H. Grimm, J. C. Marshall, & C.-W. Wallesch (Eds.), *Linguistic disorders and pathologies: An international handbook* (pp. 34–46). New York: Walter de Gruyter.

Fowler, C. A., Best, C. T., & McRoberts, G. W. (1990). Young infants' perception of liquid coarticulatory influences on following stop consonants. *Perception and Psychophysics, 48,* 559–570.

Fowler, C. A., Brown, J. M., & Mann, V. A. (1999). Compensation for coarticulation in audiovisual speech perception. In J. J. Ohala, Y. Hasegawa, M. Ohala, D. Granville, & A. C. Bailey (Eds.), *Proceedings of the 14th International Congress of Phonetics Sciences* (Vol. 1, pp. 639–642). Berkeley: University of California Press.

Goldsmith, J. (1985). Vowel harmony in Khalkha Mongolian, Yaka, Finnish, and Hungarian. *Phonology Yearbook, 2,* 253–275.

Goldstein, L. (1983). *Vowel shifts and articulatory-acoustic relations.* Paper presented at the 10th International Congress of Phonetic Sciences, August 1983. Utrecht, The Netherlands.

Hajek, J. (1997). *Universals of sound change in nasalization.* Boston: Blackwell.

Harms, R. T. (1987). What Helmholtz knew about neutral vowels. In R. Channon & L. Shockey (Eds.), *In honor of Ilse Lehiste: Ilse Lehiste Pühendusteos* (pp. 381–399). Dordrecht: Foris.

Hawkins, S. (1995). Arguments for a non-segmental view of speech perception. In K. Elenius & P. Branderud (Eds.), *Proceedings of the 13th International Congress of Phonetic Sciences* (Vol. 3, pp. 18–25). Stockholm: KTH and Stockholm University.

Hyman, L. (1972). Nasals and nasalization in Kwa. *Studies in African Linguistics, 3*(2), 167–205.

Hyman, L. (1975). Nasal states and nasal processes. In C. A. Ferguson, L. M. Hyman, & J. J. Ohala (Eds.), *Nasálfest. Papers from a symposium on nasals and nasalization* (pp. 249–264). Stanford: Language Universals Project, Stanford University.

Hyman, L. (1982). The representation of nasality in Gokana. In H. van der Hulst & N. Smiths (Eds.), *The structure of phonological representations*, Part I (pp. 111–130). Dordrecht: Foris.

Kavanagh, M. L., Fee, E. J., Kalinowski, J., Doyle, P. C., & Leeper, H. A. (1994). Nasometric values for three dialectal groups within the Atlantic provinces of Canada. *Journal of Speech and Language Pathology and Audiology, 18*(1), 7–13.

Kawasaki, H. (1986). Phonetic explanation for phonological universals: The case of distinctive vowel nasalization. In J. J. Ohala & J. J. Jaeger (Eds.), *Experimental phonology* (pp. 81–103). Orlando: Academic Press.

Kent, R. D., Carney, P. J., & Severeid, L. R. (1974). Velar movement and timing: Evaluation of a model of binary control. *Journal of Speech and Hearing Research, 17*, 470–488.

Kingston, J., & Macmillan, N. A. (1995). Integrality of nasalization and F1 in vowels in isolation and before oral and nasal consonants: A detection-theoretic application of the Garner paradigm. *Journal of the Acoustical Society of America, 97*, 1261–1285.

Krakow, R. A. (1993). Nonsegmental influences on velum movement patterns: Syllables, sentences, stress, and speaking rate. In M. K. Huffman & R. A. Krakow (Eds.), *Nasals, nasalization, and the velum* (pp. 87–113). New York: Academic Press.

Krakow, R. A. (1999). Articulatory organization of syllables: A review. *Journal of Phonetics, 27*, 23–54.

Krakow, R. A., Beddor, P. S., Goldstein, L. M., & Fowler, C. A. (1988). Coarticulatory influences on the perceived height of nasal vowels. *Journal of the Acoustical Society of America, 83*, 1146–1158.

Kunisaki, O., & Fujisaki, H. (1977). On the influence of context upon the perception of fricative consonants. *Research Institute of Logopedics and Phoniatrics Annual Bulletin, University of Tokyo, 11*, 85–91.

Litzaw, L. L., & Dalston, R. M. (1992). The effect of gender upon nasalance scores among normal adult speakers. *Journal of Communication Disorders, 25*, 55–64.

Lotto, A. J., & Kluender, K. R. (1998). General contrast effects in speech perception: Effect of preceding liquid on stop consonant identification. *Perception and Psychophysics, 60*, 602–619.

Lotto, A. J., Kluender, K. R., & Holt, L. L. (1997). Perceptual compensation for coarticulation by Japanese quail. *Journal of the Acoustical Society of America, 102*, 1134–1140.

Magen, H. S. (1984). Vowel-to-vowel coarticulation in English and Japanese. *Journal of the Acoustical Society of America, 75*, S41.

Magen, H. S. (1997). The extent of vowel-to-vowel coarticulation in English. *Journal of Phonetics, 25*, 187–205.

Majors, T. (1998). *Stress-dependent harmony: Phonetic origins and phonological analysis.* Unpublished doctoral disssertation, University of Texas, Austin.

Majors, T. (1999). *Perceptually motivated phonology: The case of stress-dependent harmony.* Poster presented at "The Role of Speech Perception Phenomena in Phonology" Satellite Meeting of the International Congress of Phonetic Sciences, July 1999, San Francisco.

Mann, V. A. (1980). Influence of preceding liquid on stop-consonant perception. *Perception and Psychophysics, 28,* 407–412.

Mann, V. A., & Repp, B. H. (1980). Influence of vocalic context on perception of the [ʃ]–[s] distinction. *Perception and Psychophysics, 28,* 213–228.

Manuel, S. Y. (1987). *Acoustic and perceptual consequences of vowel-to-vowel coarticulation in three Bantu languages.* Unpublished doctoral disssertation, Yale University, New Haven.

Manuel, S. Y. (1995). Speakers nasalize /ð/ after /n/, but listeners still hear /ð/. *Journal of Phonetics, 23,* 453–476.

Martin, J. G., & Bunnell, H. T. (1982). Perception of anticipatory coarticulation effects in vowel–stop consonant–vowel sequences. *Journal of Experimental Psychology: Human Perception and Performance, 8,* 473–488.

Nguyen, N., & Hawkins, S. (1999). Implications for word recognition of phonetic dependencies between syllable onsets and codas. In J. J. Ohala, Y. Hasegawa, M. Ohala, D. Granville, & A. C. Bailey (Eds.), *Proceedings of the 14th International Congress of Phonetics Sciences* (Vol. 1, pp. 647–650). Berkeley: University of California Press.

Ohala, J. J. (1981). The listener as a source of sound change. In C. S. Masek, R. A. Hendrick, & M. F. Miller (Eds.), *Papers from the parasession on language and behavior* (pp. 178–203). Chicago: Chicago Linguistic Society.

Ohala, J. J. (1986). Phonological evidence for top–down processing in speech perception. In J. S. Perkell & D. H. Klatt (Eds.), *Invariance and variability of speech processes* (pp. 386–401). Hillsdale, NJ: Erlbaum.

Ohala, J. J. (1993). Coarticulation and phonology. *Language and Speech, 36,* 155–170.

Ohala, J. J. (1994). Hierarchies of environments for sound variation; plus implications for "neutral" vowels in vowel harmony. *Acta Linguistica Hafniensia, 27*(2), 371–382.

Pardo, J. S., & Fowler, C. A. (1997). Perceiving the causes of coarticulatory acoustic variation: Consonant voicing and vowel pitch. *Perception and Psychophysics, 59,* 1141–1152.

Petersen, N. R. (1986). Perceptual compensation for segmentally conditioned fundamental frequency perturbation. *Phonetica, 43,* 31–42.

Piggott, G. L. (1988). A parametric approach to nasal harmony. In H. van der Hulst & N. Smith (Eds.), *Features, segmental structure and harmony processes* (pp. 131–167). Dordrecht: Foris.

Recasens, D. (1987). An acoustic analysis of V-to-C and V-to-V coarticulatory effects in Catalan and Spanish VCV sequences. *Journal of Phonetics, 15,* 299–312.

Recasens, D. (1989). Long-range coarticulation effects for tongue dorsum contact in VCVCV sequences. *Speech Communication, 8,* 293–307.

Silverman, K. (1987). *The structure and processing of fundamental frequency contours.* Unpublished doctoral disssertation, Cambridge University.

Stevens, K. N. (1989). On the quantal nature of speech. *Journal of Phonetics, 17,* 3–45.

van der Hulst, H., & Smith, N. (1986). On neutral vowels. In K. Bogers, H. van der Hulst, & M. Mous (Eds.), *The phonological representation of suprasegmentals* (pp. 233–279). Dordrecht: Foris.

van der Hulst, H., & van de Weijer, J. (1995). Vowel harmony. In J. A. Goldsmith (Ed.), *The handbook of phonological theory* (pp. 495–534). Cambridge: Blackwell.

van Heuven, V. J., & Dupuis, M. C. (1991). Perception of anticipatory VCV-coarticu-lation: Effects of vowel context and accent distribution. In *Proceedings of the 12th International Congress of Phonetic Sciences* (Vol. 4, pp. 78–81). Aix-en-Provence: Université de Provence.

Vayra, M., Fowler, C. A., & Avesani, C. (1987). Word-level coarticulation and shortening in Italian and English speech. *Studi di Grammatica Italiano, 13,* 249–269.

Whalen, D. H. (1981). Effects of vocalic formant transitions and vowel quality on the English [s]–[ʃ] boundary. *Journal of the Acoustical Society of America, 69,* 275–282.

Whalen, D. H. (1984). Subcategorical phonetic mismatches slow phonetic judgments. *Perception and Psychophysics, 35,* 49–64.

Whalen, D. H. (1989). Vowel and consonant judgments are not independent when cued by the same information. *Perception and Psychophysics, 46,* 284–292.

Xu, Y. (1994). Production and perception of coarticulated tones. *Journal of the Acoustical Society of America, 95,* 2240–2253.

CHAPTER

Markedness and Consonant Confusion Asymmetries

Steve S. Chang, Madelaine C. Plauché,
and John J. Ohala
Department of Linguistics
University of California, Berkeley
Berkeley, California 94720

1. Introduction
II. Markedness
   A. Study 1
   B. Study 2
   C. Discussion
III. [ti] versus [tʃi]
   A. Study 3a
   B. Study 3b
   C. Discussion
IV. Conclusions
   Acknowledgments
   Notes
   References

79

The Role of Speech Perception in Phonology

1. INTRODUCTION

In both lab-based speech perception studies and in sound change, one finds directional asymmetries of consonant change. In each of the following examples, the CV sequences on the left have shifted diachronically to those on the right, but the reverse is rarely attested:

ki > tʃi   (e.g., Slavic, Indo-Iranian, Bantu)[1]
pi > ti   (cf. Czech dial. var: pĭːvo [pʲiːvɔ] ~ [tiːvɔ] 'beer')
ku > pu   (cf. PIE ekʷōs 'horse' Gk hippos).

For insight into this phenomenon, we turn to the domain of vision. Below are examples of unidirectional confusions made by subjects when asked to identify Roman capitalized letters in a visual perception study conducted by Gilmore *et al.* (1979):

E > F   Q > O
R > P   W > V[2]

In visual perception tasks, subjects confused 'E' with 'F,' 'R' with 'P,' and so on, but 'F' was rarely confused with 'E' and 'P' rarely with 'R,' etc. In each pair of confused characters, both are structurally similar, but the one on the left has an 'extra' feature that the one on the right lacks (Gilmore *et al.*, 1979). The perceiver is more likely to miss a distinctive part of the stimulus array than she is to imagine its presence when it is not actually there.

The same conceptual explanation may be applied to consonant confusion asymmetries. In speech, the pertinent cues for differentiation are the temporal and spectral properties of acoustic events. These acoustic cues have intrinsically different salience or robustness for the task of differentiation. For example, acoustic cues from the amplitude envelope are more auditorily salient than those from spectral details (Miller & Nicely, 1954). Irrespective of intrinsic salience, all cues are subject — probabilistically — to degradation in transmission. The second law of thermodynamics dictates an increase in entropy; entropy never decreases (absent the diversion of energy from other domains). While all cues are subject to degradation, robust cues are less likely to be compromised to the point of losing their distinctiveness. Non-robust cues, on the other hand, may be degraded to the point where they lose their distinctiveness. Significant degradation of a non-robust cue can lead to an irreversible confusion. We argue that it is precisely such an instance that gives rise to asymmetries in confusion matrices.

It has been observed that [ki] is often confused in a laboratory setting for [ti] by listeners, but [ti] is almost never confused as [ki] (Winitz *et al.*, 1972; Delogu *et al.*, 1995). Plauché *et al.* (1997) investigated the temporal and spectral properties responsible for this asymmetrical confusion in stop place. They found that, due to the resulting raised F2 of the following high vowel, the formant transitions for [ki] and [ti] are similar, neutralizing the formants' role as distinctive stop place cues. The spectra of the stop bursts, too, are similar, but the stop burst in [ki] has an "extra," non-robust feature: a compact mid-frequency spectral peak — essentially the front cavity resonance ≡F3 (Stevens & Blumstein, 1978). Plauché et al. (1997) hypothesized that this mid-frequency spectral peak functions much like the extra "foot" in the letter 'E' or the extra "tail" in the letter 'Q.' If this "extra," non-robust feature is degraded to the point of losing its contrastiveness, listeners are likely to confuse the [ki] as [ti]. [ti] will very rarely, however, be confused as [ki] since listeners are unlikely to erroneously insert a nonexistent cue into the speech signal for [ti]. This accounts for the asymmetry.

By filtering out the characteristic mid-frequency spectral peak of the velar burst in [ki], Plauché et al. (1997) succeeded in enhancing the asymmetrical confusion with [ti]. Table 4.1, adapted from Plauché et al. (1997), summarizes the results from a perceptual experiment in which English-speaking subjects were asked to identify the stop in three natural speech tokens and an edited token. The "edited ki" token was a natural [ki] whose stop burst had been band-reject filtered to effectively remove the characteristic mid-frequency peak of the velar burst.

TABLE 4.1

Confusion Asymmetry Results from
Plauché et al. (1997)

Stimuli/ response	pi	ti	ki
pi	**97%**	3%	0
ti	0	**100%**	0
ki	0	20%	**80%**
Edited ki	0	**100%**	0

As the top half of the table demonstrates, there was some asymmetric confusion evident in the natural stimuli: 3% of the naturally produced [pi] tokens and 20% of the naturally produced [ki] tokens were mistaken for [ti]. All of the [ti] tokens, however, were correctly identified. The filtered [ki] token, "edited ki," was always identified as [ti].

Two important questions were raised with respect to the results of the Plauché et al. study. First, how do we know that the acoustic properties of [ki] and [ti] (e.g., the "extra" feature consisting of the mid-frequency peak) are responsible for the consonant confusion asymmetry and not markedness? After all, alveolar stops occur with much greater frequency than velar stops in the languages of the world, and velar stops are known in general to be more marked than alveolar stops. Lyublinskaya (1966), for example, argued that frequency effects were present even at the level of phoneme identification. Aren't these sound changes and confusion asymmetries simply a favoring of the unmarked? Second, the [ki] > [ti] confusion asymmetry displayed in the laboratory is rarely attested in actual diachronic sound change. [ki] is known to change to [tʃi] in many languages, not to [ti]. Given that [ki] is so readily mistaken for [ti] in the laboratory, that [ki] > [ti] is not a more frequent sound change poses an interesting question. Why don't subjects in laboratory perception studies hear [tʃi] instead of [ti]? This study addresses both of these questions.

Study 1 replicates and expands Plauché *et al.* (1997) and demonstrates the primacy of the acoustic/auditory characteristics over markedness as an explanation for this consonant confusion asymmetry by inducing confusion in the opposite direction ([ti] > [ki]). Study 2 provides further support for the primacy of auditory cues over markedness by illustrating that stop place confusion is specific to vocalic environments in which all but one differentiating cue is neutralized, namely, the mid-frequency peak. Finally, studies 3a and 3b address the question of the apparent discrepancy between the actual ki > tʃi sound change and the [ki] > [ti] confusion asymmetry induced in the laboratory.

II. MARKEDNESS

Before addressing the role that markedness might play in asymmetrical consonant confusion, it is important to define what we mean by "markedness." The weak version of our argument would define markedness as an effect due to crosslinguistic, universal frequency of occurrence. That is, due to the relatively high frequencies with which certain sounds occur in the languages of the world, in perception, where some ambiguity may arise, such sounds are the "default" percept. Alveolar stops are more frequent and therefore less marked than velar stops. Conceivably, this fact may bias listeners to think they hear alveolar stops when presented with degraded velar stops.

The stronger version of our argument defines markedness as any non-acoustic considerations that listeners employ in the task of differentiation. Such considerations may be SPE-style (Chomsky & Halle, 1968) universal disfavoring of certain sounds based either on articulatory or perceptual (but non-acoustic) ease, a Praguean positive valence for a particular feature (Trubetzkoy, 1939), or any other traditional definitions of markedness. Under this definition of markedness, velar stops may be argued as being universally more marked than alveolar stops due to any number of reasons, for example, articulatory or perceptual.

While we acknowledge that frequency of occurrence and other universal markedness constraints may indeed contribute to consonant confusion asymmetries, we believe they are secondary and may effectively be factored out. Study 1 (§II.A) supports the explanatory primacy of acoustic cues over markedness factors in confusion asymmetries by inducing confusion from a less marked to a more marked consonant ([ti] > [ki]) by manipulating the acoustic features of the bursts. Study 2 (§II.B) further supports this hypothesis by demonstrating that the consonant confusion asymmetry is obtained only in those vocalic contexts, namely, high front vowels, where all other velar cues except the mid-frequency spectral peak are neutralized.

A. Study 1

1. Stimuli Preparation

For Study 1, three male native speakers of American English in their mid to late twenties (BB, SC, and JR) were recorded to create the test tokens. In order to obtain voiceless, unaspirated stops, the target CV tokens [ki], [pi], and [ti] were digitally extracted from the words 'skeet,' 'speak,' and 'steep,' that is, by removing the [s] and end-truncating the vowel. Voiceless, unaspirated stops were selected to (1) simulate the Spanish CV tokens in the Plauché *et al.* study and (2) avoid the messiness of editing and identifying the components of the aperiodic noise portion characteristic of English aspirated stops. The target words were read five times by each speaker in the carrier sentence 'Say ___ once.' The tokens were digitally captured using Kay Elemetrics Corporation's Computerized Speech Laboratory (CSL) with a sampling rate of 20,000.

For each subject, one [pi], one [ti], and one [ki] token, all with similar prosody, were selected. The Plauché *et al.* (1997) study filtered the characteristic velar burst of [ki] with a Hanning band-reject filter of order 10 between the frequencies 2.5 and 4.0 kHz. Here we adopt the same methodology but use four different Blackman filters designed from combinations of two orders (**Low/High**) and two bandwidths (**Narrow/Wide**). The purpose of using four different filters was to gauge the degree of degradation necessary to induce confusion asymmetries. One hundred percent of the subjects in the Plauché *et al.* study perceived the filtered token as being [ti] (Table 4.2). We wanted to demonstrate that it is indeed the "extra" feature of the mid-frequency spectral burst in [ki] that differentiates it from a [ti] by showing a graded effect on perception by degrading the spectral peak to differing degrees.

TABLE 4.2

Filter Parameters for Study 1

Filter parameters	Low order (20)	High order (35)
Narrow bandwidth (1 kHz)	KILN	KIHN
Wide bandwidth (2 kHz)	KILW	KIHW

The filters were centered at each speaker's velar mid-frequency peak. BB = 3370 Hz, SC = 3390 Hz, and JR = 2751 Hz.

In addition to the 12 filtered [ki] stimuli (4 filtered [ki] tokens per speaker), in which we removed the characteristic velar mid-frequency spectral peak, we processed 3 [ti] tokens (1 mixed [ti] token per speaker) to introduce the mid-frequency peak to the [ti] burst. In order to add energy to the mid-frequency region of the alveolar stop in [ti], we (1) generated white noise (sampling rate 20,000; duration: 48 ms), (2) band-pass filtered the white noise, using a Blackman window of order 101 from 2880 to 3880 Hz, which corresponds to the average center

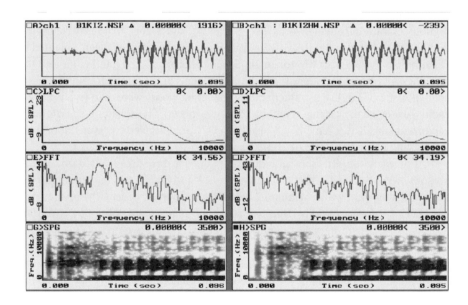

Figure 4.1. Waveform, LPC at burst, FFT at burst, and spectrogram of [ki] and KIHW. Note the characteristic mid-frequency spectral peak of the velar burst in the left column. The spectral peak in the right column has been attenuated by filtering. (Note that the spectral scales have not been normalized.)

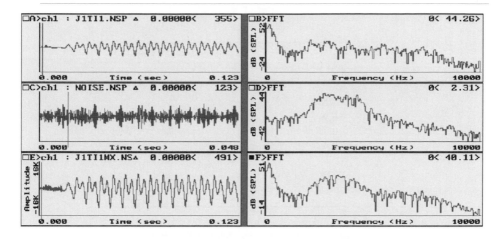

Figure 4.2. Waveform and FFT at burst of [ti] (top panel), filtered white noise (middle), and mixed [ti] (TIMX). The spectral shape of the filtered white noise, when mixed with a [ti] burst, yields a mid-frequency spectral peak akin to that found in a [ki] burst (compare with left FFT panel of Figure 4.1).

frequency of the spectral peak of [ki] across all three speakers, and (3) mixed the filtered noise with the burst of the alveolar stop in [ti].

The purpose of filtering the mid-frequency peak out of the velar bursts, as in Plauché *et al.* (1997), is to demonstrate that the spectral peak functions as an "extra" feature, potentially causing asymmetrical confusion. By introducing this peak into an alveolar stop burst, we hypothesize that some listeners will confuse the alveolar stop with a velar stop, which cannot be accounted for with a "default" markedness approach.

2. Perception Experiment

For distributional purposes, we added three additional [ti] tokens and nine additional [pi] tokens. The number of stimuli for Study 1 are listed in Table 4.3.

Sixteen speakers of American English, 12 women and 4 men, ranging in age from 19 to 33, served as subjects for the three studies. All 16 subjects were students at the University of California, Berkeley, at the time of the studies and were paid for their participation. None of the subjects had any known hearing conditions that would have affected their performance. However, one male subject's results were excluded as investigation of his data showed that he did not understand the task. The stimuli were randomized and presented over headphones in a quiet environ-

TABLE 4.3

Stimuli for Study 1

Stimulus	Number
KI	3
KILN	3
KILW	3
KIHN	3
KIHW	3
TI	6
TIMX	3
PI	12

L = low order (20), H = high order (35), N = narrow bandwidth (1000 Hz), and W = wide bandwidth (2000 Hz).

ment using Kay Elemetrics Corporation's Auditory Perception Program and Database (ASPP).

Subjects were asked to identify the consonant in each stimulus, from the choices B/P, D/T, CH, and G/K. (We were concerned with the perceived place of articulation, not the voicing of the segments in question, especially since the tokens had VOT values typical of English word-initial voiced stops but were phonemically voiceless, e.g., *skeet*.) Although the responses were not timed, the subjects were instructed to answer as quickly as possible and were not allowed to change their answers.

3. Results

The confusion matrix for the listeners' responses of Study 1 is presented in Table 4.4. Unlike the subjects from the Plauché *et al.* (1997) study, who confused natural [ki] as a [ti] 20% of the time, the subjects in the current study correctly identified 100% of the natural [ki] tokens. As expected, filtering the burst of the [ki] tokens did induce confusion with [ti]. It is interesting to note, however, that only the filter with the high order and wide bandwidth yielded significant confusion. The other three filters had a negligible effect, if any, on perception of the velar stop. This indicates that the degradation threshold at which listeners confuse [ki] for [ti] corresponds to a band-pass filter with an order of 35 and a bandwidth of 2 kHz centered around 3000 Hz. It is also worth noting that this is the first forced-choice stop place confusion study to offer both [ti] and [tʃi] as possible responses for

TABLE 4.4

Confusion matrix for Study 1 (percentages are given in parentheses)

Stimulus	Response				
	G/K (%)	D/T (%)	B/P (%)	CH (%)	None (%)
KI	45 (100)	0	0	0	0
KILN	45 (100)	0	0	0	0
KILW	43 (95.6)	2 (4.4)	0	0	0
KIHN	42 (93.3)	1 (2.2)	1 (2.2)	1 (2.2)	0
KIHW	30 (66.7)	13 (28.9)	0	2 (4.4)	0
TI	0	87 (97.8)	0	2 (2.3)	0
TIMX	4 (8.9)	31 (68.9)	6 (13.3)	4 (8.9)	0
PI	0	4 (2.2)	175 (97.2)	0	1 (0.6)

processed [ki] stimuli. Most previous consonant confusion studies have been forced-choice tasks that did not offer subjects the option of selecting either [t] or [tʃ] as the percept (e.g., Plauché et al., 1997; Miller & Nicely, 1955; Winitz et al., 1972; Wang & Bilger, 1973; Delogu et al., 1995). Guion (1998), on the other hand, only offered [k], [tʃ], [g], and [dʒ], to the exclusion of [t] and [d].

Upon further investigation, we discovered that there was a strong speaker-dependent effect, suggesting that other cues are involved in identification of stop place. Speaker BB's stimuli were responsible for the majority (12 out of 13) of the listeners' confusion of KIHW for [ti]. An examination of burst characteristics by speaker revealed that BB's velar stop token had the shortest VOT, shortest burst duration (onset of the first burst to the end of the final burst), and only three bursts (Table 4.5). We suspect that the relatively long VOT, long burst duration, and

TABLE 4.5

Confusion of KIHW by Speaker

	KIHW					
	Response				Velar characteristics	
Speaker	G/K	D/T	CH		VOT	burst	# of bursts
BB	2	12	1		26 ms	15 ms	3 bursts
SC	14	1	0		38 ms	20 ms	3 bursts
JR	14	0	1		60 ms	29 ms	4 bursts

multiple number of bursts of SC and JR's tokens provided sufficient cues for listeners to detect velarity, even after filtering with a high order and broad bandwidth. When BB's mid-frequency spectral peak is effectively filtered out, on the other hand, VOT, burst duration and the number of bursts did not provide sufficient cues for velar place.

TABLE 4.6

Confusion of TIMX by Speaker

| | TIMX | | | | | |
| | Response | | | | Alveolar characteristics | |
Speaker	G/K	D/T	B/P	CH	VOT	# of bursts
BB	0	14	0	1	13 ms	1
SC	3	9	0	3	37 ms	1
JR	1	8	6	0	16 ms	1

The processed [ti] file, in which we introduced a mid-frequency spectral peak to the alveolar burst, induced confusion as well. However, directionality toward [ki] was not evident. It would appear that for more than 30% of the TIMX tokens subjects were aware that the burst in TIMX was not alveolar, but they were unsure about the identity of the stop place, as these tokens were equally confused as [ki], [pi], and [tʃi].

These results, too, reflect some speaker-dependent effects, as summarized in Table 4.6. Speaker BB's token did not induce significant confusion, and speakers SC and JR's tokens resulted in different patterns of confusion. At least 93% (28 out of 30) of each speaker's natural [ti] tokens were correctly identified as alveolar. Three of SC's tokens were confused as velars, and three others were confused as [tʃ]. We suspect that the latter is due in part to the relatively long VOT of this token. Nearly half of JR's tokens were confused as bilabials, a result that we were not anticipating. Speaker SC's tokens best support the hypothesis adopted in this paper. Mixing in the mid-frequency spectral peak characteristic of velar stops to an alveolar burst did induce some listeners to perceive a velar stop. Moreover, some listeners perceived [tʃ], indicating that [ti] and [tʃi] are, in fact, perceptually linked, a point to which we will return in Study 3

The results from Study 1 support the view that listeners are opportunists. They make use of whatever cues are available for differentiating speech sounds.

Even when the characteristic "extra" feature of the mid-frequency spectral peak of a velar stop is removed, the presence of other velar cues may be sufficient for identification of the velar place. A further investigation of the relative salience of other acoustic cues such as VOT and the number of bursts, among others, is necessary for a fuller understanding of these phenomena. Language-specific considerations may also be important factors. In American English, for example, postalveolar fricatives and affricates are usually rounded, thus having lower center frequencies of the noise spectra than were presented in our stimuli.

B. Study 2

In Study 2 we seek to demonstrate that the [k] > [t] confusion asymmetry is specific to a high, front vocalic environment, further supporting the claim that it is the acoustic properties of [ki] and [ti] that are responsible for the consonant confusion asymmetry. A simple markedness account would be unable to explain why the confusion asymmetry is not obtained in all vocalic environments since velar stops are presumably more marked than alveolar stops regardless of the quality of the following vowel.

1. Stimuli Preparation

For Study 2, two of the speakers from Study 1, BB and SC, and a third subject, MP, a female native speaker of American English in her mid-twenties, were recorded to create the test stimuli. The target tokens for Study 2 were unaspirated, voiceless kV tokens where the vowel was one of nine American English vowels (see Table 4.7). The tokens were again digitally extracted from sC clusters in the carrier sentence "Say ___ once." For control purposes, we also elicited tV tokens in which the consonant was a voiceless, unaspirated alveolar stop. The tokens were digitally captured using Computerized Speech Laboratory (CSL) at a sampling rate of 20,000.

For each subject, one representative token from the three repetitions was selected for prosodic consistency. The burst of each token was filtered to remove the mid-frequency spectral peak. LPC and FFT spectral analyses showed that the center peak frequency for the velar burst in front of these different vowels varied little for a given speaker. Consequently, one filter was designed for all the stimuli (order 35, bandwidth 2 kHz).

The same 16 subjects from Study 1 participated in Study 2 (the data of all 16 subjects were used for this study). The subjects were asked to identify the stop in the stimuli. They were given three choices: G/K, D/T, or CH. (Again, we were concerned with the perceived place of articulation, not the voicing of the segments

TABLE 4.7

Test Stimuli for Study 2

Velar	Filtered	Alveolar
ki	ki – flt	ti
kau	kau – flt	tau
ker	ker – flt	ter
ku	ku – flt	tu
kei	kei – flt	tei
kaɪ	kaɪ – flt	taɪ
kae	kae – flt	tae
ka	ka – flt	ta
kou	kou – flt	tou

in question.) Response time was not measured, but the subjects were instructed to answer as quickly as possible and were not allowed to change their answers. Given that all the distinctive acoustic cues for velar place (except the mid-frequency spectral peak of the burst) are neutralized only before high front vowels, we predicted that confusion would not be induced by filtering velar bursts before non-high, non-front vowels.

2. Results

The results for the kV tokens are summarized in Figure 4.3. As the vast majority of the stimuli were correctly identified as velars (see the confusion matrix in Table 4.8), only the confused responses are displayed. The histogram shows that stimuli [ki], for example, induced one CH response, indicating that the remaining 47 tokens were correctly identified as velars.

As expected, the filtered [ki] file resulted in the greatest number of D/T responses. Given that it is the acoustic properties of high front vowels that give rise to consonant confusion asymmetry, it is not surprising that we get a confusion effect for the other two filtered files with front vowels: filtered [keɪ] and filtered [kæ]. A surprising result was that unfiltered [kaɪ] elicited as many D/T responses as the front vowel filtered files. Moreover, this confusion disappeared when the [kaɪ] file was filtered. Another interesting result is that some of the stimuli elicited CH responses even though none of the stimuli were heavily aspirated. Stimuli that elicited multiple CH responses were those with relatively "tight constrictions," that is, tokens with relatively high vowels such as [ki] and [ku], or in the case of

TABLE 4.8

Confusion Matrix for Natural and Filtered kV Stimuli (where V is one of nine American English vowels)

	Response			
Stimulus	G/K	D/T	CH	B/P
KA	48	0	0	0
ka–flt	48	0	0	0
kae	46	1	1	0
kae–flt	44	4	0	0
kai	44	4	0	0
kai–flt	48	0	0	0
kau	48	0	0	0
kau–flt	45	2	1	0
kei	48	0	0	0
kei–flt	44	4	0	0
ker	46	0	2	0
ker–flt	45	0	3	0
ki	47	0	1	0
ki–flt	41	5	2	0
kou	46	1	1	0
kou–flt	48	0	0	0
ku	46	0	2	0
ku–flt	48	0	0	0

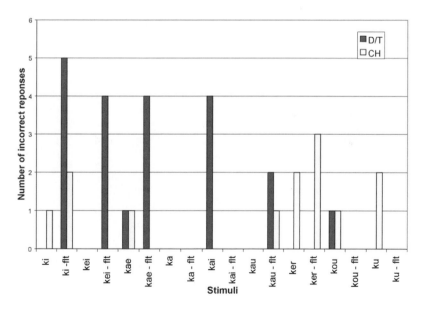

Figure 4.3. Confusion histogram for natural and filtered kV stimuli, where V is one of nine American English vowels. Only incorrect responses are shown.

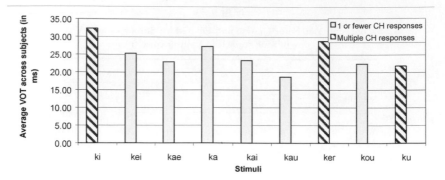

Figure 4.4. Average VOT across all three subjects of kV tokens. Those tokens that elicited multiple [tʃ] responses are cross-hatched.

[kɚ], a token with multiple constrictions (Chang, 1999) (see Figure 4.4). We hypothesize that the relatively tight constrictions of these vowels resulted in slightly longer VOT (as in [ki] and [kɚ]) or slight frication due to aerodynamic principles (Chang, 1999), leading some listeners to perceive a change in manner as well as place of articulation. Figure 4.5 charts the correlation between VOT (along the abscissa) and the number of times a token was perceived as being [tʃ] (along the ordinate). While there aren't enough data points to draw any conclusions, the results are suggestive of a potential correlation and warrants further investigation.

As expected, the tV stimuli did not induce significant confusion toward velar place (see confusion matrix in Table 4.9). We were surprised to discover, however,

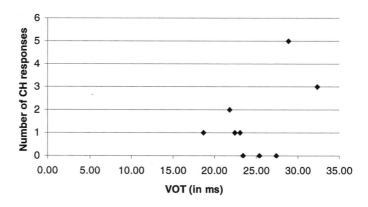

Figure 4.5. Correlation between VOT (averaged across all three subjects for kV tokens) and number of CH responses.

TABLE 4.9

Confusion Matrix for tV stimuli (where V is one of nine American English vowels)

	Response			
	G/K	D/T	CH	B/P
TA	1	42	5	0
TAE	0	47	1	0
TAU	0	38	10	0
TAI	1	47	0	0
TEI	2	46	0	0
TER	1	36	11	0
TI	0	15	0	0
TOU	0	48	0	0
TU	0	46	2	0

that four of the tV stimuli — [tɑ], [taʊ], [tu], and [tɝ] — induced multiple CH responses, as reflected in the confusion histogram in Figure 4.6, where only incorrect responses are shown. Closer investigation revealed that most of these

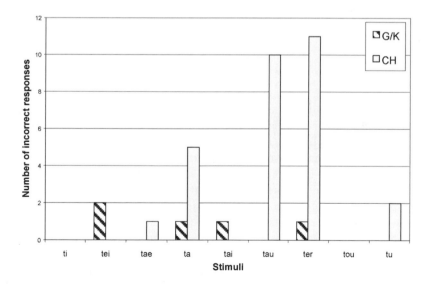

Figure 4.6. Confusion histogram from tV stimuli, where V is one of nine American English vowels. Only incorrect responses are shown.

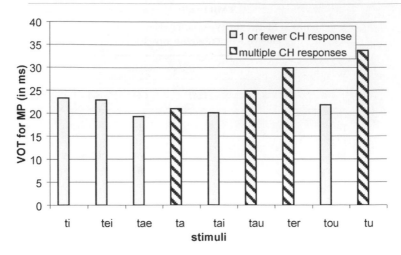

Figure 4.7.   VOT measurements for subject MP. Dark bars indicate tokens that elicited mulitple (tʃ) responses.

confusions were for tokens uttered by the same subject, MP. A histogram of VOT for MP's tV tokens (Figure 4.7) reveals that, unlike subjects BB and SC, MP's utterances of [tɑ], [taʊ], [tu], and [tɚ] had relatively high VOT values. We hypothesize that it is this relatively long VOT that induced confusion for [tʃ] for several subjects.

C. Discussion

In the first two studies we set out to demonstrate that it is the physical, acoustic characteristics of [ki] and [ti] that are responsible for the confusion asymmetry [ki] > [ti], not markedness factors. The data from these two studies support the claim that it is the physical, auditory cues that underlie this particular consonant confusion asymmetry. Study 1 supports the primacy of auditory factors over markedness factors by inducing a confusion from a less marked sound to a more marked sound by appropriately manipulating the acoustic signal. Study 2 further supports the auditory account by demonstrating that the consonant confusion asymmetry is limited to a particular environment that results in acoustic properties amenable to confusion. There is no reason according to the markedness hypothesis why one should find the [k] > [t] confusion only in the environment of a high, front vowel since velar stops are presumably more marked than alveolar stops in all vocalic environments.

III. [ti] VERSUS [tʃi]

One potential criticism of Studies 1 and 2 is that ki > ti is not a common sound change. Rather, ki ubiquitously changes to tʃi or ts in the languages of the world, not to ti.

We hypothesize that the lack of a [ki] > [tʃi] confusion asymmetry in the laboratory is due to the combination of two facts about most laboratory studies of this sort. First, as mentioned earlier, previous consonant confusion asymmetry studies that deal with [ki] > [ti] did not offer both [ti] and [tʃi] as options. Second, the stops used in many laboratory studies (including this one) are unaspirated. It is unlikely, we think, that subjects will perceive a change in the manner of articulation as well as a change in the place of articulation for unaspirated stops. We suspect that it is the aspiration noise following the degraded burst of a [kʰi] that is reanalyzed as the [ʃ] of a [tʃ], that is, the listener "hears" an alveolar burst (as demonstrated by the first study) followed by an unusual, incongruous amount of aspiration for an alveolar stop (since velars are known to engender the longest VOT, especially before the high, front vowel [i]; Cho & Ladefoged, 1999). Faced with such acoustic cues, we argue, some listeners parse the token as [tʃi].

As mentioned above, it is also worth noting that language-specific considerations may play a role. For example, American English postalveolar fricatives and affricates are usually rounded. The relatively high F3 of the filtered file may be enough of a cue for American English subjects that the stop in the filtered [ki] token is not a postalveolar segment.

A. Study 3A

1. Methodology

Taking these facts into consideration, we designed a third study that better reflects the actual sound change ki > tʃi. The three male speakers from Study 1 were recorded for the final study. The target words *key* [kʰi] and *chi* [tʃʰi] were read five times by each speaker in the carrier sentence 'Say ___ once.' For each subject, one [kʰi] and one [tʃʰi], with similar prosody, were selected.

The bursts of the velar token, *key*, were then subjected to the same four filters from Study 1. The resulting six tokens were randomized and presented to the same 16 subjects from Study 1. The subjects were asked to rate the [tʃʰi] goodness score of each token. If the token sounded like a canonical [tʃʰi], they were instructed to give it a goodness score of 1. If, however, the token did not sound like a [tʃʰi] at all, they were instructed to give it a goodness score of 7. Based on our hypothesis, we predicted that the [kʰi] token that was filtered with a high order and wide bandwidth would have better goodness scores than plain [kʰi] (see Figure 4.8).

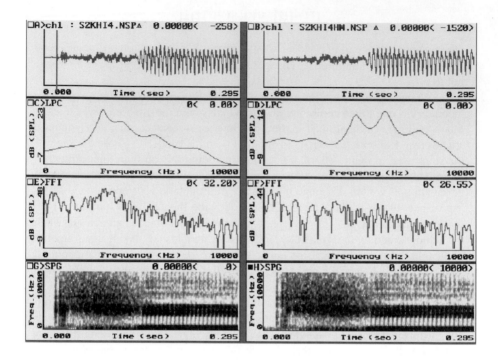

Figure 4.8. Waveform, LPC at burst, FFT at burst, and spectrogram of [kʰi] and KHIHW ([kʰi] band-reject filtered with a high order, 35, and wide bandwidth, 2 kHz.) Note the characteristic mid-frequency spectral peak of the velar burst in the left column. The spectral peak in the right column has been attenuated by filtering. (Spectral scales have not been normalized.)

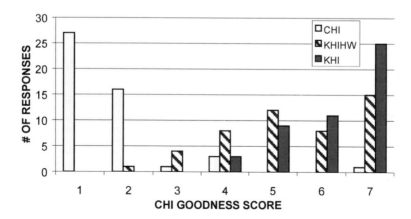

Figure 4.9. [tʃʰi] goodness scores for [tʃʰi] (CHI), [kʰi] (KHI), and filtered [kʰi] (KHIHW). '1' is the best [tʃʰi] goodness score, and '7' is the worst.

2. Results

As expected, the vast majority of [tʃʰi] tokens received a goodness score of 1 or 2, and most of the natural [kʰi] tokens received scores of 6 or 7. As in the first study, only the higher order, wider bandwidth filter resulted in a significantly different goodness score from the unfiltered [kʰi] token. These filtered [kʰi] tokens, as expected, received better goodness scores than the natural [kʰi] tokens. These results are summarized in Figure 4.9 and Table 4.10.

TABLE 4.10

**Mean [tʃʰi] Goodness Scores and Standard Deviation
for [tʃʰi] (CHI), [kʰi] (KHI), and Filtered [kʰi]
(KHILN, KHILW, KHIHN, KHIHW)**

Stimulus	Mean	Standard deviation
CHI	1.6875	1.132804
KHI	6.2083	0.966642
KHILN	6.3125	0.926128
KHILW	6.0833	0.985714
KHIHN	6.1666	0.974861
KHIHW	5.3958	1.41029

'1' is the best score, and '7' is the worst. Of the filtered tokens, only KHIHW displayed a significantly better score.

B. Study 3B

1. Methodology

According to the hypothesis adopted here, that it is the aspiration noise of [tʃʰi] in combination with the mistaken alveolar perception of filtered [kʰi] that is responsible for the [ki] > [tʃi] confusion, we would expect that the confusion would be reduced in the case of the voiced counterpart [gi] since there is no aspiration after the burst. To empirically verify this prediction, we replicated Study 3a with voiced tokens.

The same three male speakers from Study 1 were recorded for the final study. The target words ghee [gi] and gee [dʒi] were read five times by each speaker in the carrier sentence 'Say ___ once.' For each subject, one [gi] and one [dʒi], with similar prosody, were selected.

The bursts of the velar token [gi] were then subjected to the same four filters from Study 1. The resulting six tokens were randomized and presented to the same 16 subjects from Study 1. The subjects were asked to rate the [dʒi] goodness score of each token. If the token sounded like a canonical [dʒi], they were instructed to give it a goodness score of 1. If, however, the token did not sound like a [dʒi] at all, they were instructed to give it a goodness score of 7. Based on our hypothesis, we predicted that none of the filtered [gi] tokens would have better goodness scores than plain [gi] (see Figure 4.10).

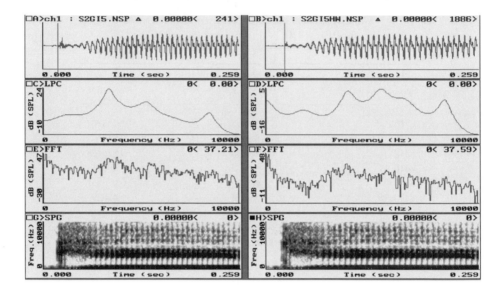

Figure 4.10.   Waveform, LPC at burst, FFT at burst, and spectrogram of [gi] and GIHW ([gi] band-reject filtered with a high order, 35, and wide bandwidth, 2 kHz.) Note the characteristic mid-frequency spectral peak of the velar burst in the left column. The spectral peak in the right column has been attenuated by filtering. (Note that spectral scales have not been normalized.)

2. Results

As expected, most of the [dʒi] tokens received a goodness score of 1 or 2, and most of the [gi] tokens received a goodness score of 6 or 7. More importantly, none of the filtered [gi] files, including the one that was filtered with a high order and a wide bandwidth (GIHW), had significantly better scores than natural [gi]. The results are summarized in Figure 4.11 and Table 4.11.

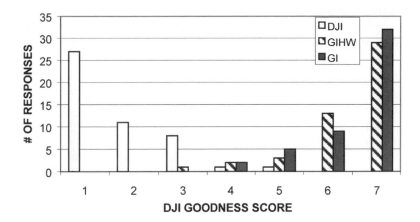

Figure 4.11. [dʒi] goodness scores for [dʒi] (DGI), [gi] (GI), and filtered [gi] (GIHW). '1' is the best [dʒi] goodness score, and '7' is the worst.

TABLE 4.11

Mean [dʒi] Goodness Scores and Standard Deviation for [dʒi] (DJI), [gi] (GI), and Filtered [gi] (GIHN, GIHW, GILN, GILW)

Stimulus	Mean	Standard deviation
DJI	1.7083	0.966642211
GI	6.4792	0.850271129
GIHN	6.3333	1.05856855
GIHW	6.3958	0.939433585
GILN	6.4375	0.872907833
GILW	6.375	1.023656359

'1' is the best score and '7' is the worst.

C. Discussion

Insofar as we were able to influence the direction of consonant confusion by targeted modification of some of the acoustic cues of stops, we believe we have demonstrated that it is acoustic–auditory factors that underlie such perceptual errors. But this study also undercuts claims that markedness plays a major role in these confusions. As far as markedness is concerned, affricates such as [tʃ] are rarer in the phonologies of the world than a plain stop like [k]. A markedness account of consonant confusion asymmetries fails to explain how the less marked velar stop could became the highly marked affricate [tʃ] in so many languages.

IV. CONCLUSIONS

In this paper, we have demonstrated consonant confusion asymmetries in the laboratory that parallel historical sound changes. Moreover, we have argued that it is the physical, acoustic properties of the sounds themselves that give rise to consonant confusion asymmetries and not markedness effects. We supported this claim through a pair of experiments in which markedness considerations were effectively factored out. We do not argue that markedness never plays a role in consonant confusion asymmetries, but rather that they are secondary to the acoustic-auditory factors. Perhaps, as we hypothesized earlier, markedness effects arise due to the physical acoustic properties of sounds. Finally, we showed that laboratory-based consonant confusion asymmetries do in fact lend insights to actual historical sound changes.

There remain some issues that warrant further scrutiny. First, an investigation of the role of the number of velar bursts, VOT, and burst duration in consonant confusion asymmetries and their relation to velar spectral characteristics may shed more light on the [ki] > [ti] consonant confusion asymmetry. Research currently underway focuses on these issues as well as exploring the relative importance of such cues (in addition to the relative amplitude of bursts versus vowel and formant transition information) in the detection and misperception of stop place in various vocalic environments.

ACKNOWLEDGMENTS

This study was funded by a National Science Foundation grant (#98-17243); Principal Investigator: John J. Ohala. The authors would like to acknowledge Sue-Wen Chiao and Julie A. Lewis for their research assistance and the editors of this volume for helpful comments.

NOTES

1. The parallelism in lab confusion studies and sound change involves the phonetic character of the sounds involved. For example, regarding the Czech palatalized labials, they are phonetically palatalized due to the palatalization being a distinctive

secondary articulation whereas in the lab studies involving English the stop in [pi] is palatalized non-distinctively due to coarticulation with the following palatal vowel.

2. In this paper, we use the notation X > Y, where "X can be confused as Y, but Y is rarely confused as X."

REFERENCES

Chang, S. C. (1999). Vowel-dependent VOT variation. *Proceedings of the XIVth International Congress of Phonetic Sciences, San Francisco, 2,* 1021.

Cho, T., & Ladefoged, P. (1999). Variation and universals in VOT: Evidence from 18 languages. *Journal of Phonetics, 27*(2), 207–229.

Chomsky, N., & Halle, M. (1968). *The sound pattern of English.* New York: Harper & Row.

Delogu, C., Paoloni, A., Ridolfi, P., & Vagges, K. (1995). Intelligibility of speech produced by text-to-speech systems in good and telphonic conditions. *Acta Acoustica, 3,* 89–96.

Gilmore, G. C., Hersh, H., Caramazza, A., & Griffin, J. (1979). On the prediction of confusion matrices from similarity judgments. *Perception & Psychophysics, 25*(5), 425–431.

Guion, S. G. (1998). The role of perception in the sound change of velar palatalization. *Phonetica 55,* 18–52.

Lyublinskaya, V. V. (1966). Recognition of articulation cues in stop consonants in transition from vowel to consonant. *Soviet Physics–Acoustics, 12*(2), 185–192.

Miller, G. A., & Nicely, P. E. (1955). An analysis of perceptual confusions among some English consonants. *Journal of the Acoustical Society of America, 27*(2), 338–352.

Plauché, M., Delogu, C., & Ohala, J. (1997). Asymmetries in consonant confusion. *Proceedings of Eurospeech '97: Fifth European Conference on Speech Communication and Technology, 4,* 2187–2190.

Stevens, K. N., & Blumstein, S. E. (1978). Invariant cues for place of articulation in stop consonants. *Journal of the Acoustical Society of America, 104*(1), 1358–1368.

Trubetzkoy, N. S. (1939). *Grundzuge der Phonologie.* Prague.

Wang, M. D., & Bilger, R. C. (1973). Consonant confusions in noise: A study of perceptual features. *Journal of the Acoustical Society of America, 54*(5), 1248–1266.

Winitz, H., Scheib, M. E., & Reeds, J. A. (1972). Identification of stops and vowels for the burst portion of /p,t,k/ isolated from conversation speech. *Journal of the Acoustical Society of America, 51*(4), 1309–1317.

CHAPTER

Effects of Vowel Context On Consonant Place Identification

Implications for a Theory of Phonologization

Jennifer Cole and Khalil Iskarous

Department of Linguistics
University of Illinois at Urbana-Champaign
Urbana, Illinois 61801

I. Phonetic Factors in Phonology
II. Evaluating Phonetic Naturalness
   A. Articulatory Factors
   B. Perceptual Factors
III. Phonetic and Phonological Evidence for Contextual Effects on Place Identification in Oral Stops
IV. Experiment
   A. Stimuli
   B. Method
   C. Results
V. Discussion
   Acknowledgments
   Notes
   References
   Appendix

The Role of Speech Perception in Phonology

I. PHONETIC FACTORS IN PHONOLOGY

A perennial question in linguistics concerns the nature of the relationship between phonology and phonetics. On casual observation, the synchronic evidence is conflicting: while phonetically "natural" phonological processes abound, for example, the palatalization of coronals preceding palatal vocoids, there are also plenty of examples of phonological processes for which phonetic motivation is not readily apparent (Anderson, 1981). The fact that phonetic conditioning factors are not always evident can be taken as support for the dual claims of phonological theory that phonological systems are defined at a level distinct from phonetics, and that phonological processes need not be held to a criterion of phonetic plausibility or naturalness. In principle, any pattern that can be defined over the units of phonological representation, in accordance with formal constraints that hold over those representations, can form the basis for a phonological rule or constraint.

Despite this separation of phonetics and phonology, phonetic considerations often play a major role in phonological analysis. Given a choice between two competing analyses for the alternation X ~ Y, /X/ → [Y], or /Y/ → [X], preference is often given to the analysis that has a plausible phonetic basis, all else being equal. It is not hard to accept that phonetic conditioning underlies certain phonological processes. For instance, few would dispute that categorical place assimilation (viewed as a phonological process) may have its roots in patterns of gradient coarticulation (viewed as a phonetic process). What has posed more of a challenge to phonological theory has been to explain why languages vary in the extent to which patterns of phonetic variation are "phonologized," that is, promoted to the status of a phonological process or constraint. In other words, why is it that in some languages the sequence /ti/ fails to undergo phonological palatalization to [tʃi], despite the fact that in the realization of [ti] the [t] may be subject to palatal "coloring" due to coarticulation?

Constraint-based approaches to phonology appear to offer a solution to this problem: phonetically motivated constraints on phonological representation may form part of a universal phonological grammar, but need not be uniformly enforced in all languages. Thus, in Optimality Theory (Prince & Smolensky, 1993; Archangeli & Langendoen, 1997) a particular constraint may be upheld in one language and violated in another, as a function of the interaction between it and other constraints in the phonological grammar. The possibility of violable constraints has reopened the door to phonetic explanation in phonology, and recent years have witnessed an increasing number of phonological analyses that draw on phonetic constraints, such as those that govern speech articulation and perception. For the sake of illustration, we cite several examples here.

Constraints arising from speech articulation are invoked to explain:

- the failure of tongue root advancement harmony to affect low vowels (Archangeli & Pulleyblank, 1994);

- the occurrence of vowel reduction and consonant lenition due to articulatory undershoot (Lindblom, 1983);

- place assimilation due to undershoot (Lindblom, 1983), reflecting patterns of coarticulation (Lee, 1999);

- the voicing of stops conditioned by place of articulation, closure duration, position in a consonant cluster, and phrasal position (Ohala, 1983; Westbury & Keating, 1986; Hayes, 1996).

- the failure of geminates to undergo lenition, viewed as a phenomenon of physical effort reduction (Kirchner, 1998).

Constraints arising from speech perception are invoked to explain:

- place assimilation arising from listener misperception (Hura *et al.*, 1992; Ohala, 1990);

- the neutralization of laryngeal contrasts in consonants conditioned by the salience of acoustic cues that signal the contrasts (Steriade, 1995).

II. EVALUATING PHONETIC NATURALNESS

While phonetic constraints may offer insight into the origin and function of a phonological pattern, their role in phonological analysis raises one fundamental question: which patterns in the phonetics may give rise to constraints that operate in phonology? Without a clear answer to this question, phonetic accounts of phonological phenomena will never make testable predictions, and thus will never offer more than convenient post-hoc analysis. This problem with functional, phonetic explanation in phonology is cited by Kenstowicz (1981) as the primary reason that functionalism has not been well received in American (generative or structuralist) linguistics, "chiefly because they [functional theories that draw on phonetic explanation (JC/KI)] require independently motivated theories of the external domain appealed to (i.e., theories of the vocal apparatus, speech perception, etc.), which are not developed to the point where appeals to these domains lead to testable empirical consequences" (p. 431). The number of phonetic patterns that can be defined along continuous acoustic and articulatory parameters and that could in principle serve as the basis for phonological generalization is much greater than the number of phonological patterns for which a phonetic basis has been claimed. We must come to know more precisely *which* patterns in phonetics may be incorporated in phonology before evaluating claims about phonetic naturalness or the consequences of phonetic variation in phonology.

A related question concerns the form in which a phonetic constraint gets expressed when it is incorporated into phonology. One view, expressed by Ohala (1990), is that phonetic constraints are imported directly into phonological grammar, without mediation or reformulation in terms of phonological features. An alternative view is that phonetic patterns are the seeds of development for phonological constraints, but that the form and even the function of the constraint may change in the mapping from the phonetic domain to the phonological domain. This is the view put forth by Hayes (1996), who argues that "there is a considerable gap between the raw patterns of phonetics and phonological constraints" (p. 5). Hayes claims that "the influence of phonetics in phonology is not direct, but is mediated by structural constraints that are under some pressure toward formal symmetry" (p. 11).

A. Articulatory Factors

Hayes's argument is based on the phonetic factor of ease of articulation, in particular, on the ease of producing voicing or voicelessness on a stop consonant based on aerodynamic factors that arise from the local environment. Constraints on stop consonant voicing that are observed to function in phonological systems reflect the relative ease of producing voicing (or voicelessness) in a particular environment. Voicing is ruled out in contexts where it is harder to produce than voicelessness, and vice versa. Under a principle of formal symmetry, the voicing constraint is extended from its phonetically determined environment to other environments that fall into the same phonological class. For example, based on the predictions of the aerodynamic model, Hayes claims that voicing is easier to produce than voicelessness for bilabial and coronal stops following a liquid, but in the same context voicelessness is easier than voicing for the velar stop (Figure 5.1). Despite the difference between the velar stop and bilabial or coronal stops, Hayes's analysis predicts that languages that suspend a voicing contrast in post-liquid position will tend to affect all three places of articulation in a uniform manner, e.g., allowing [lb, ld, lg] while disallowing [lp, lt, lk].

B. Perceptual Factors

Crucial to Hayes's account of phonetic constraints in phonology is a concrete model of the relative difficulty of producing speech sounds in various environments. The aerodynamic model Hayes uses provides an independent measure of

	p	t	k	b	d	g
l/r ___ :	45	28	15	10	20	30

Figure 5.1. Phonetic difficulty indices for oral stops in post-liquid position. High values indicate more difficulty in the production of voicelessness for [p,t,k] or voiding for [b,d,g]. Adapted from Hayes (1996).

phonetic difficulty that can be applied to evaluate the phonetic naturalness of phonological patterns of stop voicing. While Hayes's focus is on phonetic difficulty in the domain of speech production, of equal interest is phonetic difficulty arising from speech perception, and its role as a conditioning factor in phonology. As noted above, perceptual difficulty (or conversely, perceptual salience) is claimed by Ohala (1990) and Steriade (1995) as the basis for certain phonological patterns such as assimilation.

In order to fully understand how perceptual ease or difficulty may give rise to constraints that shape phonological systems, we must first have, in Hayes's terminology, a landscape of perceptual difficulty for each type of phonological distinction that languages make. Hayes evaluates production difficulty on the basis of a formal model of speech aerodynamics. In this paper, we propose that a map of perceptual diffuculty can be obtained by considering results from speech perception research. In the remainder of this paper, we report on a speech perception experiment that investigates contextual effects on the perception of consonantal place of articulation (C-Place). The goal of the experiment is to determine if there are perceptual biases for the identification of C-Place that stem from the context of the adjacent vowels. If such effects are found, then a further goal is to determine how the perceptual biases relate to known patterns in phonology governing the occurrence of contrastive C-Place features. The results of this experimental work are offered here as a first step in the construction of a complete landscape of perceptual difficulty, toward the goal of evaluating the role of perception in phonology.

III. PHONETIC AND PHONOLOGICAL EVIDENCE FOR CONTEXTUAL EFFECTS ON PLACE IDENTIFICATION IN ORAL STOPS

It is well-known that the acoustic cues that identify the place of articulation for an oral stop consonant vary according to the adjacent vowel context. The second formant transition provides an important cue to C-Place (Delattre *et al.*, 1955), but the slope of the transition varies depending on the place of articulation of the adjacent vowel (V-Place). Another important cue to C-Place is the spectrum of the release burst (Blumstein & Stevens, 1979, 1980; Stevens & Blumstein, 1978), which also varies as a function of the V-Place of the adjacent vowel. Thus, the possibility exists that the C-Place cues obtained in a specific vowel context are more salient than in other vowel contexts, for a given C-Place feature.

Consistent with the observed effects of adjacent vowel context on C-Place cues, phonological research provides evidence for the interaction between C-Place features for stop consonants and the V-Place features of adjacent vowels. Clements (1991) and Clements & Hume (1995) note that there are phonological systems in which labial consonants co-occur with round vowels, and systems in which palatal consonants co-occur with front vowels. These interactions include cases where the consonant conditions the place features of an adjacent vowel, as well as cases where the vowel feature conditions the place features of the adjacent consonant. Other evidence for interactions between C-place and adjacent V-Place comes from research on the lexical frequency of C-Place features in five languages (Janson, 1986; Kawasaki-Fukumori, 1992), as reported in Figure 5.2. Phonological theory has focused on formal models of these C-Place/V-Place dependencies, but makes no direct claims about the phonetic origins of these patterns of place dependency. Plausible explanations can be constructed both in terms of speech production, drawing on coarticulation, and in terms of speech perception, drawing on the salience of C-Place and V-Place cues. It is even conceivable that both kinds of effects conspire to render the observed distributional restrictions on place of articulation.

More frequent combinations:
■ alveolar + front V
■ labial + back, round V
■ velar + back, round V

Less frequent combinations:
■ velar + front V
■ velar + round V

Figure 5.2.   Evidence for C-Place and V-Place interaction from lexical frequency. Adapted from Janson (1986).

IV. EXPERIMENT

To investigate how the adjacent vowel context might affect the perception of C-Place in stop consonants, we conducted a speech perception experiment in which subjects were asked to identify the C-Place feature of an intervocalic stop consonant in noise. Subjects listened to noisy stimuli consisting of nonsense words containing VCV sequences, and were asked to identify the intervocalic consonant as either [b], [d], or [g]. The goal of the experiment was to determine if and how the identification accuracy for [b], [d], and [g] may vary as a function of adjacent vowel context, and how such variation relates to observed patterns of phonological C-Place and V-Place dependencies. Furthermore, since a major cue to C-Place lies in the F_2 locus of a stop consonant, our study compares C-Place identification of stops in the context of back vowels, (with a relatively low F_2) and front vowels (with a relatively high F_2).

A. Stimuli

The stimuli for the experiment were constructed from a set of 75 nonsense words of the form ómV_1CV_2. The vowels preceding (V_1) and following (V_2) the target conso-nant were chosen from the set of five tense vowel monophthongs, [i,e,u,o,a]. The intervocalic target consonant was chosen from the set [b,d,g]. The total number of distinct V_1CV_2 sequences was 75 ($5 \times 3 \times 5$), yielding a set of 75 nonsense words such as *ómadi*, *ómebu*, and *ómigo*. The nonsense words contain sounds which are readily identifiable by English listeners, but the words themselves do not sound like individual words of English, in large part because of the sequence of three syllables, each with a full vowel. Stress is located on the first syllable (expressed by an H*L pitch accent), but the second and third syllables also contain full vowels. In a typical English word, only the syllables with primary or secondary stress can contain a full vowel, and a three-syllable word would typically have only one or two stressed, full-voweled syllables, e.g., *Omaha* ['omə‚ha], *capital* ['kæpəɹəl]. The 75 nonsense words were produced in a clear and slow speaking style by one of the experimenters, a native speaker of Egyptian Arabic.[1]

The speech signals were digitally recorded (48 Hz) and checked for uniform amplitude in order to rule out the possibility that subjects would respond more accurately to an individual word due to greater loudness of the speech signal. The speech signals were transferred from tape to a Sun Ultra 5 workstation (sampled at 16 kHz, 16-bit encoding) for creation of the noisy stimuli using Entropics ESPS/Waves+. A uniform noise signal was synthesized at five different amplitude levels, ranging from 0.5 to 0.75 times the average amplitude level of the clear speech signals (the nonsense words). The waveform for each nonsense word was composed with each level of noise signal, for 375 (75×5) different noisy nonsense word signals.

B. Method

Nine subjects, all young adult native speakers of American English, listened to the stimuli through headphones in a quiet laboratory room. The 375 noisy stimuli were presented to subjects in three randomized blocks, with a 2-second response-to-stimulus interval, and a short break between successive blocks. The total session duration was between 1 and 1.5 hours. Subjects were asked to respond immediately after hearing each noisy word, identifying the target consonant as [b], [d], or [g] by selecting one of three response buttons appearing on the computer screen. Subjects were told before beginning that all nonsense words contained one of these three consonants, and were given a brief familiarization with the form of the nonsense words.

C. Results

Data for vowel contexts involving the front vowels [i,e] and the back vowels [o,u] are reported here. The results for C-Place identification are presented below in terms of the frontness or backness of the adjacent vowels, rather than in terms of individual vowel qualities. The complete set of stimulus–response data for the lowest (N0) and highest (N4) noise levels are presented in the form of confusion matrices in the appendix to this chapter. We report here on the result of statistical analysis using repeated-measures ANOVA, with separate ANOVAs run for each of the three consonants. The independent variables, all of which were within-subject variables, were: Repetition (3 levels), Vowel1 (2 levels: front, back), Vowel2 (2 levels: front, back), and Noise (5 levels: noise-to-signal ratio values ranging from 0.5 to 0.75). The dependent variable was a non-parametric measure of sensitivity (I), which normalizes the number of correct responses ($P_{(hit)}$) for each consonant by the number of false alarms ($P_{(fa)}$) for the same consonant (Hume *et al.*, 1999; Grier, 1972). The formula for I is given below; higher I values indicate greater sensitivity, which in the present case means more accurate identification of the C-Place feature:

$$I = (1 - P_{(fa)} + P_{(hit)})/2$$

Table 5.1 presents the ANOVA results for the main effects and interactions. Significant results are marked with an asterisk, and discussed individually below.

1. Effect of Noise

As can be seen in Table 5.1, the noise effect was significant for all three consonants. To find out which pairs of noise levels were significantly different and in which direction the difference occurred, a multicomparison procedure using Tukey's method was performed.

Table 5.2 presents the results of the multicomparison procedure, which are shown graphically in Figure 5.3. The significant comparisons (marked with double asterisks) were for the pairs n0–n2, n0–n3, n0–n4, n1–n3, and n1–n4.

TABLE 5.1

Results from Repeated-Measures ANOVA for Identification of Three Consonants

	Df	[b]		[d]		[g]	
		F	Pr(F)	F	Pr(F)	F	Pr(F)
Repetition	2,16	4.0295	**0.01839***	1.7476	0.17532	3.66506	**0.02634***
Vowel1	1,8	37.3732	**0.00000***	2.9592	0.08605	36.94403	**0.00000***
Vowel2	1,8	419.5836	**0.00000***	106.5299	**0.00000***	3.47781	0.06282
Noise	4,24	2.6459	**0.03295***	5.1583	**0.00048***	8.31169	**0.00001***
Repetition: Vowel1	2,16	2.3654	0.095026	1.5098	0.222024	2.01918	0.133909
Repetition: Vowel2	2,16	1.0353	0.355909	0.3171	0.728446	0.06798	0.934286
Vowel1: Vowel2	1,8	28.2962	**0.00000***	3.8650	**0.04988***	0.01908	0.890188
Repetition: Noise	8,64	1.1614	0.320894	1.4208	0.185106	1.11276	0.352948
Vowel1: Noise	4,24	1.7508	0.137674	0.5176	0.722862	1.17001	0.323222
Vowel2: NoiseL	4,24	0.2616	0.902521	1.1498	0.332404	0.75257	0.556641
Repetition: Vowel1: Vowel2	2,16	2.7247	0.066599	0.7964	0.451550	1.51826	0.220159
Repetition: Vowel1:Noise	8,64	1.0416	0.403526	1.1382	0.335903	0.83546	0.571641
Repetition: Vowel2:Noise	8,64	1.1220	0.346686	0.6296	0.753070	0.93863	0.484064
Vowel1: Vowel2: Noise	4,24	0.0567	0.994008	0.0929	0.984671	0.49019	0.742964
Residuals	472						

Subject Df = 8.

Figure 5.3 shows the confidence interval for the paired comparisons. Confidence intervals in the positive range indicate that identification was better at the lower noise level. In general, the closest differences (e.g., n0–n1) did not have significant effects on the sensitivity, but the larger differences (e.g., n0–n2) did, with confidence intervals well in the positive range. The largest effect of noise is seen in paired comparisons between n0 (the lowest noise level) and n3–n4 (the two highest noise levels), and between n1 and n4. These results show that the noise factor had the expected degrading effect on identification: identification at the highest noise levels was significantly worse than at the lowest noise levels.

TABLE 5.2

Multicomparison of Noise Levels

	Estimate	Std. error	Lower bound	Upper bound
n0–n1	0.0100	0.0208	–0.046800	0.0669
n0–n2	**0.0571**	**0.0208**	**0.000273**	**0.1140****
n0–n3	**0.0679**	**0.0208**	**0.011100**	**0.1250****
n0–n4	**0.0733**	**0.0208**	**0.016500**	**0.1300****
n1–n2	0.0471	0.0208	–0.009760	0.1040
n1–n3	**0.0579**	**0.0208**	**0.001040**	**0.1150****
n1–n4	**0.0633**	**0.0208**	**0.006450**	**0.1200****
n2–n3	0.0108	0.0208	–0.046000	0.0676
n2–n4	0.0162	0.0208	–0.040600	0.0730
n3–n4	0.0054	0.0208	–0.051400	0.0622

2. Effect of Adjacent Vowel Quality

We look next at the effect of the adjacent vowel quality on C-Place identification. The vowel contexts were defined in terms of two vowel groups: the front vowels [i,e] and the back vowels [u,o] (Table 5.3). Responses for the low vowel [a] were not included in this phase of the analysis in order to keep the comparison sets of equal size and diversity. The four contexts are defined in terms of the quality of the preceding and following vowels, and are identified below using the example

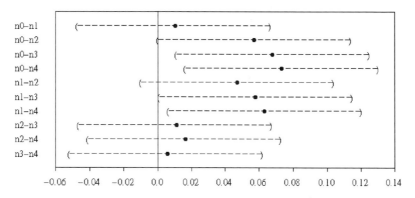

Figure 5.3. Multicomparison of noise level. Simultaneous 95% confidence limits determined by Tukey's method. Significance is detected by lack of intersection between confidence interval and 0 level.

TABLE 5.3

Vowel Context Groups for [g] Stimuli

F1	Preceding vowel is front:	*igV, egV*
F2	Following vowel is front:	*Vgi, Vge*
B1	Preceding vowel is back:	*ugV, ogV*
B2	Following vowel is back:	*Vgu, Vgo*
F1_G_F2		*igi, ige, egi, ege*
F1_G_B2		*igu, igo, egu, ego*
B1_G_F2		*ugi, uge, ogi, oge*
B1_G_B2		*ugu, ugo, ogu, ogo*

of the target consonant [g]. Similar labels identify vowel contexts for the target consonants [b,d].

a. Response patterns for [g] stimuli. The ANOVA results for [g] from Table 5.1 indicate a significant effect of the preceding vowel. Figure 5.4 plots the interaction between Vowel1 and Vowel2 for [g] identification at the highest noise level (N4). The effect of the preceding vowel is seen in the higher sensitivity values for B1 compared to F1. This is the only significant vocalic effect on the identification of [g]; no comparable difference is found for B2 and F2. The interaction between the two factors is also not significant for this consonant.

b. Response patterns for [d] stimuli. Table 5.1 shows that for [d] identification there is one significant main effect of vocalic quality and one interaction.

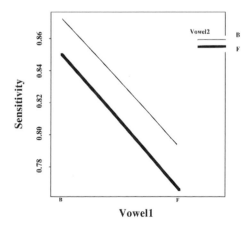

Figure 5.4. Interaction plot for the factors Vowel1 and Vowel2 in the identification of [g] at noise level N4.

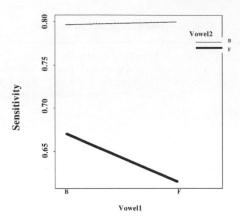

Figure 5.5.   Interaction plot for the factors Vowel1 and Vowel2 in the identification of [d] at noise level N4.

These findings are shown for the noise level N4 in the interaction plot in Figure 5.5. When V2 is back, sensitivity is significantly greater, regardless of the quality of V1. A significant interaction between V1 and V2 is found only when V2 is front: under that condition, sensitivity is greater when V1 is back.

 c. Response patterns for [b] stimuli. The results for [b] identification from Table 5.1 are similar to those for [d], with the addition of a significant main effect of V1. In all, there are two significant main effects and one significant interaction for [b], illustrated by the interaction plot in Figure 5.6 for the noise level N4. As

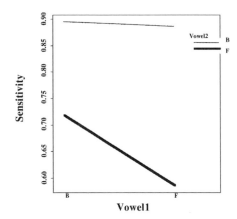

Figure 5.6.   Interaction plot for the factors Vowel1 and Vowel2 in the identification of [b] at noise level N4.

with [d], sensitivity for [b] is higher when V2 is back than when V2 is front. And as with [g], sensitivity is higher overall when V1 is back, though the effect is much greater under the condition that V2 is front. This interaction between V1 and V2 is significant for [b], as seen above for [d].

3. Summary of Results

Noise is seen to have the expected effect of degrading C-Place identification. The greatest effect of noise is found in comparing results from stimuli that differed by more than one step on the noise gradient. Overall, the clearest stimuli were identified with highest accuracy and the noisiest stimuli were identified with the lowest accuracy.

To summarize the effect of adjacent vowel quality, identification of [g], [d], and [b] is facilitated when the first vowel is back, although for [d] the effect of first vowel backness is dependent on the second vowel being front. Also, [d] and [b] identification is strongly facilitated when the second vowel is back. A generalization that emerges from this experiment, therefore, is that facilitation of identification of all three consonants occurs in the context of a back vowel. A related fact is that identification for all three consonants is worst when both preceded and followed by a front vowel.

V. DISCUSSION

Before discussing the main results from the perception study described above, we give consideration to two possible objections to the study. First, the nonsense words used as stimuli were spoken by a native speaker of Egyptian Arabic (the second author), whose consonant and vowel productions may differ from those of American English, the native language of all of the subjects. The possibility may exist that the subjects' response patterns might be influenced by this language difference. While we do not claim that the speaker produced speech sounds just as in American English, we think that the idiosyncratic features of his pronunciation did not reduce the subjects' ability to discriminate between his [b], [d] and [g] sounds. In support of our claim, we note that none of the subjects had any difficulty in understanding the speaker's productions in the clear, not even those subjects who had no prior experience hearing the speaker's voice. Even at the lowest noise level, when the noise signal was at half the amplitude of the clear signal, C-Place identification was very good. Moreover, the speaker produced the nonsense words with clear, hyperarticulated speech, in a style known to exhibit the least effects of coarticulation of the sort that might affect C-Place perception (Lindblom, 1990;

Lee, 1999). We expect that the effects of vowel context on C-Place identification might be even greater under more casual, hypoarticulated speech styles.

The second objection that might be raised concerns the perception bias that is introduced by the native language of the listener. There is evidence that listeners with different native languages attend differently to the acoustic cues that signal phonological distinctions between sounds. For example, Hume *et al.* (1999) demonstrate that listeners whose native language is Korean show a different sensitivity to C-Place cues than listeners whose native language is American English. These findings suggest the possibility that the response patterns obtained in our study reflect a bias on the part of the listeners that stems from their native language experience with American English phonetics and phonology. Although we do not dispute the Hume *et al.* finding, we do not think that our findings suggest a primary effect of the subjects' native language. None of the response patterns (e.g., facilitation of [d] and [b] identification by a following back vowel, facilitation of [g] identification with a preceding front vowel, or inhibition of all C-Place identification with preceding and following front vowels) reflect any property of American English phonology or phonetics known to us. Furthermore, the nonsense words did not resemble existing English words, especially in the sequencing of syllables with full, long vowels, so the VCV contexts the subjects heard should not have been very familiar to them based on their knowledge of English word structure.[2]

The results show that identification for [b] and [d] was conditioned by the following vowel, with a following front vowel conditioning lower sensitivity to C-Place identification. The fact that sensitivity to C-Place is reduced in the context of a following front vowel is consistent with evidence in phonology that front vowels (especially /i,e/) frequently condition phonological place assimilation (palatalization). If certain place features are less distinct preceding a front (i.e., palatal) vowel, then it is possible that palatalization may serve to further enhance the perceptual distinction. Neutralization between [b] and [d], for example, may be avoided if one of them is replaced by a palatal or palatalized sound in the context of a following front vowel. This account offers a perceptual motivation for palatalization, but does not rule out an articulatory motivation as well, and does not indicate whether one source for the phonological process is primary. One possibility is that a sound change, such as palatalization, is conditioned in the first place by coarticulation, but then may offer additional advantages for perception.

One important difference between our findings and patterns of phonological palatalization concerns the behavior of the bilabial stop. Phonological palatalization processes only very rarely affect bilabial consonants (Lee, 1999), while in our data the effect of a following front vowel is even slightly greater for the bilabial [b] than it is for the coronal [d]. If the perceptual pattern serves (even partially) as the basis for phonological patterns of palatalization, then based on our findings we would expect to find similarity in the behavior of [b] and [d], with more or less equal occurrences of bilabial and coronal palatalization. It may be that the rarity of bilabial palatalization compared with coronal palatalization reflects articulatory differences between bilabials and coronals; the lingual gesture for a front vowel is more likely to affect the lingual gesture of a preceding [d] than it will affect the labial gesture of a preceding [b], and thus there may be a greater articulatory basis for palatalization with coronals than for bilabials. This line of reasoning suggests that the primary motivation for palatalization may lie in the articulatory domain, with a perceptual benefit for the discrimination of bilabials and coronals that does not by itself motivate the sound change for bilabials.

It is of interest to note that the vocalic effects on [b] identification are not at all problematic when viewed from the perspective of the interaction between labial consonants and round vowels, as mentioned in section III. [b] identification is best when the following vowel is back and round, which is consistent with observed phonological patterns of co-occurrence between bilabials and round vowels. In a language with the five-vowel inventory used in the present experiment, a consequence of enforcing a co-occurrence restriction between bilabials and back, round vowels is that bilabials would then fail to appear in the palatalizing context of a following front (unrounded) vowel — precisely the environment where bilabials are perceptually less salient.

Oddly, our findings do not show a significant effect of a following front vowel for [g] identification, despite the observation that phonological palatalization commonly affects velars in CV structures (Lee, 1999). Our data indicate that it is the preceding vowel that influences [g] identification, with a preceding front vowel inhibiting identification. In fact, the inhibitory effect of a preceding front vowel is also found with [b] and [d] identification, but only when the following vowel is also front. This effect of a preceding front vowel is at odds with patterns of coarticulation and phonological palatalization. In her study of the acoustic evidence for coarticulation, Lee (1999) finds a greater coarticulatory influence of a vowel on an adjacent consonant in CV structures than in VC structures for bilabial, coronal, *and* velar place of articulation. She relates her finding to attested patterns of phonological palatalization, which also occur with much greater frequency in CV structures than in VC. In sum, the effects of a preceding front vowel on the perceptual patterns for C-Place identification are not consistent with the phonological patterns of palatalization, which points further to an articulatory rather than a perceptual basis for palatalization of velars.

A clear pattern that emerges for all three consonants in our study is that the context in which both the preceding and the following vowel are front is the worst overall for C-Place identification. This is a kind of "double-palatalizing" context, and suggests itself as a prime context for a phonological palatalization or, even more drastically, for the phonological suspension of a C-Place contrast altogether. Once more, we find a poor fit between the perceptual patterns and phonological patterns of place assimilation. In phonological systems, restrictions on the occurrence of C-Place features are typically one-sided. C-Place features may be restricted on the basis of a following vowel, as in palatalization, or the preceding vowel, as in the restriction of retroflex place of articulation to post-vocalic positions (Steriade, 1995). But it is rarely, if ever, the case that a consonantal place feature is restricted on the basis of the combined preceding and following vowel contexts.[3]

Of course, we recognize that there are phonological patterns that are restricted to VCV environments. For example, lenition processes typically affect stop consonants in intervocalic position, where the presence of both the preceding and following vowels are critical to the process, as in Spanish (Cole *et al.*, 1999). But in that case the vowel quality is not a factor, and all vowels equally condition the lenition process. The two-sided environment with front vowels that inhibits C-Place identification in our study is more specific with respect to vowel quality than the contexts that are found to condition the distribution of C-Place in phonological systems.

To summarize, the perceptual patterns of C-Place identification from our study are partially consistent with phonological patterns of palatalization for coronal consonants: a following front vowel reduces the perceptual distinctiveness of the coronal (and bilabial) place feature. Our findings are also consistent with the phonological patterns of co-occurrence between bilabial consonants and back, round vowels. The parallel between perceptual and phonological patterns breaks down, however, when we consider the effects of a preceding front vowel on the bilabial and coronal, and, even more clearly, on the velar consonant. Phonological palatalization processes are not typically conditioned by a preceding front vowel. Furthermore, we observe that the strongest influence of vocalic context occurs only when both the preceding and following vowels are front. The special status of this "two-sided" context is not observed in phonological processes that restrict C-Place features, such as palatalization. This finding presents us with indirect evidence about the kinds of structures that can serve as conditioning factors for phonological patterns. Although two-sided contexts may condition perception, to the extent that these perceptual patterns serve as a basis for phonological constraints, their incorporation into phonology may involve a process of generalization that locates the conditioning factor on either the preceding or following context, but not both. Or, perhaps, the conditioning factor may be interpreted solely in terms of the sequencing of C and V, disregarding the vowel quality (as in the example of lenition).

The findings from our study offer at best a loose fit between perceptual patterns and contexts for phonological constraints on the occurrence of C-Place. But we have considered thus far only those phonological processes that most fully respond to the perceptual effect: complete loss or assimilation of a C-Place feature. Another possibility is that languages respond to perceptual patterns not in an absolute way by *eliminating* less salient structures, but in a gradient way, by exhibiting such structures with lower frequency than the more-salient structures. Thus, an analysis of VCV structures in the lexicon of a given language might reveal, consistent with our findings, that many fewer words exhibit the [b/d/g] place contrast in the context of flanking front vowels than in other contexts. Similarly, it is possible that the inhibiting effect of a preceding front vowel on [g] identification is reflected in a lower incidence of [igV] and [egV] sequences compared to [ugV] or [ogV]. It is also possible that the perceptual patterns found in our study are reflected in patterns of sporadic language change, with less-salient structures more frequently undergoing sound changes that increase their overall perceptual salience. We leave these matters for future exploration, noting here only that the effort to relate patterns of lexical frequency or sound change to perception requires in the first place a thorough understanding of the perceptual landscape and the contexts that affect perceptual salience for a given sound feature.

In conclusion, we find that the precise nature of the mapping from perceptual constraint to phonological constraint is not yet clear, but the findings from our study support the view that the mapping is not direct. We observe some robust perceptual patterns that lack counterparts in phonological systems, and others that have phonological counterparts defined over contexts that are more general than those defined by the perceptual patterns alone. These findings suggest to us the use of caution and careful consideration in appealing to perceptual "explanations" of phonological phenomena, and the need for more research on the perceptual salience of speech sounds as a function of phonological context.

ACKNOWLEDGMENTS

This research was supported by NSF grant SBR 98-73450. The authors are grateful for the assistance of Joo-Kyeong Lee in running subjects for the experiment reported here, and for helpful advice from Gary Dell. Errors or omissions in this work are the full responsibility of the authors.

NOTES

1. The Egyptian Arabic speaker was chosen over an American English speaker in order to get clear, monophthongal vowel qualities. Had the stimuli included the diphthongal vowels (of the sort produced by speakers of American English) in positions adjacent to the target consonant, we would not be able to make comparisons of individual vowels in pre-consonantal vs. post-consonantal position.
2. One type of VCV vowel context with two full vowels that is found in English includes sequences where the second vowel is a word-final long /i/, as in *Edie, baby, Bobby, ruby,* and *Toby.* Though listeners had greater experience with this context compared

to others, we do not observe a consistent effect in either direction for contexts with a following front vowel.

3. We exclude here processes which are conditioned by position in prosodic structure, an effect of hierarchical rather than linear position in the phonological representation.

REFERENCES

Anderson, S. (1981). Why phonology isn't natural. *Linguistic Inquiry* 12, 493–539.

Archangeli, D., & Langendoen, D. T. (1997). *Optimality theory*. Cambridge: Blackwell.

Archangeli, D., & Pulleyblank, D. (1994). *Grounded phonology*. Cambridge: MIT Press.

Blumstein, S., & Stevens, K. (1979). Acoustic invariance in speech production: Evidence from measurements of the spectral characteristics of stop consonants. *Journal of the Acoustical Society of America, 66*, 1001–1017.

Blumstein, S., & Stevens, K. (1980). Perceptual invariance and onset spectra for stop consonants in different vowel environments. *Journal of the Acoustical Society of America, 67*, 648–662.

Clements, G. N. (1991). Place of articulation in consonants and vowels: A unified theory. *Working Papers of the Cornell Phonetics Laboratory*, no. 5, pp. 77–123.

Clements, G. N., & Hume, E. (1995). The internal organization of speech sounds. In J. Goldsmith (Ed.), *The handbook of phonological theory* (pp. 245–306). Cambridge: Blackwell.

Cole, J., Hualde, J., & Iskarous, K. (1999). Segmental and prosodic effects on /g/ lenition in Spanish. In O. Fujimura, B. Joseph, & B. Palek (Eds.), *Proceedings of linguistics and phonetics 1998* (pp. 575–589). Prague: Charles University Press.

Delattre, P., Liberman, A., & Cooper, F. (1955). Acoustic loci and transitional cues for consonants. *Journal of the Acoustical Society of America, 27*, 769–773.

Grier, J. B. (1972). Nonparametric indexes for sensitivity and bias: Computing formulas. *Psychological Bulletins, 75*, 424–429.

Hayes, B. (1996). *Phonetically driven phonology: The role of optimality theory and inductive grounding*. Unpublished manuscript, University of California at Los Angeles.

Hume, E., Johnson, K., Seo, M., Tserdanelis, G., & Winters, S. (1999). A cross-linguistic study of stop place perception. *Proceedings of the XIVth International Congress of Phonetic Sciences, 9*, 2069–2072.

Hura, S., Lindblom, B., & Diehl, R. (1992). On the role of perception in shaping phonological assimilation rules. *Language and Speech, 35*, 59–72.

Janson, T. (1986). Cross-linguistic trends in the frequency of CV sequences. *Phonology Yearbook, 3*, 179–195.

Kawasaki-Fukumori, H. (1992). An acoustical basis for universal phonotactic constraints. *Language and Speech, 35*, 73–86.

Kenstowicz, M. (1981). Functional explanations in generative phonology. In D. L. Goyvaerts (Ed.), *Phonology in the 1980s* (pp. 431–444). Ghent: Scientific Publishers.

Kirchner, R. (1998). *Geminate inalterability and lenition.* Unpublished manuscript, University of California at Los Angeles.

Lee, J.-K. (1999). *A phonetic examination of C-to-V place assimilation.* Unpublished doctoral dissertation, University of Illinois, Urbana.

Lindblom, B. (1983). Economy of speech gestures. In P. F. MacNeilage (Ed.), *The production of speech* (pp. 217–245). Heidelberg: Springer.

Lindblom, B. (1990). Explaining phonetic variation: A sketch of the H&H theory. In W. Hardcastle & A. Marchal (Eds.), *Speech production and speech modeling* (pp. 403–439). Dordrecht: Kluwer.

Ohala, J. (1983). The origin of sound patterns in vocal tract constraints. In P. F. MacNeilage (Ed.), *The production of speech* (pp. 189–216). New York: Springer.

Ohala, J. (1990). The phonetics and phonology of aspects of assimilation. In J. Kingston & M. Beckman (Eds.), *Papers in laboratory phonology*, Vol. 1: *Between the grammar and the physics of speech* (pp. 258–275). Cambridge: Cambridge University Press.

Prince, A., & Smolensky, P. (1993). *Optimality theory: Constraint interaction in generative grammar.* Unpublished manuscript, Rutgers University, New Brunswick, NJ, and the University of Colorado, Boulder.

Steriade, D. (1995). *Positional neutralization.* Unpublished manuscript, University of California at Los Angeles.

Stevens, K., & Blumstein, S. (1978). Invariant cues for place of articulation in stop consonants. *Journal of the Acoustical Society of America, 64,* 1358–1368.

Westbury, J., & Keating, P. (1986). On the naturalness of stop consonant voicing. *Journal of Linguistics, 22,* 145–166.

APPENDIX: CONFUSION MATRICES

Front-Front Noise 0		Response		
		b	d	g
Stimulus	b	58	50	0
	d	36	66	5
	g	7	18	83

Front-Back Noise 0		Response		
		b	d	g
Stimulus	b	105	3	0
	d	23	78	7
	g	11	7	88

Back-Front Noise 0		Response		
		b	d	g
Stimulus	b	81	25	0
	d	0	106	0
	g	8	3	95

Back-Back Noise 0		Response		
		b	d	g
Stimulus	b	92	8	6
	d	11	93	3
	g	6	3	97

Front-Front Noise 4		Response		
		b	d	g
Stimulus	b	34	70	2
	d	18	72	18
	g	7	32	69

Front-Back Noise 4		Response		
		b	d	g
Stimulus	b	97	9	2
	d	19	71	17
	g	15	29	64

Back-Front Noise 4		Response		
		b	d	g
Stimulus	b	37	65	6
	d	6	92	10
	g	6	11	91

Back-Back Noise 4		Response		
		b	d	g
Stimulus	b	60	29	19
	d	9	89	9
	g	10	8	90

CHAPTER

Adaptive Design of Sound Systems

Some Auditory Considerations

Randy L. Diehl, Michelle R. Molis,
and Wendy A. Castleman

Department of Psychology
University of Texas
Austin, Texas 78712

I. Introduction
II. Auditory Enhancement Hypothesis
III. Preference for Realizing Phonological Contrasts
   as Qualitative Distinctions
IV. Simplicity of Phonological Category Boundaries
V. Conclusions
   Acknowledgments
   Notes
   References

The Role of Speech Perception in Phonology

I. INTRODUCTION

The theme of this paper is neatly captured by a famous remark of Roman Jakobson's: "we speak to be heard in order to be understood" (Jakobson *et al.*, 1963, p. 13). Following Lindblom (1986, 1990), a qualification might be added: in striving to be heard (so that we may be understood), we tend to expend only as much articulatory effort as necessary. Evidently, the aim of talkers is not to make phonological contrasts maximally distinctive but rather to make them *sufficiently* distinctive given the conditions that apply in any particular communication situation (e.g., the amount of knowledge shared between the talker and the listener, the auditory capabilities of the listener, the level and spectral characteristics of environmental noise, and the information content of the message).

We suggest that most aspects of phonological systems that are universal or widely attested derive from the requirement of sufficient distinctiveness and the principle of least effort (broadly construed to include ease of learning to produce a phonological contrast as well as ease of executing it once it is learned). However, we will not try to defend this claim here. Rather, we will attempt to illustrate how the need for auditory distinctiveness shapes the structure of sound systems, focusing on three empirical generalizations:

1. Language communities tend to implement phonological contrasts using an implicit strategy of "auditory enhancement."

2. Where possible, language communities tend to implement phonological contrasts as qualitative (not merely quantitative) distinctions.

3. Phonological category boundaries — at least in the case of vowels — may be expressible in auditorily quite simple terms.

II. AUDITORY ENHANCEMENT HYPOTHESIS

A striking fact about phonological segment inventories is that they tend to under-exploit the range of sounds producible by human vocal tracts (Lindblom, 1986; Diehl & Lindblom, 2000). Vowels and consonants are individually produced as sets of coordinated vocal-tract movements or gestures. A vowel, for example, usually consists of movements of the tongue root, dorsum and tip, pharyngeal walls, jaw, lips, velum, and vertical position of the larynx. The selection of component gestures that make up segments is anything but random; rather, the gestures tend to covary in systematic ways.

Many linguists and speech scientists have tended to appeal exclusively to physical or physiological constraints on production in order to explain common patterns of gestural covariation (for reviews, see Diehl & Kluender, 1989; Diehl, 1991; Kingston & Diehl, 1994). Although the role of such constraints is undeniable, it appears that they underdetermine the patterns of gestural covariation observed in languages. Along with other colleagues, we have proposed that talkers can in principle exercise a rather high degree of independent control over most of the component structures used in speech production. That is, within the limits imposed by physics and physiology, talkers have sufficient articulatory degrees of freedom to produce many segments that are not in fact attested very often in languages. Why, then, are only a subset of possible segments regularly used? We think that an important part of the answer is given by what we refer to as the Auditory Enhancement Hypothesis (Diehl & Kluender, 1989; Kingston & Diehl, 1994). This hypothesis states that the phonetic properties of vowels and consonants covary as they do largely because language communities tend to select properties that have mutually reinforcing auditory effects.

The strategy of auditory enhancement is well illustrated with respect to the vowel /u/, which occurs in about 84% of the world's languages. The acoustic property that distinguishes /u/ from most other vowels is a low second formant frequency (F_2). (The vowel /u/ also has a low first formant frequency, F_1, but it shares this property with other high vowels such as /i/.) What settings of the vocal tract contribute to the distinctively low F_2 of /u/? A general acoustic framework for answering this and similar questions is provided by the classic work of Chiba & Kajiyama (1941/1958) and Fant (1960). Given a tube-like configuration such as the vocal tract, there are in principle three independent ways to lower (raise) a tube resonant frequency:

1. Lengthen (shorten) the tube.

2. Constrict (dilate) the tube at any maximum in the standing volume-velocity wave corresponding to that resonance.

3. Dilate (constrict) the tube at any minimum in the standing volume-velocity wave corresponding to that resonance.

Now consider how these theoretical options are exploited to produce a distinctively low F_2 in the case of /u/. Vocal-tract lengthening may be achieved either by protruding the lips or by lowering the larynx. It is well known that, crosslinguistically, lip protrusion is a very common correlate of this vowel. In addition, relative to most other vowels, /u/ is associated with larynx lowering (Fant, 1960; MacNeilage, 1969; see also Riordan, 1977). Next, consider the options of constricting the vocal tract at volume-velocity maxima and dilating it at volume-velocity minima. For the second vocal-tract resonance (corresponding to F_2), there are just two maxima and two minima in the standing volume-velocity waveform. The maxima occur at the lips and in the region of the velum. In the case of /u/, it turns out that just these regions have major constrictions (Fant, 1960). As for the volume-velocity minima, they occur in the prepalatal region and in the lower pharyngeal area, and vocal tract dilation occurs for /u/ in just these regions (Fant, 1960). Thus, every theoretical possibility for lowering F_2 appears to be exploited by talkers in canonical productions of /u/. This is a good example of what is meant by the claim that talkers follow an implicit strategy of auditory enhancement of phonological contrasts. Analogous enhancement accounts can be given for the other point vowels /i/ and /a/ as well for the vowel /ɝ/ (Ohala, 1985), which has a distinctively low third formant frequency (F_3).

III. PREFERENCE FOR REALIZING PHONOLOGICAL CONTRASTS AS QUALITATIVE DISTINCTIONS

The second empirical generalization about the design of phonological sound systems is that, where possible, language communities tend to implement phonological contrasts as qualitative — not merely quantitative — distinctions.

This generalization is at the heart of the Quantal Theory of Speech (Stevens, 1972, 1989), although the case to be considered here is not closely tied to that theory. The case involves a tendency for languages to exploit inverse covariation of acoustic segment durations. Maddieson (1985) has documented that almost all languages with consonant length distinctions exhibit differences in preceding vowel duration, such that long consonants are preceded by short vowels and short consonants by long vowels. Another well-attested example of such inverse durational patterning occurs with medial and final [voice] distinctions. Specifically, [+voice] consonants, which tend to be shorter than their [–voice] counterparts, are usually preceded by longer vowels, such that vowel duration is an effective perceptual cue to voice status (Raphael, 1972; Kluender et al., 1988). Given the inverse patterning of vowel and consonant durations in the [voice] distinction, Kohler (1979) and Port & Dalby (1982) suggested incorporating both durations into a single measure such as the consonant/vowel duration ratio.

Some might attribute these instances of inverse durational patterning to a general tendency to maintain a uniform syllable or utterance length. However, it is not at all obvious why such a tendency would be favored on motoric grounds. Moreover, in many cases the inverse durational patterning does not actually result in uniform overall durations, and the deviations from uniformity appear to be quite systematic. For example, in Norwegian, syllables consisting of a short vowel followed by a long (or geminate) consonant tend to be reliably shorter than those consisting of a long vowel followed by a short consonant (Fintoft, 1961).

We propose that the use of inverse acoustic segment durations to signal phonological distinctions may have a perceptual motivation. Figure 6.1 shows three hypothetical ways in which phonological distinctions based on duration differences might be implemented. One way would be for a single acoustic interval to vary in duration. Another would be for two adjacent acoustic intervals to covary positively, that is, Short–Short versus Long–Long. A third way, illustrated by the facts under discussion, is for two adjacent acoustic intervals to covary inversely, that is, Short–Long versus Long–Short. What the first two approaches have in common is that they reflect only a quantitative difference or a difference in scale. The third approach instead reflects a qualitative difference in pattern. There is evidence, across perceptual modalities, that such differences in pattern are easier to discriminate and identify than simple differences in scale (Weintraub, 1971; Macmillan & Ornstein, 1993).

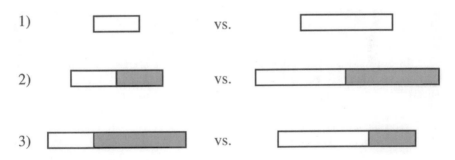

Figure 6.1.   Three ways (in principle) to implement phonological distinctions based on duration differences.

With these considerations in mind, we draw your attention to the distinction between [+continuant] and [–continuant] consonants, particularly the distinction between /tʃ/ and /ʃ/. Figure 6.2 shows spectrograms of the utterances "Say shop" and "Say chop." Two visually salient differences between these cases are that the affricate /tʃ/ contains a significant interval of silence that is lacking in the fricative, and the frication duration is longer for the fricative. Although these correlates have often been noted, most discussions of the [+continuant]/[–continuant] distinction have focused on differences in the initial amplitude envelope or rise time of the frication (Gerstman, 1957; Cutting & Rosner, 1974; Howell & Rosen, 1983; Stevens & Keyser, 1989; Weigelt *et al.*, 1990).

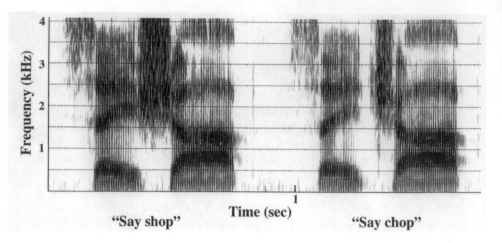

Figure 6.2. Spectrograms of "Say shop" (left) and "Say chop" (right) (Diehl & Castleman, 1996). Notice that "shop" begins with a longer interval of frication and is not preceded by a significant interval of silence.

In our laboratory, Castleman (1997, see also Diehl & Castleman, 1996) recorded six adult talkers (four male, two female) of American English saying five pairs of words ("sheep" versus "cheap," "shop" versus "chop," "ship" versus "chip," "share" versus "chair," and "shoe" versus "chew") differing only in the initial consonant — /tʃ/ vs. /ʃ/. The words were embedded in the carrier sentence "Say _____ once more." Emphatic stress was placed either on the target word or on the following word "once." Each sentence was repeated three times for a total of 60 sentences per speaker (2 target phonemes × 5 vowel contexts × 2 stress conditions × 3 repetitions).

Several acoustic measurements were made on the fricatives and affricates including silence interval (if any), frication duration, and amplitude rise time of the frication noise. (The latter measure was defined as the interval of increase in rms amplitude at the onset of the fricative until there was a noticeable flattening in slope.)

A multivariate analysis of variance showed that each of these measures differed significantly between affricates and fricatives. As expected, silence intervals were longer for affricates than fricatives [$F(1,337) = 1804.86$, $p < 0.001$], while frication durations and rise times were shorter [$F(1,337) = 281.16, p < 0.001$; $F(1,337) = 50.79$, $p < 0.001$, respectively] for affricates than fricatives.

Figures 6.3, 6.4, and 6.5 present frequency histograms of several acoustic measures, pooled across emphatically stressed and unstressed conditions. Figure 6.3 displays histograms of the amplitude rise time measurements for both affricates and fricatives. Notice that the two categories are very poorly distinguished on the basis of this measure. Figure 6.4 shows a frequency histogram for the frication duration measurements. Clearly, the categories are better separated by this measure than by rise time, but there remains a good deal of overlap. In Figure

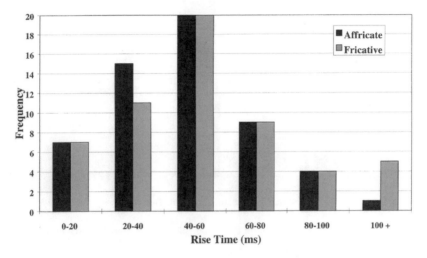

Figure 6.3. Frequency histograms of amplitude rise time measurements for affricates and fricatives (Diehl & Castleman, 1996).

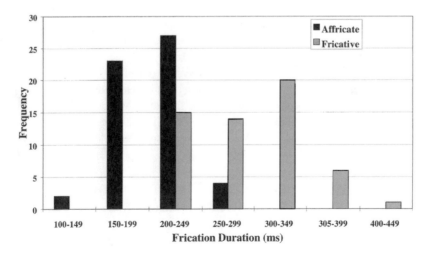

Figure 6.4. Frequency histograms of frication duration measurements for affricates and fricatives (Diehl & Castleman, 1996).

6.5, the histogram is a plot of the ratio of silence interval to frication duration (S/F ratio). There is a clear separation between the affricate category, with its long silence interval followed by a short frication, and the fricative category, with its short (or zero) silent interval followed by a long frication.

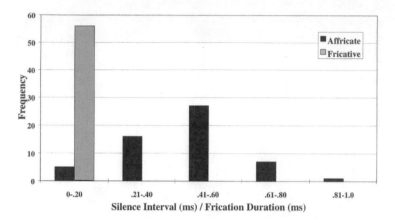

Figure 6.5. Frequency histograms of the ratio of silence interval to frication duration for affricates and fricatives (Diehl & Castleman, 1996).

Discriminant function analyses confirmed what is revealed in the histograms. Rise time alone successfully classified only 56.9% of the tokens (with chance equal to 50%).[1] Frication duration alone performed much better, correctly classifying 82.9% of the tokens. However, the best discriminator was S/F ratio, which classified 98.6% of the tokens correctly.

This example illustrates the use of inverse durational patterning (in this instance, between silence interval and frication duration) to enhance the perceptual robustness of phonological contrasts. Again, the key point is that qualitative or pattern differences appear to be an adaptive design feature of phonological systems.

IV. SIMPLICITY OF PHONOLOGICAL
CATEGORY BOUNDARIES

The third and final empirical generalization is that phonological category boundaries — at least in the case of vowels — may be expressible in auditorily quite simple terms.

Vowel perception studies from several languages have documented an interesting fact about the nature of category boundaries among vowel categories: they tend to be fairly linear, especially if represented in an auditorily motivated frequency space with dimensions of Mel, Bark, or log units. For example, Mushnikov & Chistovich (1971, reported in Karnickaya et al., 1975) had three listeners identify synthetic tokens of four Russian vowels. The boundaries between /i/ and /e/ and between /o/ and /a/ were linear and normal to the F_1 axis; the boundary between /e/ and /o/ was linear and normal to the F_2 axis, and the boundary between /e/ and /a/ was a linear diagonal in the $F_1 \times F_2$ space, corresponding to a constant difference between log F_2 and log F_1. Hose et al. (1983, reported in Rosner & Pickering, 1994) obtained similar identification results for eight synthetic German vowels. All but one of the category boundaries were linear and normal to either the F_1 or F_2 axes. (The exception was the /a/–/æ/ boundary, which was a linear diagonal corresponding to the difference between F_2 and F_1.) Finally, in an identification study of nine synthetic Swedish vowels, Carlson et al. (1970) found that all category boundaries were linear with respect to a Mel-scaled $F_1 \times F_2$ space and were either normal to the F_1 axis or diagonal within the $F_1 \times F_2$ space corresponding to the difference between, or else the average of, F_1 and F_2.

In each of these studies, the vowel stimuli were restricted to two formants, and it is reasonable to ask whether boundary linearity is an artifact of the simple stimulus structure. On the basis of recent work conducted in our laboratory, it appears that linearity may hold also for multiformant stimuli.

Molis (1999) synthesized a set of five-formant vowel stimuli, represented by the diamonds in Figure 6.6. F_2 varied from 1081 (9.0 Bark) to 2390 Hz (14.2 Bark) in 0.4-Bark steps, while F_3 varied from 1268 (10.0 Bark) to 2783 Hz (15.2 Bark), also in 0.4-Bark steps. F_1, F_4, and F_5 were held constant at 455 (4.5 Bark), 3250 (16.2 Bark), and 3700 Hz (17.0 Bark), respectively. The stimuli were 225 ms in length. Fundamental frequency was held constant at 132 Hz for the initial 150 ms and thereafter fell linearly to 127 Hz.

This larger stimulus set was sampled in order to form three partially overlapping stimulus subgroups, one for each of the three possible binary identification tasks (see Figure 6.6). The 24 stimuli used for the /ʊ/ versus /ɪ/ subgroup consisted of four separate series differing in F_3 in steps of 0.4 Bark, with each 6-item series varying in F_2 in steps of 0.8 Bark. Each of these stimuli was presented in 20 randomized blocks (480 trials/subject) to 17 listeners. The 27 stimuli used for the /ɝ/ versus /ɪ/ subgroup formed three series differing in the value of $F_3 - F_2$. Within each nine-item series, the stimuli varied according to the numerical average of F_2 and F_3. In this case, the series lay along positive diagonals of the stimulus space. The stimuli in this subgroup were presented in 20 randomized blocks (540 trials/subject) to 18 listeners. The 30 stimuli used for the /ʊ/ versus /ɝ/ subgroup comprised six series differing in F_2 and varying in F_3 within each 5-item series.

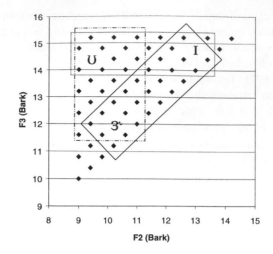

Figure 6.6. Boxes enclose three partially overlapping stimulus subgroups used in three binary identification experiments (Molis, 1999). Phonetic symbols indicate the stimuli that represent the closest matches to average second- and third-formant frequencies for these vowels produced by male speakers (Hillenbrand *et al.*, 1995).

Eighteen randomized blocks of this stimulus subgroup (540 trials/subject) were presented to 21 listeners.

Three separate groups of Introductory Psychology students from the University of Texas at Austin served as listeners in exchange for partial course credit. All reported normal hearing and were native speakers of American English. In each condition, listeners responded by pressing one of two response buttons labeled with key words corresponding to the relevant vowel sounds ("hood," "hid," or "heard").

Logistic regression functions were used to estimate category boundaries. An attempt was made to share as many of the regression parameters as possible across series within a subgroup; parameter values were allowed to vary across series only if it significantly improved the overall fit of the regression.

Labeling of all four series in the /ʊ/ versus /ɪ/ condition (see Figure 6.7, top panel) could be described using a single logistic function with a common slope and identification boundary [$F(6,400) = 1.20$, $p = 0.31$]. The 50% identification boundary was located at 11.78 Bark along the F_2 axis.

While the three logistic functions in the /ɝ/ versus /ɪ/ condition (see Figure 6.7, middle panel) shared a common slope, the fit of the logistic regression was significantly improved if each series had a unique boundary value [$F(3,482) = 3.27$, $p < 0.05$]. Although identification boundaries varied, they did fall within a very narrow range: 0.1 Bark. Boundary values for the three series along the

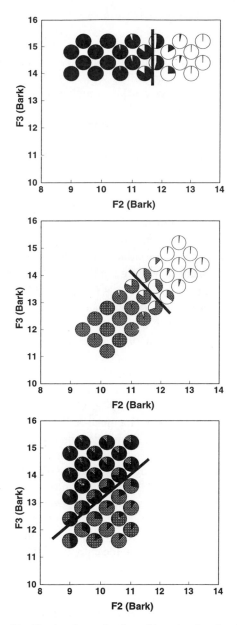

Figure 6.7. Group identification data and estimated boundary locations for each of three binary identification experiments (top panel: /ʊ/ versus /ɪ/; middle panel: /ɝ/ versus /ɪ/, bottom: /ʊ/ versus /ɝ/). Pie charts indicate the relative percentages of category response to individual stimuli (black: /ʊ/; white: /ɪ/; grey: /ɝ/).

positive diagonal and in order of increasing $F_3 - F_2$ distance were 12.52, 12.57, and 12.62 Bark.

Compared with the results of the other two conditions, there was greater variability in the /ʊ/ versus /ɝ/ condition in boundary location among subjects and between F_2 series. Data for this condition were described with a single logistic function, which minimized the error in the simultaneous fit of the six F_2 series through rotation of stimulus axes. The data were fit with an axis rotation of 43.2°, which roughly translates into a consistent boundary with a value of $F_3 - F_2 = 3.0$ Bark.

Boundary linearity is significant for at least two reasons. First, it gives us important clues about how vowel sounds are represented auditorily. The linear functions reported by Molis and by the earlier investigators appear to be of three types: (1) horizontal or vertical lines in a two-dimensional formant space reflecting the exclusive role of one formant value or the other in determining categorization (e.g., in Figure 6.7, top panel, the /ɪ/–/ʊ/ boundary corresponds to the function $F_2 = 11.78$ Bark);[2] (2) a negative diagonal line reflecting a dependence on the *average* of two formant values (e.g., in Figure 6.7, middle panel, the /ɪ/–/ɝ/ boundary corresponds to the function $[F_2 + F_3]/2 = 12.57 \pm 0.05$ Bark), or (3) a positive diagonal line reflecting a dependence on the *difference* between two formant values (e.g., in Figure 6.7, bottom, the /ʊ/–/ɝ/ boundary corresponds to the function $F_3 - F_2 = 3.0$ Bark). Both of the diagonal cases suggest the possibility of averaging of closely spaced formant peaks in the auditory representation of vowel categories. In particular, the location of the /ʊ/–/ɝ/ boundary hints at a possible role for the 3-Bark auditory integrator posited by Chistovich and her colleagues (Chistovich & Lublinskaya, 1979; Chistovich et al., 1979; see also Syrdal, 1985; Syrdal & Gopal, 1986; Hoemeke & Diehl, 1994).

A second reason why boundary linearity is significant is that it could greatly simplify our theories of vowel categorization. Currently, the most influential models of categorization within cognitive psychology are prototype models (Reed, 1972; Cohen & Massaro, 1992), which assume that diverse stimulus tokens are mapped onto a single abstract mental representation of the category, and exemplar models (Medin & Schaffer, 1978; Nosofsky, 1986; Johnson, 1997), which assume that the mental representation of the category includes a large sample of instances or exemplars of the category rather than a single abstract representation. Johnson & Mullennix (1997) have correctly noted that prototype models require a simple form of mental representation but a complex mapping between stimulus tokens and the category prototype, whereas for exemplar models the requirements are exactly reversed (i.e., the mental representation is complex but the mapping is simple). However, if a category can be defined by the boundaries that separate it from other categories and if those boundaries are simple in form, then both the mental representation and the stimulus mapping can be described in theoretically simple terms (Ashby & Maddox, 1998; Maddox & Ashby, 1998).

Experiments are now being planned in our laboratory to investigate whether boundary linearity is preserved under talker- or context-dependent shifts in boundary location and, if so, whether the boundary slope is also preserved. Linearity- and slope-invariance under boundary shift would imply that listeners are using the same acoustic or auditory variables (e.g., Bark-scaled F_2, $F_3 - F_2$, or $[F_2 + F_3]/2$) to assign stimulus tokens to categories but are simply changing the criterion value of those variables. Evidence that such behavior is the norm would impose an important constraint on theories of vowel categorization.

V. CONCLUSIONS

In summary, phonological structure may often be explained on auditory-perceptual grounds. Examples include tendencies of language communities: to structure phonological contrasts by using an implicit strategy of auditory enhancement, to implement phonological contrasts as qualitative or pattern distinctions, and to use auditorily simple (e.g., linear) phonological category boundaries.

Several important theories of speech perception, including the Motor Theory (Liberman et al., 1967; Liberman & Mattingly, 1985) and the Direct Realist Theory (Fowler, 1986, 1989), assert that listeners perceive articulatory gestures (Direct Realism) or the neural commands underlying articulatory gestures (Motor Theory). The generalizations outlined in this chapter point, we think, to an alternative view of speech perception. According to this view, the primary objects of speech perception consist of auditory, rather than articulatory, events.

ACKNOWLEDGMENTS

This work was supported by Research Grant No. 5 R01 DC00427-10, 11 from the National Institute on Deafness and Other Communication Disorders, National Institutes of Health.

NOTES

1. These results differ markedly from those of Weigelt et al. (1990), who found that a rate of rise measure successfully distinguished fricatives from plosives (including affricates) at a rate of 96.8%. One difference between the two studies is that the target phonemes in the Weigelt et al. study appeared in isolated words, all of which were presumably stressed. Half of the tokens in Castleman's study were unstressed, and in the unstressed condition, rise times were actually greater for affricates than for

fricatives (although the opposite was true in the stressed condition). In any case, we do not wish to suggest here that rise time is never a perceptually useful correlate of the affricate/fricative distinction.

2. This result is incompatible with a claim of Syrdal (1985, Syrdal & Gopal, 1986) that the perceptual boundary between [+back] and [-back] vowels in American English occurs at an $F_3 - F_2$ difference of 3 Bark. However, a fairer test of the Syrdal's hypothesis would require synthetic vowels that imply a variety of different talkers varying in age and sex.

REFERENCES

Ashby, F. G., & Maddox, W. T. (1998). Stimulus categorization. In M. H. Birnbaum (Ed.), *Measurement, judgment, and decision making* (pp. 251–301). San Diego: Academic Press.

Carlson, R., Granström, B., & Fant, G. (1970). Some studies concerning perception of isolated vowels. *Speech Transmission Laboratory: Quarterly Progress and Status Report, 2–3*, 19–35.

Castleman, W. A. (1997). Integrated perceptual properties of the [±continuant] distinction in fricatives and affricates. Unpublished doctoral dissertation, University of Texas at Austin.

Chiba, T., & Kajiyama, M. (1941). *The vowel: Its nature and structure.* Tokyo: Tokyo-Kaiseikan. (Reprinted by the Phonetic Society of Japan, 1958.)

Chistovich, L. A., & Lublinskaya, V. V. (1979). The "center of gravity" effect in vowel spectra and critical distance between the formants: Psychoacoustical study of the perception of vowel-like stimuli. *Hearing Research, 1*, 185–195.

Chistovich, L. A., Sheikin, R. L., & Lublinskaja, V. V. (1979). "Centres of gravity" and spectral peaks as the determinants of vowel quality. In B. Lindblom & S. Öhman (Eds.), *Frontiers of speech communication research* (pp. 143–157). London: Academic Press.

Cohen, M. M., & Massaro, D. W. (1992). On the similarity of categorization models. In F. G. Ashby (Ed.), *Multidimensional models of perception and cognition* (pp. 395–447). Hillsdale, NJ: Lawrence Erlbaum.

Cutting, J. E., & Rosner, B. S. (1974). Categories and boundaries in speech and music. *Perception & Psychophysics, 16*, 564–570.

Diehl, R. L. (1991). The role of phonetics within the study of language. *Phonetica, 48*, 120–134.

Diehl, R. L., & Castleman, W. A. (1996). Integrated perceptual properties: The affricate/fricative distinction. In A. P. Simpson & M. Pätzold (Eds.), *Sound patterns of connected speech: Proceedings of the symposium held at Kiel University on 14–15 June 1996* (pp. 191–200). Arbeitsberichte #31. Kiel: Institut für Phonetik und digitale Sprachverarbeitung, Universität Kiel.

Diehl, R. L., & Kluender, K. R. (1989). On the objects of speech perception. *Ecological Psychology*, *1*, 121–144.

Diehl, R. L., & Lindblom, B. (2000). Explaining the structure of feature and phoneme inventories. In S. Greenberg, W. A. Ainsworth, A. Popper, & R. Fay (Eds.), *Speech processing in the auditory system*. New York: Springer-Verlag. In press.

Fant, G. (1960). *Acoustic theory of speech production*. The Hague: Mouton.

Fintoft, K. (1961). The duration of some Norwegian speech sounds. *Phonetica*, *7*, 19–39.

Fowler, C. A. (1986). An event approach to the study of speech perception from a direct-realist perspective. *Journal of Phonetics*, *14*, 3–28.

Fowler, C. A. (1989). Real objects of speech perception: A commentary on Diehl and Kluender. *Ecological Psychology*, *1*, 145–160.

Gerstman, L. J. (1957). Perceptual dimensions for the friction portion of certain speech sounds. Unpublished doctoral dissertation, New York University.

Hillenbrand, J. M., Getty, L. A., Clark, M. J., & Wheeler, K. (1995). Acoustic characteristics of American English vowels. *Journal of the Acoustical Society of America*, *97*, 3099–3111.

Hoemeke, K. A., & Diehl, R. L. (1994). Perception of vowel height: The role of $F_1 - F_0$ distance. *Journal of the Acoustical Society of America*, *96*, 661–674.

Hose, B., Langner, G., & Scheich, H. (1983). Linear phoneme boundaries for German synthetic two-formant vowels. *Hearing Research*, *9*, 13–25.

Howell, P., & Rosen, R. (1983). Production and perception of rise time in the voiceless affricate/fricative distinction. *Journal of the Acoustical Society of America*, *73*, 976–984.

Jakobson, R., Fant, G., & Halle, M. (1963). *Preliminaries to speech analysis*. Cambridge: MIT Press.

Johnson, K. (1997). Speech perception without speaker normalization: An exemplar model. In K. Johnson & J. W. Mullennix (Eds.), *Talker variability in speech processing* (pp. 145–165). San Diego: Academic Press.

Johnson, K., & Mullennix, J. W. (1997). Complex representations used in speech processing. In K. Johnson & J. W. Mullennix (Eds.), *Talker variability in speech processing* (pp. 1–8). San Diego: Academic Press.

Karnickaya, E. G., Mushnikov, V. N., Slepokurova, N. A., & Zhukov, S. J. (1975). Auditory processing of steady-state vowels. In G. Fant & M. A. A. Tatham (Eds.), *Auditory analysis and perception of speech* (pp. 37–53). New York: Academic Press.

Kingston, J., & Diehl, R. L. (1994). Phonetic knowledge. *Language*, *70*, 419–454.

Kluender, K. R., Diehl, R. L., & Wright, B. A. (1988). Vowel-length differences before voiced and voiceless consonants: An auditory explanation. *Journal of Phonetics*, *16*, 153–169.

Kohler, K. J. (1979). Dimensions in the perception of fortis and lenis plosives. *Phonetica*, *36*, 332–343.

Liberman, A. M., & Mattingly, I. (1985). The motor theory of speech perception revised. *Cognition*, *21*, 1–36.

Liberman, A. M., Cooper, F. S., Shankweiler, D. P., & Studdert-Kennedy, M. (1967). Perception of the speech code. *Psychological Review, 74*, 431–461.

Lindblom, B. (1986). Phonetic universals in vowel systems. In J. J. Ohala & J. J. Jaeger (Eds.), *Experimental phonology* (pp. 13–44). Orlando: Academic Press.

Lindblom, B. (1990). Explaining phonetic variation: A sketch of the H&H theory. In W. Hardcastle & A. Marchal (Eds.), *Speech production and speech modeling* (pp. 403–439). Dordrecht: Kluwer.

Macmillan, N. A., & Ornstein, A. S. (1993). *Mean-integrality of rectangles: A detection-theory approach.* Paper presented at a meeting of the Psychonomic Society, Washington, DC.

MacNeilage, P. M. (1969). *A note on the relation between tongue elevation and glottal elevation in vowels.* Monthly Internal Memorandum, University of California, Berkeley, January 1969, pp. 9–26.

Maddieson, I. (1985). Phonetic cues to syllabification. In V. A. Fromkin (Ed.), *Phonetic linguistics: Essays in honor of Peter Ladefoged* (pp. 203–221). Orlando: Academic Press.

Maddox, W. T., & Ashby, F. G. (1998). Selective attention and the formation of linear decision boundaries: Comment on McKinley and Nosofsky (1996). *Journal of Experimental Psychology: Human Perception and Performance, 24*, 301–321.

Medin, D. L., & Schaffer, M. M. (1978). Context theory of classification learning. *Psychological Review, 85*, 207–238.

Molis, M. (1999). Perception of vowel quality in the F_2/F_3 plane. *Proceedings of ICPhS'99, San Francisco*, 2 August, pp. 191–194.

Mushnikov, V. N., & Chistovich, L. A. (1971). Auditory description of vowels, I. In *Analiz rechevykh signalov chelovekom.* Leningrad.

Nosofsky, R. M. (1986). Attention, similarity, and the identification–categorization relationship. *Journal of Experimental Psychology: General, 115*, 39–57.

Ohala, J. J. (1985). Around flat. In V. A. Fromkin (Ed.), *Phonetic linguistics: Essays in honor of Peter Ladefoged* (pp. 223–241). Orlando: Academic Press.

Port, R. F., & Dalby, J. (1982). Consonant/vowel ratio as a cue for voicing in English. *Perception & Psychophysics, 32*, 141–152.

Raphael, L. F. (1972). Preceding vowel duration as a cue to the perception of the voicing characteristic of word-final consonants in English. *Journal of the Acoustical Society of America, 51*, 1296–1303.

Reed, S. K. (1972). Pattern recognition and categorization. *Cognitive Psychology, 3*, 382–407.

Riordan, C. J. (1977). Control of vocal-tract length in speech. *Journal of the Acoustical Society of America, 62*, 998–1002.

Rosner, B. S., & Pickering, J. B. (1994). *Vowel perception and production.* Oxford: Oxford University Press.

Stevens, K. N. (1972). The quantal nature of speech: Evidence from articulatory-acoustic data. In E. E. David & P. B. Denes (Eds.), *Human communication: A unified view* (pp. 51–66). New York: McGraw-Hill.

Stevens, K. N. (1989). On the quantal nature of speech. *Journal of Phonetics, 17,* 3–45.

Stevens, K. N., & Keyser, S. J. (1989). Primary features and their enhancement in consonants. *Language, 65,* 81–106.

Syrdal, A. K. (1985). Aspects of a model of the auditory representation of American English vowels. *Speech Communication, 4,* 121–135.

Syrdal, A. K., & Gopal, H. S. (1986). A perceptual model of vowel recognition based on the auditory representation of American English vowels. *Journal of the Acoustical Society of America, 79,* 1086–1100.

Weigelt, L. F., Sadoff, S. J., & Miller, J. D. (1990). Plosive/fricative distinction: The voiceless case. *Journal of the Acoustical Society of America, 87,* 2729–2737.

Weintraub, D. J. (1971). Rectangle discriminability: Perceptual relativity and the law of pragnanz. *Journal of Experimental Psychology, 88,* 1–11.

CHAPTER

The Limits of Phonetic
Determinism in Phonology

*NC Revisited

Larry M. Hyman

Department of Linguistics
University of California
Berkeley, California, 94720

I. Introduction
II. The Place of Phonetics in Phonology
  A. Phonetics ≠ Phonology
  B. Diachronic Phonology ≠ Synchronic Phonology
  C. Summary
III. Nasal+Obstruent Interactions
  A. Postnasal Voicing
  B. Postnasal Devoicing
  C. Why Postnasal Devoicing?
  D. Other Languages
  E. Other Processes
IV. Conclusions
  Acknowledgments
  Notes
  References

141

The Role of Speech Perception in Phonology

I. INTRODUCTION

Virtually since the founding of modern phonology, there have been recurrent proposals for the incorporation of phonetic insights into phonological theory. Phonological rules frequently resemble phonetic processes, which in turn have natural explanations in the physiology, acoustics, and perception of speech. As numerous studies have shown (e.g., Wang & Fillmore, 1961; Chen, 1970; Ohala, 1974), the "seeds" of such phonological rules can be traced to the intrinsic variations in speech that become phonologized into the grammars of languages.[1] That "naturalness" is prized by many phonologists is, thus, not surprising. It is, however, surprising when individual phonologists insist that all phonology must be executed in phonetic terms: phonological rules must derive from phonetic principles, and whatever is not characterizable as phonetically determined is, thus, not phonology. According to this view, language-specific generalizations that appear to have no phonetic justification must be relegated to the morphology (e.g., as morpholexical rules) or are dismissed as historical residue that has simply to be listed in individual allomorphs. Others, standing opposed to phonetic determinism, deny that phonology need be constrained by phonetic considerations at all. Such scholars typically emphasize the formal and cognitive nature of (abstract) phonology as part of grammar versus the (concrete) phonetic substance from which phonological systems derive historically.[2]

All of this discussion essentially reduces to the basic question: what is the proper relation between phonetics and phonology? While addressed over and over in the history of modern linguistics, the question has recently returned to the fore with attempts to phoneticize Prince & Smolensky's (1993) Optimality Theory (OT). Prince & Smolensky propose that the diverse properties of phonological systems result from the different rankings of universal and violable constraints. In their implementation, developed further in McCarthy & Prince (1993, 1994) and elsewhere, these constraints are phonological, for example, MAX (don't delete), DEP (don't epenthesize), IDENT(I/O) (the input and output should be identical). In many cases, specific phonetic substance is the subject of a constraint. Pater (1996, 1999), for instance, proposes a constraint *NT that penalizes consonantal sequences of [+nasal] followed by [−voice].[3] The effects of this constraint can be both distributional and processual. First, many languages have prenasalized voiced stops, but lack prenasalized voiceless stops. Second, as Pater shows, the relative high ranking of *NT accounts for the fact that the voiceless stop of a heteromorphemic N+T sequence is deleted in Malay, while the corresponding voiced stop of N+D sequences is not. Hayes (1995, 1997) further emphasizes the phonetic motivation of the frequent process by which obstruents become voiced after nasals, that is, NT → ND, whose effect is to respect Pater's constraint *NT. Both Hayes (1997, pp. 18–19) and Flemming (1995, p. 3) claim that an opposite, counter-phonetic process, ND → NT, whereby an obstruent becomes devoiced after a nasal, is unattested. Hayes accounts for this by showing that *NT is "phonetically driven," while a corresponding constraint *ND, which would rule out a sequence of nasal+voiced stop, is not. On the assumption that phonological constraints must be phonetically driven, further developed in Kirchner (1998), there can be no constraint *ND, and, hence, it is claimed, no language that has postnasal devoicing.

I have two goals in this paper. First, I would like (once more) to address the general relation between phonetics and phonology. I will argue in section II that phonetic determinism ought not to be a synchronic principle, but rather is relevant only in the diachronic domain. As Ohala (1989, 1993) has argued in a number of publications, commonly occurring sound changes have the character they do because of their direct phonetic source. The same can be said about the phonetic naturalness of resulting phonological rules: "the reason natural rules are the way they are is that they are deeply grounded in the universal phonetic properties of speech" (Hyman 1975a, p. 171). The position argued below is that, once such natural phonetic processes are "phonologized," they enter into the realm of grammar and are subject to different principles.[4]

My second goal in section III is to reconsider Pater's *NT constraint, and particularly, the implications that Hayes draws from it. Citing Bantu examples, I shall provide evidence for the constraint *ND that "counter-balances" *NT. I shall show that postnasal devoicing does in fact occur, for example, in the Sotho-Tswana subgroup. I will demonstrate that a number of languages allow NT without allowing ND. I shall suggest that the reason these languages "prefer" NT over ND is perceptual. I then consider a number of other nasal+consonant processes to determine the role that perception may play in motivating such "counter-processes" as postnasal devoicing. I end with a brief conclusion in section IV.

II. THE PLACE OF PHONETICS IN PHONOLOGY

In this section, I consider the role of phonetics in phonology. I note first that there are at least four intuitive arguments for incorporating phonetics into phonology.

First, an "economy argument" is sometimes given: phonetics and phonology utilize a common alphabet. Both use descriptive terms such as "voiceless stops" and "nasalized vowels." As this argument goes, it would be more economical, therefore, to treat the two as one, meaning that phonology should be executed in phonetic terms, that is, phonology = phonetics.[5]

Second, there is no well-defined boundary between phonetics and phonology. In many cases it is at best difficult to determine whether a "low-level" process is a post-lexical phonological process or part of the language-specific phonetics of a language.[6]

Third, phonetics is often "explanatory" of phonology. Given the goal of linguistics to be an explanatory science, it has seemed natural to incorporate "the explanation" directly into the formulation of grammar.[7]

Finally, it is at least implicit in much of this work that the phonetics can constrain phonology. Given the difficulty in developing a restrictive theory of phonology (or grammar in general), perhaps if we were to require that phonology must mimic phonetics we would be that much closer to determining what is possible within phonology.

For some or all these reasons, some phonologists propose to do phonology in increasingly phonetic terms. Flemming (1995), for instance, proposes various auditory constraints within OT that refer directly to formant structure. These, then, function directly in individual phonologies. In this way, as one gets closer to the raw material (and its auditory effect), the resultant phonologies should have a less arbitrary character, deriving in all cases from the ranking of universal phonetic constraints. As Hayes (1997, p. 14) puts it, "it is reasonable to suppose [. . .] that virtually all of segmental phonology [. . .] is driven by considerations of articulatory ease and perceptual distinctness." On the other hand, we find opposing statements: "although phonological processes are expressed in phonetic terms, they do not have underlying phonetic motivations" (Kaye, 1989, p. 53). Kaye instead sees phonology as an aid to parsing. Rather than seeing phonology as "phonetically driven," an opposing view is that it is computationally driven: "the phonology is a computational system that manipulates abstract categories and does not incorporate information about phonetic naturalness" (Buckley, 1999, p. 6). Similarly, Hale & Reiss (1998, pp. 6–7) "assume that the substance of phonological entities is never relevant to how they are treated by the computational system, except in *arbitrary, stipulative* ways" (their emphasis). According to Hale & Reiss, "Phonology is not and should not be grounded in phonetics since the facts which phonetic grounding is meant to explain can be derived without such grounding."

In order to sort out these issues, it is useful to reconsider two common dichotomies: phonetics vs. phonology and synchrony vs. diachrony.

A. Phonetics ≠ Phonology

The question at issue might be phrased as "how phonetic is phonology?" First, most scholars begin with the notion that there is a distinction. While phoneticians often have an interest in phonology (and phonologists often have an interest in phonetics), there are considerations of both subfields that more naturally interact (or intersect) than others. If phonetics deals with the production, acoustics, and perception of speech sounds, then phonology can be defined as in (1):

(1) Phonology = "the intersection of phonetics and grammar"

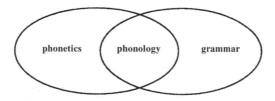

As seen, I have represented phonetics and grammar as two large elipses, the intersection of which is phonology. This meeting of speech sounds with grammar is what drives the distinction between phonetics and phonology.[8]

As an illustration of the need to view phonology as the intersection of phonetics and grammar, consider Ohala's (1990) generalization concerning the creation of geminates by place assimilation. Ohala points out that, when place assimilation occurs in a heterorganic sequence of stops, C_1C_2 tends to become C_2C_2, rather than C_1C_1, for example, Latin *septem, *octo# > Italian sette, otto (not *seppe, *okko). Ohala's explanation is that C_1 tends to be unreleased, hence less salient perceptually than C_2, which, in the examples considered, is necessarily released into the following vowel. It is thus to be expected that the non-released C_1 will assimilate to the released C_2, whose perceptual cues are more prominent, rather than the reverse. A similar explanation is offered to explain why homorganic nasal assimilation (HNA) results in changes such as /np, ŋt/ → [mp, nt] rather than *[nt, ŋk], where the stop assimilates to the place of the preceding nasal.[9]

While I agree with Ohala's generalization and explanation for it, there are, however, important counterexamples to it. The one I shall cite here comes from the realization of the progressive suffix /-te/ in Noni, a Bantoid language spoken in Cameroon (Hyman, 1981). The relevant data are presented in (2).

(2) Realization of the progressive suffix in Noni

a.	cím	'dig'	cim-tè	'be digging'
	dvum	'groan'	dvùm-tè	'be groaning'
b.	bín	'dance'	bin-è	'be dancing'
	kfun	'hit'	kfùn-è	'be hitting'
c.	cíŋ	'tremble'	ciiŋ-kè	'be trembling'
	káŋ	'fry'	kaaŋ-kè	'be frying'
d.	kéy	'cough'	key-tè	'be coughing'
	kfúy	'trim'	kfuy-tè	'be trimming'
e.	jíw	'blacken'	jii-kè	'be blackening'
	law	'pay'	làà-kè	'be paying'

f.	cii	'drag'	cìì-lè	'be dragging'
	dɛɛ	'cook'	dèè-lè	'be cooking'
g.	bi	'follow'	bì-ì	'be following'
	tó	'itch'	to-ò	'be itching'

The forms in (2a) show that /-te/ is realized without change after a root-final /m/. In (2b) it can be seen that its /t/ drops out after the homorganic root-final consonant /n/. It is the examples in (2c) that interest us here: the input sequence /ŋ+t/ is realized [ŋk]. The /t/ has assimilated to the velar place of the preceding [ŋ]. The development of the prenasalized stop is accompanied by compensatory lengthening in presumably the same way as discussed by Tucker (1962) and Clements (1986) for (lu-)Ganda. In Noni, the only coda consonants allowed are nasals and glides. The forms in (2d–g) show how the progressive suffix is realized after all of the remaining monosyllabic root structures. In (2d) it is realized as –te, while in (2e) we see that it assimilates to the velarity of the preceding [w], which drops out, again producing compensatory lengthening. Finally, the progressive suffix is realized –le after a CVV root in (2f) and as vowel lengthening after CV roots in (2g).

     Given the generality of Ohala's observation, the question is why the Noni progressive suffix works differently. I would like to suggest that Noni constitutes a principled counterexample that can be explained by reference to the view of phonology in (1). The reason why the [t] of the progressive suffix /-te/ assimilates to a preceding velar is that it is a suffix. Besides phonetic principles, phonology is subject to (possibly conflicting) grammatical ones. The relevant principle here is a paradigmatic one: languages frequently preserve base features over affixal ones. We know that affixal morphemes are frequently subject to greater reduction, for example, assimilation, than root morphemes. This has recently been expressed by McCarthy & Prince (1995) as "root faithfulness." What I would like to suggest is that, where root faithfulness is low ranked, Ohala's phonetic explanation will have maximal effect. However, where root faithfulness is ranked high, that is, higher than affix faithfulness, a Noni-like effect will instead occur.[10]

     To summarize, Ohala claims in his study that the nasal of a heterorganic N+C sequence should assimilate to the following consonant, as seen in the informal feature geometric representation in (3a).

(3) Need for assimilations/autosegmental spreading in both directions:

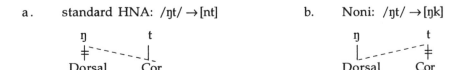

a.   standard HNA: /ŋt/ → [nt]   b.   Noni: /ŋt/ → [ŋk]

As indicated, such right-to-left place assimilation aptly captures standard homorganic nasal assimilation. Ohala goes on, however, to say that the reverse process formulated in (3b) ought not to occur. He criticizes feature geometry for its ability to express the disfavored left-to-right place assimilation process indicated in (3b) as easily as the favored right-to-left HNA in (3a). However, this is exactly what is needed: the Noni example shows that an input sequence /ŋ+t/ may undergo place assimilation in either direction. In light of such counterexamples to Ohala's generalization, we are faced with two possible responses. The first response would be to say that Noni-type counterexamples are simply rare, that is, "marked" in phonological terminology. A more explanatory response would be to say that the Noni data constitute a principled counterexample that can be accounted for by reference to the grammatical (here, paradigmatic) side of phonology. The prediction we are left with is that rules such as (3b) should not readily occur unless motivated other than by perceptual phonetics.

As the above demonstrates, the bipolar view of phonology schematized in (1) can actually have the effect of saving phonetic generalizations that otherwise would be obscured if grammar were not simultaneously taken into consideration.

B. Diachronic Phonology ≠ Synchronic Phonology

The second dichotomy I would like to briefly consider is that between diachronic and synchronic phonology. As pointed out numerous times in the history of generative phonology — and despite frequent resemblances — the synchronic analysis of phonological systems is not equivalent to going through the historical changes that produced them. Phonological systems are the way they are not only because of the phonetic conditioning of sound changes, but also because of telescoping, restructuring (e.g., by analogy), and borrowing. The result can be quite "unnatural."

(4) Labial palatalization in Ndebele (Bantu; Zimbabwe) (cf. Sibanda, 1998)

	Active		Passive	
a.	boph-a	'tie'	boc-w-a	'be tied'
	vuβ-a	'mix together'	vuc'-w-a	'be mixed together'
	dob-a	'pick up'	doj-w-a	'be picked up'
	bumb-a	'mould'	bunj-w-a	'be moulded'
	thum-a	'send'	thuɲ-w-a	'be sent'
b.	dal-a	'create'	dal-w-a	'be created'
	thuk-a	'curse'	thuk-w-a	'be cursed'

	Active		Passive	
c.	fumbath-a	'clench (hand)'	funjath-w-a	'be clenched'
	vumbulul-a	'uncover, unearth'	vunjulul-w-a	'be uncovered'
	phambukis-a	'lead aside'	phanjukis-w-a	'be led aside'
	gombolozel-a	'encircle, surround'	gonjolozel-w-a	'be encircled'
d.	βal-a	'read'	βal-w-a	'be read'
	βik-a	'announce'	βik-w-a	'be announced'
e.	aphul-a	'break, snap off'	aphul-w-a	'be broken, snapped off'
	aβel-a	'share, allot to'	aβel-w-a	'be shared, allotted'
	amuk-a	'deprive, take away'	amuk-w-a	'be deprived, taken away'

As an example, consider the palatalization of labial consonants in southern Bantu languages, illustrated here in Ndebele (cf. Sibanda, 1998). As seen in (4a), the labial consonants /ph/, /β/, /b/, /mb/, and /m/ are realized, respectively, as c [tʃ], c′ [tʃ′], j [dʒ], nj [ɲdʒ], and ɲ when followed by the passive suffix -w-, where c′ = ejective. There are at least four reasons why Ndebele labial palatalization represents a synchronic restructuring.

First, the change of labials to palatals before [w] in (4a) is synchronically unnatural, the result of telescoped sound changes, that is, *Bwa > Bɥa > By(w)a > BJ(w)a > J(w)a (Tucker, 1929; Ohala, 1978), where B and J = labial vs. palatal consonants, respectively.[11] As often remarked (Ohala, 1978; Kawasaki, 1982; Flemming, 1995), sequences of labial + [w] are frequently missing, or, as we see here, modified so as to avoid such sequences. However, this observation cannot in itself predict why labials should become palatalized (with the [w] remaining), nor why, /B/ should alternate with ejective [tʃ′].[12]

Second, as seen in (4b), only labials are affected by palatalization vs. the more usual palatalization of coronals and/or velars: "Palatalization is less easily introduced on labials than on dentals and velars; and if introduced, it is more easily lost" (Hock, 1991, p. 133). An alternation between [m] and [ɲ] has to be viewed as less "natural" than one between either [n] and [ɲ] or between [ŋ] and [ɲ].

Third, as seen in (4c), the labial/palatal alternations have been analogized to apply at-a-distance. In the examples cited, morpheme-internal /mb/ is realized [ɲdʒ] because of the passive suffix -w- with which it is not contiguous. Thus, even if we could rationalize the palatalization of labials in (4a) as a response to Flemming's (1995) auditory constraint *Bw, we would be hard put to explain how the putative phonetic constraint *Bw can have such a long-distance effect.

Finally, there is again a morphological consideration. As seen in (4d), root-initial labials are exempt from at-a-distance palatalization, an apparent case of positional faithfulness (Beckman, 1997). The vowel-initial roots in (4e) in fact show that a following labial consonant also escapes palatalization (cf. Downing, 2000). The generalization thus appears to be that the first consonant of a root, if labial, is not palatalizable.[13]

It thus seems relatively clear that the present state of Ndebele labial palatalization has involved both the telescoping of several sound changes as well as the analogizing of palatalization to noncontiguous environments. The question, then, is whether it should be the concern of synchronic phonology to make the situation look more "natural," particularly from a phonetic deterministic point of view. I suggest that it isn't. In order to see why not, let us briefly contrast the goals of diachronic phonology with those of synchronic phonology.

The goals of diachronic phonology are threefold.

First, diachronic phonology seeks to determine where phonology comes from. The answer, largely, has been that it derives via phonologization, the process by which "natural," quasi-universal variations in the speech signal come to be part of the phonological system of a language (Hyman, 1977).

Second, diachronic phonology seeks to determine how phonology changes — while still remaining phonology. This means studying the processes of telescoping, rule inversion, and other forms of restructuring. As seen in the Ndebele case, this includes analogy.

Finally, the third goal of diachronic phonology is to determine where phonology goes, that is, how does phonology cease to be phonology — for example, via morphologization, lexicalization, paradigmatic leveling, and rule loss.

For most linguists, the goals of synchronic phonology are quite different.

First, synchronic phonology seeks to determine the universal properties of sound patterns in languages. The key question here is: "What is a possible phonology?"

Second, synchronic phonology seeks to determine what's going on in the heads of speakers with respect to sound patterns.

Given the different goals of diachronic and synchronic phonology, we can now return to the question of phonetic determinism in phonology. It is quite clear that the phonetics plays a major role in diachronic phonology. The crucial question is: does phonetically driven phonology help us with the above two synchronic goals?

With respect to the first goal, can the phonetics determine universal properties of phonological systems? That is, can the phonetics constrain phonology (limit the class of "possible phonologies")? I am interested here in considering whether the phonetics can rule out "impossible" phonologies. I attempt to show in section III that it does not. Because of the restructurings that take place, phonetic universals are readily violated in synchronic phonologies.

Second, do speakers "know" phonetics? Is their knowledge of phonology stored in phonetic terms? Whereas the preceding question asks whether the phonetics rules out certain phonological systems, this second question, instead, asks whether it is "better" from a learnability point of view for synchronic phonological rules to mimic the phonetics? The answer has never been convincingly demonstrated, experimentally or otherwise. The evidence from actually occurring historical developments seems, largely, to be negative. Aside from the fact that phonological rules begin their existence as "natural," given the phonologization process, the rest of their history seems to be on a downward slide from the phonetic point of view. As frequently noted, phonologicalized processes are typically subject to subsequent developments, which include further modifications of the input and output segments, including the conditioning environments, which ultimately can be lost entirely. The results are familiar: opacity, morphologization, exceptionality, etc. If naturalness were such an important factor, synchronically, why do natural rules so readily become denaturalized?

What kind of evidence might one, then, seek to justify the view that phonetic naturalness is an important criterion in synchronic phonology? Most examples cited involve phonetically driven rule activation, which I have relegated to the phonologization process. At least two other types of evidence, however, might be sought. First, one might look for instances of phonetically driven rule inhibition, that is, situations where otherwise general phonological rules are blocked from applying just in case the result would constitute an "unnatural" output. The hypothetical example cited in Hyman (1975a, p. 181) is reproduced in (5).

(5)

| a. | /papi/ | → | | → | [papə] |
| b. | /paki/ | → | [pači] | | (↛ *pačə) |

In (5a), final [i] reduces to schwa by rule. In (5b), final [i] palatalizes the preceding /k/ to [č]. Because of phonetically driven rule inhibition, final reduction of [i] to schwa is blocked — for then the palatalization rule would be rendered opaque. Such situations are highly restricted at best, and, where occurring, have a different explanation.[14]

A second type of evidence for phonetic naturalness might be termed phonetically driven rule loss. If non-naturalness represents a relative complexity in learnability, less natural phonological rules should be more readily (i.e., earlier) lost than more natural ones. The place to look would be paradigms that provide both natural and unnatural alternations in otherwise comparable environments. Such a situation exists in (lu-)Ganda and several Bantu languages spoken in the Lake Victoria area. As seen in (6),

(6) Illustration from Ganda showing the neutralization of *p, *t, *k > [s]
and *b, *d, *g > [z]

	Proto-Bantu			Ganda		Corres-pondence
a.	*-pída	'pus'	>	(ma)-síra	'pus'	*p > s
	*-kapí	'oar'	>	(n)-kasî	'oar'	*p > s
	*-bín-	'dance (v.)'	>	-zín-a	'dance (v.)'	*b > z
	*-bímb-	'swell (v.)'	>	-zímb-a	'swell (v.)'	*b > z
b.	*-tíd-	'rub, grind'	>	-sil-a	'rub, pulverize'	*t > s
	*-dím-	'extinguish'	>	-zím-a	'extinguish'	*d > z
c.	*-kɪd-	'be silent'	>	-sílik-a	'be silent'	*k > s
	*-gɪd-	'be taboo'	>	-zil-a	'be taboo'	*g > z

Ganda underwent a series of consonant changes whereby tautomorphemic stops
ultimately became fricatives before Proto-Bantu tense *i̧: *p, *t, *k > [s], while
*b, *d, *g > [z]. The alternations in (7) show that root-final alveolar and velar
stops continue to undergo these "frications" synchronically when followed by one
of the three indicated suffixes reconstructed with *i̧:

(7) Frication of *t, *d, *k, and *g before causative *-i̧-, agentive *-i̧, and
perfective *-i̧d-e

a.	*-déet-i̧-	'bring '+ -i̧-	>	-lées-i̧-	'make bring'	*t > s
	*-ded-i̧-	'care for' + -i̧-	>	-lez-i̧-	'make care for'	*d > z
	*-ji̧duk-i̧-	'run' + -i̧-	>	-'ddus-i̧-	'make run'	*k > s
	*-jig-i̧-	'learn' + -i̧-	>	-yiz-i̧-	'make learn'	*g > z
b.	*-déet-i̧	'bring' + i̧	>	mu-lées-i̧	'bringer' (rain)	*t > s
	*-ded-i̧	'care for' + i̧	>	mu-lez-i̧	'caretaker'	*d > z
	*-ji̧duk-i̧	'run'+ i̧	>	mú-ddus-i̧	'fugitive'	*k > s
	*-jig-i̧	'learn'+ i̧	>	mu-yiz-i̧	'apprentice'	*g > z
c.	*-déet-i̧	'bring' + i̧d-e	>	-lées-i̧	'brought'	*t > s
	*-ded-i̧	'care for' + i̧d-e	>	-lez-i̧-e	'cared for'	*d > z
	*-ji̧duk-i̧	'run' + i̧d-e	>	-'ddus-i̧-e	'ran'	*k > s
	*-jig-i̧	'learn' + i̧d-e	>	-yiz-i̧-e	'learned'	*g > z

On the other hand, the forms in (8) show that the labials *p and *b do not fricate
before these suffixes:

(8) Non-frication of *p, *b before causative *-j-, agentive *-j, or perfective
    *-jd-e

a.	*-puup-j-	'blow' + -j-	>	-puuy-j-	'make blow'	*p > w > y[15]
	*-djb-	'fish' + -j-	>	-vub-j-	'make beat'	*b > b
b.	*-puup-j	'blow' + j	>	mu-puuy-j	'horn-blower'	*p > w > y
	*-djb-j	'fish' + j	>	mu-vub-j	'fisherman'	*b > b
c.	*-puup-j	'pay' + jd-e	>	puuy-j-e	'blew'	*p > w > y
	*-djb-	'fish' + jd-e	>	vub-j-e	'fished'	*b > b

Recall from (6) that labials, alveolars, and velars all become fricated tautomorphemically before *j. So, why should it only be the labials that do not alternate
before the suffixes in question?

    One hypothesis that can be considered here is that it has to do with the
relative naturalness of the three alternations. Arguably, alternations such as p/s and
b/z are less natural than either t/s and d/z or k/s and g/z. Both spirantization of
alveolars and "velar softening" are well known to phonologists. Alternations of
p/s and b/z seem more restricted (although known particularly to Africanists).
Could it be that Ganda originally underwent these frications across the board, but
that the heteromorphemic p/s and b/z alternations were leveled out specifically
because they represented less natural relations between segments? Again, this is a
question that has not been resolved. Do such considerations of naturalness play a
role in suppressing synchronic alternations — that is, ultimately rule curtailment
and loss? I believe the case is not strong here either.[16]

C. Summary

I have thus far argued, first, that phonology should be viewed as the intersection
of phonetics and grammar (§II.A) and, second, that one should be careful to
distinguish synchronic and diachronic phonology (§II.B). In this last regard, one
has to be careful not to fall into the alluring trap of confusing the goals of
synchronic vs. diachronic phonology or the difference between transparent
phonologization vs. what we might call "mature phonology." Much of the discussion on phoneticizing phonology slips into this "trap." Recall Ohala's (1990)
position on place assimilation in the creation of geminates and homorganic na-
sal+consonant sequences. Ohala begins by observing, first, that some phonologi-
zations are unidirectional, and second, that current models of phonology are
inadequate to capture this unidirectionality. Thus, a sequence such as VŋtV could
develop into VntV, but not into *VŋkV. He points out that, because feature
geometry can just as easily express both the attested as well as the allegedly

unattested (or rare) changes, as we saw in (3a) vs. (3b), it and other formal theories should be rejected on this basis.[17] However, we have seen that the phonetic tendency in question can be overridden by other considerations, for example, the ranking of morphological constraints: Root Faithfulness > Affix Faithfulness. In other words, the explanation of the tendency noted by Ohala is not a synchronic phonological one, but rather a diachronic phonetic one. Rather than deploring feature geometry's ability to express (3b), its proponents may take comfort that feature geometry, a *phonological* framework, can still formulate the rarer alternation.

What I conclude from the above discussion is the following:

    i. Although there is much of phonology that is not phonetically arbitrary, there is little evidence that this is more than the consequence of the phonologization process: universal phonetics determines in large part what will become a language-specific phonetic property, which ultimately can be phonologized to become a structured, rule-governed part of the grammar.

    ii. Once part of the grammar, phonology may be further subjected to structural or systemic principles. What has been phonologized is thus often telescoped, analogized to broader contexts, subject to rule inversion, and/or morphologized.

    iii. It is possible to get relatively "unnatural" synchronic systems as a result of the interactions of "natural" processes.

In the next section, I return to Pater's (1996) constraint *NT, which Hayes (1995, 1997) has invoked in support of phonetically driven phonology. I will show that this constraint, although "phonetically grounded," does not get us closer to the two goals of synchronic phonology cited earlier: it neither constrains the class of possible phonologies, nor does it help us understand cognitive aspects of phonology, for example, what is going on in the heads of Sotho-Tswana speakers.

III. NASAL+OBSTRUENT INTERACTIONS

In this section I apply the conclusions of section II to the study of nasal+obstruent (N+C) sequences, particularly as they are realized in Bantu languages. Surveys such as Herbert (1986), Rosenthal (1989), Steriade (1993), and others show a wide array of "natural" sound changes/resulting phonological rules affecting input N+C sequences. In what follows I shall use the following abbreviations:

(9)

N	= nasal consonant	S	=	voiceless fricative
C	= (oral) obstruent	Z	=	voiced fricative
T	= voiceless stop	TS	=	voiceless affricate
D	= voiced stop	DZ	=	voiced affricate

Based on their distribution, as well as the processes that affect them, the following hierarchy has been assumed, where ⊃ can be read either as "is better than" or "is implied by the presence of":[18]

(10)

$$ND \quad ⊃ \quad NZ \quad ⊃ \quad NT \quad ⊃ \quad NS$$

As seen, the most "natural" combination of nasal+obstruent is ND. Many languages permit only ND (i.e., disallowing lower combinations in the hierarchy), either in their underlying system and/or in the phonetic output. Others generalize the system to include ND and NZ, while still others allow ND, NZ, and NT, disallowing only NS. Both these distributional generalizations and the recurrent processes that affect nasal+obstruents have "natural" phonetic explanations (e.g., Ohala, 1975; Ohala & Ohala, 1993; Hayes, 1995, 1997; Huffman & Hinnebusch, 1998). In addition, most of these generalizations apply equally well whether the N+C sequences are: (i) prenasalized consonants (NC); (ii) tautosyllabic sequences (.NC); or (iii) heterosyllabic sequences (N.C). As the above studies indicate, N+C realizations provide a wealth of data for the study of the phonetics–phonology interface.

A. Postnasal Voicing

In this section, I consider the voicing of obstruents after nasals, that is, NT → ND. As stated by Herbert (1986, p. 236), "Perhaps the most common process to apply to the oral consonant in nasal–oral sequence is postnasal voicing of voiceless consonants." In fact, of all environments, the postnasal context appears to have the greatest effect on voicing: "A healthy supply of languages voice obstruents after nasals, but not after vowels, glides, or liquids" (Hayes, 1995, p. 2). As an example, consider in (11) the data from (ci-)Yao, a Bantu language spoken in Mozambique and parts of Tanzania and Malawi:

(11) Yao postnasal voicing (Hyman & Ngunga, 1997; Ngunga, 2000)

    a. When the following consonant is voiceless, it becomes [+voice]

ku-N-péleka	→	kuu-m-béleka	'to send me'
ku-N-túma	→	kuu-n-dúma	'to order me'
ku-N-cápila	→	kuu-ɲ-jápila	'to wash for me'
ku-N-kwéela	→	kuu-ŋ-gwéela	'to climb on me'

    b. When the following consonant is voiced, it deletes

ku-N-búúcila	→	kuu-múúcila	'to be angry with me'
ku-N-lápa	→	kuu-nápa	'to admire me'
ku-N-jíima	→	kuu-ɲíima	'to begrudge me'
ku-N-góneka	→	kuu-ŋóneka	'to make me sleep'
ku-N-mála	→	kuu-mála	'to finish me'
ku-N-néma	→	kuu-néma	'for me to do incorrectly'
ku-N-ɲála	→	kuu-ɲála	'to cut me into small pieces'
ku-N-ŋáándila	→	kuu-ŋáándila	'to play around with me'

    c. An exception to the preceding is /d/, which does not delete

ku-N-dípa	→	kuu-n-dípa	'to pay me'
ku-N-délela	→	kuu-n-délela	'to understimate me'

    d. The nasal deletes when followed by /s/ (=the only voiceless fricative)

ku-n-sóosa	→	kuu-sóosa	'to look for me'

As seen in (11a), voiceless stops become voiced after the first person singular prefix N–.[19] This same rule applies in a number of other Bantu languages, for example, Kikuyu, (ki-)Nande, and Bukusu, where the output voiced consonants merge with the corresponding underlying voiced consonants. As seen in (11b), however, there is no such merger in Yao. Instead, voiced consonants delete after the nasal prefix — thereby neutralizing /b, l, j, g/ with /m, n, ɲ, ŋ/. As seen in (11c), the one exception to this deletion process is /d/. Finally, (11d) shows the common process of nasal effacement before the voiceless fricative /s/.[20] In all cases the vowel that precedes an input NC is lengthened.

    The alternations in (11a) could be multiplied by quite a number of other Bantu languages in support of the claim that postnasal voicing is a natural phonological rule. As Pater (1996) and Hayes (1995, 1997) suggest, it is best seen as an active response to the constraint *NT. That is, a common means by which languages avoid NT is by voicing the oral consonant.

    A second, *passive* response to *NT comes from potential cases where an otherwise general rule is blocked from applying just in case the result would be NT. Such cases are rare, one possible instance being the following from Basaá, a Bantu language spoken in Cameroon.[21] Ignoring affricates, the stop system of Basaá is presented in (12), as realized in three different environments:

(12) Basaá stop system

a.	stem-initial			b.	phrase-final			c.	elsewhere		
	p	t	k		p	t	k		b	d	g
	mb	nd	ŋg		mb	nd	ɲg		mb	nd	ŋg

As seen, the Basaá oral stops /p, t, k/ are realized voiceless in both stem-initial and phrase-final positions. Examples are seen in (13).

(13)

a.	lì-pàn	'forest'		b.	lì-yép	'poverty'	(lì- = class 5 prefix)
	lì-tám	'fruit'			lì-yɔ́t	'anger'	
	lì-kùŋ	'owl'			lì-lɔ̀ìk	'dancing'	

In other environments these stops are realized voiced, for example, in prefixes, as seen in (14a), or phrase-internally, as in (14b).[22]

(14)

a.	bi-jék	'food' (cl. 8)		b.	lì-yéb lí mût	'poverty of a person'
	di-nuní	'birds' (cl. 13)			lì-yɔ́d lí mût	'anger of a person'
					lì-lɔ́g lí mût	'dancing of a person'

As also indicated in (12), however, the prenasalized stops /mb, nd, ŋg/ appear as voiced in the same three environments. Crucially, postnasal voicing is maintained in the two devoicing environments, stem-initial (15a) and phrase-final (15b).

(15) Stem-initial and phrase-final ND

a.	lì-mbóó	'kind'		b.	lì-ùmb	'alcohol'
	lì-ndám	'round basket'			lì-pènd	'barrier'
	lì-ŋgén	'fountain'			lì-séŋg	'parasol-holder'

While one might attribute the non-devoicing of ND in (15a) to the fact that the N is stem-initial, not the D, this will not work in (15b), where it is the D that stands at the end of the phrase. This suggests that the universal tendency that prenasalized stops be voiced takes precedence over both the language-specific constraint that stem-initial stops be voiceless and the universal tendency for phrase-final obstruents to devoice.[23] In OT terms, the correct output is derived by ranking *NT higher than Final Devoicing, as in (16a).

(16)   Basaá   Non-Basaá

a.	/ùmb/	*NT	FinDev
☞	ùmb		*
	ùmp	*!	

b.	/ùmb/	FinDev	*NT
	ùmb	*!	
☞	ùmp		*

Had Final Devoicing been ranked higher than *NT, as in (16b), the incorrect output *ùmp would have been obtained.

B. Postnasal Devoicing

Taken together, the Yao & Basaá data show how *NT can either motivate a change of NT to ND, or inhibit a change of ND to NT. We are safe in concluding, along with others before us, that the postnasal environment is particularly conducive to voicing. On the other hand, the reverse rule, ND → NT, would be quite "un-phonetic" according to Flemming (1995, p. 3) and Hayes (1997, p. 18), who hypothesize that it is "rare or unattested." Similarly, we should not expect an otherwise general voicing rule to be inhibited by a preceding nasal.

However, postnasal devoicing is attested in Bantu, particularly in the Sotho-Tswana group and closely related Makua (Janson, 1991/1992), as well as in Bubi and certain other languages in the northwest Bantu area. In this section, I shall document postnasal devoicing in Tswana, where, I shall claim, there is a need for a constraint *ND that is higher ranked than Pater's *NT.

I begin by presenting the Tswana consonant system in (17), based on Krüger & Snymann (n.d., pp. 80–81):

(17) Tswana consonant system

p′	t′	k′		voiceless ejective stops
pʰ	tʰ	kʰ		voiceless aspirated stops
b	(d)			voiced stops (re [d], see below)
	tl′			ejective voiceless lateral affricate
	tlʰ			aspirated voiceless lateral affricate
	ts′	tʃ′		ejective voiceless affricates
	tsʰ	tʃʰ	kxʰ	aspirated voiceless affricates
ɸ	s	ʃ	x	voiceless fricatives
	r̥		h	voiceless resonants
w	l	y		voiced resonants
m	n	ɲ	ŋ	voiced nasals

Shown above are the consonants of Tswana minus cases of NC, discussed below. Of concern to us are the voiced stops. As seen in (18), these devoice after the same first person singular object prefix N– exemplified in Yao in (11) above:[24]

(18) Devoicing after 1 sg. object prefix N–

a.	bón-á	'see'	b.	m-pón-á	'see me!'	
	dís-á	'watch'		n-tís-á	'watch me!'	
	áráb-á	'answer'		ŋ-káráb-á	'answer me!'	(< -gáráb-)

While the devoicing of m+b and n+d to [mp] and [nt] in (18b) is straightforward in the first two examples, the last example shows an alternation between the lack of a consonant in [áráb-á] and the [k] in [N-káráb-á]. As indicated to the right, however, such forms originally began with *g, which also devoiced after the nasal prefix, as seen.

Postnasal devoicing is, in fact, quite general in Tswana. The data in (19a) show devoicing after the class 9/10 prefix N– (PB = Proto-Bantu):

(19) Devoicing after class 9, 10 prefix N–

    a.   n-tá   'louse'   PB   *n-dá

         n-twa   'battle, war'   PB   *n-du-a (cf. *-du-a > lw-a 'to fight')

    b.   pútsó   'question'   cf.   bútsó   'to ask'

         /n-bʊts-o/   le-búts-í 'interrogative'

         tiro   'work, deed'   cf.   dir-a   'to work, to do'

         /n-dir-o/   mo-dir-i 'worker'

    c.   lʊ-bú   'salty terrain'   pl.   di-m-pú

         lʊ-di   'twine, bark string'   pl.   di-n-ti   [tone not indicated]

    d.   lʊ-bone   'lamp'   pl.   di-pone   < di-m-bone

         lʊ-eto   'trip'   pl.   di-keto   < di-ŋ-geto

         lʊ-úpá   'ashes'   pl.   di-kúpá < di-ŋ-gúpá

When the noun roots are monosyllabic, as they are in (19a), the nasal both devoices the following consonant and remains. When the roots are longer, as in (19b), the nasal, which is present structurally and is responsible for the devoicing, drops out by rule.[25] Thus, the roots of the nouns *pútsó* 'question' and *tiro* 'deed', underlyingly /n-bʊts-o/ and /n-dir-o/, are realized with initial [b] and [d] in the related forms to the right. The remaining data involve a class 11 singular prefix lʊ-, which is replaced in the plural by the complex class 10 prefix *di-N-*. In the plurals in (19c) the nasal devoicing the following consonant (and remains, since the noun roots are monosyllabic). The same devoicing is observed in the plurals in (19d), where, however, the nasal drops out, since the roots are bisyllabic.

Finally, note in (20) that the same postnasal devoicing occurred historically within roots, where there is no possibility of alternation:

(20) Historical postnasal devoicing + nasal loss within morphemes

    a. PB   *-bumb- 'mould, create'   >   Tsw.   -búp-   'mould, create'

    b. PB   *-gend-   'walk, go'   >   Tsw.   -et-   'travel'

    c. PB   *-teŋg-   'buy'   >   Tsw.   -rék-   'buy'

To summarize thus far, it should be clear that Tswana has a rule of postnasal devoicing, the exact opposite of the more widespread rule of postnasal voicing. According to the demonstrations in Hayes (1995, 1997), such a phonetically unnatural rule is not supposed to exist. Someone wishing to dismiss the above evidence might therefore respond by attempting to relegate devoicing after N–prefixes to the morphology, thereby sparing the phonology of the need to account for the alternations via phonetically driven constraints.[26] The problem I see with this move is that it is typically opportunistic, that is, taken only when needed.[27] Many studies that have reported on the phonetic motivations of phonological rules have not bothered to distinguish whether the rules cited have a morphological character or not.

In fact, it is difficult to dismiss postnasal devoicing as simply a morphological issue (or, worse, as "historical residue"). The same scholars who argue for the phoneticization of phonology, for example, Flemming (1995), consider as part of their charge to account for static distributions within words and morphemes. With this in mind, consider the following table of distributions of NC in Tswana, based on Creissel's (1996) lexicon of ca. 5700 entries:

(21) Distribution of NC in Tswana, based on Creissels (1996)

	mp	mph	mb	nt	nth	nd	ntl	ntlh	nts	ntsh	ŋk	ŋkh	ŋg
C_1	5	3	–	1	–	–	4	2	10	4	8	–	–
C_2	22	2	2	21	1	–	8	3	5	14	16	–	–
C_3	4	–	–	3	2	–	7	–	2	8	4	–	–
C_4	–	–	–	5	–	–	–	–	–	–	–	–	–

Exceptions: ámbúlénsí 'ambulance'; bámbáɲèχà 'gratter fort'

The distribution of NC in all positions of stems up to four syllables $(C_1VC_2VC_3VC_4V)$ were investigated, not counting the nasal, which is itself syllabic. As seen, only two exceptional forms were found that had ND, one of which is clearly a recent borrowing.[28] What is then in need of explanation is why Tswana has [b] and [d], but not [mb] and [nd]. I maintain that it is because of an active constraint *ND.

The two pieces of evidence adduced thus far in favor a constraint *ND are, first, that it would motivate postnasal devoicing and, second, that it would account for the absence of phonetic ND anywhere in the Tswana lexicon. A third argument is also quite telling. The proposed constraint *ND has the properties of a classic "conspiracy" (Kisseberth, 1970). We see this in two situations where ND is avoided not by postnasal devoicing, but by postnasal nasalization:

(i) The [ʊ] of the various *mʊ*- prefixes in the language obligatorily deletes before a root-initial /b/. In principle, when [ʊ] deletes, /mʊ+b/ should become [mb]. As seen in (22), however, /mʊ+b/ → [mm] (not *mb):

(22) mʊ+b → mm (where mʊ– is a prefix)

   a.   class 1   mʊ-bús-í   →   m-mús-í   'governor'   cf. bús-á 'to govern'
         class 3   mʊ-bús-ó   →   m-mús-ó   'government'
         class 1 object mʊ-bús-é   →   m-mús-é   'govern him!'

   b.   class 3   mʊ-bútlá   →   m-mútlá   'hare'   cf. mɪ-bútlá (pl.)

   c.   class 1 object mʊ-bón-é   →   m-món-é   'see him!'   cf. bón-á 'see'
                        mʊ-bíts-é   →   m-míts-é   'call him!'   bíts-á 'call'

These examples show the deletion of the [ʊ] of three different mʊ– prefixes: noun class 1, noun class 3, and the class 1 object prefix. Related forms are provided to show that the root-initial consonant is indeed /b/. Recall that ʊ-deletion is obligatory when the root-initial consonant is /b/, and does not apply when the following consonant is non-labial.[29]

    (ii) The second situation in which ND is avoided by postnasal nasalization concerns the perfective suffix -ile, illustrated in (23a).

(23) n+l (→ n+d) → nn in forming the perfective stem with the suffix -ile

   a. regular rék-á   'buy'   →   rek-ile
                tsʊ́m-á 'hunt'   →   tsʊ́m-ile

   b. CVn–   xan-a   'refuse'   →   xan-ile   →   xan-n-e (Cole, 1955/1992, p. 227)
               non-a   'be fat'   →   non-ile   →   non-n-e
               men-a   'fold'   →   men-ile   →   men-n-e
               bin-a   'dance'   →   bin-ile   →   bin-n-e

   c. Lobedu han-a   'refuse'   →   han-ile   →   han-d̩-e (Kotze, 1998, p. 16)
               non-ile 'be fat'   →   non-ile   →   non-d̩-e
               vun-a   'harvest'   →   vun-ile   →   vun-d̩-e

    As seen in (23b), the [i] of this suffix deletes after (monosyllabic) CVn– roots. However, the result is CVn-ne, not *CVn-de, as we would expect from other Bantu languages. One can see the relevance of the constraint *ND by considering comparable forms in Lobedu, an outlying northern Sotho dialect. As Kotze (1998) shows, this dialect in the Sotho–Tswana subgroup was not affected by postnasal devoicing. Therefore, as seen in (23c), when the [i] of the -ile perfective suffix is deleted, its /l/ hardens as (dental) [d̩]. As Dickens (1977, p. 165) shows, [d̩] is the regular reflex of *nd in Lobedu.[30]

    My interpretation of both sets of facts is that *ND functions as a conspiracy: when the deletion of the [ʊ] of mʊ- prefixes threatens to produce [mb], and the deletion of the [i] of the -ile perfective suffix threatens to produce [nd], *ND enters into the picture and guarantees that this will not occur. The conspiratorial nature of *ND is shown by the fact that Tswana has two ways of avoiding ND: postnasal devoicing and postnasal nasalization.[31]

C. Why Postnasal Devoicing?

The most straightforward conclusion to draw from the preceding, therefore, is that Tswana requires the constraint *ND. What I would like to suggest is that *ND exists in other languages, but is normally ranked below *NT, as seen in (24a).

(24) The constraint *ND may be ranked below or above *NT

a. "normal"

	/m-bona/	*NT	*ND
☞	m-bona		*
	m-pona	*!	

b. Sotho-Tswana

	/m-bona/	*ND	*NT
	m-bona	*!	
☞	m-pona		*

As was seen in section III.A, the potential effect of *NT in such languages is to condition (or protect) postnasal voicing. In most Sotho-Tswana dialects, however, the ranking is reversed, as in (24b), and, as indicated, the effect is postnasal devoicing.

The Tswana situation raises two important questions:

(i) Is *ND phonetically "grounded" in the sense of Archangeli & Pulleyblank (1994)? Hayes (1997, pp. 17–18) suggests that it is among those rare or non-attested constraints that are not phonetically driven (in his terminology). If, on the other hand, *ND is available as a universal, but violable contraint — and if all such constraints must be phonetically driven — what is the elusive phonetic motivation that drives *ND? One cannot help noting that the output of postnasal devoicing is (variably) ejective. Perhaps postnasal ejectives are favored in some way that makes NT' "better" than NT. It is not clear, however, that NT' represents an improvement over ND. On the other hand, if we reject phonetic determinism as a criterion in synchronic phonology, we can simply draw the conclusion that *ND is an actually occuring constraint, as in Tswana.

(ii) The second question, then, is why Tswana should be different from other languages. I take this to be not a synchronic question, but rather a diachronic one: how did *ND come to outrank *NT, historically? It is this second question that I would like now to consider.

In (25), based on such sources as Tucker (1929), Dickens (1977, 1984), Krüger & Snyman (n.d.), and Creissels (1999), I show the correspondences between Proto-Bantu stops and early Sotho-Tswana:

(25) Sound correspondences between Proto-Bantu and early Sotho-Tswana

			N __	Elsewhere					N __	Elsewhere
a.	*p	>	pʰ	ɸ	b.	*b	>	b	β	
	*t	>	tʰ	r̥		*d	>	d	l	(~ [ɽ])
	*k	>	kʰ, kxʰ	h, x[32]		*g	>	g	ɣ	(> Ø)

Two environments are distinguished: the postnasal environment is shown in the first column, while the second column represents the realization of the Proto-Bantu consonants in other contexts. Several observations should be made. First, concerning the proto system, some scholars begin instead with Proto-Bantu aspirated stops, that is, *pʰ, *tʰ, *kʰ, and/or with Proto-Bantu voiced continuants, that is, *β, *l, *ɣ (Meinhof, 1932). The choice of proto system does not seriously affect the historical analysis. Either way, we see in (25a) that the voiceless series is realized as aspirated after a nasal, but as voiceless continuants in other environments.[33] As a result, present-day Tswana also has alternations between voiceless continuants and aspirated stops such as in (26).

(26)

	a.	ɸeɲ-a	'conquer'	b.	m-pʰeɲ-a	'conquer me!'
		rát-á	'love'		n-tʰát-á	'love me!'
		xát-á	'trample'		ŋ-kxʰát-á	'trample me!'

Returning to (25b), in early Sotho-Tswana, the proto voiced consonants were stops postnasally, but continuants elsewhere. At this stage *b was pronounced [β] and *g was pronounced [ɣ] (which subsequently dropped out). The alveolar continuant [l] had the allophone [ɽ], a retroflex flap, before the high tense vowels *i and *u.

With this background, we can now account for the rise of *ND in the following way. The devoicing of *mb, *nd, *ŋg to mp, nt, ŋk (with potential loss of the nasal) can be seen as the result of a prohibition against voiced stops in general in early Sotho-Tswana. In other words, with *b, *d, *g pronounced as continuants when not postnasal, the subsequent devoicing of voiced stops can be seen, historically, as context-free: *b, *d, *g > p, t, k. Compare Dickens's (1984) view, who assumes proto *β, *l, *ɣ and sees postnasal devoicing as the result of two distinct processes: "*stopping*, which converted voiced continuants (fricatives and l) into non-continuants after a nasal, for example, m+βona → mbona 'see me' (lit. me+see). [. . .] *devoicing*, whereby voiced non-continuants (the outputs of *stopping*) became voiceless and sometimes ejected, after a [. . .] nasal, for example, mbona → mpona 'see me'" (p.97).[34]

A summary of the historical development of the Sotho-Tswana consonant system is given in (27).

(27) Historical stages involved in postnasal devoicing

		non-postnasal	postnasal	
a.	Stage I	*p, *t, *k	*mp, *nt, *ŋk	(Proto-Bantu)
		*b, *d, *g	*mb, *nd, *ŋg	
b.	Stage II	ɸ, r̥, x	mpʰ, ntʰ, ŋkxʰ	(spirantization;
		β, l ~ ɾ, ɣ	mb, nd, ŋg	aspiration[35])
c.	Stage III	ɸ, r̥, x	mpʰ, ntʰ, ŋkxʰ	(stop devoicing;
		β, l~ ɾ, Ø	mp, nt, ŋk	ɣ > Ø)
d.	Stage IV	ɸ, r̥, x	(m)pʰ, (n)tʰ, (ŋ)kxʰ	(nasal deletion)
		β, l~ ɾ, Ø	(m)p, (n)t, (ŋ)k	
e.	Stage V	ɸ, r̥, x	(m)pʰ, (n)tʰ, (ŋ)kxʰ	(β > b, ɾ > d)
		b, l~d, Ø	(m)p, (n)t, (ŋ)k	

In (27a) I begin with Proto-Bantu in Stage I, where it is arbitrarily assumed that the proto consonants in question were (unaspirated) stops. In (27b), where Stage II represents early Sotho-Tswana, the six consonants are realized as continuants when not following a nasal. At this point the voiceless series is unquestionably aspirated in the postnasal environment. Postnasal devoicing takes place in Stage III in (27c), and [ɣ] is lost. In Stage IV in (27d), nasals are lost intramorphemically and on nouns whose roots are polysyllabic. Finally, in Stage V in (27e), [β] and [ɾ] become [b] and [d] in Standard Tswana.

This last change is important in that it reintroduces voiced stops in Standard Tswana. Today, Tswana /b/ is pronounced [b], although it used to be pronounced [β]. Tswana [d] is an allophone of /l/ found only before the high tense vowels /i/ and /u/. As indicated in (27b–d), it used to be pronounced [ɾ], as it is in certain Sotho-Tswana dialects.[36] These facts are crucial in understanding postnasal devoicing as a historical process. As stated by Krüger & Snyman (n.d.), "[b] still acts according to its historical fricative features represented as [β]. [d] is a positional (complementary) variant of /l/ before the high vowels /i/ and /u/. /ɣ/ is a voiced velar fricative which underwent historical elision before vowel commencing stems, but which appears again in plosivated form, /k/, when these stems are preceded by /N/" (p. 122). So, as a possible *synchronic* solution to postnasal devoicing, why not "pretend" that Tswana [b] and [d] are still /β/ and /l/? In this case, we could derive postnasal devoicing by invoking the constraint *D, which, given the relative complexity of voiced stops, is non-controversially phonetically driven. With /β/ and /l/, we could then replace the tableaux in (24) with those in (28).

(28) Historical scenario involving the constraint ranking *D > *NT:

a. "normal"

/m-βona/	*NT	*D
☞ m-bona		*
m-pona	*!	

b. Sotho-Tswana

/m-βona/	*D	*NT
m-bona	*!	
☞ m-pona		*

In the "normal" situation in (28a), *NT is ranked higher than *D, so the input /m-βona/ is realized [m-bona], as it is in most of Bantu. (A separate constraint will require that /β/ be realized as a stop by postnasal hardening.) In the Sotho-Tswana situation in (28b), on the other hand, *D is ranked higher than *NT, and devoicing occurs. However, in this interpretation, /mβ/ is realized [mp] (instead of [mb]) not because of the postnasal environment, but because high-ranked *D forbids voiced stops in all positions in this analysis (as it did historically).

 Despite the fact that this analysis avoids the constraint *ND, the historical scenario no longer "works" in present-day Tswana. At least two problems arise. First, if *D is highly ranked, as in (28b), why is /β/ allowed to be pronounced [b], that is, bón-á 'see' (not *[βón-á])? Second, if *D is highly ranked, why are /li/ and /lu/ realized as [di] and [du]? Examples such as in (29a) clearly show that /l/ devoices to [t] after a nasal:

(29) More alternations involving l, d and t

	a.	lw-a	'fight'	→	n-twa	'battle, war'	
		lóm-á	'bite'	→	n-tǒmá	'bite me!'	
	b.	ópél-á	'sing'	→	mo-ópéd-í	'singer'	
		bul-a	'open'	→	bud-ile	(perfective)	
	c.	dúél-á	'pay'	→	n-túél-á	'pay me!'	(< /-lúél-/ 'pay')

In this analysis, one would say that [nd] is avoided in (29a) so as to satisfy the constraint *D. But why doesn't *D force the /l/ of /li/ and /lu/ to devoice to [ti] and [tu] in (29b)? Similarly, why is /lu/ realized as [du] in forms such as (29c)?[37]

We might argue one of two responses. First, we might pretend that [b] and [d] remain [β] and [ɾ] throughout the phonology, becoming [b] and [d] only in the phonetic implementation. Or, second, we might introduce a new family of constraints: I/O faithfulness to absolute onset-initial position. In this case we would say (i) that /β/ and /ɾ/ may not surface as such, but (ii) must maintain their [+voice] specifications in absolute onset-initial position. It is clear, however, that these ad hoc responses are merely "tricks" to avoid having to refer to the postnasal environment. On the other hand, once we admit the constraint *ND, everything falls into place. It is in fact hard not to accept *ND as motivating this important aspect of Tswana phonology.

D. Other Languages

To summarize the preceding subsections, we conclude, first, that most dialects within the Sotho-Tswana subgroup have an "unphonetic" process of postnasal devoicing. The process is non-neutralizing, since the proto voiceless stops spirantized to ɸ, ɾ̥, x, as was seen in (26) and (27b). The historical scenario included hardening of the voiced continuants β, l, ɣ to b, d, g after nasals, then devoicing, as in (27c). As we have said, the historical devoicing of mb, nd, ŋg to mp, nt, ŋk could have been the result of general devoicing of voiced stops, because these occurred only after nasals. However, the historical explanation is not available as a synchronic solution, because Tswana now contains [b] and [d], which do not devoice, for example, /li, lu/ → [di, du], not *[ti, tu]. I therefore propose a constraint *ND that functions as a conspiracy, as was seen in (22) and (23).

While generally overlooked in studies on NC, Herbert (1986) mentions postnasal devoicing in Sotho-Tswana, which he sees as non-general. He seems to have Sotho-Tswana in mind when he states that "no language which exhibits distinctive voicing in consonants limits prenasalized consonants to only voiceless consonants, although all prenasalized consonants may be voiceless in a language without a voice contrast in the consonant system" (p. 249). We might therefore hypothesize that *ND > NT was "allowed" to occur in Tswana, because of two pecularities of the system. First, there was no D other than in postnasal position, that is, there was no distinctive voicing on stops at the point in which the change took place. Voiced stops are very often spirantized in Bantu languages. Thus, many have surface oppositions between [p, t, k] vs. [β, l, ɣ], with the latter being realized [b, d, g] after a homorganic nasal. If the lack of a (non-postnasal) contrast between voiced and voiceless stops is a sufficient condition for postnasal devoicing, we should then find *ND > NT in many other Bantu languages. Since *ND > NT is rare, perhaps it depends not on the absence of [b, d, g], but on another property of early Sotho-Tswana: Prior to the introduction of postnasal devoicing, *T had already spirantized, and *NT had become NT^h, such that the change *ND > NT (> T) did not create any mergers. In other words, at the stage just prior to postnasal devoicing, the actual contrast was between NT^h and ND. Thus, the voicing of D had become redundant, with VOT constituting the major perceptual cue. Under this latter interpretation, the voicing of D could have become undone by a process that Ohala (1993) terms "hypercorrection": listeners could have "misparsed" the voicing of the D of ND, attributing it not to the D, but instead to the preceding N.[38]

Whether other factors contribute to the ND > NT process can only be determined by studying the effects of this change in other languages where it occurs. Postnasal devoicing also applies in Makua, which, however, may have shared this innovation with Sotho-Tswana (Janson, 1991/1992). In order to find other cases of postnasal devoicing, it is necessary to travel thousands of miles away to the Northwest of the Bantu zone. Janssens (1993) has shown that *ND is realized T in Bubi, spoken off the coast of Cameroon on the island of Fernando Po. Among the Proto-Bantu/Bubi correspondences noted by Janssens (1992) are the following:

(30)   Proto-Bantu   Bubi
    a.   *-cɨmbà   'wildcat'   -cìpà
    b.   *-gènd-   'walk'   -ét-à
    c.   *-gàngá   'root'   -àká

Note the striking resemblance of Bubi -ét-à 'walk' in (30b) with Tswana -et-a 'travel' in (20b), both from *-gènd-. What is important about the ND > T process in Bubi is that the output frequently merges with *T, as seen in the following correspondences also provided by Janssens:[39]

(31)   Proto-Bantu   Bubi
    a.   *-pàpá   'wing'   -pàpá
    b.   *-jútó-   'body'   -ótó

It thus appears that the result of the *ND > T process can be merger.

Mergers also occur in Punu, a northwest Bantu language spoken in Gabon. As seen in (32a), the first person singular prefix N– conditions the stopping and devoicing of voiced continuants (Fontaney, 1980):

(32) Postnasal devoicing (+ hardening) in Punu [northwest Bantu]
(Fontaney, 1980, pp. 73–74)

a.	m+β → mp	-βég-	'give' →	m-pégi dibága	'give me the knife'
	n+r → nt	-rónd-	'love' →	é n-tondi	'he loves me'
	ŋ+ɣ → ŋk (~ŋg)	-ɣirig-	'light' →	n-kírigili múji	'light the fire for me'
b.	m+p → mp	-pas-	'split' →	m-pásiri mwî:ri	'split wood for me'
	n+t → nt	-tábul-	'cut' →	n-tábulili pé:mbi	'cut bread for me'
	ŋ+k → ŋk	-kap-	'tie' →	átsí ŋ-kápa	'he tied me up'

Here we see that the voiced continuants [β, r, ɣ] not only become non-continuants postnasally, but also devoice (variably, in the case of the velar). (The nasal prefix also optionally deletes before a voiceless stop.) In (32b) we observe that there is a merger with /p, t, k/, so we are at a loss to explain, phonetically, why this devoicing takes place.[40] From a synchronic perspective, it would seem that postnasal hardening is accompanied by devoicing — even though the inputs /m+b/ and /n+d/ are not.

Up until now, all of the examples have come from Bantu. There is, however, reason to believe that *ND exerts an effect outside Bantu as well. Court (1970), for instance, reports on developments such as in (33) in certain Indonesian languages:

(33) Evidence for *ND in Indonesian languages (Court, 1970)

	Stage I		Stage II		Stage III
a.	NV	>	NṼ	>	NṼ
b.	NDV	>	N^{D}V	>	NV

The languages in question begin with a contrast between /NV/ and /NDV/ in what I have identified as Stage I. In Stage II, the vowel of /NV/ in (33a) is subject to progressive nasalization (which continues until checked by an antagonistic consonant — or the end of the word). At or subsequent to Stage II, the oral release of /ND/ becomes weakened in (33b), shown by the subscripted D. As shown in Stage III, the oral release may subsequently be lost. The original opposition between /N/ vs. /ND/ thereby becomes transphonologized as a contrast between [+nasal] and [-nasal] on the following vowel. Examples from Court (1970) are presented in (34).

(34) Examples showing NDV > N^{D}V > NV (Court, 1970)

a. Sundanese	[mānĩ]	'very'	[mān^{d}i] (mandi)	'to bathe'
b. Ulu Muar Malay	[mŋ$^{(g)}$oet]	to twitch	[mŋōẽ)ʔ]	'to bellow'
c. Sea Dayak	[nāŋ$^{(g)}$a] (nangga)	to set up ladder	[nāŋā] (nanga)	'to straighten'
d. Mĕntu Land	[əm$^{(b)}$ak]	'gong stick'	[əmāk]	'sleeping mat'
Dayak	[ɲin$^{(d)}$aʔ]	'to love'	[ɲĩnāʔ]	'snake (sp.)'

The significance of these data for our study is that /NT/ is not altered in these languages. The endpoint of the changes in (33) is thus one not unlike Sotho-Tswana: NT is found, but ND is not — ruled out, presumably, by *ND, which, again, must be higher ranked than *NT. Instead of satisfying *ND by postnasal devoicing, these languages invoke postnasal D-deletion.

Given the teleological orientation of phonetic OT, it is interesting to ask why ND should become N in the first place. The apparent gain appears to be the avoidance of ND (the most natural NC!) — and at quite an expense: an earlier N/ND opposition is transphonologized as one of [±nasal] on the following vowel. By so doing, these languages create an unusual situation, where nasalization on vowels is contrastive only if a nasal consonant precedes. In Hyman (1975b), I speculated that because of progressive nasalization, the [±nasal] opposition on vowels becomes more salient to speakers than the N/ND opposition.[41]

That such a transphonologization is not required for the change ND > N to occur is seen from the Scots facts in (35).

(35) Nasal cluster simplification in Scots (Harris, 1994, pp. 85–86)

a.	[mp] :	pump, lamp, limp	b.	[m] :	thimble, tremble, number, limb, dumber
	[nt] :	rant, sent, flint		[n] :	handle, bundle, thunder, hand, send
	[ŋk] :	sink, sank, donkey, wrinkle		[ŋ] :	bangle, single, finger, hunger, linger, anger, sing, strong,

In (35a) we see that NT is not modified in Scots, while ND is clearly avoided in (35b).

Finally, note in (36) the similar avoidance of ND by gemination in southern Italian dialects, compared to standard Italian (in parentheses):[42]

(36) Southern Italian dialects, where mb > mm, nd > nn (Rohlfs, 1949)

		Within morphemes			Across morphemes		
a.	Roman	piommo	(piombo)	'lead'	'm mettò	(un bottone)	'a button'
		palomma	(palomba)	'wooddove'			
		monno	(mondo)	'world'	un nitu	(un dito)	'a finger'
		quanno	(quando)	'when'			
b.	Neap.	tammurro	(tamburo)	'drum'	nom mòglio	(non voglio)	'I don't want'
		sammuco	(sambuco)	'elderberry'	nom mène	(non viene)	'he doesn't come'
		gónnola	(gondola)	'gondola'			
		vénnere	(vendere)	'to sell'			
c.	Sicilian	sammucu	(sambuco)	'elderberry'	um masu	(un bacio)	'a kiss'
		chiummu	(piombo)	'lead'	nom manu	(non vanno)	'they don't come'
		munnu	(mondo)	'world'	un niri	(non dire)	'to not say'
		quannu	(quando)	'when'	un nòrmu	(non dormo)	'I don't sleep'

Certain of the relevant Italian dialects provide evidence that *ND is higher ranked than *NT. While all of Italian originally contrasted NT and ND, (37) shows how each of these have been affected across dialects:

(37) Typology of NT/ND in Italian dialects

a.	Type I :	NT > NT	ND > ND	e.g., Tuscan, Northern Italian [i.e. no change]
b.	Type II :	NT > NT	ND > NN	e.g., Romanesco, Salentino
c.	Type III :	NT > ND	ND > NN	e.g., Neapolitan, Sicilian
d.	Type IV :	NT > ND	ND > ND	[unattested]

What is crucial are the type II dialects, where ND is modified to NN without NT being affected. Thus, in Romanesco, *cantare* 'to sing' is realized *cantà*. Type III is the most widespread pattern in the affected area. As Michele Loporcaro puts it, "What you find in southern Italy is type III, with two side-belts, as it were, north and south of type II: in other words, the area of NT > ND is included in that of ND" (personal communication, 1999). Thus, as seen in (37d), there is no type IV dialect where NT > ND occurs without the gemination of *ND. This provides strong evidence that ND > NN is the prior process and that *ND is ranked higher than *NT in southern Italy.

E. Other Processes

In the preceding subsections we have seen that, although many languages have post-nasal voicing, thereby motivating the constraint *NT, the reverse process of postnasal devoicing is also attested. In part to account for this, the constraint *ND was proposed. Synchronic phonology must therefore recognize both *NT and *ND, constraints which, ranked differently, account for the contradictory processes of postnasal voicing and devoicing. These results are in fact not isolated, nor limited to this pair of constraints. A close look at the different developments of NC throughout the Bantu language family shows a number of such contradictory synchronic processes, summarized in (38).

(38) Postnasal processes/"counter-processes" in Bantu

Process	Schema	Language	Counter-process	Schema	Language
Postnasal voicing	NT > ND	Yao, Kikuyu, Nande, Bukusu	Postnasal devoicing	ND > NT	Sotho-Tswana, Makua, Bubi
Postnasal affrication	NS > NTS NZ > NDZ	Kongo, Yaka, Tuki, Venda	Postnasal de-affrication	NTS > NS NDZ > NZ	Shona, Rwanda, Kinga
Postnasal aspiration	NT > NT^h	Cewa, Swahili, Pokomo	Postnasal deaspiration	NT^h > NT	Zulu, Ndebele, Xhosa, Swati
Postnasal nasalization	ND > NN	Ganda, Matuumbi	Postnasal de-nasalization	NN > ND	Kongo, Yaka, Punu

Another common postnasal process is the affrication of fricatives. Examples are seen from (ki-)Kongo in (39), where again the first person singular prefix N-conditions the changes:

(39) Postnasal affrication in Kongo (Carter, 1984)

    a.   /ku-N-fíl-a/   →   kú-m-pfil-a   'to lead me'

         /ku-N-síb-a/   →   kú-n-tsib-a   'to curse me'

    b.   /ku-N-vun-á/   →   kú-m-bvun-á   'to deceive me'

         /ku-N-zól-a/   →   kú-n-dzol-a   'to love me'

On the other hand, many Bantu languages exhibit postnasal de-affrication. In the Shona examples in (40a), for instance,

(40) Postnasal-deaffrication in Shona (Hannan, 1959/1987)

    a.   bvum-a   'agree, admit'   →   m-vum-o   'permission, agreement'

    b.   mu-dzúwe   'swing'   ~   n-zúwe   'swing'

the initial /bv/ of the verb root -bvum- becomes [v] when nominalized with the homorganic class 9 prefix N–. The examples in (40b) show the dialectal realization of the same root /-dzúwe/ 'swing' in two different noun classes: class 9 vs. class 3. As seen, /dz/ is realized as [z] after the class 9 prefix N–.[43]

    Another example concerns aspiration. It is frequently pointed out that voiceless stops tend to aspirate after homorganic nasal prefixes. Examples are again cited from Kongo in (41).

(41) Postnasal aspiration in Kongo (Carter, 1984)

    a.   /ku-N-pun-á/   →   kú-m-p^{h}un-á   'to deceive me'

    b.   /ku-N-tál-a/   →   kú-n-t^{h}al-a   'to look at me'

    c.   /ku-N-kiyíla/   →   kú-N-k^{h}iyíl-a   'to visit me'

However, the reverse process is found in the Nguni languages in southern Africa. Thus, as seen in the Ndebele examples in (42), aspirated stops are deaspirated (and usually ejectivized) when preceded by a nasal prefix:[44]

(42) Postnasal de-aspiration in Nguni (Pelling, 1971; Galen Sibanda, personal communication)

    a.   ulu-t^{h}i   'stick'   pl.   izin-ti

    b.   u(lu)-p^{h}ondo   'horn'   pl.   im-pondo

         u(lu)-p^{h}awu   'sign, mark'   pl.   im-pawu

    c.   u(lu)-k^{h}uni   'firewood'   pl.   iŋ-kuni

         u(lu)-k^{h}alo   'waist'   pl.   iŋ-kalo

The forms on the left involve the class 11 prefix *ulu-*, which can be simplified to u- if the noun stem has at least two syllables. The plural forms to the right are in class 10, which is marked by *iziN-* if the root is monosyllabic, otherwise by *iN-*.

Finally, Bantu languages have been found that nasalize vs. de-nasalize consonants in the postnasal environment. In the first case, I cite examples of Meinhof's Rule in Ganda:

(43) Postnasal nasalization ("Meinhof's Rule") in Ganda (Katamba & Hyman, 1991)

a.	N-bomba	→	m-momb-a	'I escape'	(*mbomba)
	N-banda	→	m-mand-a	'I open up a way'	(*mbanda)
	N-banja	→	m-manj-a	'I demand payment'	(*mbanja)
	N-banga	→	m-mang-a	'I begin'	(*mbanga)
b.	N-limba	→	n-nimb-a	'I lie'	(*ndimba)
	N-londa	→	n-nond-a	'I choose'	(*ndonda)
	N-langa	→	n-nang-a	'I announce'	(*ndanga)
c.	N-jamba	→	ɲ-ɲamb-a	'I help'	(*njamba)
	N-jonda	→	ɲ-ɲond-a	'I twine'	(*njonda)
	N-jonja	→	ɲ-ɲonj-a	'I make smart'	(*njonja)
	N-junga	→	ɲ-ɲung-a	'I join'	(*njunga)
d.	N-gamba	→	ŋ-ŋamb-a	'I say'	(*ngamba)
	N-genda	→	ŋ-ŋend-a	'I go'	(*ngenda)
	N-gengewala	→	ŋ-ŋengewal-a	'I become a leper'	(*ngengewala)

The examples in (43) show the nasalization of a voiced non-continuant when preceded by a nasal prefix and followed by a ND in the next syllable. On the other hand, postnasal denasalization is attested in Kongo dialects, Yaka, Punu and a few other languages in the general vicinity. The examples in (44) are cited from Yaka:

(44) Postnasal denasalization in Yaka (Kidima, 1991; Hyman, 1995)

a.	N+b	→	mb	e.g.	[N-[bak-idi]]	→	m-bak-idí	'I caught'
	N+d	→	nd	e.g.	[N-[duuk-idi]]	→	n-duuk-idí	'I became wise'
b.	N+m	→	mb	e.g.	[N-[mak-idi]]	→	m-bak-iní	'I carved'
	N+n	→	nd	e.g.	[N-[nuuk-idi]]	→	n-duuk-iní	'I smelt'
	N+ɲ	→	ndy	e.g.	[N-[ɲem-idi]]	→	n-dyem-ené	'I pushed"

As seen, the N+D inputs in (41a) surface as unchanged. On the other hand, the N+N inputs in (44b) are realized ND. Although the initials merge in these examples, note that the perfective suffix, realized *-idi* in (41a), is modified to *-ini* when the root begins with an underlying N.

While it is not clear what is motivating the denasalization process in (44b), it is hard to see how this process, completely general in the language, can be seen as the result of a phonetically driven process (cf. §IV).[45]

IV. CONCLUSIONS

On the basis of the preceding discussion, I conclude the following:

(i) "Phoneticizing" phonology by incorporating *NT does not constrain phonology as implied in phonetically driven phonology.

(ii) ND → NT exists as a process in Sotho-Tswana, which allows surface NT, but not *ND.

(iii) The historical change, ND > N (with the transphonologization of the N/ND opposition as one of [±nasal] on following vowel), also creates a distribution where NT is allowed, but ND is not (Měntu Land Dayak, etc.).

(iv) Other NC phenomena involve analogous contradictory processes (affrication vs. de-affrication, aspiration vs. de-aspiration, nasalization vs. de-nasalization).

On the one hand, these specific conclusions might be interpreted to support the general proposition developed in section II that phonetic determinism is not a property of synchronic phonologies, and therefore should not be incorporated as the driving force within synchronic phonological theory. On the other hand, the existence of what I'm calling "processes" vs. "counter-processes" may simply highlight the richness and complexity of the phonetic-phonology interface. Either way, we are left with the problem of explaining such bidirectionalities as those in section III.E. There are at least two possible explanations for the existence of the contradictory processes in (38).

First, the indicated processes are indeed phonetically driven, while the corresponding counter-processes are the result of non-phonetic factors, for example, restructuring, analogy, grammatical factors.

Second, both the processes and counter-processes are phonetically driven, but by different, sometimes contradictory demands.

It is this latter possibility that I would like to consider in this brief conclusion. As indicated in (45a)), postnasal devoicing, affrication, aspiration, and denasalization fall within the class of processes frequently referred to as fortition, vs. the lenition processes of voicing, deaffrication, deaspiration, and nasalization in (45b).

(45)

    a. fortition: devoicing, affrication, aspiration and denasalization
    b. voicing: deaffrication, deaspiration, nasalization

It is tempting to attribute these contradictory processes to what Dressler (1985, pp. 41–42) refers to as the "age-old distinction between clarity (optimization of perception) and ease of articulation." Could the process/counter-process distinction be due to this dichotomy? Specifically, can the processes in (45b) have an articulatory motivation — on the assumption that they would require less effort — while those in (45a) serve the function of reinforcing perceptual cues needed to make relevant contrasts in the respective languages?

Several colleagues have proposed to me that, although favored as an NC articulation, ND is perceptually non-optimal in terms of its opposition with N. Thus, when ND → NT in Tswana, the result is an output articulation that is more perceptually distinct from N than the input ND. The perceptual precariousness of an N/ND opposition would, in this interpretation, be resolved in favor of N/NT in Tswana, but would result in merger in situations such as in Sea Dayak, repeated in (46).

(46)

a.	NV	>	NṼ
b.	NDV	>	NV

However, as I have already commented, it is hard to see what is "advantageous" or "optimized" in (46), where an opposition is created between oral and nasalized vowels only after nasal consonants. It would appear that one precarious perceptual contrast (N/ND) is replaced by an even worse one — nasalized vs. oral vowels contrasting only after nasal consonants. Presumably, (46b) is not articulatorily driven or these languages would have "fixed up" the nasal+voiceless stop sequence first. Thus, if certain of the NC counter-processes are perceptually rather than articulatorily driven, the force behind them may not be optimization.[46] An alternative diachronic interpretation, based on Ohala (1993), is indicated in (47).

(47) Alternative diachronic interpretation, based on Ohala (1993)

a.	NS > NTS	hypocorrection	[–cont, –nasal] transition between N & S is misinterpreted as intentional/structural
b.	NTS > NS	hypercorrection	[–cont, –nasal] spec. of TS is misinterpreted (factored away) as transition between N & S

In the case of postnasal affrication in (47a), the [–cont, –nasal] transition between a nasal and a voiceless fricative is misinterpreted as intentional and therefore phonologized as a structural property of the language. The counter-process in (47b), deaffrication, occurs when the [–cont, –nasal] specification of the voiceless fricative is misinterpreted as an intrinsic transition between the nasal a fricative (and hence factored away). Ohala's notions of hypocorrection and hypercorrection thus allow for the bidirectional postnasal processes in (38), but need to be further validated in the other cases.

Whether phonological states and processes reflect a tug of war between articulation and perception or between phonetics and grammar, or both, I hope to have shown that one does not predict what is attested vs. not attested on the basis of a single dimension alone. For reasons we have considered, synchronic input/output relations that mimic phonetically motivated sound changes will be more frequent than those that do not. Input/output relations will be less frequent if they require the interplay of more than one sound change and/or a restructuring which draws on the grammatical side of phonology, for example, the paradigm. Characterizing a phonological state as rare is, potentially, quite different from claiming that it is unattested. A phonological property may be unattested for one of two reasons.[47] First, we may not yet have found a language in which the right set of factors have interacted to produce such a state. In this case the property is, in principle, attestable. On the other hand, a phonological property may be unattested because it is ruled out by some universal principle of language. In this case, we might instead refer to it as unattestable. As pointed out in section II, a major goal of phonological theory has been to characterize what is a possible phonological system, that is, what is attestable vs. unattestable. Scholars will disagree with respect to how successful this program has been. As indicated, phonetic determinism is essential in understanding what is likely to become phonology. It appears to have less to say about developments subsequent to the phonologization process, since languages do develop "crazy rules" (Bach & Harms, 1968).

The major outstanding question, therefore, is the following. If the phonetics does not constrain post-phonologized phonology, what does? What determines the limits on "denaturalized" phonology? The general response has been to seek cognitive constraints on phonological computability. However, even admitting such limitations, we are still left with a vast array of possible phonologies. This is the negative result. The positive result of this study is that it is possible to gain insight into the workings of phonology by viewing it as the mediator of two poles — the phonetics and the grammar — and by taking an essentially diachronic perspective.

ACKNOWLEDGMENTS

This paper was developed as part of a joint seminar that I taught in the Fall of 1998 with John Ohala entitled "Phonetics in Phonogy: Where It Is, Where It Isn't," and presented in various versions at the Institut de Phonétique (Paris III), the Laboratoire Dynamique du Langage (Université Lumière Lyons/CNRS), the Linguistic Society of America Annual Meeting (1999, Los Angeles), UCLA, Stanford, UC Santa Cruz, and ICPhS Satellite Meeting on the Role of Perceptual Phenomena in Phonology. I am grateful to these audiences for their feedback as well as to Denis Creissels, Laura Downing, Sharon Inkelas, Paul Kiparsky, Michele Loporcaro, Jaye Padgett, Janet Pierrehumbert, Charles Reiss, Donca Steriade, and Ugo Vergnuzzi, who provided email comments on an earlier draft of the paper. Research on comparative Bantu has been supported in part by National Science Foundation Grant #SBR96-16330.

NOTES

1. Anderson (1981, 1985) traces this view back to Baudouin de Courtenay (1895/1972). Many generative phonologists in the late 1960s and early 1970s were particularly impressed by the study of natural rules, culminating in the movements known as "natural phonology" (Stampe, 1969; Donegan & Stampe, 1979) and "natural generative phonology" (Vennemann, 1974; Hooper, 1976).

2. A number of intermediate positions can doubtless be distinguished between phonetic integration, on the one hand, and phonological autonomy on the other.

3. Pater's constraint is given as *NC, where he uses C to stand for voiceless obstruents. In this study I use T to stand for voiceless stops, D for voiced stops, and C to stand for any obstruent.

4. This point has, of course, been repeatedly made in the literature (see especially Anderson, 1981). In my own work (Hyman, 1975a,b), I have emphasized the potential differences between synchronic and diachronic naturalness. The distinction is particularly useful in the case of tone (Hyman & Schuh, 1984). Many eastern and southern Bantu languages have a synchronic process by which a high tone is shifted to a metrically strong position, for example, the penultimate syllable, which can be several tone-bearing units to the right. Goldsmith (1987) has attributed this to a synchronic principle, the Tone–Accent Attraction Principle, whose effect would be to accomplish this shift. However, it is clear that such a long-distance shift could not have taken place in a single step, diachronically. Rather than a rule of high tone shift, other languages from throughout the Bantu zone have a rule of high tone SPREADING to a metrically strong position, which creates a sequence of high tone-bearing units. Some of these languages variably lower all but the last of these highs. The high-tone shift languages are, thus, those where this subsequent lowering process has become obligatory. Wherever evidence is available (see especially Cassimjee & Kisseberth, 1992, and Downing, 1990), it invariably points to the synchronically natural rule of high-tone shift deriving from the "telescoping" of the natural diachronic processes of high tone spreading and high tone lowering.

5. The opposite conclusion would be equally valid by the economy argument. In order not to duplicate, one should keep phonetics out of phonology: "Duplication of the principles of acoustics and acquisition inside the grammar constitutes a violation of Occam's razor and thus must be avoided" (Hale & Reiss, 1998, p. 7).

6. Interestingly, the most common demonstration of complementary distribution in introductory linguistics courses may have this character: the (non-)aspiration of voiceless stops in English.

7. Thus, compare Vennemann's statement offered as a prelude to his arguments in favor of incorporating the syllable into then-current phonological theory: "I require of a theory of grammar that it provide a notational framework in which grammatical processes are formulizable in a general and explanatory way. It is not sufficient to require generality of a grammatical formulation. An intelligent linguist can express any grammatical process in any framework without loss of generality. The more important requirement is that of explanatoriness. A language-specific grammatical formula (i.e., a rule in a grammar) must directly refer to its own motivation, i.e., its explanation in the metatheory, the theory of grammar" (Vennemann, 1971, p. 1).

8. The intersection of phonetics and grammar in (1) can, in turn, be interpreted on different planes, for example, synchronic, diachronic, and sociolinguistic, and must also intersect with semantics and pragmatics.

9. Note that Ohala makes another prediction. If the C_1 of a VC_1C_2V sequence *is* released, then we do not expect place assimilation at all. In fact, cases of "antigemination" (McCarthy, 1986) bear this out. In Afar (Bliese, 1981), a syncope rule derives digb-é 'I married' from /digib-é/. The same rule fails to apply to /adad-é/ 'I/he trembled,' thus realized [adad-é], because the ungrammatical output *add-é would result in two identical consonants in sequence (an OCP violation, as McCarthy points out). Bliese (1981, p. 25) expresses his surprise at this condition: "Since the language accepts geminates, it is not obvious why they are avoided here." The answer comes from the fact that coda consonants are released in Afar: "Nonhomorganic consonants have an audible transition when contiguous. The sound of the release precedes that of the onset of the following consonant. Between fricatives and voiced consonants, and after voiced consonants, the release is a shwa. [. . .] After other voiceless consonants, the release can be heard by the escaping of the oral air trapped behind the closure before the beginning of the next closure" (Bliese 1981, p. 246), that is, the above-cited form digb-é is pronounced [digᵇbé]. Thus, what would be expected if syncope applied to /adad-é/ is [adˀd-é]. I conclude that what is thus avoided in Afar is a sequence of homorganic *released* consonants (cf. Odden, 1988 for additional discussion of anti-germination in terms of release).

10. There are other examples as well. One that is particularly striking comes from Hayu, a Himalayish language spoken in Nepal (Michailovsky, 1988). In this language a suffix-initial velar consonant will assimilate in place to a preceding labial-final root consonant, for example, /dip-ŋo/ 'he pinned me (in wrestling)' → dipmo (→ diʔmo by other rules). Also presumably related to the base/affix distinction are the suffixing languages in which C-initial suffixes drop their C when the base to which they are attached ends in a consonant.

11. The reason for placing the [w] in parenthesis is that it remains present only when a labial immediately precedes passive -w-. In other cases it is lost, for example, Proto-Bantu *i-N-búa> i-n-ja 'dog.'

12. Sibanda (1998) speculates that this has to do with the fact that Ndebele [β] corresponds to implosive [ɓ] in other Nguni languages, for example, Xhosa. The palatalized consonant thus appears to preserve the historical glottality.

13. Interestingly, non-suffixed -VC- roots take the passive allomorph -iw-, which does not condition palatalization. Thus, -eβ-a 'steal' passivizes as -eβ-iw-a 'be stolen', not *-ec'w-a (Sibanda, 1998).

14. The best known inhibitory factors appear not to be segmental, but rather prosodic, for example, rules that are sensitive to syllabification. Thus, the restricted environment VC__CV in which syncope applies in Yawelmani (Kisseberth, 1970) is designed to guarantee that there will be no complex onsets or codas in a Yawelmani syllable. Another example is the anti-gemination phenomenon cited in note 9, which also is a response to impending syncope. Much rarer are similar inhibitory effects to strictly segmental rulesr. Cf. in this connection the discussion in section III.A concerning the non-devoicing of prenasalized consonants in Basaá.

15. Where *p does not fricate to [s], it instead weakens to [w], for example, *-pá- → -wá- 'give', except before *j and lax *i, where *p > y, for example, *-pít- > -yít- 'pass'. This has nothing to do with the frication process under discussion here.

16. In Hyman (1997), I argued for the opposite interpretation: frication began tautomorphemically and later spread to heteromorphemic contexts, not quite reaching the labials. In this interpretation, one must, however, ask why only *p and *b are exempt from frication in derived environments.

17. Cf. "it is only through a fine-grained phonetic analysis that a true and general account of phonological processes may be gained" (Ohala, 1997).

18. AIso ultimately to be considered are sequences such as N+TS, N+DZ, N+L, N+G, and N+N, where L = liquids and G = glides.

19. Although the likely underlying form of this prefix is alveolar, that is, n–, I show it here as N–. Note also that the consonants written c, j are affricates, that is [tʃ, dʒ].

20. Interestingly, Bantu languages that voice stops after nasals split in their treatment of N + voiceless fricatives. Yao and Bukusu have nasal effacement (NS → S), while Kikuyu and Nande have voicing (NS → NZ).

21. What one would ideally like to find is a language where an NV– prefix loses its vowel before a consonant-initial root unless that consonant is a voiceless stop, for example, mu-bVCV → m-bVCV, but mu-pVCV does not become *m-pVCV. While I have not found any such case, see the discussion in section III.B of an analogous rule in Tswana that has direct relevance to this issue.

22. The voiced variants may also be pronounced as the continuants [β, r, ɣ], particularly intervocalically.

23. Since I do not have instrumental data, I cannot state with certainty that there is a complete lack of phonetic devoicing of ND phrase-finally. However, these consonants have always been transcribed and described as voiced, including by native speakers: "la présence d'une nasale non syllabique précédente sonorise la consonne et exige que l'on marque la variante sonore. On aura ainsi [ámb] et non [ámp]. [. . .] les lois du langage exigent que le phonème soit sonorisé" (Lemb & de Gastines, 1973, p. 25). This conforms with my own observations, having worked on Basaá myself with several speakers.

24. Unaspirated stops are variably ejectivized in Tswana, which most scholars consider to be a redundant feature of unaspirated stops, perhaps "enhancing" their contrast with aspirated stops.

25. This is reminiscent of what happens when NT undergoes aspiration. Whereas some languages, for example, ki-Kongo and ci-Cewa, have NT → NT^h, others such as Swahili and Venda lose the conditioning nasal and have NT → T^h.

26. The view that devoicing has become morphologized has been expressed by certain Sotho-Tswana specialists. Dickens (1977, pp. 166–167), for instance, takes this position because the reflexive prefix i- also has this devoicing effect: i-pon-e 'see yourself!,' i-tis-e 'watch yourself!,' i-karab-e 'answer yourself!' Dickens supposes that an earlier form of the reflexive prefix was *in-, with the nasal dropping out in all environments.

27. This is not to say that there is no difference between "phonological rules of different types" (Anderson, 1975). Within lexical phonology and morphology (Kiparsky, 1982, 1985), it is known that so-called stratum 1 rules may have different properties from either stratum 2 or post-lexical rules. Perhaps it is, then, stratum 1 rules that need not be phonetically driven. Since stratum 1 typically refers to the stem domain in Bantu, while the first person singular prefix N– comes in at stratum 2, we would have to treat these alternations as stem alternates if we were to seriously pursue this proposal.

28. The table in (21) includes only N + [–cont] consonants. Creissels also include a few borrowings that have nasal + voiceless fricative, for example, émɸìlʼpɔ́ 'envelope', khánsàtá 'concert', pénsélé 'pencil' (cf. also the last syllable of ám̀búléǹsí 'ambulance'). These forms are exceptional in that we expect postnasal affrication, that is, NS → NTS^h, in Tswana. Thus, non-exceptional N+ɸ and N+s becomes [mp^h] and [nts^h], respectively (cf. (26)).

29. It also apparently doesn't apply when the root begins with /m/. However, it optionally applies, with dialectal variation as well, when the root-initial consonant is /ɸ/ (from Proto-Bantu *p). When it does apply in this context, /ɸ/ obligatorily becomes [h], for example, mu-ɸáxó ~ m-háxó 'food for a journey' (Cole, 1955/1992, p. 48).

30. Thus, *mu-tánd-é 'love him!' is realized mʊ-rát-é in Tswana vs. mʊ-rád̪-é in Lobedu.

31. Of course, the interesting question is why /b/ and /l/ do not undergo devoicing here, as they do after the first person sg. object prefix N–. I will demonstrate below that postnasal devoicing is a consequence of postnasal hardening, which applied only to input N+C.

32. Generally speaking, *k is realized [k^h, h] before *u and [kx^h, x] before other vowels.

33. Recall, however, from note 26, that the proto consonants have the same realization after reflexive *i- (or *iN–?) as they do after *N.

34. In Dickens (1977), the same author assumes that *ND was first simplified to D, which then became T'. In my survey of Bantu I have, curiously, not found any language where *ND > D. On the other hand, as seen in (30) below, some quite distant languages have undergone the same *ND → T change as in Sotho-Tswana. Dickens does indicate in his note 9 that *ND > NT' > T' might also be a possible interpretation (and, in any case, would have to be assumed where the N is not deleted).

35. As indicated above, it is also possible that aspiration already occurred on Proto-Bantu voiceless stops, in which case it was preserved postnasally, but fed affrication + deaffrication in other contexts (k^h > kx^h > x).

36. This change from [ṛ] to [d] in Tswana and elsewhere in Sotho-Tswana is quite recent. Cole (1955/1992, p. 28) still records it as such, but indicates that [d] "is now used by most of the younger generation of Tswana speakers." Other scholars with whom I have spoken indicate that they have never encountered [ṛ].

37. The same questions arise in an analysis that would represent these two consonants as underspecified for [continuant].

38. Besides using hypercorrection as a "wild card," Ohala actually would be suspicious of this interpretation for two reasons. First, he does not consider the feature [voice] to be a good candidate for dissimilation. Second, he does not expect dissimilatory processes to create new segments. The only source of unaspirated (variably ejective) voiceless stops is from *ND in Sotho-Tswana.

39. Bubi falls within those northwest Bantu languages that have "double reflexes" of the Proto-Bantu consonants (Janssens, 1993). Thus, *p also sometimes corresponds to [h], while *t sometimes corresponds to [l]. *k seems always to drop out, however.

40. Diachronically we can assume that there has been a rule inversion, that is, that [β, r, ɣ] were originally voiceless stops, preserved as such in postnasal position. For further discussion, see Blanchon (1991).

41. In Ohalian terms, listeners parse the NDV sequence not as the original, intended ND-V, but rather as N-DV, where the oral release of the nasal is attributed to the orality on the V (which in turn stands in contrast to the nasalized vowel of /NV/). As a consequence, they then hypocorrect and subsequently leave out the oral release D altogether. Cf. Ladefoged & Maddieson (1996, pp. 103–104) for further discussion of the phonetic issues involved.

42. Only the labial and dental changes are indicated in (36), although ɲj > ɲɲ is also often attested. On the other hand, Italian dialects show a reluctance to extend the process to create a geminate velar nasal (ŋg > ŋŋ). The reason for this appears to be one of structure-preservation, since [ŋ] otherwise occurs only before a velar stop in Italian. It is interesting that Romance languages avoid the velar nasal, while Germanic languages seem to welcome the new "phoneme" (e.g., all varieties of English have lost the final *g in words like sing, strong). The difference appears to have to do with the origins of the ND simplifications. Whereas the process first affects ND in coda position in Germanic (and then spreads to intervocalic position), ND > NN is an intervocalic process in Italian. Thus, what appears to be avoided in the latter case is pre-vocalic [ŋ]. As has often been noted, [ŋ] appears to be privileged in coda position and avoided in onset position. Many languages restrict [ŋ] to coda position, where diachronic *m, *n > ŋ also frequently occurs (see, e.g., Chen, 1973).

43. While postnasal affrication is a form of postnasal hardening, involving an intrusive or emergent stop (Clements, 1987; Ohala, 1997), postnasal de-affrication is, I assume, a false parse or hypercorrection (Ohala, 1993).

44. While researchers have tended to view the opposition as one of VOT, again, the issue of unaspirated vs. ejective comes up. Perhaps the process can be viewed as postnasal ejectivization, rather than postnasal deaspiration (which I have, thus far, not found to be attested without concomitant glottalization). It is possible that we have an areal feature here. The Nguni languages have been in contact with the Sotho-Tswana languages — and both have NT'. What is interesting is that the former develop NT' from deaspiration, while the latter develop NT' from devoicing.

45. Meinhof (1932) speculates that an analogy is involved, perhaps a false extension in undoing Meinhof's rule.

46. There is the additional problem of finding support for the claimed optimizations. One might, for example, claim that denasalization occurs so as to enhance the N/NN distinction, which now becomes N/ND. However, what about the resulting merger of /NN/ with /ND/? Does it matter? Do certain claimed perceptually driven processes depend on their being (or not being) a prior opposition? Some of these issues are taken up by Flemming (1995) and others, but more work is clearly needed in this area.

47. See Hyman (1975a), Anderson (1981), Janda (1984), Blevins & Garrett (1998), Dolbey & Hansson (1999), among others, for further discussion.

References

Anderson, S. R. (1975). On the interaction of phonological rules of various types. *Journal of Linguistics*, *11*, 39–62.

Anderson, S. R. (1981). Why phonology isn't natural. *Linguistic Inquiry*, *12*, 493–539.

Anderson, S. R. (1985). *Phonology in the twentieth century*. Chicago: University of Chicago Press.

Archangeli, D., & Pulleyblank, D. (1994). *Grounded phonology*. Cambridge: MIT Press.

Bach, E., & Robert T. H. (1972). How do languages get crazy rules? In R. P. Stockwell & R. K. S. Macaulay (Eds.), *Linguistic change and generative theory* (pp. 1–21). Bloomington: Indiana University Press.

Baudouin de Courtenay, J. (1972). An attempt at a theory of phonetic alternations. In E. Stankiewicz (Ed.), *A Baudouin de Courtenay anthology* (pp. 144–212). Bloomington: Indiana University Press. (Original work published 1895.)

Beckman, J. (1997). Positional faithfulness, positional neutralization and Shona vowel harmony. *Phonology*, *14*, 1–46.

Blanchon, J. A. (1991). Le pounou (B.43), le mpongwé (B.11a) et l'hypothèse fortis/lenis. *Pholia*, *6*, 49–83. Laboratoire Dynamique du Language, CNRS/Université Lumière Lyons.

Blevins, J., & Garrett, A. (1998). The origin of consonant–vowel metathesis. *Language*, *74*, 508–556.

Bliese, L. F. (1981). *A generative grammar of Afar*. Arlington: Summer Institute of Linguistics.

Buckley, E. (1999). *On the naturalness of unnatural rules*. Paper presented at the Workshop on American Indigenous Languages, University of California, Santa Barbara, 14–16 May 1999. Unpublished manuscript, University of Pennsylvania, Philadelphia.

Carter, H. (1984). Geminates, nasals and sequence structure in Kongo. *Oso, 3*, 1, 101–114.

Cassimjee, F., & Kisseberth, C. W. (1992). On the tonology of depressor consonants: Evidence from Mijikenda and Nguni. In *Special session on tone system typology: Proceedings of the 18th Annual Meeting of the Berkeley Linguistics Society* (pp. 26–40). Berkeley: Berkeley Linguistics Society.

Chen, M. (1970). Vowel length variation as a function of the voicing of the consonant environment. *Phonetica, 22*, 129–159.

Chen, M. (1973). Cross-dialectal comparison: A case study and some theoretical considerations. *Journal of Chinese Linguistics, 1*, 38–63.

Clements, G. N. (1986). Compensatory lengthening and consonant gemination in Luganda. In L. Wetzels & E. Sezer (Eds.), *Studies in compensatory lengthening* (pp. 37–77). Dordrecht: Foris.

Clements, G. N. (1987). Phonological feature representation and the description of intrusive stops. In *Papers from the parasession on autosegmental and metrical phonology: Chicago Linguistics Society* (pp. 29–50). Chicago: Chicago Linguistics Society.

Cole, D. T. (1992). *An introduction to Tswana grammar*. Cape Town: Longmans. (Original work published 1955.)

Court, C. (1970). Nasal harmony and some Indonesian sound laws. In S. A. Wurm & D. C. Laycock (Eds.), *Pacific linguistics*, Series C, No. 13. Canberra: Australian National University.

Creissels, D. (1996). *Lexique Tswana-Français on diskette*. Lyons.

Creissels, D. (1999). Remarks on the sound correspondences between Proto-Bantu and Tswana (S.31), with particular attention to problems involving *j (or *y), *j and sequences *NC. In J.-M. Hombert & L. M. Hyman (Eds.), *Recent advances in bantu historical linguistics* (pp. 297–334). Stanford: CSLI.

Dickens, P. R. (1977). Grammar simplification vies with rule inversion: The effect of historical deletion of nasals on modern Sotho. *African Studies, 36*, 161–170.

Dickens, P. R. (1984). The history of so-called strengthening in Tswana. *Journal of African Languages and Linguistics, 6*, 97–125.

Dolbey, A. E. & Hansson, G. O. (1999). *Phonetic naturalness is not encoded in synchronic phonology*. Paper presented at HILP.

Donegan, P., & Stampe, D. (1979). The study of natural phonology. In D. Dinnsen (Eds.), *Current approaches to phonological theory* (pp. 126–173). Bloomington: Indiana University Press.

Downing, L. (1990). Local and metrical shift in Nguni. *Studies in African Linguistics*, *21*, 261–317.

Downing, L. (2000). Prosodic stem ≠ prosodic word in Bantu. *Proceedings of Berlin Conference on the Phonological Word.* In press.

Flemming, E. (1995). *Auditory features in phonology.* Unpublished doctoral disssertation, University of California, Los Angeles.

Fontaney, L. (1980). Le verbe. In F. Nsuka-Nkutsi (Ed.), *Eléments de description du punu* (pp. 51–114). Lyons: Université Lyons.

Goldsmith, J. (1987). Tone and accent, and getting the two together. *Berkeley Linguistic Society*, *13*, 88–104.

Hale, M., & Reiss, C. (1998). *Substance abuse and dysfunctionalism: current trends in phonology.* Unpublished manuscript, Concordia University, Montréal.

Hannan, M. (1987). *Standard Shona Dictionary.* Harare: The College Press. (Original work published 1959.)

Harris, J. (1994). *English sound structure.* Oxford: Blackwell.

Hayes, B. (1995). *A phonetically driven, optimality-theoretic account of post-nasal voicing.* Paper presented at the Tilburg Derivationality Residue Conference.

Hayes, B. (1997). *Phonetically driven phonology: The role of optimality theory and inductive grounding.* Unpublished manuscript, University of California, Los Angeles. (Written for the 1996 Milwaukee Conference on Formalism and Functionalism in Linguistics.)

Herbert, R. K. (1986). *Language universals, markedness theory, and natural phonetic processes.* Berlin: Mouton de Gruyter.

Hock, H. H. (1991). *Principles of historical linguistics.* Berlin: Mouton de Gruyter.

Hooper, J. B. (1976). *An introduction to natural generative phonology.* New York: Academic Press.

Huffman, M., & Hinnebusch, T. (1998). The phonetic nature of "voiceless" nasals in Pokomo: Implications for sound change. *Journal of African Languages and Linguistics* *19*, 1–19.

Hyman, L. M. (1975a). *Phonology: Theory and analysis.* New York: Holt, Rinehart & Winston.

Hyman, L. M. (1975b). Nasal states and nasal processes. In C. A. Ferguson, L. M. Hyman, & J. J. Ohala (Eds.), *Nasálfest: Papers from a symposium on nasals and nasalization* (pp. 249–264). Stanford: Language Universals Project, Stanford University.

Hyman, L. M. (1977). Phonologization. In A. Juilland (Ed.), *Linguistic studies presented to Joseph H. Greenberg* (pp. 407–418). Saratoga: Anma Libri.

Hyman, L. M. (1981). *Noni grammatical structure.* Southern California Occasional Papers in Linguistics, No. 9. Los Angeles: University of Southern California.

Hyman, L. M. (1995). Nasal consonant harmony at a distance: The case of Yaka. *Studies in African Linguistics*, *24*, 5–30.

Hyman, L. M. (1997). La morphologie et la "fricativation" diachronique en bantou. *Mémoires de la Société de Linguistique de Paris, Grammaticalisation et reconstruction*, 5, 163–175.

Hyman, L. M., & Ngunga, A. (1997). Two kinds of moraic nasal in Ciyao. *Studies in African Linguistics*, 26, 131–163.

Hyman, L. M., & Schuh, R. G. (1984). Universals of tone rules: Evidence from West Africa. *Linguistic Inquiry*, 5, 81–115.

Janda, R. (1984). Why morphological metathesis rules are rare: On the possibility of historical explanation in linguistics. *Berkeley Linguistic Society*, 10, 87–103.

Janson, T. (1991/1992). Southern Bantu and Makua, *Sprache und Geschichte in Afrika*, 12/13, 1–44.

Janssens, B. (1992). Correspondances PB > bubi. Unpublished manuscript, Université Libre de Bruxelles.

Janssens, B. (1993). *Doubles reflexes consonantiques: Quatre études sur le bantou de zone A*. Unpublished doctoral disssertation, Université Libre de Bruxelles.

Katamba, F., & Hyman, L. M. (1991). Nasality and morpheme structure constraints in Luganda. *Africanistische Arbeitspapiere*, 25, 175–211.

Kawasaki, H. (1982). An acoustical basis for universal constraints on sound sequences. Unpublished doctoral disssertation, University of California, Berkeley.

Kaye, J. (1989). *Phonology: a cognitive view*. Hillsdale, NJ: Lawrence Erlbaum.

Kidima, L. (1991). *Tone and accent in KiYaka*. Unpublished doctoral disssertation, University of California, Los Angeles.

Kiparsky, P. (1982). Lexical phonology and morphology. In *Linguistics in the Morning Calm* (pp. 3–91). Seoul: Hanshin.

Kiparsky, P. (1985). Some consequences of lexical phonology. *Phonology [Yearbook]*, 2, 85–138.

Kirchner, R. (1998). *An effort-based approach to consonant lenition*. Unpublished doctoral disssertation, University of California, Los Angeles.

Kisseberth, C. W. (1970). On the functional unity of phonological rules. *Linguistic Inquiry*, 1, 291–306.

Kotze, A. (1998). *Notes on perfective formation in Lobedu*. Unpublished manuscript, University of South Africa.

Krüger, C. J. H., & Snyman, J.W. (n.d.). *The sound system of Setswana*. Via Afrika Limited.

Ladefoged, P., & Maddieson, I. (1996). *The sounds of the world's languages*. Oxford: Blackwell.

Lemb, P., & de Gastines, F. (1973). *Dictionnaire basaá-français*. Douala: Collège Libermann.

McCarthy, J. (1986). OCP effects: Gemination and antigemination. *Linguistic Inquiry*, 17, 207–263.

McCarthy, J., & Prince, A. (1993). Generalized alignment. In G. Booij & J. V. Marle (Eds.), *Yearbook of morphology* (pp. 79–153). Dordrecht: Kluwer.

McCarthy, J., & Prince, A. (1995). Faithfulness and reduplicative identity. In J. Beckman, et al. (Eds.), *Papers in optimality theory* (pp. 249–384). Amherst: University of Massachusetts.

Meinhof, C. (1932). *Introduction to the phonology of the Bantu languages.* Berlin: D. Reimer. Reprinted Glueckstadt: J. J. Augustin. (English translation of *Grundriss einer Lautlehre der Bantusprachen*, 1899; translated, revised and enlarged in collaboration with the author and Dr. Alice Werner by N. J. van Warmelo.)

Michailovsky, B. (1988). *La langue Hayu.* Paris: Editions du Centre National de la recherche scientifique.

Ngunga, A. (2000). *Lexical phonology and morphology of the Ciyao verb stem.* Stanford: CSLI. In press.

Odden, D. (1988). Anti-antigemination and the OCP. *Linguistic Inquiry, 19,* 451–475.

Ohala, J. J. (1974). Experimental historical phonology. In J. M. Anderson & C. Jones (Eds.), *Historical linguistics, II: Theory and description in phonology* (pp. 353–379). Amsterdam: North-Holland.

Ohala, J. J. (1975). Phonetic explanations for nasal sound patterns. In C. A. Ferguson, L. M. Hyman, & J. J. Ohala (Eds.), *Nasálfest: Papers from a symposium on nasals and nasalization* (pp. 289–316). Stanford: Language Universals Project, Stanford University.

Ohala, J. J. (1978). Southern Bantu vs. the world: The case of palatalization of labials. *Berkeley Linguistic Society, 4,* 370–386.

Ohala, J. J. (1989). Sound change is drawn from a pool of synchronic variation. In L. E. Breivik & E. H. Jahr (Eds.), *Language change: Contributions to the study of its causes* (pp. 173–198). Berlin: Mouton de Gruyter.

Ohala, J. J. (1990). The phonetics and phonology of aspects of assimilation. In J. Kingston & M. Beckman (Eds.), *Papers in laboratory phonology*, Vol. 1: *Between the grammar and physics of speech* (pp. 258–275). Cambridge: Cambridge University Press.

Ohala, J. J. (1993). The phonetics of sound change. In C. Jones (Ed.), *Historical linguistics: Problems and perspectives* (pp. 237–278). London: Longmans.

Ohala, J. J. (1996). The relation between phonetics and phonology. In W. Hardcastle & J. Laver (Eds.), *Handbook of phonetics* (pp. 674–694). Oxford: Blackwell.

Ohala, J. J. (1997). *Emergent stops.* Paper presented at Seoul International Conference on Linguistics.

Ohala, J. J., & Ohala, M. (1993). The phonetics of nasal phonology: Theorems and data. *Phonetics and Phonology, 5,* 225–249.

Pater, J. (1996). *NC. *Proceedings of the North East Linguistic Society, 26,* 227–239.

Pater, J. (1999). Austronesian nasal substitution and other NC effects. In R. Kager, H. van der Hulst, & W. Zonneveld (Eds.), *The prosody–morphology interface* (pp. 310–343). Cambridge: Cambridge University Press.

Pelling, R. J. N. (1971). *A practical Ndebele dictionary.* Harare: Longmans Zimbabwe.

Prince, A., & Smolensky, P. (1993). *Optimality theory: Constraint interaction in generative grammar.* Unpublished manuscript, Rutgers University, New Brunswick, NJ, and the University of Colorado, Boulder.

Rohlfs, G. (1949). *Historische Grammatik der Italienischen Sprache und ihrer Mundarten.* Bern: A. Francke.

Rosenthal, S. (1989). *The phonology of nasal-obstruent sequences.* Unpublished master's thesis, McGill University, Montreal, Canada.

Sibanda, G. (1998). *Labial palatalization in the Ndebele passive.* Unpublished manuscript, University of California, Berkeley.

Stampe, D. (1972). *How I spent my summer vacation.* Unpublished doctoral disssertation, University of Chicago.

Steriade, D. (1993). Closure, release and nasal contours. In M. Huffman & R. Krakow (Eds.), *Nasals, nasalization, and the velum* (pp. 401–470). Orlando: Academic Press.

Tucker, A. N. (1929). *The comparative phonetics of the Suto-Chuana group of Bantu languages.* London: Longmans, Green and Co.

Tucker, A. N. (1962). The syllable in Luganda: A prosodic approach. *Journal of African Languages, 1,* 122–166.

Vennemann, T. (1971). On the theory of syllabic phonology. *Linguistische Berichte, 18,* 1–18.

Vennemann, T. (1974). *Words and syllables in natural generative phonology.* In *Papers from the parasession on autosegmental and metrical phonology: Chicago Linguistics Society* (pp. 346–374). Chicago: Chicago Linguistics Society.

Wang, W. S.-Y., & Fillmore, C. (1961). Intrinsic cues and consonant perception. *Journal of Speech and Hearing Research, 4,* 130–136.

CHAPTER

Contrast Dispersion and Russian Palatalization

Jaye Padgett

Department of Linguistics
Stevenson College
University of California
Santa Cruz, California 95064

I. Introduction
II. Russian Palatalization: Background
III. Russian Palatalization: i vs. ɨ
IV. Contrast Shift
V. Russian Velarization
VI. Phonetic Investigation
   A. Methods
   B. Results
   C. Discussion
VII. Conclusions
   Appendix: The Carrier Sentences
   Acknowledgments
   Notes
   References

The Role of Speech Perception in Phonology

Будет ей рот раздирать до ушей небы-
валый, невозможный звук «ы».
Her mouth will be rent to the ears by the fantastic,
impossible sound "ï".

Osip Mandelshtam

I. INTRODUCTION

The hypothesis that phonological patterns are at least in part explained by functional phonetic considerations has a long history. Martinet (1952, 1964, 1974)
advocated a view in which the sometimes conflicting needs of articulatory economy and perceptual distinctiveness both played important roles. Such notions arise
again, in more explicit formulations, in the work of Liljencrants & Lindblom
(1972) and Lindblom (1986, 1990). Other representative works on the functional
underpinnings of phonology include Ohala (1983, 1990), Kohler (1990), and
Kingston & Diehl (1994), among many others.

    Yet the role that functional notions have played in the history of generative
phonology can be described at best as indirect and peripheral. Two apparent
reasons for this cleft between generative phonology and functionalism will be
mentioned here, though there are certainly others. First is the fact that languages
differ from each other in systematic and often categorical ways. If phonology is
determined by facts of the mouth and ear in some respects (to put it crudely), then
why aren't all languages the same in these respects? This objection loses its force
for many phonologists in the context of Optimality Theory (Prince & Smolensky
1993), since this widely adopted formal theory works precisely by deriving
explicit, categorical, language particular results from a prioritization of often
conflicting constraints that are considered universal. Optimality Theory has in fact
paved the way for a reemergence of functional explanations within phonological
theory (Flemming 1995; Ní Chiosáin & Padgett, to appear; Steriade, 1995—to
name just a few.[1])

    Second, I would argue, is a tension between the goals of description and
explanation. Though formal phonologists differ in how they practice, many consider it part of the job description to provide a characterization of a significant and
sometimes intricate range of facts within a particular language that is not only
theoretically revealing, but descriptively rigorous and complete. Chomsky &
Halle (1968) is a paragon example of this kind of work, even though it is itself
only a fragmentary description of English phonology. Yet it seems no easier to
derive a complete description of even a small portion of English phonology, based
on very general functional principles, than it is to derive a complete description
of, say, the sea lion, based on general evolutionary principles. Those who seek the
functional explanations necessarily pay a price in terms of descriptive coverage.

This article is a case in point, since it focuses on a single allophonic rule of Russian, a rule by which /i/ is said to emerge as [ɨ] after plain (non-palatalized) consonants. One goal of this paper is to argue for a significantly different understanding of the generalization. Specifically, non-palatalized *consonants* before *i* are *velarized*. At a more theoretical level, the paper advocates the goal of seeking explanations for allophonic processes, particularly non-assimilatory ones, rather than simply stating them or focusing on questions of distribution. In the case examined, and perhaps many others, the explanation depends on functional considerations, in particular the requirement that contrasts be sufficiently distinct. Most broadly, these results imply that the terminological distinction between 'contrastive' or 'phonemic' on the one hand and 'allophonic' on the other conceals a deeper unity between the two: allophonic processes at least sometimes serve the goal of contrast preservation.

II. RUSSIAN PALATALIZATION: BACKGROUND

Russian has the five vowel phonemes — *i*, *e*, *a*, *o*, and *u* — according to most analysts. The qualification concerns a sixth vowel, *i* (often transcribed *y* by Slavic specialists), which will be our main focus below. The consonantal phonemes of Russian are given in (1). Most of these are 'paired,' contrasting palatalized versus plain versions, notated C′ versus C here, following the practice of Slavic literature. The remaining, 'unpaired,' consonants are highlighted within bolded cells. The velars are palatalized before front vowels, otherwise plain; the rest are either invariably palatalized (*j* naturally falls within this group) or invariably not. (ʃ′ arguably can be analyzed as ʃ+tʃ′ in some dialects, as in Halle, 1959).[2]

(1)

	Labial	Dental	Post-alveolar	Palatal	Velar
Stop	p p′ b b′	t t′ d d′			k/k′ g/g′
Fricative	f f′ v v′	s s′ z z′	ʃ (ʃ′:) ʒ		x/x′
Affricate		ts	tʃ′		
Nasal	m m′	n n′			
Lateral		l l′			
Rhotic		r r′			
Glide				j	

Some examples illustrating the palatalization contrast are given below. Contrasts as in (2a–b) are prevalent in the language, while (2c) is more limited due to assimilations and neutralizations in that context.[3]

(2)

a. Before back vowels

mat	'foul language'	*m′at*	'crumpled (past part.)'
rat	'glad'	*r′at*	'row'
vol	'ox'	*v′ol*	'he led'
nos	'nose'	*n′os*	'he carried'
nu-ka	'now then!'	*n′uxa*	'scent (gen.sg.)'
suda	'court of law (gen.sg.)'	*s′uda*	'here, this way'

b. Word-finally

mat	'foul language'	*mat′*	'mother'
krof	'shelter'	*krof′*	'blood'
ugol	'corner'	*ugol′*	'(char)coal'
v′es	'weight'	*v′es′*	entire'

c. Before another consonant

polka	'shelf'	*pol′ka*	'polka'
tanka	'tank (gen. sg.)'	*tan′ka*	(name)
v′etka	'branch'	*f′et′ka*	(name)
gorka	'hill'	*gor′ko*	'bitterly'

The palatalization contrast before *e* is very limited. Consonants were allophonically palatalized in this environment historically, therefore rendered 'unpaired,' as shown in (3a). However, the existence of loan words such as *tennis* and *tent*, with a plain consonant before *e*, has effectively introduced the contrast in roots, at least for certain speakers. It remains true that *suffixation* of –*e* invariably palatalizes a preceding consonant, as shown in (3b).

(3)

a. Before *e* in roots (ignoring borrowings)

s′est′	'to sit down'	**sest′*	*n′et*	'no'	**net*
p′et′	'to sing'	**pet′*	*gd′e*	'where'	**gde*
v′et′er	'wind'	**veter*	*l′eto*	'summer'	**leto*

b. Before *e* under suffixation

dom	*dom′e*	'house, home (nom.sg./prep.sg.)'
brat	*brat′e*	'brother (nom.sg./prep.sg.)'

III. RUSSIAN PALATALIZATION: i vs. ɨ

Of particular interest here is the one remaining environment: before the phoneme *i*. Paired consonants *do* contrast here; however, this contrast is normally transcribed as shown below:

(4)

v'it'	'to twist, weave'	vit'	'to howl'
bi't	'beaten'	bit	'way of life'
t'ikat'	'to tick'	tikat'	'to address in familiar form'
xod'i	'walk!'	xodi	'gaits'
s'ito	'sieve'	sito	'sated (neut.)'

That is, after plain consonants we find not *i* but *i*. The following is the nearly ubiquitous statement, abstracting across theoretical schools — for example, Trubetzkoy (1969), Avanesov & Sidorov (1945), Halle (1959), Hamilton (1980), Sussex (1992) — there is one phoneme *i*, which is realized as *i* after plain (non-palatalized) consonants, so long as no pause intervenes, that is, within something like the phonological phrase.

This allophonic rule is quite productive in Russian. In (5a) are examples of word-initial *i* varying with *i*, the latter occurring in the standard pronunciation when a plain consonant precedes. This can lead to minimal pairs of the sort shown in (5b) (see Gvozdev, 1949; Reformatskii, 1957; Halle, 1959, and references therein).

(5)

a.	ivan	'Ivan'	**k** ivanu	'to Ivan'
			brat ivana	'Ivan's brother'
	ital'ija	'Italy'	**v** ital'iju	'to Italy'
			nad ital'ijej	'above Italy'
b.	**k**'ir'e	'Kira (dat.sg.)'	**k** ir'e	'to Ira'
	v'ital'iju	'Vitalij (dat.sg.)'	**v** ital'iju	'to Italy'

Indeed, *i* does not occur word-initially (unless preceded in the phrase by a word-final plain consonant, as above), so that there are no words such as **ivan*, **italija*. Nor does *i* occur following a vowel in Russian, for example, **poigrat'*, **poiskat'*, cf. occurring *poigrat'* 'to play a little,' *poiskat'* 'to look around for.'

We find the variation also within words, for example when a root that is otherwise *i*-initial is prefixed with a morpheme ending in a plain consonant, as shown in (6a), or when a suffix which is otherwise *i*-initial occurs following a plain stem-final consonant (6b). Many morphemes display this variation within a word.[4] It is also found in so-called stump compounds such as *p'edinst'itut* derived from *p'edagog'itʃesk'ij inst'itut* 'pedagogical institute.'

(6)

a.	igrat'	'to play (imperf.)'	sigrat'	'to play (perf.)'
	iskat'	'to search (imperf.)'	otiskat'	'to find'
b.	ugol	'corner (sg.)'	ugli	(pl.)
	ugol'	'(char)coal (sg.)'	ugl'i	(pl.)

Finally, (7) shows examples of a reduction characteristic of Russian patronymics. The sequence *ov/ev* found in patronymics is omitted in the reduced form,
causing a preceding consonant to come together with a following would-be *i*. If
the consonant in question is plain, then the vowel is realized as *ɨ*, as shown in (7b)
(compare (7a)). Such short forms are essentially lexicalized; the examples shown
here are from *War and Peace*, where reduced forms are sometimes spelled in
dialogue:

(7)

a.	*al'eks'ejitʃ*	<	*al'eks'ejev'itʃ*	b.	*ivanitʃ*	<	*ivanov'itʃ*
	andr'ejitʃ	<	*andr'ejev'itʃ*		*k'ir'il'itʃ*	<	*k'ir'ilov'itʃ*

Throughout the large literature on Russian, this allophonic variation is
discussed in a way that would be familiar to any phonology student: the comple-
mentarity of *i and ɨ* is pointed out, and the generalization stated above regarding
their distribution is noted. Yet there are questions one might pose about it. Why,
for example, should *i* become *ɨ* after plain consonants? As stated, such a requirement makes no obvious sense. Why should a *plain* consonant exert any such
effect? We might also ask, is there a reason why this requirement holds of Russian
in particular, and not of other languages that are abounding in plain consonants?
In principle, could such a rule occur in English? Finally, why is *ɨ* limited to *only*
this environment, following plain consonants within a phonological phrase?

IV. CONTRAST SHIFT

Another language with a palatalization contrast is Irish. Ní Chiosáin & Padgett (to
appear) discuss the Irish facts, noting that the actual realization of consonants
varies between palatalized, velarized, and plain, depending on the following
vowel. These facts, illustrated below, hold only of consonants before long vowels.
(Short vowels take their backness value from neighboring consonants.) As seen in
(8a–c), before back vowels the contrast is realized as palatalized versus plain.
However, when the following vowel is front, as in (8d–e), the contrast is realized
as *plain* versus *velarized*, respectively.

(8)

a.	fʲuː	'worth'	fuːə	'hate'
b.	bʲoː	'alive'	boː	'cow'
c.	fʲɔːn	'skin, flay'	fɔːn	'straying, wandering'
d.	biː	'be (IMP.)'	bˠiː	'yellow'
e.	beːl	'mouth'	bˠeːl/bˠiːl	'danger'

Why should the facts turn out this way? There is a relatively straightforward answer that calls on the notion of contrast dispersion: sounds in contrast should be sufficiently distinct. (See the references cited in the introduction.) To begin simply, consider the contrast between a *j*-vowel sequence and the same vowel alone, as in *ja* versus *a* and so on. (9) gives a rank ordering of such contrasts, for the five common vowels, based on the movement of the second vowel formant. In the transition from *j* to *i*, F2 moves very little; it moves farther in the transition from *j* to *e*, and so on. Therefore the difference between *ji* and *i* is smaller than that between *je* and *e*, etc., judging in this way. Differences in F2 are well known to roughly correlate with differences in perceived backness (as well as roundness), and the ranking shown in (9) is impressionistically clear at least for *ji–i* through *ja–a*:

(9) *ji–i* < *je–e* < *ja–a* < *jo–o* < *ju–u*

Assuming that there is a tendency for languages to favor more distinct contrasts over less distinct ones, all else being equal, then (9) makes markedness predictions. Considering again just *ji–i* through *ja–a*, for example, there should be languages that allow all three contrasts, languages that rule out specifically *ji–i*, and languages that rule out *ji–i* and *je–e*. An example of the first is English, with contrasts such as [i:st] 'east'/[ji:st] 'yeast,' [e:l] 'ale'/[je:l] 'Yale,' and [ɑn] 'on'/[jɑn] 'yon.' Spanish is an example of the second; it lacks the first contrast, but has pairs such as [el] 'he'/[jel] 'gall' and [a'ser] 'to do'/[ja'ser] 'to rest.' Japanese exemplifies the last kind of language, lacking the first two, but having *ja–a* (Itô & Mester 1995), for example, [aki] 'autumn'/[jaki] 'to sear.' (All of these languages in addition allow *jo–o* and *ju–u*.) On the other hand, there should *not* be languages that allow specifically *ji–i* while ruling out *je–e* and *ja–a*, or languages allowing *ji–i* and *je–e* while ruling out *ja–a*, all else being equal. This certainly seems to be the correct prediction. Putting aside these markedness implications, however, the crosslinguistic tendency to avoid *ji–i* and *je–e* is well documented and has an evident auditory basis. (See especially Maddieson & Precoda 1992.) Similar reasoning extends to the contrasts *wu/u*, *wo/o*, and *wa/a*.

Though a contrast in palatalization is more complex, with other phonetic properties such as frication or burst potentially contributing to the distinction, we can nevertheless posit, by the same reasoning again, that the contrast *Cʲa* versus *Ca* should be favored over *Cʲe* versus *Ce*, and that both of these should do better than *Cʲi* versus *Ci*, all else equal, where *C* is any consonant. There is a good deal of evidence that this is the case. In Northern Estonian, and in Karakaštan, the plain versus palatalized contrast is neutralized before front vowels, according to Kawasaki (1982) and Ohala & Kawasaki-Fukumori (1997). The same holds of Japanese (Itô & Mester, 1995). Turning to Slavic, the contrast is also neutralized before front vowels in Bulgarian and Polabian (the latter a West Slavic language now extinct), and before *i* in Polish.[5] Macedonian lacks a general palatalization contrast, but contrasts *ł* versus *l*. (The latter can be pronounced as palatalized.) This contrast is neutralized before *i* and *e*. (For an overview of the Slavic facts discussed in this paper, and references, see the papers in Comrie & Corbett, 1993.) Significantly, there are no cases where a palatalization contrast is favored specifically before *front* vowels, nor to my knowledge are there languages Contrasting C^ji versus Ci, but not C^je versus Ce, that is, the implications for possible glide-vowel contrasts discussed earlier appear to hold for palatalization as well.

This independent evidence that the contrast plain versus palatalized is avoided before front vowels in languages bears significantly on the Irish facts. Irish can be seen as a language that takes a more assertive approach to the problem than those mentioned above. A contrast is not lost but maintained in this environment in Irish, but its realization is *shifted* from plain versus palatalized to velarized versus plain, respectively. Hence it would be better to call the Irish contrast one of frontness/backness, and not simply of palatalization. This contrast shift implies that Irish requires the frontness/backness contrast to be at least as distant as γi–*i*, which is roughly on the order of *ja–a*, again judging by F2 transitions. In this regard, Irish resembles Japanese. It is different in that it maintains all contrasts by invoking velarization before front vowels, while Japanese does not maintain the contrast before front vowels. Ní Chiosáin & Padgett (to appear) give an account of the Irish facts along these lines within Optimality Theory.

There is an alternative account for such facts well known to phonologists, involving the Obligatory Contour Principle (OCP), a constraint prohibiting adjacent identical elements (Leben, 1973; Goldsmith, 1976; McCarthy, 1986). For the case at hand the restriction would involve occurrences of [–back][–back], ruling out forms such as *je* and *ji*. The OCP account is significantly different from one appealing to contrast, since the latter does not specifically disfavor forms such as *ji* and *je*. Rather, it disfavors the *contrasts ji/i* and *je/e*, while leaving open the possibility that a language without these contrasts will favor *either ji* and *je*, or *i* and *e*, depending on other factors such as the requirement of an onset, or assimilation, versus articulatory or structural minimalism.[6]

There are several important disadvantages to the OCP account. First, it does not predict the markedness implications just detailed. Why is *ji/i* worse than *je/e*, since *ji* and *je* both involve sequences of [–back]? One could address this issue by assuming that the OCP not only disfavors sequences of [–back], but also checks the relevant segments for identical values for [high] and [low] (see Padgett, 1995, for similar proposals), and disfavors sequences more if they have more of these features in common. Such an account acquires some of the advantage of the contrast-based approach, specifically in calling on a kind of *scale* of similarity. However, there is a divide between the formal account and the intended explanation: it remains *formally* mysterious why just these features are involved together in the prohibition. A direct appeal to the acoustic/perceptual element of F2, on the other hand, avoids this problem.

Second, since the OCP is often invoked to account for long-distance dissimilations, we would expect long-distance effects involving these glide-vowel cooccurrences, ruling out for example the cooccurrence of i and palatalization in ip^ja (where p^ja is fine). (In fact, this would not even count as long-distance within something like the feature geometric framework of Sagey, 1986.) Yet no such restriction holds of any language surveyed here. In the contrast-based approach it follows immediately that such forms are acceptable, even when p^ji versus pi is not, since the problem of acoustic/perceptual similarity arises precisely under adjacency of the palatalization off-glide and the vowel.

Third, though such an account predicts that bi and not b^ji occurs in Irish, it does *not* explain why a language such as Irish might *require* $b^\gamma i$. It is important to ask why the presence of a palatalization contrast should *correlate* with the presence of velarization, especially bearing in mind that b^γ is articulatorily more complex than plain b and is considered more marked in phonology. Marshallese is another language having both palatalization and velarization (Bender, 1969; Choi, 1992, 1995), and so is Russian, the case we return to below. Assuming that velarization involves more articulatory effort and/or markedness than a plain consonant, we can only understand the tendency for it to accompany palatalization as a means of enhancing a contrast, as Trubetzkoy (1969, p. 130) does.

V. RUSSIAN VELARIZATION

A tendency for the 'plain' consonants of Russian to be velarized has often been noted (Trubetzkoy, 1969; Reformatskii, 1958; Fant, 1960; Öhman, 1966; Purcell, 1979; Lyovin, 1997, p. 64, and many others), though the amount of velarization, and the consonants affected by it, are matters of disagreement. (See Evans-Romaine, 1998, for a thorough overview of this question and references.) I argue below that the role of velarization is actually underestimated in phonological accounts of Russian, a fact that is unfortunate, since its presence bears in an important way both on phonological theory and on Russian phonology.

Considering the broader theory first, the occurrence of velarized segments in languages having contrastive palatalization points up a markedness paradox. Taking the specific example shown in (10a), there are languages with a contrast among plain, palatalized, and velarized laterals, including Bernera Scots Gaelic, at least one dialect of Irish (see Ladefoged & Ladefoged, 1997, on both of these), and Marshallese (Bender, 1969; Choi, 1992, 1995). There are languages contrasting palatalized and velarized laterals, including Irish and Russian (ɫ is the segment

that is most uncontroversially velarized in Russian). Finally, there are languages
having just one contrastive lateral. Though the latter is counted as 'plain' in (10a),
there can of course be variation in a sole lateral phoneme's realization.[7] Since a
plain lateral, however, is the most widespread kind across languages, markedness
theories single it out as the best. It is therefore a surprise, as Lyovin (1997) notes,
that Russian has no plain lateral, and the same can be said of Irish.

(10)

a.	l' vs. l vs. $ɫ$	Bernera Scots Gaelic
	l' vs. $ɫ$	Russian, most Irish dialects
	l	Many languages
b.	i vs. $ɨ$ vs. u	Guaraní
	i vs. u	Many languages
	$ɨ$	Kabardian

The situation here is closely analogous to that of (10b). Theories of markedness
developed within formal phonology are typically 'unidimensional,' to use a term
from Ní Chiosáin & Padgett (to appear), in the sense that they rate segments along
a *single* scale of goodness. Assuming that the best segments are those found across
most languages, such theories favor i and u over $ɨ$, just as they favor l over l' and
$ɫ$. Yet in Kabardian, just as in Russian and Irish, the 'best' segments are *disfavored*.
The facts instead support a view in which markedness is determined along more
than one dimension. On the one hand, l and i are best from the point of view of
articulatory simplicity (except where coarticulatory influences dictate otherwise).
On the other, when a language contrasts two segments, it can be more important
that the contrast be well dispersed perceptually. This latter requirement conflicts
with the first, since l' and $ɫ$ make the best such pair, just as i and u do, the F2 values
differing the most in each case. To the extent that other 'plain' consonants of
Russian are in fact velarized, they raise the same problem for unidimensional
markedness.

   Turning now to a closer look at Russian, the most important reason why the
existence of velarization in Russian is underestimated is that it is scarcely recog-
nized just where it is most prevalent and systematic: on non-palatalized consonants before i. Here we have in mind $ɨ$: though described and transcribed as a
central vowel in most of the literature, Russian $ɨ$ is typically pronounced as a
diphthong $[ɨ͡i]$ or $[ɯ͡i]$, at least when stressed. This observation tends to be confined
to the more phonetic literature, and occurs there only occasionally, for example,
Meillet (1951), Boyanus (1967), Jones & Ward (1969), Bondarko (1977), Derkach
et al. (1983, pp. 27–28), and Antonova (1988). Even in these works, the potential
relevance of this fact to the presence of contrastive palatalization is not addressed.
The Russian facts are strikingly similar to those of Irish, and the points raised in

the previous section suggest that this is not likely to be coincidental. An alternative transcription of the Russian forms we saw in section III is shown in (11).[8]

(11)

vit'	'to twist, weave'	$v^y it'$	'to howl'
bit	'beaten'	$b^y it$	'way of life'
tikat'	'to tick'	$t^y ikat'$	'to address in familiar form'
xodi	'walk!'	$xod^y i$	'gaits'
sito	'sieve'	$s^y ito$	'sated (neut.)'

As with Irish, palatalization before i is not transcribed. More important, Russian i is reinterpreted as *velarization of the consonant before i*. This is a more accurate transcription in two important respects. First, in a minimal pair such as bit versus $b^y it$, it is the latter that phonetically bears the greater burden of the contrast. That is, the velarization in $b^y it$ is much more discernable than is the palatalization in bit. Second, this distinguishing phonetic property is localized at the *release* of the consonant, just as we find with palatalization.

We are now in a position to address some of the questions raised earlier about the Russian allophonic rule. First, why should i become i after plain consonants? The answer offered here is that there *is no i* in the sense usually intended, that is, no phonetic (let alone phonemic) category i, nor any plain consonant. Instead, there is $C^y i$. Second, why should i be limited to occurring *only* following a 'plain' consonant within a phonological phrase? Obviously, this restriction follows without comment if i in fact represents velarization of the preceding consonant. To the question, could such a rule exist in English, or in any of the myriad languages having 'plain' consonants, the answer suggested is no; velarization before i in Russian is directly related to the presence of contrastive palatalization in that language, and it is just one instance of a crosslinguistic tendency to avoid contrasts such as $C^j i$ versus Ci. The prediction is that we should not find a similar rule in a language such as English.

Let us consider (11) in more detail. First, our choice to omit palatalization in forms such as bit is not crucial, since the point of interest is that the velarization in $b^y it$ is *more* significant from the perspective of contrast dispersion. However, people trained in transcription are not generally tempted to record palatalization in forms such as bit, just as they are not for Irish, and the indiscernability of palatalization (in the sense of off-glide j) before i is noted in various works on Russian, including Jones & Ward (1969) and Zubkova (1974). The facts are not so simple when we consider non-labial places of articulation. For example, coronal stops in forms such as $xodi$ are typically affricated, the degree of affrication depending on the speaker and the dialect. In this sense they are more notably 'palatalized.' This point bears interestingly on the claim that contrasts such as $C^j i$ versus Ci are deficient, since affrication is another means (besides velarization) by which the contrast dispersion of such a pair can be improved. We will return to this point later.

The more important claim of (11) is that Russian Ci should be understood as $C^{\gamma}i$. In spite of discussion of velarization in other contexts (that is, not before i) found in the literature on Russian, and despite occasional mention of the diphthongization of i in particular, apparently no one has suggested that C^{γ} should be understood as $C^{\gamma}i$. It is difficult to say why this is, though part of the problem may be that the extent of the diphthongization is not considered convincing enough. Most who note the diphthongization state that it ends short of Russian [i] (hence Russian "[i]"), for example, Jones & Ward (1969), and Lyovin (1997), who transcribe [ɯ͡i]. (On the other hand, Bondarko, 1977, among others, is clear in stating that i ends in Russian i.) The eminent Russian phonologist Shcherba (1912) explicitly argued that there is *no* diphthongization of i, though it is difficult to reconcile this opinion with observed fact.[9] A third consideration is that i is in fact less diphthongized, or not diphthongized at all (i.e., occurring as [ɨ] or something similar), in unstressed syllables. This last fact presents no serious obstacle to the claim here, however. No one would deny the existence of, for example, $C^{j}a$ in Russian, as in $p^{j}at'$ 'five,' even though when not under main stress such a syllable reduces to Ci or $Cɪ$ as in $piti$ 'five (gen.sg.).' Ci is a plausible outcome under reduction for a syllable that is $C^{\gamma}i$ under stress. (One also finds reductions of this syllable to $Cə$ or nearly so.)

VI. PHONETIC INVESTIGATION

How can we further explore the claim that Russian Ci is $C^{\gamma}i$? Two tests suggest themselves. First, if Ci is $C^{\gamma}i$, then a comparison of Russian Ci and Ci should reveal that these syllables are very different at the release of the consonant, but similar at their conclusion. Second, it is worth comparing the Russian facts to those of another language that is said to have $C^{\gamma}i$ uncontroversially, in order to get a baseline on what a 'real' case of velarization before i is like. To these ends an experiment was conducted comparing Russian and Irish.

A. Methods

Three Russian speakers and three Irish speakers were recorded speaking the syllables bi, $b^{\gamma}i$, di, $d^{\gamma}i$ as portions of real words. (From here on $C^{\gamma}i$ will be written instead of Ci, to keep the comparison between Russian and Irish forms clear.) The Russian speakers were from Moscow or nearby, were approximately in their forties or fifties, and had been living in the United States for up to ten years. The

Irish speakers all spoke Northern (Donegal) Irish, were in their twenties and thirties, and lived in Dublin, Ireland.[10] There were two women and one man in each case.

The words used for recording are shown below. Irish contrasts 'long' and 'short' vowels, though it is as much a contrast in quality as quantity. The vowels in these Irish words are 'long.' For both languages, examples with both initial *b* and initial *d* were examined because various works suggest that diphthongization in Russian C^yi is stronger after bilabials, with the vowel ending further forward, for example, Meillet (1951), Boyanus (1967), Jones & Ward (1969):

(12)

The Russian words:	[rʌ'bʸi] 'slaves'	[vˌʌdʸi] 'water (gen.sg.)'
	[drʌ'bi] 'stamp your feet!'	[xʌ'di] 'walk!'
The Irish words:	[bʸiː] 'yellow'	['dʸiːhɪ] 'to her'
	[biː] 'be (imp.)'	[diː] 'drink (gen.sg.)'

The words were embedded in carrier sentences. There were four contexts, each intended in its own way to elicit something like a careful or hyperarticulated pronunciation (see Lindblom, 1990, Moon & Lindblom, 1994, and Johnson *et al.*, 1993, on hyperarticulation). The reasoning was that C^yi and Ci stand the best chance of being similar at their endpoints under such maximally unreduced conditions. As it happens, the different contexts had no entirely systematic effect of interest on the results. Though they were treated as a factor in the statistical analyses, they are not discussed here. These carrier sentences, along with more about the materials, are shown in the Appendix.

There were three repetitions for each of the four contexts, giving 12 tokens of each word per Russian speaker. The number of tokens varied more in the case of the Irish speakers. (Some speakers did not repeat materials the requested three times in every task, so that the number of tokens went down.) Since there were four target words per language, this meant (ideally) 48 tokens per speaker.

Analyses were performed on a Kay Elemetrics CSL 4300. The target words were digitized at 10 kHz. Formants 1–3 were estimated by Linear Predictive Coding, using a 10-ms window and 10, 12, or 14 coefficients, the choice depending on the speaker. Measurements were taken at two positions: at consonantal release, and at peak F2, that is, where F2 was highest. If F2 rose and then plateaued, then the measurement was taken at the end of the voiced portion of the vowel. These positions were determined using a waveform and spectrogram together.

There is evidence that not only F2, but F3 figures into the perception of frontness, in particular in the case of [i], where F2 is close enough to F3 to be perceptually integrated with it (Carlson *et al.*, 1970). Based on some of the spectrograms, in fact, it seemed that some of the perceived glide toward [i] in $C^y i$ was contributed by the upward movement of F3. It therefore seemed wise to take both F2 and F3 into account. A well-known means of doing this employs the formula (due to Carlson *et al.*) deriving F2′ ("F2 prime") shown in (13). As it turned out, F2′ means at peak F2 for Ci versus $C^y i$ were more significantly different than either peak F2 or F3 means alone, for most speakers. (For one it made no significant difference, and one subject was not checked.) Thus, using F2′ made it more difficult to demonstrate that Ci and $C^y i$ are similar at their end-points.[11]

(13)

$$F2' = F2 + 0.5 \ (F3 - F2) \ ((F2 - F1)/(F3 - F1))$$

B. Results

Figure 8.1 shows representative spectrograms from the first Russian speaker and Irish speaker analyzed (both male). As can be seen, bi differs from $b^y i$ similarly in the two languages based on this informal inspection. In particular, the second formant of $b^y i$ in both languages begins low, and (more interestingly) ends somewhere very similar to its position for i in bi.

Figure 8.2 shows the mean F2′ values for the Russian speakers and Irish speakers, with consonant type (b or d) and speakers lumped together within each language. The numbers at the bottom indicate the number of tokens of each type; thus, there were altogether 144 Russian tokens, and 104 Irish tokens. As this figure makes clear, the F2′ values are indeed more similar at the end of the syllables Ci versus $C^y i$ than they are at the beginning. The figures show 95% confidence intervals around each mean as well; any two means within a confidence interval of each other are not significantly different. As can be seen here, there was no significant difference between the Irish palatalized versus velarized syllables at peak F2, while the Russian means were significantly different: $F(1,128) = 8.1, p < 0.005$.

There is a great deal of variation in formant values between speakers, particularly due to gender. Hence it is more informative to consider each speaker separately. For each speaker, a three-factor analysis of variance (Anova) was performed comparing the F2′ means of $C^y i$ versus Ci at consonantal release, and at peak F2. The factors were palatalized versus velarized syllable (i.e., Ci versus $C^y i$), consonant type (b versus d), and context (see appendix).[12] The most imme-diate result was that Ci is significantly different from $C^y i$ at each point for most of the speakers (five out of six). Specifically, the F2′ means of $C^y i$ versus Ci were

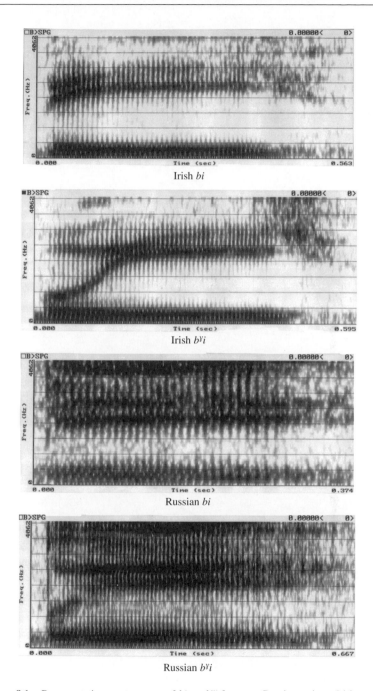

Figure 8.1. Representative spectrograms of *bi* vs. *bʸi* from one Russian and one Irish speaker.

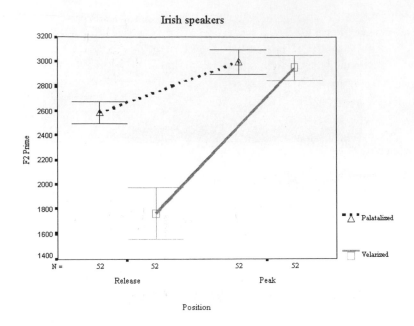

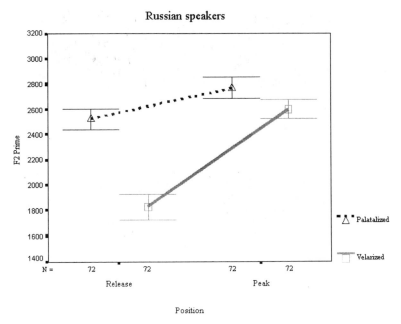

Figure 8.2.   Mean F2′ values for Irish speakers and Russian speakers, with 95% confidence intervals.

significantly different at both the point of consonantal release and at peak F2, for five speakers. For one Irish speaker they were not significantly different at peak F2.

The finding that the F2′ values of $C^{y}i$ differ from those of Ci at consonantal release is no surprise, and would be expected whether $C^{y}i$ is understood as $C^{y}i$ or Ci. Indeed, the magnitude of the difference between F2′ means at this point is huge in comparison to that at peak F2, for all speakers. The table in (14) gives the mean F2′ values at consonantal release, and the Anova results, for all consonants grouped together.

(14) Mean F2′ values in Hertz and Anova results at consonantal release

Subject	Russian 1 (male)	Russian 2 (female)	Russian 3 (female)	Irish 1 (male)	Irish 2 (female)	Irish 3 (female)
Ci	2138	2833	2602	2245	3008	2519
$C^{y}i$	1606	2044	1832	1583	1958	1754
Difference	532	789	770	662	1050	765
Result of Anova	$F(1,32)$ $= 530$ $p < 0.001$	$F(1,32)$ $= 2066$ $p < 0.001$	$F(1,32)$ $= 310$ $p < 0.001$	$F(1,16)$ $= 598$ $p < 0.001$	$F(1,32)$ $= 435$ $p < 0.001$	$F(1,24)$ $= 1039$ $p < 0.001$

A similar table in (15) reports the mean F2′ values at peak F2. As the graphs of Figure 8.2 suggest, these differences are much smaller. However, they are statistically significant for five of the six subjects, all except Irish speaker 3.

(15) Mean F2′ values in Hertz and Anova results at peak F2

Subject	Russian 1	Russian 2	Russian 3	Irish 1	Irish 2	Irish 3
Ci	2283	2986	3032	2541	3452	3001
$C^{y}i$	2192	2869	2741	2477	3359	2998
Difference	91	117	291	64	97	3 Hz
Result of Anova	$F(1,32)$ $= 29$ $p < 0.001$	$F(1,32)$ $= 17$ $p < 0.001$	$F(1,32)$ $= 75$ $p < 0.001$	$F(1,16)$ $= 10$ $p < 0.01$	$F(1,32)$ $= 5.6$ $p < 0.05$	$F(1,24)$ $= 0.1$ n.s.

Figure 8.3 shows the mean F2′ values for Russian speaker 1 and Irish speaker 1, broken down according to initial consonant type, b versus d. As can be seen, at the point of consonantal release, the F2′ means differ much more following

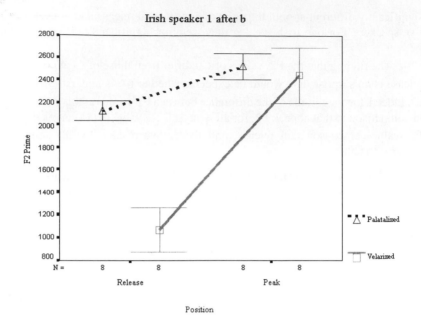

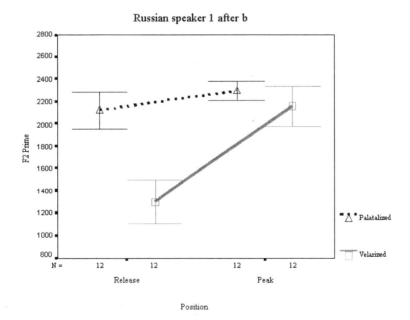

Figure 8.3.   Mean F2′ values by consonant, with 2 ∗ standard deviation.

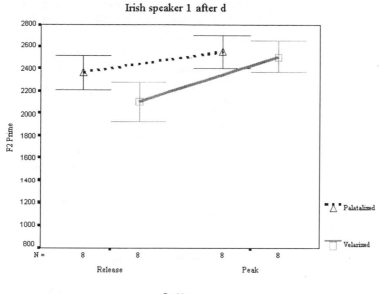

Irish speaker 1 after d

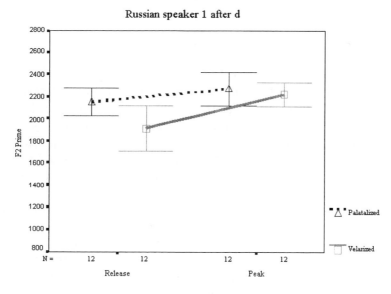

Russian speaker 1 after d

b than following *d*, for both of these speakers. In other words, the contrast between the velarized and palatalized forms is much greater following the bilabial, as judged solely by these F2′ values. Note that the range shown around the means in this figure is no longer the 95% confidence interval but a larger one.[13]

The table in (16) presents the Anova results for all speakers at consonantal release. For every subject, the difference between F2′ means was much larger following the bilabial consonant, an interaction (velarized/palatalized versus consonant type) that is highly significant. For Russian speakers 1 and 2 only, this difference by consonant persisted even to peak F2 position, though it was much smaller there. (Speaker 1: 134 versus 47 Hz, $F(1,32) = 6.8$, $p < 0.05$; speaker 2: 207 versus 28 Hz, $F(1,32) = 9.8$, $p < 0.01$.)

(16) Difference between mean F2′ values by consonant, at release

Subject	Russian 1	Russian 2	Russian 3	Irish 1	Irish 2	Irish 3
bi vs. b$^{\gamma}$i	826 Hz	1189 Hz	1009 Hz	1061 Hz	1842 Hz	1395 Hz
di vs. d$^{\gamma}$i	238 Hz	390 Hz	532 Hz	263 Hz	257 Hz	136 Hz
Results of Anova	$F(1,32)$ $= 161$ $p < 0.001$	$F(1,32)$ $= 529$ $p < 0.001$	$F(1,32)$ $= 30$ $p < 0.001$	$F(1,16)$ $= 218$ $p < 0.001$	$F(1,32)$ $= 249$ $p < 0.001$	$F(1,24)$ $= 694$ $p < 0.001$

C. Discussion

In spite of the statistically significant differences seen in (15), the results here support the view that Russian *Ci* is indeed *C$^{\gamma}$i*. First and most obviously, these results show that the contrast between *C$^{\gamma}$i* and *Ci* is much greater at the release of *C* than in the following vowel, indicating that *C$^{\gamma}$i* versus *Ci* (or *C^{j}i*) is indeed a better representation of the facts than is *Ci* versus *C^{j}i*. In fact, the striking similarity between the Russian and Irish facts extends to the different treatment of *b* and *d*, and this difference also points up the importance of consonantal release to the contrast, a point we turn to momentarily.

Second, there is a good deal of overlap in the F2′ values for individual tokens of *C$^{\gamma}$i* versus *Ci* at peak F2, even within the same speaker. Figure 8.3 shows a range of two standard deviations around the means, a range that includes roughly 95% of the data for the respective means (assuming normal distribution). Even though F2′ values for *Ci* versus *C$^{\gamma}$i* were significantly different at peak F2 for each of these speakers, Figure 8.3 shows that there was quite a bit of overlap in the relevant tokens, regardless of language or consonant type. There was similar overlap in F2′ values at peak F2 for all speakers.[14]

Third, another perspective on the significance of these results can be had by inquiring how robust these differences in Hertz are to the human ear. A conservative estimate of the "just noticeable difference" between vowel formants in the range of F2 is 3% of the formant value, judging by the studies summarized in Kewley-Port & Watson (1994).[15] For the F2' values shown in (15), this means roughly 80 Hz. The actual differences found between the F2' means are roughly this amount or less in the case of Irish, implying that the difference in that language between Ci and C^yi at their endpoints is virtually inconsequential auditorily. The actual differences are larger overall in the case of Russian, but only modestly so for speakers 1 and 2.

Though the Irish F2' means are closer together in (15) in comparison to those of Russian, a difference between languages at this level of detail in the realization of a phoneme such as i, assuming it were to hold up across more subjects, is not at all unusual. The fact that the vowel in C^yi falls a bit short of that in Ci in either language due to preceding velarization could be modeled in one of several ways. First, C^yi and Ci might have the same phonetic target at the syllable endpoint, but this target is undershot more in the case of C^yi due to the contrary tug of velarization. Second, the vowel i might have different *targets* according to phonetic context, that is, the target realization for this vowel after a velarized consonant is not quite so front as that of i in other contexts. Third, the target of i might be a 'window' in the sense of Keating (1990), that is, a *range* of acceptable realizations within which variation according to context is possible. This last position can be seen as a compromise between the first two. All of these possibilities reflect well-known approaches to dealing with contextual realization of phonemes.

The difference found between b and d supports the observation made by Meillet (1951), Boyanus (1967), Jones & Ward (1969), and others, that the diphthongization of i — or rather, velarization of the consonant preceding i — is greater when the preceding consonant is a bilabial. (Judging by the data obtained, however, this effect is not because the vowel ends further forward, as the latter two report; rather, F2' *begins* much lower after bilabials.) The question arises whether this difference is related in any interesting way to the fact of a palatalization contrast, or whether it merely reflects an inherent difference between bilabials and dentals in their effects on formant transitions, apart from considerations of palatalization. According to the latter view, these would be just the acoustic results to expect from combining one and the same palatalization gesture with a bilabial versus a dental on the one hand, and doing the same for a velarization gesture on the other.

There is indeed evidence supporting the latter view. For example, Sussman *et al.* (1991) carried out a study of coarticulation between consonants and following vowels, with the goal of demonstrating invariant acoustic cues for stop place of articulation. The study involved English speakers ranging over various dialects, and it showed that formant values for bilabials at release vary to a much greater degree due to a following vowel than do those for alveolars, a result that held across English vowel types. These results are consistent with earlier findings that a much more stable F2 "locus" exists for alveolars at release compared to bilabials. This difference may be due to the relative freedom of the tongue body to assume the posture of a neighboring vowel when the stop closure is bilabial, compared to presumed constraints that a tongue blade articulation places on tongue body movement. (See Sussman *et al.*, 1991, for references and discussion.) Purcell's (1979) study of coarticulation in Russian VCV sequences found a similar difference between non-palatalized bilabials and dentals across vowel contexts. (Not surprisingly, the F2 values of palatalized consonants at release vary much less due to vowel context.) It also revealed that a difference such as that in (16) between palatalized and non-palatalized bilabials, compared to the dentals, holds whether the following vowel is *i*, as here, or a different Russian vowel. That is, it is seen not only in *bi/bʲi* versus *di/dʲi*, but in *bʲa/ba* versus *dʲa/da*, and so on. The data observed here are consistent with this general difference between *b* and *d*. As Figure 8.3 shows, the *overall* variation in F2′ values following *b* is much larger. Indeed, the means for *d* vary so much less that values for palatalized versus velarized *d* actually overlap for all Irish speakers, and two of the Russian speakers, in terms of the 2× standard deviation range indicated. There is never such overlap in the case of *b*.

On the other hand, a comparison of Irish and Russian dialects suggests that there is more to the story. There is a way in which the contrast in the case of dentals is much *more* variable in comparison to bilabials. The Irish subjects analyzed here speak a northern variety of the language that is characterized by very heavy affrication of the palatalized dentals, as shown in (17).[16] In comparison, the same sequences in western dialects are much less affricated. At the same time the non-palatalized dentals before *i* are velarized very little by these subjects in comparison to the norm in western dialects, so little as to sometimes give no impression of velarization at all. Standard Russian is more similar to western Irish. However, some dialects, in north and central European Russia especially, also heavily affricate the palatalized dentals (Kuznetsova, 1969). In the recorded speech of one such speaker I obtained, the non-palatalized dentals before *i* are velarized surprisingly little, similarly to those of the Irish subjects.

(17)

| Northern Irish: | bi | bʲi | dʑi | d⁽ʸ⁾i |
| Western Irish: | bi | bʲi | di | dʸi |

A more systematic study would be required in order to determine whether heavy affrication and weak velarization indeed correlate across dialects. Such a correlation would suggest an independent reason why the palatalizaton contrast involves more extreme F2′ movements in the case of bilabials, even in Standard Russian. Palatalized dentals are somewhat affricated even in Standard Russian and western Irish, providing a further acoustic cue to palatalization, while bilabials lack this possibility of affrication. Assuming that the two kinds of cue to palatalization can be traded off, it follows that a smaller F2 difference between palatalized and non-palatalized dentals could suffice for a perceptually robust contrast, in comparison to bilabials. Zubkova (1974) suggests just this explanation for the greater velarization in the case of bilabials. Seen in this light, the overlap mentioned above between F2′ values for palatalized and velarized d, even within speakers, might not be surprising: F2′ values are not solely responsible for ensuring the palatalization contrast in the case of d.

These differences between dentals and bilabials most likely bear on a crosslinguistic phonological pattern. Labials are more restricted than coronals in their ability to contrast in palatalization. For example, though Polish, Belorussian, and Russian all contrast palatalized and non-palatalized labials, this contrast is neutralized in favor of plain labials syllable-finally in Polish (Rothstein, 1993), Belorussian (Mayo, 1993), and in some Russian dialects (Kuznetsova 1969), while the contrast is retained in the case of coronals. Further, several of the Slavic languages have no contrast at all between palatalized and non-palatalized labials, but have one in the case of coronals, for example, Czech, Slovak, and Ukranian. There are no cases in which the contrast is preferred for labials rather than coronals. Takatori (1997) notes this markedness implication in a survey of palatalization in Slavic languages, and proposes an Optimality Theoretic account in which constraints against palatalized labials universally outrank those against palatalized coronals. This universal might well be grounded in facts of perceptual contrast dispersion once again: the more dependent a palatalization contrast is on F2 transition cues, especially upon release, the more this contrast will suffer in positions not conducive to audible release, including syllable-finally. (See Kingston, 1990, Lombardi, 1991/1994, and Steriade, 1995, on the connection between consonantal release and the maintenance of certain contrasts.) Labials are more dependent on these cues than coronals, and are disfavored accordingly. The fact that palatalized labials are dispreferred even apart from position might follow from the very fact that the number of cues to palatalization for labials is fewer than those for coronals.[17]

Before concluding this section, it is worth making some final comments on the treatment of Russian Ci as C^yi. This approach helps make sense of a longstanding controversy over whether Russian "i" is a phoneme or not. In spite of the considerable evidence seen in section III that i and i are not in contrast, there has been much disagreement on this point for decades, and descriptions of Russian often include i in the chart of vowel phonemes. One forceful, if somewhat nebulous, reason for this follows from an old notion that sub-phonemic differences are not normally something that speakers are aware of, while Russian speakers are highly aware of "i," an argument Gvozdev (1949) makes, for example.[18] Consider this argument in light of our earlier discussion of the phonetic realization of the contrast Ci versus C^yi: though the former may be perceived as palatalized to some degree (especially if affricated), the velarization in C^yi is most important to perceiving the contrast. If C^yi is understood as 'plain' $C + i$, then this amounts to saying that it is the *vowel i* that is most important to perceiving the contrast. Put differently, it is impossible to perceive the 'plainness' of C apart from i. (Zubkova, 1974, among others, makes this observation.) Once we understand Ci as C^yi instead, however, then we identify the crucial property as one involving the *consonant* (namely, velarization), rendering this situation analogous to that of C^ja, in which it is likewise a property of the consonant (palatalization) that is at issue. The problem of the status of "i" disappears.

This gain in parallelism comes at the cost of a loss of parallelism in another sense: it is no longer possible to treat Russian as having a contrast 'plain' versus palatalized regardless of environment. It is the temptation of parallelism that leads researchers to infer from the contrast 'plain' versus palatalized in back vowel environments that the contrast must be the same before i: hence palatalized $C'i$ versus plain Ci in the usual Slavic transcription. A basic claim of this paper, however, is that Russian consonants contrast in *frontness/backness*, and that the realization of this contrast is intimately tied to the phonetic environment, as we have seen. It is only this interpretation of the facts that brings some reason to the otherwise mysterious allophonic rule of Russian we began with.

VII. CONCLUSIONS

Phonological descriptions are rife with allophonic rules such as "/i/ → [ɨ] after plain C." Judging by the discussion these processes generally receive, one might infer that the major reason such rules exist is to help teach students the concept of the phoneme. A basic point of this paper has been that more attention to both phonetic detail and phonetic theories might aid in understanding what such rules are really about. This focus on understanding hinges, at least in this case, on some appeal to the functional notion of perceptual dispersion of contrast. Though the idea that *assimilatory* rules might have a basis in phonetics has a long history, this idea comes up much more rarely in the case of other kinds of allophonic rule such as this Russian one. To take another example, virtually all discussions of the rule by which English voiceless consonants are aspirated at the beginnings of words and stressed syllables limit themselves to stating this fact, sometimes also using it to draw the inference that the syllable is an important unit of phonology. Yet it is possible to explain this rule in part as the result of a contrast shift much like that of Russian (see Kingston & Diehl, 1994, and references therein). A contrast such as *b* versus *p* is disfavored at the beginning of words or utturances, since voicing of obstruents is difficult in that position; hence "voiced" *b* is often realized as *p*. At the same time, the plain voiceless phoneme is shifted to voiceless aspirated p^h. Whether or not aspiration word-initially is truly the result of maintaining a perceptually good contrast in that position, the point is that it is worthwhile to pursue these questions rather than settle for statements about phonemes and distributions of allophones. It may be that the traditional terminological dichotomy between "allophonic" and "phonemic" processes, though serving an important purpose in phonology, has been unhelpful in this regard. The idea suggested here is that "/i/ → [ɨ] after plain C" is all about maintaining a phonemic contrast.

APPENDIX: THE CARRIER SENTENCES

The Russian and Irish materials were designed to be similar. There were two different tasks, one providing two of the carrier conditions, the other two more. Subjects were given written instructions in Russian or Irish respectively. For the first task, the instructions were as follows:

> Now we will read some short dialogues together. My portion of the dialogue is in parentheses. In each dialogue, I'll ask what word you said, as though I am hard of hearing, and you will repeat the word. Please repeat the word clearly, but not loudly. We'll read each dialogue three times.

The dialogues had the following form (the target word is underlined, and was capitalized on the third line). Translations are loose.

Russian

ja skʌˈʒu ˈslovə rʌˈbʸi tiˈpˈerˈ)	I'll say the word slaves now
(kʌˈkojiˈslovə?)	(Which word?)
rʌˈbʸi	SLAVES

Irish

bʸiː ə'derhə mə ə'nɪʃ	yellow (is what) I'll say now
(ken 'fəkəl eː ʃɪn?)	(What word is that?)
bʸiː	YELLOW

The second task had the following instructions:

> Please read the following sentences three times each. Each time, try to
> stretch the last word out for two seconds.

For the Russian words, the effect of these instructions was to get the stressed syllable lengthened. (Subjects of both languages were very mixed in their ability to hold words in this way.) These materials had the following form:

Russian

ja skʌˈzal ni rʌˈbʸi, ʌ drʌˈbi   I said not <u>slaves</u>, but <u>stamp your feet</u>!

Irish

ni <u>bʸiː</u> ə duːrˈtʲ mə, ax <u>biː</u>   (It was) not <u>yellow</u> that I said, but <u>be</u>!

For the first task, materials with the target words were interspersed with materials with filler words having other vowels and consonants. Though this was true also of the second task, this task was intended to elicit a pronunciation contrasting similar target words, so that any idea of concealing the task was moot.

ACKNOWLEDGMENTS

I am grateful to Dorothy Evans-Romain, José Ignacio Hualde, Beth Hume, Keith Johnson, Máire Ní Chiosáin, Nathan Sanders, Marija Tabain, Rachel Walker, and the audience at the ICPhS satellite workshop "The Role of Perceptual Phenomena in Phonological Theory" for their very helpful comments. Special thanks to John Kingston, who read the paper closely and provided commentary leading to many improvements, and to Campbell Leaper, who helped rescue me from the jaws of SAS. Any remaining errors of judgement are solely my responsibility.

NOTES

1. A question that remains open, however, even assuming that functional forces play an important role in shaping phonologies, is the extent to which they have any place in a synchronic, "psychologically real," description, that is, are they in direct play within the grammar of a language, as functional work within Optimality Theory might be taken to imply, or is their role indirect, shaping language through patterns of language change over time? (It is certainly possible to recast functional work within Optimality Theory in this latter way, though it is not a trivial move.) Though this question is

important, it is worth keeping in mind that much useful work can be done without our knowing the answer to it. This article is meant to be neutral on the subject.

2. Another phoneme sometimes reported, $\check{z}'$ occurs marginally or not at all in contemporary Standard Russian. Palatalized velars might be considered phonemes due to historically borrowed words such as *lik'or* 'liqueur,' *leg'um* 'legume,' etc. k' is in fact very marginally phonemic based on the native vocabulary, due to one (Standard) Russian verb *tkat'* 'to weave,' which in some forms presents k' before *o*, e.g., *tk'oš* 'you weave.'

3. The transcriptions in this paper abstract away from predictable vowel quality effects due to assimilation and vowel reduction.

4. As is well known, however, there are derivational suffixes that begin with *i* and, rather than undergo this rule, remain *i* and actually palatalize the preceding otherwise plain consonant, e.g., lis + it͡sa → lis'it͡sa (*l'isit͡sa) 'fox (fem.)' (Gvozdev, 1949). The output respects the allophonic rule, but the causality seems to be reversed. Such facts invite analysis making use of some notion of lexical level (as in Kiparsky 1982, 1985), or morphologically-governed phonology.

5. The situation in Polish is actually similar to that of Irish and Russian. There is a 'palatalization' contrast before /i/; however, /i/ is realized as a 'semi-high retracted front vowel' (Rothstein, 1993) after the plain consonants. See Szpyra (1995) for a recent treatment of Polish palatalization.

6. For example, Japanese consonants before *i* might be transcribed as palatalized; similarly, though Russian rules out a palatalization contrast before *e* under suffixation and in native roots, a consonant before *e* is palatalized, not plain. (See (3).) Similarly, under conditions of hiatus such as *a + i* and *a + u*, the realizations *aji* and *awu*, respectively, are common.

7. In fact, there is evidence that 'plain' laterals are inherently velarized to some degree. See Sproat & Fujimura (1993) and Walsh Dickey (1997).

8. It is worth mentioning that velarization before *e* is often overlooked as well. Though consonants are palatalized before this vowel in native words, there are many borrowings violating this regularity, and velarization is then evident, e.g., *ka'fʲe* 'coffee.' (This velarization is most evident on stressed syllables, where vowel reduction does not take place.) Also, *e* does not palatalize a preceding consonant across a word boundary in Russian, leading to frequent pronunciations such as *vʲetəm* for *v+etəm* 'in this.'

9. Shcherba suggests that those who hear diphthongization are observing *i* before a palatalized consonant, as in *bit'* 'to be,' in which case there is indeed an *i*-like offglide from the vowel, as there is for other vowels before a palatalized consonant. Many other descriptions note this effect. However, the diphthongization of *i* has a firm reality apart from this context. See below, as well as the references cited earlier. Shcherba also allows that *i* might indeed be diphthongized in dialects other than his own.

10. I am very grateful to Máire Ní Chiosáin for arranging and conducting the Irish recording sessions, and for helping me construct the Irish materials.

11. An issue that arises when seeking some measure of the 'frontness' peak is that peak F2 as seen on a spectrogram may or may not coincide in time with peak F3 (or the trough of F1). Since it isn't really possible to guess what position would give the highest F2′ according to the formula, F2 peak was taken as the best measurement position.

12. Irish speaker 2 provided only one repetition of tokens in two of the four sentential contexts employed. Therefore only a 2-factor Anova was performed on that data, taking consonant type, and palatalized versus velarized syllable, as factors.

13. The error bars in Figure 8.3 indicate a range equal to twice the standard deviation. This measure of dispersion is broader than the 95% confidence intervals used in Figures 8.1 and 8.2, and was chosen in order to make it more clear where there is token overlap. See the discussion in the text that follows.

14. Displays for the other four speakers can be viewed at http://ling.ucsc.edu/~padgett/papers.html, or contact the author.

15. Kewley-Port & Watson (1994) and Hawks (1994) report just noticeable differences as low as about 1.5% for this frequency range. However, these values are obtained by highly trained subjects under optimal listening conditions, and Hawks concludes that "discriminability of vowels in natural speech communication modes should be based in larger perceptual units." Previous studies mostly report values in the 3 to 5% range, as Kewley-Port & Watson note.

16. Jim McCloskey informs me that this heavy affrication is a feature of the speech of younger speakers in Northern Ireland in particular.

17. As José Hualde reminds me, there may also be an articulatory explanation for the preference for palatalized coronals: palatalization has its roots in coarticulation with a palatal vocoid, and such coarticulation would more directly affect lingual consonants (i.e., velars and coronals) than labial ones. John Kingston, on the other hand, notes an alternative perceptual account. Given the greater F2 variation in the case of bilabials noted above, independent of palatalization, a more extreme difference between F2 values for palatalized versus non-palatalized bilabials might be required to render the contrast perceptually robust, in comparison to coronals. This could be true apart from any consideration of affrication. The discussion here is consistent with either of these possibilities, but is intended to suggest that the *number of perceptual cues* matters as well. The fact that palatalized bilabials are disfavored in syllable-final or pre-consonantal position, in particular, would not follow from either of these alternative accounts alone.

18. A contributing factor here is that Russian has a letter for "ɨ" that is separate from the letter for *i*, and the Russian name for this letter is in fact pronounced [ʲɨ], or perhaps [ʔʲɨ]. This is in part why Russians are highly aware of this sound. In our terms, this means that Russian uses a separate letter to spell velarization of a preceding consonant before *i*. Russian handles the spelling of palatalization before vowels precisely analogously: each vowel is spelled differently depending on whether the previous consonant is palatalized or not.

REFERENCES

Antonova, D. N. (1988). *Fonetika i intonatsiia*. Moscow: Russkii Iazyk.

Avanesov, R. I., & Sidorov, V. N. (1945). *Ocherk grammatiki russkogo literaturnaia iazyka*. Chast' 1: *Fonetika i morfologia*. Moscow: Gosudarstvennoe Uchebno-Pedagogicheskaia Izdatel'stvo.

Bender, B. W. (1969). *Spoken Marshallese*. Honolulu: University of Hawaii Press.

Bondarko, L. V. (1977). *Zvukovoi stroi sovremennogo russkogo iazyka*. Moscow, Prosveshchenie.

Boyanus, S. C. (1967). *Russian pronunciation*. Cambridge: Harvard University Press.

Carlson, R., Granström, B., & Fant, G. (1970). Some studies concerning perception of isolated vowels. *Speech Transmission Laboratory Quarterly Progress and Status Report, Royal Institute of Technology, Stockholm, 2–3,* 19–35.

Choi, J. (1992). *Phonetic underspecification and target-interpolation: An acoustic study of Marshallese vowel allophony*. Unpublished doctoral disssertation, University of California, Los Angeles.

Choi, J. (1995). An acoustic–phonetic underspecification account of Marshallese vowel allophony. *Journal of Phonetics, 23,* 323–347.

Chomsky, N., & Halle, M. (1968). *The sound pattern of English*. New York: Harper & Row.

Comrie, B., & Corbett, G. C. (Eds.) (1993). *The Slavonic languages*. New York: Routledge.

Derkach, M. F., Gumetskii, R. Ia., Gura, B. M., & Chaban, M. E. (1983). *Dinamicheskie spektry rechevykh signalov*. Lvov: Vishcha Shkola.

Evans-Romaine, D. K. (1998). *Palatalization and coarticulation in Russian*. Unpublished doctoral disssertation, University of Michigan, Ann Arbor.

Fant, G. (1960). *Acoustic theory of speech production*. The Hague: Mouton.

Flemming, E. (1995). *Auditory representations in phonology*. Unpublished doctoral disssertation, University of California, Los Angeles.

Goldsmith, J. (1976). *Autosegmental phonology*. New York: Garland.

Gvozdev, A. N. (1949). *O fonologicheskikh sredstvakh russkogo iazyka: Sbornik statei*. Moscow, Izdatel'stvo Akademii Pedagogicheskikh Nauk RSFSR.

Halle, M. (1959). *The sound pattern of Russian*. Mouton: The Hague.

Hamilton, W. S. (1980). *Introduction to Russian phonology and word structure*. Columbus: Slavica Publishers.

Hawks, J. W. (1994). Difference limens for formant patterns of vowel sounds. *Journal of the Acoustical Society of America, 95*(2), 1074–1084.

Itô, J., & Mester, A. (1995). Japanese phonology. In J. Goldsmith (Ed.), *Handbook of Phonological Theory* (pp. 817–838). Cambridge: Blackwell.

Johnson, K,, Flemming, E., & Wright, R. (1993). The hyperspace effect: Phonetic targets are hyperarticulated. *Language, 69*(3), 505–528.

Jones, D., & Ward, D. (1969). *The phonetics of Russian.* Cambridge: Cambridge University Press.

Kawasaki, H. (1982). *An acoustical basis for universal constraints on sound sequences.* Unpublished doctoral disssertation, Univesity of California, Berkeley.

Keating, P. A. (1990). The window model of coarticulation: Articulatory evidence. In J. Kingston & M. Beckman (Eds.), *Papers in laboratory phonology*, Vol. 1: *Between the grammar and the physics of speech* (pp. 451–470). Cambridge: Cambridge University Press.

Kewley-Port, D., & Watson, C. S. (1994). Formant-frequencey discrimination for isolated English vowels. *Journal of the Acoustical Society of America, 95*(1), 485–496.

Kingston, J. (1990). Articulatory binding. In J. Kingston & M. E. Beckman (Eds.), *Papers in laboratory phonology*, Vol. 1: *Between the grammar and the physics of speech* (pp. 406–434). Cambridge: Cambridge University Press.

Kingston, J., & Diehl, R. L. (1994). Phonetic knowledge. *Language, 70*(3), 419–454.

Kiparsky, P. (1982). Lexical phonology and morphology. In In I. S. Yang (Ed.), *Linguistics in the morning calm* (Vol. 2, pp. 3–91). Seoul: Hanshin.

Kiparsky, P. (1985). Some consequences of lexical phonology. *Phonology, 2*, 85–138.

Kohler, K. J. (1990). Segmental reduction in connected speech in German: Phonological facts and phonetic explanations. In W. J. Hardcastle & A. Marchal (Eds.), *Speech production and speech modeling* (pp. 69–92). Dordrecht: Kluwer Academic Publishers.

Kuznetsova, A. M. (1969). Nekotorye voprosy fonticheskoi kharakteristiki iavleniia tverdosti — miagkosti v russkikh govorakh. In S. S. Vysotskii (Ed.), *Eksperimental'no-fonticheskoe izuchenie russkikh govorov* (pp. 35–137). Moscow: Nauka.

Ladefoged, P., & Ladefoged, J. (1997). Phonetic structures of Scottish Gaelic. *UCLA Working Papers in Phonetics, 95*, 114–153.

Leben, W. (1973). *Suprasegmental phonology.* Unpublished doctoral disssertation, Massachusetts Institute of Technology, Cambridge.

Liljencrants, J., & Lindblom, B. (1972). Numerical simulation of vowel quality systems: The role of perceptual contrast. *Language 48*(4), 839–862.

Lindblom, B. (1986). Phonetic universals in vowel systems. In J. Ohala & J. Jaeger (Eds.), *Experimental phonology* (pp. 13–44). Orlando: Academic Press.

Lindblom, B. (1990). Explaining phonetic variation: A sketch of the H&H theory. In W. J. Hardcastle & A. Marchal (Eds.), *Speech production and speech modeling* (pp. 403–439). Dordrecht: Kluwer Academic Publishers.

Lombardi, L. (1991). *Laryngeal features and laryngeal neutralization.* Unpublished doctoral disssertation, University of Massachusetts, Amherst. (Published 1994, New York: Garland.)

Lyovin, A. V. (1997). *An introduction to the languages of the world.* Oxford: Oxford University Press.

McCarthy, J. J. (1986). OCP effects: Gemination and antigemination. *Linguistic Inquiry, 17*, 207–263.

Maddieson, I., & Precoda, K. (1992). Syllable structure and phonetic models. *Phonology*, *9*, 45–60.

Martinet, A. (1952). Function, structure, and sound change. *Word*, *8*(1), 1–32.

Martinet, A. (1964). *Elements of general linguistics*. Chicago: University of Chicago Press.

Martinet, A. (1974). *Economía de los cambios fonéticos*. Madrid: Editorial Gredos. (Originally published as *Économie des changements phonétiques*, 1955.)

Mayo, P. (1993). Belorussian. In B. Comrie & G. G. Corbett (Eds.), *The Slavonic languages* (pp. 887–946). New York: Routledge.

Meillet, A. (1951). *Obshcheslavianskii iazyk*. Moscow: Izdatel'stvo Innostrannoi Literatury. (Translation into Russian of *Le Slave Commun*, 2nd ed.)

Moon, S. J., & Lindblom, B. (1994). Interaction between duration, context, and speaking style in English stressed vowels. *Journal of the Acoustical Society of America*, *96*(1), 40–55.

Ní Chiosáin, M., & Padgett, J. (to appear). Markedness, segment realisation, and locality in spreading. In L. Lombardi (Ed.), *Segmental phonology in optimality theory*. Cambridge: Cambridge University Press.

Ohala, J. J. (1983). The origin of sound patterns in vocal tract constraints. In P. MacNeilage (Ed.), *The production of speech* (pp. 189–216). Springer Verlag, New York.

Ohala, J. J. (1990). The phonetics and phonology of aspects of assimilation. In J. Kingston & M. Beckman (Eds.), *Papers in laboratory phonology*, Vol. 1: *Between the grammar and the physics of speech* (pp. 258–275). Cambridge: Cambridge University Press.

Ohala, J. J., & Kawasaki-Fukumori, H. (1997). Alternatives to the sonority hierarchy for explaining segmental sequential constraints. In S. Eliasson & E. H. Jahr (Eds.), *Language and its ecology: Essays in memory of Einar Haugen* (pp. 343–365). Berlin: Mouton de Gruyter.

Öhman, S. E. G. (1966). Coarticulation in VCV utturances: Spectrographic measurements. *Journal of the Acoustical Society of America*, *39*, 151–168.

Padgett, J. (1995). *Stricture in feature geometry*. Stanford: CSLI Publications.

Prince, A., & Smolensky, P. (1993). *Optimality theory: Constraint interaction in generative grammar*. Unpublished manuscript, Rutgers University, New Brunswick, NJ, and the University of Colorado, Boulder.

Purcell, E. T. (1979). Formant frequency patterns in Russian VCV utterances. *Journal of the Acoustical Society of America*, *66*(6), 1691–1702.

Reformatskii, A. A. (1957). Fonologicheskie zametki. *Voprosy iazykoznaniia*, *6*(2), 101–102.

Reformatskii, A. A. (1958). O korrelatsii "tverdykh" i "miagkikh" soglasnykh (v sovremennom russkom literaturnom iazyke). In *Mélanges linguistiques offerts à Emil Petrovici par ses amis étrangers a l'occasion de son soixantième anniversaire* (pp. 494–499). Bucharest: Editura Academiei Republicii Populare Romine.

Rothstein, R. A. (1993). Polish. In B. Comrie & G. G. Corbett (Eds.), *The Slavonic languages* (pp. 686–758). New York: Routledge.

Sagey, E. (1986). *The representation of features and relations in nonlinear phonology.* Unpublished doctoral disssertation, Massachusetts Institute of Technology, Cambridge.

Shcherba, L. V. (1912). *Russkie glasnye v kachestvennom i kolichestvennom otnoshennii.* St. Petersburg: Tipografiia Iu. N. Erlikh.

Sproat, R., & Fujimura, O. (1993). Allophonic variation in English /l/ and its implications for phonetic implementation. *Journal of Phonetics, 21,* 291–311.

Steriade, D. (1995). *Laryngeal neutralization and laryngeal features.* Unpublished manuscript, Univesity of California, Los Angeles.

Sussex, R. (1992). Russian. In W. Bright (Ed.), *International encyclopedia of linguistics* (pp. 350–358). New York: Oxford University Press.

Sussman, H. M., McCaffrey, H. A., & Matthews, S. A. (1991). An investigation of locus equations as a source of relational invariance for stop place categorization. *Journal of the Acoustical Society of America, 90*(3), 1309–1325.

Szpyra, J. (1995). *Three tiers in Polish and English phonology.* Lublin: Wydawnictwo Uniwersytetu Marii Curie-Sklodowskiej.

Takatori, Y. (1997). *A study of constraint interaction in Slavic phonology.* Unpublished doctoral disssertation, Yale University, New Haven.

Trubetzkoy, N. (1969). *Principles of phonology.* Berkeley: University of California Press.

Walsh Dickey, L. (1997). *The phonology of liquids.* Unpublished doctoral disssertation, University of Massachusetts, Amherst.

Zubkova, L. G. (1974). *Foneticheskaia realizatsiia konsonantnykh protivopolozhenii v russkom iazyke.* Moscow: Universitet Druzhby Narodov.

CHAPTER

Directional Asymmetries in Place Assimilation

A Perceptual Account

Donca Steriade

Department of Linguistics
University of California
Los Angeles, California 90024-1543

  I. Introduction
 II. Major Place Assimilation
III. Apical Assimilation
 IV. Likelihood of Assimilation
  V. Manner Effects in Apical Assimilation
 VI. The Grammar of Perceptibility Effects
VII. The Innocent Misapprehension Theory of Assimilation
VIII. The P-Map
    A. Poetic Equivalence and the P-Map
    B. Loan Adaptation and the P-Map
 IX. P-Map-Based Analyses of Place Assimilation
    Acknowledgments
    Notes
    Appendix: Patterns of Word-Internal Apical Assimilation
    References

The Role of Speech Perception in Phonology

I. INTRODUCTION

The project presented here seeks to explain observed regularities in the direction of place assimilation. The best known among these is the fact that assimilation proceeds regressively in intervocalic clusters composed of alveolars, palatoalveolars, labials, or velars. This fact is consistent with a variety of interpretations, some of which are discussed below. However, the range of analyses narrows down drastically once we observe that assimilation is consistently *progressive* in clusters composed of retroflexes and alveolars. These two observations are schematically illustrated below. Instances of each type are presented in the body of the chapter.

(1) **Regressive** assimilation in VC_1C_2V:

$C_1,C_2 \in \{(Palato)\text{-Alveolar, Labial, Velar}\}$

(a)	{Alveolar, Labial}	anpa → ampa;	amta → anta
(b)	{Velar, Labial}	aŋpa → ampa;	amka → aŋka
(c)	{Alveolar, Velar}	anka → aŋka;	aŋta → anta
(d)	{Palatoalveolar, Labial}	aɲpa → ampa;	amtʃa → aɲtʃa

(2) **Progressive** assimilation in VC_1C_2V:

$C_1, C_2 \in \{Alveolar, Retroflex\}$

anṭa → anta;   anta → anṭa

Assimilation is a form of contrast neutralization: it reduces, in a C_1C_2 sequence, the number of potential bearers of place features from two (each of C_1 and C_2) to one (the whole C_1C_2 cluster). Neutralization can also take non-assimilatory forms. Thus, the [s]–[ʃ] contrast is neutralized pre-consonantally in English, as only [ʃ] occurs before [r] and only [s] occurs before obstruents, nasals, and [l]. This is in part a non-assimilatory effect: the fricative in [sp], [sm], and [sk] cannot contrast for anteriority but remains unassimilated to the following C. Similarly, in Chumash (Poser, 1982), the [s]–[ʃ] contrast is reduced to [ʃ] before the non-strident coronals [t, l, n]: clusters like [ʃn] have an unassimilated, but place-neutralized first member.

Place-assimilation patterns correspond to patterns of non-assimilatory place neutralization. Contrasts between alveolars, labials, velars, and palatoalveolars (abbreviated here as *major C-place contrasts*) are typically neutralized in pre-consonantal or domain-final position, that is, *in consonants not followed by vowels*. Thus, the pre-consonantal C_1 in the clusters in (1) is not only the typical target of assimilation, as in (1), but also, in non-assimilating cases, the typical target of place neutralization. This is the pattern observed above for English and Chumash fricatives: pre-consonantal strident fricatives neutralize, while prevocalic fricatives continue to contrast for anteriority. An extension of this pattern is the case in which word-final and pre-consonantal C's are place neutralized. Thus, the alveolar–labial contrast between ancient Greek [n] and [m] is eliminated through assimilation before a C, and in non-assimilatory fashion word-finally, where only [n] is permitted.

Non-assimilatory neutralization also affects the contrast between api-coalveolars and retroflexes (referred to here as the *apical* — or t/ʈ — *contrast*). In this case, however, it is typically the domain-initial and post-consonantal positions that are place-neutralized, that is, the apicals *not preceded by a vowel*. Thus, C_2 in the clusters in (2) is not only the typical target of apical place assimilation but also the position in which the apical contrast is generally neutralized. An instance of this sort is the distribution of apicals in the Murinbata morpheme internal clusters (Hamilton, 1996): in this language, apicals contrast with retroflexes postvocali-cally (in V_# and V_C), but the t/ʈ contrast is suspended after C's. Post-consonan-tal apicals are uniformly realized as alveolars after non-apicals (e.g., [ɳd], [ɲt], [md]), and as homorganic with a preceding apical C (e.g., [nd], [ɳɖ]). Miriwung (Hamilton, 1996) is an extension of this system: the apical contrast is realized in all postvocalic positions, and neutralized post-consonantally, as in Murinbata. In addition, the Miriwung t/ʈ contrast is neutralized word-initially: only alveolars surface initially. The observations about contexts of non-assimilatory neutraliza-tion are summarized below (cf. Hamilton, 1996, and Steriade, 1999a, for more details):

(3) Contexts of non-assimilatory place neutralization for major place contrasts:

Pre-C: [s]–[ʃ] contrast reduced to [ʃ]/_[t,l,n] (Chumash)
Domain-final: [n]–[m] reduced to [n]/__# (ancient Greek)

(4) Contexts of non-assimilatory place neutralization for major place contrasts:

Post-C: [t]–[ʈ] contrast reduced to [t] in C_ (Murinbata)
Domain-initial: [t]–[ʈ] contrast reduced to [t] in C_ ; #_ (Miriwung)

We have observed that assimilatory and non-assimilatory neutralization draw the same distinctions between contexts but that these distinctions are contrast specific. Major C-place contrasts are shielded in pre-V position from both types of neutralization.[1] The apical contrast, on the other hand, is shielded, again from both forms of neutralization, in the post-V context, while post-C and initial apicals are potential targets to both processes. The task before us is to provide an expla-nation for this systematic pattern and a framework for its phonological analysis.

The gist of the argument developed is that both varieties of neutralization select their targets on the basis of a hierarchy of perceived similarity between the input and output strings. One key assumption is that the perception of phonological similarity is influenced by auditory factors such as the availability of cues to the relevant contrast: the terms of poorly cued contrasts being more similar than those of a better cued contrast. The comparison between major place and apical contrasts is revealing because we know independently that their perceptual correlates have a different contextual distribution: this perceptual difference matches observed differences in neutralization and assimilation patterns. A more general principle emerges from the comparison between apical and major place assimilation: *assimilation for any feature F targets positions in which the F contrast, if realized, would be less salient.*

Perceptual factors identify not only the direction of assimilation but also the likelihood that it will occur at all; we observe that different CC clusters give rise to considerably different rates of place assimilation, depending again on the salience of place contrasts in each one of the cluster's components. Assimilation is infrequent in cases where each C carries cues that allow a reliable identification of its place category; assimilation is prevalent if one C lacks its primary place correlates. Taken together, the observations about predictability of direction and incidence in assimilation suggest the hypothesis in (5):

(5) Perceptual similarity to input:

> The likelihood that a lexical representation R will be realized as modified R' is
> a function of the perceived similarity between R and R'.

Thus, if [n] in a sequence /anpa/ is confusable with [m], then the lexical representation /anpa/ is similar to an assimilated variant [ampa]; then regressive assimilation is likely. If a progressively assimilated variant [anta] is perceived as more dissimilar to the lexical form /anpa/, then progressive assimilation is correspondingly less likely. Finally, if neither [n] is perceived as similar to [m] nor [p] to [t] in the original /anpa/, then neither form of place assimilation is likely to occur. The reference to *perceived* similarity in (5) is meant to convey the central idea here: that perceptual factors — among them cue distribution — play a critical role in defining degrees of similarity between lexical forms and their conceivable modifications.

Although the focus here is on establishing the link between cue distribution, assimilatory direction, and rates of assimilation, this chapter touches also on the form taken by speakers' knowledge of similarity and the evidence that this knowledge has consequences for grammatical organization.

II. MAJOR PLACE ASSIMILATION

The initial evidence for linking assimilatory direction to perceptibility in regressive place assimilation comes form studies by Fujimura *et al.* (1978), Ohala (1990), and Jun (1995). The first two works have established selective attention on the part of speakers to release-related cues to place (CV transitions) to the detriment of transitional place cues clustered at the onset of closure (VC transitions). In stimuli containing an interlude with the duration of a single C and contradictory place cues (VC transitions excised from one C; CV transitions excised from another; no burst) listeners identify the C on the basis of CV transitions. Longer interludes allow the hearer to interpret the contradictory information as evidence of a heterorganic CC cluster. However, as the interlude duration decreases, the interpretation shifts to a single C and this sets the stage for a forced choice between conflicting place cues. In this forced choice, the CV transitions are given preference over VC transitions. It is just the CV transitions alone, without the burst, that can have this effect (Fujimura *et al.*, 1978).

A further detail makes it likely that we are dealing here with a language-independent perceptual bias that can be safely invoked in explaining crosslinguistic patterns. Fujimura and colleagues compared the performance of Japanese and English subjects, based on the observation that Japanese phonotactics make the VC transitions redundant; in careful speech, all Japanese coda C's are homorganic with following onsets. The CV transitions, on the other hand, are indispensible for the identification of word-initial place features. Therefore, the Japanese phonotactics may train the speakers to ignore VC transitions; this may be the language-specific, phonological origin of the CV dominance effect. But in English there is a much smaller asymmetry between pre- and postvocalic C's with respect to the range of place contrasts: place features contrast in stops in all positions. Therefore, as the English subjects displayed exactly the same bias in favor of the CV transitions, their behavior cannot be attributed to the effect of language-specific phonotactics.

Fujimura's experiment thus settled, for this case, the issue of phonotactically dependent perception biases and allowed a direct comparison of the relative contribution of CV and VC transitions, independently of information present in bursts. Further, it showed that the CV-bias does not have an articulatory basis; when played backwards, the stimuli were processsed in the same way, with the CV transitions (now originating as VC transitions) dominating the percept again. This means that the effect of CV transitions could not have been due to an asymmetry in coarticulation. This result invites one to speculate then that major place assimilation targets C_1 in VC_1C_2V simply because C_1's place cues are less well attended to and hence a place-modified C_1 is a lesser departure from the input than an altered C_2.

The notion that assimilation asymmetries have a perceptual basis is further supported by the observation that manner classes differ in their propensity to assimilate in ways that mirror confusion rates for place features. Kohler (1990) notes that nasals are more likely to assimilate than stops, and stops in turn are more likely than fricatives, an observation confirmed by Jun's (1995) survey. Thus, final [bn] in German assimilates progressively to [bm] (*haben* [habm̩]), but final [pt] does not (*liebt* [li:pt], *[li:tt][2]). Medial [t] assimilates to a following obstruent (*mitbringen* [mipbriŋən]) but [s] does not (*Ausfahrt* *[auffaːrt]). The correspondence between place assimilability and rates of place confusion was later established by Hura *et al.* (1992), who presented listeners with word sequences of the form $XVC_1\#C_2VY$, where C_1 varied between a stop, a nasal, and a fricative, and C_2 was a heterorganic stop. The resulting misperception rates display the hierarchy nasals > stops > fricatives, with nasals being the most confusable class. Kohler's and Hura *et al.*'s studies suggest that both the incidence of assimilation and its direction are controlled by perceptibility differences. We return to this point below.

However, if we limit our attention to major place assimilation, three interpretations of the directionality data are possible, as outlined by Fujimura *et al.* (1978). The first possibility is that the CV transitions are dominant in the perception of major place contrasts, but not necessarily for other contrasts; this is the contrast-specific interpretation of perceptibility differences that I pursue here. A different view has become the standard syllable-based interpretation (cf. Jun, 1995, and Beckman, 1998): assimilation is regressive because the target C_1 is a coda and the trigger C_2 an onset. Perceptibility is controlled by syllable position because listeners pay more attention to onsets than to codas. Finally, the third possible interpretation is that the information encoded in C_2 is dominant simply because C_2 is more recent.

The contrast-specific account of assimilation predicts that assimilation will work regressively only for features cued primarily by CV transitions. Progressive assimilation is not ruled out; indeed, it is predicted for any feature cued mainly by VC transitions. Since C_2 in a VC_1C_2V sequence lacks the VC transitions and C_1 possesses them, assimilation for any features cued by VC transitions should target C_2. In contrast, the syllable-based and the recency accounts of regressive assimilation do not differentiate among feature types, or at least do not do so on the basis of cue distribution: there is no reason why it should be major place features, and not others, that spread from onsets to codas or from more to less recent C's. Both these accounts lead one to expect, wrongly, that all forms of local intervocalic assimilation will be regressive, regardless of the feature involved.

III. APICAL ASSIMILATION

We turn now to the t/ṭ apical contrast. The reason to consider this case is that cues to the t/ṭ distinction lie primarily in the VC transitions, as noted by Ladefoged & Maddieson (1986, p. 12), Dave (1976) for Gujarati, Stevens & Blumstein (1975) for Hindi, and Bhat (1973, p. 235) in a crosslinguistic survey of retroflexion. The VC transitions preceding retroflexes point to distinctively low F3, F4 values relative to those of dentialveolars: typical F3 loci are at 1800 Hz for retroflexes,

2700 Hz for dentialveolars; F4 loci at 2750 for retroflexes and 3500 Hz for dentialveolars (based on Gooniyandi data reported by McGregor, 1990, and Gujarati data in Dave, 1976). In contrast, the CV transitions of the two classes are similar or indistinguishable.[3] There is a clear articulatory explanation for this asymmetry: during the retroflex closure, the tongue tip slides forward; at release, it reaches a site nearly identical to that of an apicoalveolar (Butcher, 1995; Henderson, 1997). Therefore, the release-related cues, including the CV transitions, are misleading if both apicals are released from the same constriction point.

The VC transitions are not the only acoustic properties distinguishing retroflexes from alveolars. Thus, Anderson & Maddieson (1994) show that Tiwi [t] and [ʈ] are distinguished by closure duration (shorter for [ʈ]), VOT values (shorter for [ʈ]), and burst amplitude (lower for [ʈ]). Similarly, Dart (1991, p. 127) finds that the t/ʈ contrast of Malayalam involves small differences in VOT values (shorter for [ʈ]). Some of these properties may serve as cues for the t/ʈ distinction in initial and post-C position: for languages like Hindi, where the apical contrast is maintained initially and after C's, this is a necessary assumption.

This said, the data reviewed thus far suggest two differences between the perception of the apical contrast and that of major place contrasts. First, it suggests a reversal in the status of CV and VC transitions in the perception of apical classes relative to the role of transitions in the perception of major place contrasts: VC transitions provide unambiguous information distinguishing among apical classes, in contrast to the CV transitions. By contrast, we have seen earlier that the CV transitions dominate in the perception of major place categories. Second, if transitions represent the main source of place information, then apical contrasts differ from major place contrasts in yet another way: apicals should be more confusable in the absence of VC transitions than major place classes should be in the absence of CV transitions. That is because the apicals' CV transitions are ambiguous, whereas the VC transitions of major class categories are not, in most vocalic contexts. This second point is borne out informally by scores of Australianists who report their inability to distinguish auditorily among initial apicals.[4] By contrast, few, if any, field workers report difficulties in distinguishing postvocalic unreleased [p˺] from [t˺] and from [k˺]. A more rigorous confirmation of this point comes from the results of Anderson's (1997) perceptual confusion experiment with speakers of Western Arrente. Anderson compared rates of identification of the medial C in aCə words and in Cə word fragments extracted from aCə; the identification rates were similar in the two conditions for labials, velars, and laminals, but listeners' performance dropped to chance levels in distinguishing t/ʈ in the truncated Cə fragments. More interestingly, the rates of apical confusion reported in Anderson's experiment far exceed the rates of confusion among major place classes ([p], [k], coronals) reported in a symmetrical experiment by Ohala

& Ohala (1998), in which listeners had to identify Hindi consonants based on VC stimuli with bursts excised. Ohala & Ohala's aC stimuli — the closest symmetric counterparts to Anderson's Arrernte Cə stimuli — showed that labials, velars, and coronals as a class continued to be reliably identified (although loss of release caused confusion between [tʃ] and [t]).[5]

Thus, if the relative perceptibility of place distinctions determines (a) the sites of non-assimilatory place neutralization, (b) the direction of assimilation, and (c) the incidence of place assimilation, then we predict (a) that apicals will have place distinctions neutralized typically in initial and post-C contexts, where they lack VC transitions, (b) that apical assimilation will be triggered by the better-cued C_1 and undergone by the poorly cued C_2 in VC_1C_2V sequences, and (c) that progressive place assimilation will be considerably more common in apical clusters (where C_2 lacks reliable transitional cues) than any form of place assimilation should be in non-apical clusters (where C_1 continues to be identifiable, after at least some V's).

These points are verified below, beginning with the predictions concerning place neutralization in apicals. This process targets mainly contexts lacking VC transitions: initial and post-C positions. The main trends observed in the distribution of apical neutralization are summarized below.

(6) Patterns of apical neutralization:

  (a) **The Law**: if the t/ʈ contrast occurs in a language, it occurs after V.

  (b) **The General Case**: t/ʈ contrast *only* after V.

  (c) **The Initial Deviation**: t/ʈ contrast only after V and in #__
       (e.g., Djinang; Waters, 1979).

  (d) **The I-Deviation**: t/ʈ contrast after central and back V; reduced to [t]
       after [i] (e.g., Maʈuʈuniʈa; Dench, 1995).

The generalization in (6a) is self-explanatory; the context of optimal perceptibility for apical subtypes is after a vowel. This is also the first context where the contrast surfaces, if it occurs at all. Neutralization in all other contexts is widespread (6b). The initial deviation (6c) is a general effect, not specific to this contrast and will not concern us further here (cf. Steriade, 2000). The i-deviation (6d) is more revealing for a perceptually based analysis: in at least some languages, iC transitions do not distinguish clearly t/ʈ (Dave, 1976, p. 103), and it/iʈ confusions have been reported (Ohala & Ohala, 1998). The cause of this is the conflict between the gesture of tongue body fronting and raising (for [i]) and the curling back of the tongue tip required for [ʈ]: if the conflict is resolved in [i]'s favor, the result is a diminished retroflexion gesture and thus a perceptually reduced t/ʈ contrast.[6] Thus, not only the general law regarding the context of apical neutralization but also the details support a link between differential perceptibility and the selection of neutralization targets.

The patterns of apical assimilation support the same view. There are a number of clear generalizations that can be supported regarding the direction of assimilation in this case. Beginning with the best-documented and most striking one, place assimilation is progressive in the vast majority of apical clusters, and it is 100% progressive in apical clusters that belong to the same word and are of identical stricture level (both stops, or both fricatives, or both nasals, or both liquids). The Appendix summarizes relevant cases. Major points are outlined as follows.

(7) Patterns of inter-apical assimilation:

    (a) **The Law**:   all else equal, assimilation is progressive in apical clusters.

    (b) **Final deviation**:   assimilation may be regressive across the boundary of content words; for example, Sanskrit (Allen, 1962) and Punjabi (Malik, 1995).

    (c) **Nasal deviation**:   assimilation may be regressive in nasal-stop clusters, for example, Sanskrit (Allen, 1962) and Malayalam (Asher & Kumari, 1997).

The data in the Appendix show that progressive assimilation is encountered with clusters of identical or different stricture, in retroflex+dentialveolar as well as dentialveolar+retroflex sequences. The latter are harder to document, because retroflexes are rare in suffixes, but enough relevant cases occur to ensure that what we analyze as progressive assimilation (i.e., [ʈt] → [ʈʈ], [tʈ] → [tt]) cannot be reanalyzed as a retroflex-dominance effect ([tt] → [ʈʈ], [tʈ] → [ʈʈ]). The two deviations noted in (7) are systematic. The final deviation (7b) indicates the attested possibility that a word-initial C will trigger regressive assimilation. This effect may be invariant, and it is likely to reflect contrast-independent factors, as it has counterparts in hiatus resolution (Casali, 1996): word-initial segments, whether poorly cued or not, are more likely to be invariant. The nasal deviation (7c) records the occasional occurrence of regressive inter-apical assimilation in nasal+stop clusters. This can be attributed to the fact that F3 is attenuated by nasal zeroes: since F3 is a diagnostic value for the alveolar/retroflex distinction, this means that in an apical+apical cluster where C_1 is a nasal and C_2 is a stop, there may be no constant perceptual advantage of C_1 over C_2, as there is in other heterorganic apical clusters. The variable direction of assimilation in N-stop clusters may be tied to this fact.

The overall number of apical assimilations attested is small, but the trend is very clear. If there is assimilation in word-internal apical clusters with identical manner, the direction is exclusively progressive. The direction is predominantly progressive also in clusters of apicals with different manner: word-internally, regressive assimilation is documented only among nasal-stop clusters.

Returning to points made at the outset, I note that the direction of place assimilation is contrast-specific. Apical assimilation targets C_2 while major place assimilation targets C_1. In both cases the consonant undergoing F-assimilation — for any F — possesses fewer or weaker F cues. This generalization poses an analytical challenge: if the synchronic analysis of individual systems is to reflect crosslinguistic markedness properties, then the analysis of assimilation must succeed in identifying its targets on the basis of *relatively reduced perceptibility*. The question is how, and whether, to build this notion into a synchronic analysis.

IV. LIKELIHOOD OF ASSIMILATION

However, before addressing the formal issue, I verify a different prediction of the central hypothesis in (5): assimilation should affect more frequently clusters in which place features are not reliably identified in one component of the sequence, less frequently clusters where both components are reliably cued. This conjecture extends Kohler's (1990) and Hura *et al.*'s (1992) ideas to systems in which both apical and major place assimilation can in principle occur.

A source of relevant data is Hamilton's (1996) survey of morpheme internal phonotactics in 115 Australian languages. This represents the largest known group of languages contrasting t/ʈ and thus allows a comparison between rates of apical vs. major place assimilation. Hamilton's survey contains 76 relevant languages: these permit CC clusters and contrast apical types in some contexts. In this group, we observe first that apical clusters are virtually always homorganic, in contrast to clusters consisting of apicals and non-apicals. Second, assimilation between apical in C_1 and non-apical in C_2 is uncommon and implied by all other assimilation types: if any unassimilated CC is allowed, that sequence consists of apical+non-apical. A further heterorganic cluster that occurs frequently in Hamilton's corpus is that consisting of a palatal in C_1 and a non-coronal in C_2. The least common unassimilated sequence are the apical clusters. The count in (8) substantiates these points. The languages are grouped by types of heterorganic CC clusters they permit morpheme internally, with the * sign marking impermissible heterorganic clusters in a given language group. All but one language permit homorganic CC sequences: languages listed as disallowing all heterorganic clusters, permit homorganic NC, LC.

(8) Incidence of heterorganic cluster types in Hamilton's (1996)
     Australian corpus:

Number of languages	Apical+ non-apical (e.g., ŋp, np, nk, ŋk)	Palatal+C (e.g., ɲp, ʎk)	Non-apical+C (e.g., mk, ʈp, mc, ŋp)	Apical+apical (e.g., ɳt, nʈ, ɭn, ɳl)
2 (3%)	*	*	*	*
12 (15%)	√	*	*	*
40 (53%)	√	√	*	*
21 (28%)	√	√	√	*
1 (1%)	√	√	√	√

The first striking fact in these data is the near-absence of heterorganic apical clusters. We ask first whether this fact has an articulatory basis: perhaps the only clusters avoided in this corpus are those in which two successive C's engage the same active articulator. But this cannot be the reason: in apical+laminal clusters (e.g., [nʈ], [lʈ] [ɳc]), the tongue blade must form in quick succession two distinct constrictions. Yet these heterorganic clusters occur in 49 (64%) of the 76 languages, frequently yielding contrasts of the form [nt]–[nc], [ɳʈ]–[ɳc], [nt]–[nʈ], [ɳʈ]–[ɳʈ]. Conversely, a retroflex+alveolar (e.g. [ɳt]) should pose no articulatory difficulty, as its trajectory is similar to that involved in a single retroflex: recall that the tongue tip reaches a site close to the alveolar region anyway by the end of the retroflex closure. But in fact, the only retroflex+alveolar cluster in the corpus, [ɳt], is reported in only one language, Nyigina, and its status remains debatable according to Hamilton.

     The factor determining which clusters assimilate is not ease of articulation but rather the perceived similarity between the assimilated output and the input. The implicational relation between assimilation of the four types of clusters identified in (8) follows from the contextual distribution of cues to place. We have seen that, for all intents and purposes, there are no cues to the apical contrast in the CV transitions. Then if a language contrasts apicoalveolars and retroflexes, this very fact trains the speakers to attend primarily to the VC transitions of all apicals, as it is these transitions that reliably distinguish apical subtypes. In this way, the VC transitions become a major cue to place — and the unique transitional cue — for all apicals, whether retroflex or not. Consider now an apical+non-apical cluster in intervocalic position, for example, [ʈk]. The apical [ʈ] is identified by its major transitional cue (the VC transitions); and so is the non-apical [k], for which the CV transitions serve this role. The place features of the two C's are then equally salient in this cluster. We predict that place assimilation is least likely to affect this sequence, because modifying either C_1 or C_2 will result in an equally noticeable departure from the perceived properties of the input. For Australian languages, this is indeed the case.[7]

Compare now heterorganic apical+apical clusters (e.g., [nt̪], [n̪t]) with heterorganic clusters consisting of two non-apicals (e.g. [mk], [ŋp]). There is a clear difference in Hamilton's corpus between these two types: the apical clusters are virtually always assimilated, while non-apical [ŋp], [mk] clusters surface unassimilated in 22 (29%) of the 76 languages. If we include in the count the palatal+non-apical sequences, then 62 languages (81%) possess heterorganic non-apical+non-apical clusters. Why this difference in the rate of assimilation between apicals and non-apicals? The apical clusters contain one member — C_2 — that lacks all transitional cues to place distinguishing it from another apical.[8] In contrast, place is identifiable in each consonant of the non-apical clusters on the basis of some contextual cue: CV or VC transitions. If cue distribution contributes to perceived similarity, then the similarity between assimilated and unassimilated apical clusters ([tt̪] and [tt], [t̪t] and [t̪t̪]) is greater than that between assimilated and unassimilated non-apicals ([kp] and [pp], [pk] and [kk]); hence, the much greater likelihood that an assimilatory sound change will be initiated for [tt̪], [t̪t] clusters. The chances of detecting and repressing incipient assimilation in the two types of clusters discussed — [tt̪], [t̪t] vs. [kp], [pk] — are thus very different, and this is reflected in the rate of success of such innovations and, ultimately, in their effects on phonotactic typology.

V. MANNER EFFECTS IN APICAL ASSIMILATION

Manner differences have an effect on the direction and incidence of place assimilation. We have seen that place contrasts are more confusable among stops than among sibilants (Hura *et al.*, 1992) and that this correlates with different rates of regressive assimilation. Progressive apical assimilation displays the same asymmetry, as observed in Sanskrit (Allen, 1962; Steriade, 1995); word-internal clusters with identical manner features (two nasals, two stops, or two fricatives) assimilate in an obligatorily and strictly progressive manner. I attribute this to the fact that C_1 possesses the major transitional cue to the apical contrast and C_2 lacks it (cf. (9a)). In this case, C_2 has no compensating perceptual advantage. In the case where C_1 is a fricative and C_2 is a stop or nasal, C_1 possesses both transitional and internal cues (the latter representing the fricative's noise spectrum) while C_2 possesses neither. Here, too, assimilation is progressive, as predicted (cf. (9b)). Nasals assimilate regressively to stops and progressively to any preceding apicals (9b–c); the possibility of regressive assimilation in nasal-stop clusters was discussed above and may be tied to the reduced perceptibility of place distinctions in nasals. (I do not, however, understand the difference between the Sanskrit and the Australian patterns where all apical clusters, including N+stop, assimilate progressively.) Finally, we consider (9d), the case where C_1 is a retroflex stop [ʈ] and C_2 is an alveolar sibilant [s]. In this case, [ʈ] could have been identified through VC transitions and [s] through its noise spectrum.[9] In this case, no assimilation takes place and VʈsV surfaces intact. One can speculate that this case is comparable to the heterorganic apical+non-apical clusters of Hamilton's corpus; it is likely that the fricative's noise spectrum alone provided place information that was comparable to that encoded in the stop's VC transitions. If so, then the members of the [ʈs] cluster were equally well cued, although in different ways, and any assimilatory realization — [ts] or [ʂʈ] — would have been avoided as too dissimilar to the lexical form.

(9) Manner effects in Sanskrit apical assimilation (Allen, 1962; Whitney, 1889):

    (a) same manner apical clusters: **progressive assimilation**

i. fricative–fricative:	ṣs → r	(jyotiṣ-su → jyotiṣṣu)
ii. stop–stop:	ḍ-dʰ → ḍḍ	(piṇḍdʰi → piṇḍḍʰi)
	ḍ-t → ʈʈ	(iḍ-te → iʈ)
iii. nasal–nasal:	ṇ-n → ṇṇ	(ṣaṇ-na:m → ṣaṇṇa:m)

    (b) fricative-C clusters: **progressive assimilation**

i. fricative-stop:	ṣt → ʂʈ	(iṣ-ta → iʂʈa)
ii. fricative-nasal:	ṣn → ṣṇ	(uṣ-na → uṣ-ṇa)

    (c) nasal-obstruent clusters: **regressive assimilation**

i. ṇ-t [nt]	expected	kaɽ-aṇti, actual kaɽ-anti
ii. ṇ-dʒ [ṇdʒ]	expected dʒaⁿṇʒaṇa, actual dʒandʒaṇa

    (d) stop-fricative clusters: **no assimilation**

        ʈs [ts]   viʈ-su

    I have been unable to locate other languages with a sound pattern comparable to that of Sanskrit — especially /ʈs/ and /ʂʈ/ lexical sequences — and thus cannot determine how representative this pattern of apical assimilation is.

VI. THE GRAMMAR OF PERCEPTIBILITY EFFECTS

In the remainder of this chapter, I consider two questions relating to the analysis of the assimilation patterns discussed so far. First, is it necessary that the perceptual account of assimilation have some synchronic counterpart? Second, what would a perceptually based, synchronic analysis of assimilation look like?

It is easier to address the second question first. To allow perceptibility effects into the analysis of place assimilation, we must adopt two assumptions, one justifiable and the other unoriginal. The first assumption is that speakers can compute relatively consistent similarity values for sound differences and that this computation of similarity takes into account cue distribution. This assumption is defended in section VIII. The unoriginal second assumption is that constraint rankings in an Optimality Theoretic model of phonology can be indexed to phonetic scales (Prince & Smolensky, 1993); the rankings we will discuss are those of correspondence constraints and the scales these rankings are indexed to are scales of perceived similarity. The idea is that if two contrasts a–b and x–y are known to differ in degree of similarity, with a–b more similar than x–y, then correspondence constraints that prohibit an a–b difference between input (a pronunciation norm) and output (a modified realization of it) are lower ranked than correspondence constraints that ban an x–y difference between input and output. What is needed is to link similarity scales to the ranking of correspondence constraints. This point is sketched in section IX and developed in more detail in Steriade (2000).

The issue of necessity — must similarity scales play this role in the grammar of assimilation internalized by native speakers? — is addressed in the next section by considering the incipient stages in an assimilatory sound change.

VII. THE INNOCENT MISAPPREHENSION THEORY OF ASSIMILATION

The argument advanced here is that the speakers who initiate assimilation as a sound change select a specific modification of a lexical norm on the basis of two factors: perceived similarity to the original form and optimized articulation. Any modification must be tolerably similar to the original, and must involve an improvement, in articulation, perception, or paradigm structure, over the original. This echoes Lindblom *et al.*'s (1995), Kohler's (1990), and Hura *et al.*'s (1992) view of assimilation as "perceptually *tolerated* articulatory simplification." The simplification, in the case of place assimilation, consists of eliminating one of the two original constrictions. The critical assumption then is that speakers exert some control over the incipient sound change — that they do so, in part, by computing the distance in perceptual space between a lexical norm and potential modifications of it. In what follows, references to *the synchronic analysis of assimilation* are references to this computation.

An alternative view of assimilatory sound change has been put forth by Ohala in passages like this:

> A non-teleological view of sound change [. . .]: neither the speaker nor the hearer chooses — consciously or not — to change pronunciation. [. . .] Rather variation occurs due to innocent misapprehensions about the interpretation of the speech signal. [. . .] [Sound change] does not optimize speech in any way: it does not make it easier to pronounce, easier to detect, or easier to learn. (Ohala, 1990, p. 266)

The perceptually based asymmetries in place assimilation reported in this chapter would be consistent with Ohala's view if the relative frequencies of sound changes that turn a's into b's matched the likelihood of a perceptual confusion between a and b. If that were the case, we could conclude that listeners mistake an intended a for a b and, if the b for a mistake is frequent, the b-forms become lexically entrenched and the $a \rightarrow b$ change becomes part of the grammar.

However, the patterns of perceptual confusion observed in the laboratory do not exactly match attested sound changes. More specifically, the experimental evidence on perceptual confusion correctly identifies strings more likely to be modified by sound change but does not match the *actual* modification. Recall, for instance, the place-confusability hierarchy nasals > stops > fricatives established by Hura *et al.* (1992). This matches observed tendencies in the selection of assimilation targets. But the patterns of confusion observed by Hura *et al.* were mostly non-assimilatory, with a bias in favor of the alveolar stops and nasals regardless of context. Thus, the greater inclination of nasals to assimilate relative to stops cannot be attributed to higher rates of grammaticalized misperception for nasals vs. stops. Nasals do tend to be misperceived, but not primarily in assimilatory ways. Therefore, bare misperception is unlikely to be the root of assimilation. Asymmetries in assimilation may arise from the fact that speakers are aware of the relative rates of confusion by manner class and by position and deliberately put this knowledge to use in their own production: they target the nasals more and the stridents less in place assimilation because they know that it is safer — perceptually more tolerable, as Hura *et al.* put it — to modify the nasals' place features than to modify the stridents. This may be an example of knowledge of perceptibility used as a phonological tool.

Continuing the defense of the optimizing intent in sound change, I consider now a different process, which plausibly involves an improvement not in articulation but in perception. Hume (1998) has discussed metathesis as a case of perceptual optimization. I would like to spell out this argument for a goal-directed sound change using the example of stop-sibilant metathesis (as in Southern English *ask-* $\rightarrow$ *aks*). Central to the discussion is the different perceptibility of place in stops and sibilants: place identification in stops is dependent on transitions and burst quality while sibilants benefit, in addition to the vocalic transitions, from the place cues inherent in their noise spectrum. In general this means that the constriction information survives, for sibilants, in contexts where it could not be maintained for unreleased stops: initially before a stop, finally after a stop, or interconsonantally. There are four different cases of metathesis seen below (data from Brugmann, 1903/1933; Grammont, 1933; Stroop, 1981; Hume, 1998; Harkema, 1999):

(10) Metathesis in stop+s, s+stop clusters:

    (a) VTsV → VsTV   (T = stop):
        rural Latin *ipse* → *ispe*; *wepsa* → *wespa*;
        Anc. Greek: *euk^{h}samenos* → *eusk^{h}amenos*
        Old Dutch: *wepse* → *wespe*
        19th cent. Parisian French: fiksə → fiskə, ɛ̃deksa → ɛ̃dɛskə

    (b) #TsV → #sTV
        Anc. Greek: *p^{h}syk^{h}e:* > *sp^{h}yk^{h}e*
        Latin: *psallere* → *spallere*
        Dutch (children): *psychologe* → *spychologe*

    (c) VsTC → VTsC
        Lithuanian: *dresk-ti:* → *dreks-ti*

    (d) sT# → Ts#:
        Dutch (dialects and children): *wesp* → *weps*
        Southern American English *wasp* → *waps*

Hume points out that, in the VTsV → VsTV case (10a), the stop moves to a position where it will have CV transitions, the preferred source of place information for major place distinctions. More systematic is the case of initial metathesis, (10b): #Ts → #sT. Here the stop is moving from a position where it possesses no transitional cues at all and where, if it were to remain, its common diachronic fate would be deletion. In cases of #Ts to #sT metathesis, a minor perceptual loss for [s] is offset by a major gain for the stop. Metathesis operates in the opposite direction in cases (10c) and (10d), where the stop is trapped between a sibilant and another obstruent or the end of the word. Here, too, the movement positions the stop so that it will be flanked at least on one side by a vowel: this too is a major gain for the stop and a minor loss for [s]. To summarize, the common types of s//T metathesis seem to have the consequence of providing the stop with the best transitional cues locally available.

    In principle, however, metathesis as a sound change can arise as a form of listener error. Given this, we ask a second question: is s//T metathesis equally well attested in both directions? Note that confusability is, in principle, symmetric: if *aks* is confusable with *ask*, then *ask* is also confusable with *aks* and any bias in favor of one of these forms requires explanation. If the sound change is initiated as misperception, there would be no reason to expect metathesis in one direction and not in the other. In fact, however, the direction of metathesis is highly constrained. Only certain types of reversal, which can be identified as perception-optimizing, are frequent and systematic, as shown both by Grammont's comments and by individual studies like Stroop (1981) and Harkema (1999).

(11) *Ts-sT* Metathesis in the Dutch children's speech (Harkema, 1999):

> Word-final   sT → Ts common: *asterisk ~ asteriks, wesp ~ weps* 'wasp'
>
> Ts → sT not found: *tʃips* 'chips', never °*tʃisp*,
>
> *gips* 'plaster', not **gisp*
>
> Word-initial   Ts → sT attested: *psychologe → spychologe*
>
> sT→ Ts not found: *spriŋhaan* 'grasshopper' not **psriŋhaan*

The same can be said about most other cases of systematic metathesis: when the reordering of C's becomes a regular sound change rather than lexical fluctuation, it systematically locates the stop in a position of improved perceptibility in its local context. This generalization fits the data in Grammont's (1933) and Hume's (1998) surveys.[10]

The metathesis data are consistent in two respects with the view of sound change presented here. On the one hand, it does suggest an attempt at perceptual improvement. Metatheses that involve no gain or a net loss of perceptibility are not systematic. On the other hand, drastic dislocations — such as *psykʰe* → **pykʰes* or *æsk* → **kæs* — are strictly unattested even when they do improve the perceptibility of all consonants involved.

These remarks do not exclude the possibility of sound change originating as genuine, non-optimizing, misperception but make it likely that some modifications of lexical norms are *selected* by speakers because they pass the two tests mentioned earlier: perceived similarity to the original form and improved functionality.

VIII. THE P-MAP

The idea that potential sound innovations are subjected to a similarity test is inspired by Lindblom's proposal (1990; Hura *et al.*, 1992; Lindblom *et al.*, 1995) that speakers constantly tune their articulation to the perceptual needs of their listeners. As Lindblom puts it (1990, p. 403), the speaker is guided by his "tacit awareness of the listener's sources of information independent of the signal," and compensates for the absence of this signal-independent information or for anticipated gaps in the signal itself. The idea central to Lindblom's H&H hypothesis is that speaker behavior is guided by a *model of the listener's lexical access mechanisms*, which draw on both signal-dependent and signal-complementary information. But in addition to this model of lexical access, it is likely that the speaker's activity is also guided by *a model of the generic listener's perceptual abilities and biases*.

I call this second model the P-map. The P-map is the repository of speakers' knowledge, rooted in observation and inference, that certain contrasts are more discriminable than others, and that the same contrast is more salient in some positions than in others. One function of the P-map is to identify the margins of articulatory freedom for the speaker: the regions of relative safety within which he may deviate from established pronunciation norms while minimizing the risk of being "found out." Thus, if an innovative speaker contemplates articulatory simplification in a VC_1C_2V cluster, it is the P-map that will identify the optimal target of simplification: the consonant whose modification is least likely to be detected by his interlocutors. Other P-map functions include identifying more vs. less salient morphological alternations (Steriade, 1999b), and generating the judgments of similarity needed for rhyming, loan adaptation, speech disguise, and in experimental situations.

One can conceive of the P-map as a set of statements, each of which assigns a similarity value to a contrast realized in a specific context. By *contrast* I mean a perceived difference between two strings, regardless of its phonemic status. I leave open the source of the similarity knowledge contained in the P-map: for our immediate purposes it matters only that this knowledge exists in the minds of speakers. Whether it results from observations of confusion rates (Shepard, 1972), or is deduced from a similarity computation, the end result of interest here is just the actual set of similarity statements. We will, however, have to assume that among the factors that shape similarity judgments, relative perceptibility plays a role: we see below that contrasts realized in less informative contexts, where they lack some of their perceptual correlates, are judged more similar than the same contrasts realized in more informative contexts. This may indicate that a deductive theory of similarity — one that attributes to speakers the ability to anticipate similarity relations among pairs of strings, without necessarily relying on observed confusion rates — will be based on a calculus of perceptual correlates to contrasts, rather than on a calculus of distinctive features. The following P-map fragment in (12) illustrates this hypothesis. The vertical axis lists segmental contrasts generated by anteriority differences among apicals (t/ṭ, s/ṣ, n/ṇ, etc.). The horizontal axis lists six of the contexts where each of these sounds might in principle occur: the contexts are arrayed from left to right in the order of the number and likely weight of potential cues to retroflexion available in each position. The cells thus defined are labeled with characters whose sizes code hypothesized similarity values: larger characters stand for contrasts assumed to be less similar, hence more salient.

(12) Hypothetical P-map fragment: similarity of apical pairs by context:

	V_V	V_#	V_C	#_V	C_V	C_C
s/ʂ	S/ʂ	S/ʂ	s/ʂ	s/ʂ	s/ʂ	s/ʂ
t/ʈ	t/ʈ	t/ʈ	t/ʈ	t/ʈ	t/ʈ	t/ʈ
n/ɳ	n/ɳ	n/ɳ	n/ɳ	n/ɳ	n/ɳ	n/ɳ

Letter size reflects hypthesized similarity: bigger letter = less similar pair.

A number of basic observations, all independent of the issue of assimilation, lead one to postulate the P-map. I outline these below.

A. Poetic Equivalence and the P-Map

Speakers can provide relatively consistent judgments of sound similarity, in experimental situations or in versification. Some similarity judgments are reflected by linguistic mechanisms already in place but others cannot be so understood. Thus, *cumulative* similarity effects — for example, the fact that [ɪn]–[ɛn] is a more similar pair than [ɪn]–[ɛd] — are explained by any framework that uses the features [±high] and [±nasal]. On the other hand, if the pair [ɪm]–[ɪn] emerges as systematically more similar than [ɪb]–[ɪd], then some supplement to distinctive feature theory is needed to record the judgment, as the same feature of labiality separates [b]–[d] and [m]–[n].

The perceptual similarity literature and the literature on poetic uses of similarity contain enough examples of the second sort to suggest that knowledge of similarity does not emerge straightforwardly from the feature count. English rhyming practices (Zwicky, 1976) disregard place of articulation differences in final nasals much more frequently than in final stops, revealing that [ɪm]–[ɪn] is indeed judged more similar than [ɪb]–[ɪd]; this fact mirrors differences discussed earlier in the perceptibility of place distinctions between nasals and stops. Further, pairs of front lax vowels that differ in height ([ɪ]–[ɛ]) rhyme much more frequently than corresponding tense pairs ([i]–[e]) (Zwicky, 1976), and this effect corresponds to differences in rates of perceptual confusion (Peterson & Barney, 1951). Note that the same height difference contributes more to dissimilarity in a longer vowel than in a shorter one. A third example is the fact that the contrast between a C̆ and its absence evokes much stronger dissimilarity judgments in positions adjacent to a vowel; pairs like [drɪft]–[drɪf] are judged more similar than [drɪft]–[drɪt] (Wingstedt & Schulman, 1988; Fleischhacker, 2000). Correspondingly, poets frequently count as equivalent, in rhyme and assonance, VC_0C–$VC_0\emptyset$ pairs like *man–hand*, while VCC_0–$V\emptyset C_0$ pairs like *loud–ground* seldom function in this way (Zwicky, 1976). Something like the P-map must be assumed as a supplement to distinctive feature theory, as the latter fails to draw any of the distinctions observed here.[11]

B. Loan Adaptation and the P-Map

The ability of speakers to compute the closest equivalent, in their native inventory, to a non-native string is a further reason to postulate the P-map. A single example of this sort is mentioned here, drawing on research by Silverman (1992) into loan adaptation patterns from English into Cantonese. The case of interest to us is a similarity ranking between two contrasts: stop vs. zero and [s] vs. zero. This ranking is revealed by the different treatment of sibilants and stops in complex syllable margins. Sibilants surface in all contexts, including in pre-obstruent onsets and post-obstruent codas: *stamp* is borrowed as [sitʰam], *tips* as [tʰipsi], *forecast* as [fokʰasi]. Stops, in contrast, surface only when adjacent — in the English word — to a vowel or liquid: *post* becomes [pʰosi], not *[pʰosit(i)], *lift* [lip], not *[liptʰi] or [lipʰit(i)]. An optimality-theoretic analysis of these data will treat sibilant recovery (formalized as context-free MAX(strident)) as undominated; but corresponding faithfulness conditions for stops must rank lower and must depend on the input context. In particular, MAX(stop)/C_# ranks below DEP (cf. *lift* → [lip]) and below Contiguity (cf. *post* → [posi]). But both DEP and Contiguity are outranked by MAX (strident) (*stamp* → [sitʰam]). The different ranking of various MAX(C) constraints suggests that contrasts between different segment classes and Ø have different similarity values. I summarize this point below using the notation in (12).

(13) P-map reflecting the treatment of two C/Ø contrasts in Cantonese loans:

	_ (L)V	V(L)_	#_T	VN_	T_#
s/Ø	s/Ø	s/Ø	s/Ø	s/Ø	s/Ø
T/Ø	T/Ø	T/Ø	—	T/Ø	T/Ø

The similarity rankings observed here do not mirror Cantonese alternations or distributional asymmetries and thus could not have been projected from the speakers' knowledge of their native sound system. Nor do they reflect processes at work in English: English labials do not delete in complex codas (cf. *stamp* → [sit^{h}am]). Rather, the rankings are likely to reflect evaluations by Cantonese speakers of the distinct degrees of auditory salience of the C/Ø contrasts listed. And, once again, these ranked similarity relations do not derive from a distinctive feature count: [s] does not possess more features than [p], on any version of feature theory, but [s] is preserved in contexts where [p] is not.

IX. P-MAP-BASED ANALYSES OF PLACE ASSIMILATION

In the early part of this chapter, I had documented the fact that the direction and incidence of place assimilation are influenced by perceptibility factors. These factors are contrast specific — they operate differently for apical and major place assimilation — and thus spelling out their effect on place assimilation requires enumerating the perceptual cues to different place categories as affected by context, internal and external to the segment. In a later section, I noted that an analysis of place assimilation in which perceptibility plays an explicit role is necessary. We must explain the basis on which innovative speakers select modifications of lexical norms: a factor in this selection must be the similarity between the assimilated form and the unassimilated original. Finally, I have shown in the last section that speakers are indeed able to perform similarity computations in which perceptibility factors play a role. The result of such computations is the P-map. The final question is how the contents of the P-map can be linked to the grammar, so as to control the functioning of assimilation.

The answer is the idea that rankings among correspondence constraints (McCarthy & Prince, 1995) must be indexed to the perceived similarity of the input–output differences they refer to. A correspondence constraint prohibits a certain type of difference between a lexical form and its surface realization: but, as we have seen, some differences are more salient than others. The proposal is that if two contrasts a–b and x–y differ in perceived salience in a given language, the correspondence constraints "a must not surface as b" and "x must not surface as y" are predictably ranked relative to each other: the more salient contrast projects the higher ranked constraint. Thus if s–Ø is a more noticeable contrast than t–Ø then both MAX(s) ranks above MAX(t), and DEP(s) ranks above DEP(t). The Cantonese data discussed earlier requires a ranking of this type: linking up the correspondence system to the P-map explains where the speakers' knowledge about the ranking comes from, a fact that up to now has remained mysterious.

Similarly, assume that the t-ʈ/V_C (the apical contrast as realized in V_C) is more salient than t-ʈ/C_V (the apical contrast realized in C_V), an assumption built into the P-map fragment in (12). We are justified to suppose this, given the difference between the information relevant to apical identification that is carried by VC vs. CV transitions. Then the constraint Ident(anterior)/V[_,apical,stop]C — which requires identity of anteriority values between apical stops in V_C — must rank above Ident(anterior)/C[_,apical,stop]V — which refers to apicals in C_V. Under this fixed ranking, the direction of apical assimilation is invariably progressive. The illustrations below simplify matters by using a blanket constraint (*Agree*, cf. Lombardi, 1999) against heterorganic C's.

(14) Apical assimilation:

a./t–ʈ/ → [tt]

/pat-ʈal/	*Agree*	Ident[ant]/ V[_apical,stop]C	Ident[ant]/ C[_apical,stop]V
☞ pattal			*
patʈal		*!	
patʈal	*!		

b. /ʈ–t/ → [ʈʈ]

/-ʅeʈ-tu/	*Agree*	Ident[ant]/ V[_apical,stop]C	Ident[ant]/ C[_apical,stop]V
☞ -ʅeʈʈ-tu			*
-ʅettu		*!	
-ʅeʈʈu			

Note that we continue to predict the possibility of crosslinguistic variation in the application of apical assimilation, that is, a function of the ranking of *Agree* relative to the lower Ident[anterior] constraint. However, if apical assimilation is to occur at all, then the effect of cue distribution on perceived similarity guarantees under our proposal that the assimilation will be progressive.

The same mechanism that projects rankings of correspondence constraints from differences in contrast salience ensures the progressive direction of apical assimilation and, at the same time, the regressive direction of major place assimilation. Here I assume that the terms of major place contrasts are perceived as more similar in post-V position than pre-V, an assumption partially justified by the results on cue weighting in place perception due to Fujimura *et al.* (1978). It is these differences in distinctiveness that will ensure that Ident[place]/_V systematically outranks Ident[place]/V_ (where *place* refers to major place features), and this in turn will guarantee the regressive direction of assimilation.[12]

(15) Major place assimilation:

a. /atpa/ → [pp]

/atpa/	*Agree*	Ident[place]/C_V	Ident[place]/V_C
☞ appa			*
atta		*!	
atpa	*!		

b. /pt/ → [tt]

/apta/	*Agree*	Ident[place]/C_V	Ident[place]/V_C
☞ -atta			*
appa		*!	
apta	*!		

Note that the Ident constraints we must use are highly specific: they do not simply refer to the identity of, say, anteriority values, but rather to anteriority values as realized in specific segment types (stops, nasals, fricatives) and specific contexts. There is no question, given the data reviewed earlier, that only these highly specific constraints can characterize complex assimilation patterns like those of Sanskrit, in which the apical's stricture degree and the external context interact. The question is rather where the knowledge of this vast set of correspondence constraints is coming from. The P-map provides a plausible answer here too if we assume that any two P-map cells with distinct similarity indices project distinct, and ranked, correspondence constraints. Thus, the speaker derives his knowledge that there exist at least the two Ident[anterior] constraints used in (14) from his knowledge, encoded in the P-map, that the pair t̪–t sounds significantly different after a vowel, but is quite similar in other contexts. A complementary assumption is that P-map cells with identical similarity indices are unranked relative to each other and identically ranked relative to other correspondence constraints. Under this assumption, the learner who knows that the similarity of the t/t̪ contrast is identical to that of d/ḍ in all contexts also expects, without further investigation, that patterns of apical assimilation should not be affected by voicing differences.

Earlier I had asserted that the P-map contains sets of statements that assign specific similarity values to contrasts. One reason to make this assumption is that absolute values of similarity can easily translate into relative similarity rankings for any pair of P-map cells: this is very useful in understanding how the choice is made between multiple repair strategies for a given phonotactic violation (Steriade, 2000). But for the cases discussed here, the idea that the P-map contains not just similarity rankings among constraints but rather absolute similarity values is potentially useful in explaining the role of perceptibility in determining the rate of assimilation. So far we have employed the constraint *Agree* to force place assimilation in any CC sequence, and we have observed that *Agree* should be able to outrank or be outranked by the conflicting Ident constraints, in order to characterize assimilating as well as non-assimilating languages. Then we still need to explain the asymmetries in assimilation rates — for instance, the fact that apical clusters almost always assimilate, especially when compared to the very low rate of assimilation in apical+non-apical clusters. Such facts suggest a partition of P-map cells into three classes: those with very high similarity indices, whose terms are perceived as nearly identical; those with very low similarity indices, whose terms are perceived as highly distinct; and all others. The assumption we must make is that the correspondence constraints matching two of these three classes have nearly invariant rankings relative to phonotactic constraints like *Agree*. First, we must assume that all phonotactics typically outrank correspondence constraints projected from the high similarity class. This will ensure that the goal of phonotactic improvement will typically be pursued if the similarity cost — in terms of deviation from the input — is low. An example of this low ranking constraint corresponding to a high-similarity P-map cell is Ident[anterior]/[_apical,stop]V, which is systematically violated in virtually all Australian languages possessing retroflexes. Second, we must assume that all phonotactics are typically outranked by correspondence constraints projected from the low similarity class of contrasts. This will ensure that the phonotactic improvements, no matter how dramatic, simply cannot be sought at the expense of a highly noticeable deviation from the original. Possible examples of the low similarity–high ranking class of constraints are variants of the Linearity constraint that prohibit certain long distance reordering of segments: we observed earlier that local *ps–sp* reversals are well documented, while distal reversals of the form *asp–pas* seem impossible, despite the fact that they turn highly marked into nearly optimal syllables. Our suggestion was that this and other sound changes are missing because there is *an absolute dissimilarity limit to phonotactic improvement*: to encode this we will need absolute similarity values. Finally, the third class of correspondence constraints — all others — are the ones whose ranking relative to phonotactics is genuinely unpredictable. This proposal must remain sketchy in the absence of a model of similarity computation. If implemented, it may allow us to place realistic limits on the still excessive amount of crosslinguistic variation predicted by allowing free ranking of correspondence and phonotactics.

I close by identifying one more of the many questions that remain open in this investigation of the interplay between perceived similarity and phonological patterns. Recent work by Harnsberger (1999) and Hume *et al.* (1999) demonstrates that the perception of similarity can be influenced by language-specific factors. It follows then that certain P-map properties should be expected to differ from language to language. Such cases have not been discussed here for two reasons. First, no testable phonological consequences could be computed from the language-specific similarity effects documented so far. Second, the results of Fujimura *et al.* (1978), reviewed earlier, suggest that language-specific factors (e.g., the rich range of place contrasts available postvocalically in English) do not necessarily obliterate language-independent perceptual biases (in this case, the bias in favor of CV transitions). Cases that may eventually shed light on the interplay between language-specific and language-independent similarity factors are those in which the two types of factors enter in conflict. These must be left for future work.

ACKNOWLEDGMENTS

The author would like to thank Beth Hume and Keith Johnson for comments on an early draft.

NOTES

1. Word-final consonants undergo major C-place assimilation in phrasal contexts; here,, too assimilation is invariably regressive. The picture is more complex in the case of apical assimilation applying at word boundaries (see section III).

2. The progressive assimilation in the case of final [bn] does not invalidate observations made earlier, which pertain only to intervocalic clusters.

3. The following is Dave's (1976, p. 98) description of representative Gujarati data: "A comparison between formant transitions in vowels adjacent to dental and retroflex consonants shows that the vowels [a], [ə], [u], [o] before retroflex stops have a very clear negative transition of F3 and F4 which is not found before dental stops. [. . .] The vowels *following* dental and retroflex consonants do not show any consistent differences except that [o] has a lower F4 after retroflex C's and [a] has a significantly lower F3 and higher F2 after retroflex C's." But, although [ta] and [ʈa] CV transitions are distinguishable, those of [ka] and [ʈa] are not (p. 118): only the VC transitions distinguish the retroflexes from all other consonant classes, across vocalic contexts.

4. Some of these reports are cited in Hamilton (1996) and Steriade (1995).

5. In different vocalic contexts, the rates of misidentification went up in the Ohala & Ohala (1998) study for the coronals (after [i]) and velars (after [u]).

6. Inspection of the palatograms in Dave (1976, pp. 38–39) for [aṭa]–[uṭu]–[iṭi] reveals that retroflex contact is initiated at a point considerably further front after [i] than after

[a] and [u]. Thus the [aṭa]–[ata] and [uṭu]–[utu] pairs are much better differentiated than [iṭi]–[iti] in terms of constriction site.

7. I lack information about the distribution of cues to lamino-palatals in the languages discussed and thus cannot comment on the frequent occurrence of palatals in the C_1 position of unassimilated clusters and on the virtual exclusion of the other laminal class, the dentals, from this context. It is possible that the preceding V is heavily influenced by the palatals as well.

8. Place-neutralized apicals can occur in the C_2 position of heterorganic clusters; they do so in 7 (9%) of the languages in the corpus.

9. Cf. LaRiviere *et al.* (1975) on the noise spectrum as the major place cue in fricatives.

10. Grammont is an explicit defender of the teleological aspect of CC metathesis (although he assumes that metathesis optimizes syllable structure rather than perceptibility, an assumption that is difficult to defend in detail). Here is a typical quote stressing teleology: "L'interversion est toujours déterminée par un principe d'ordre et de moindre effort. Elle a souvent pour object de réparer les désastres causés par les évolutions brutales. [. . .] Elle ne crée jamais des monstres mais elle les redresse quand il s'en présente" (1933, p. 249). Grammont identifies a few unusual cases of metathesis (such as Sorabian initial ʃk becoming kʃ: kʃit 'shield' from earlier ʃkit, a loanword) that are said to be motivated by the need to avoid clusters unusual in the language. The Sorabian case, about which we lack further details, belongs in this class.

11. Only a subset of the similarity facts mentioned here can be accommodated by Frisch, Broe, and Pierrehumbert's (1997) model, which builds into the computation of similarity the effect of phonological redundancy. This model is an important advance in the study of similarity, but it does not attempt to encode the effects of context on perceived similarity and the link between similarity and perceptibility.

12. No evidence has been presented so far that listeners have any awareness of their own CV bias in place perception. The argument here rests heavily on the fact that listeners show awareness of *some* of their own perceptual biases: the conjecture is that the CV bias is among these.

APPENDIX: PATTERNS OF WORD-INTERNAL APICAL ASSIMILATION

		Retro–alveolar		Alveolar–retro
Language	Source	Same manner	Different manner	Different manner
Kuvi	Reddy (1979)	/uɭ-t-eʔe)/[uʈʈeʔe)] (drink-past-1sg)	/hoɭ-du/[hoɭɖu] (run-pl)	
Kannada	Sridhar (1990) Rajapurohit (1982)	/heeɭ-al-illa/[heeɭɭilla] (tell-inf-neg)	•/toʈʈilu/[toʈɭu] 'cradle' • /kaaɳ-d-e/[kaɳɭe] (see-past-1sg)	/maɖ-id-aɭu/ (do-past-3sgfem) [maɖidlu]
Urali	Lal (1991)	• /eɳ-nuuru/[eɳɳuuru] (hundred-8 = '800') • /keɖ-t-a-/[keʈʈa-] ('spoil-intrans')	• /iruɭ-ti/[iruɭʈi] (Irula-woman)	
Telugu	Kostič et al. (1977)	• /guɖilu/[guɭɭu] (temples) • /waaɖini/[waaɳɳi] (him)		
Tulu	Bhat (1967)		• /uɳ-dɛ/[uɳɖɛ] (I eat) • /uɳ-la/[uɳɭa] (eat!) • /paaɖɪ-la/[paaɖɭa] (put!) • /kaʈɪ-la/[kaʈɭa] (tie!)	
Tamil	Kothandaraman (1997)	/viʈ-t-aan/[viʈʈaan] (read-past-3sg)		
Malaya-lam	Asher & Kumari (1997) Nayar (1973, p. 41)	•/keeɭ-tu/[keeʈʈu] (hear-past) • /peʈ-tu/[peʈʈu]	(eat-rice-past) /uɳ-tu/[uɳʈu]	
Indic				
Middle Indic	Mojumder (1972)	Skt. vaɻdʰɳa MI baɖɖaɳa 'growth'		Skt. suutɻam MI suttam 'sutra'
Marathi	Bloch (1970, p. 173)	"ɭ-l is almost ɭɭ"		

| | | Retro-alveolar | | Alveolar-retro |
		Same manner	Different manner	Different manner
Language	Source			
Indic, cont'd				
Sanskrit	Whitney (1889), Wackernagel (1958), Allen (1962)	• /av-iɖ-dʰi/ 'favor!' [aviɖɖʰi] • /ṣaṇ-na:m/ 'of six' [ṣaṇṇa:m] • /jyotiṣ-su/ 'in planets' [jyotiṣṣu]	• /iṣ-ta / 'sacrificed' [iṣṭa] • /uṣ-na / 'hot' [uṣṇá] • /gi:ṛ-su/ in songs [gi:ṛṣú!]	
E. Arrernte	Henderson (1997, p. 63)	/ar-əɭ-t-an-əm/ 'see-pl' [arəɭʈanəmə]		
Murinbata	Street & Mollinjin (1981)	• /ɳuɖu-ɭɛɭ-nu/ [ɳuɖuɭɛɭɳu] 'roll-FUT'		/pan-ʈal/ [pantal] 'he/she cut it' /ma-n-ɭař-nu/ [manlařnu] 'wrap-them -FUT'
Yukulta	Keen (1983)	/mipuɭ-ti/[mipuɭʈi] (threat-verb)		
Wambaya	Nordlinger (1998)	• /RED-labaŋga/ [laba(ɳ)-ɭabaŋga] (branch of tree)		
Kalkatungu	Blake (1979)	• /ulaaɳ-ta/ [ulaaɳʈa] (sun-locative)		
Burarra	Glasgow (1981, p. 85)			/an-ɖeta/[andeta] 'strong one'

REFERENCES

Allen, W. S. (1962). *Sandhi*, The Hague: Mouton.

Anderson, V. (1997). The perception of coronals in Western Arrernte. *Proceedings of Eurospeech '97: Fifth European Conference on Speech Communication and Technology*, *1*, 389–392.

Anderson, V., & Maddieson, I. (1994). Acoustics of Tiwi consonants. *UCLA Working Papers in Linguistics*, *87*.

Asher, R. E., & Kumari, T. C. (1997). *Malayalam*. Routledge, London.

Beckman, J. (1998). *Positional faithfulness*. Unpublished doctoral disssertation, University of Massachusetts, Amherst.

Bhat, D. N. S. (1973). Retroflexion: An areal feature. *Working Papers on Language Universals*, *13*, 27–58.

Bhat, S. (1967). *Descriptive analysis of Tulu*. Poona: Deccan College.

Blake, B. J. (1979). *A Kalkatungu grammar*. *Pacific linguistics*, Series B, No. 57.

Bloch, J. (1970). *The formation of the Marathi language*. New Delhi: Motilal Banarsidass.

Broe, M. (1993). *Structured specification*. Unpublished doctoral disssertation, University of Edinburgh.

Brugmann, K. (1933). *Kurze Vergleichende Grammatik der Indogermanischen Sprachen*. Trübner: Strassburg. (Original work published 1903.)

Butcher, A. (1995). The phonetics of neutralization: The case of Australian coronals. In J. Windsor-Lewis (Ed.), *Studies in general and English phonetics*). London: Routledge.

Casali, R. (1996). Vowel elision in hiatus: Which vowel goes? *Language*, *73*, 493–533.

Dart, S. (1991). Articulatory and acoustic properties of apical and laminal articulations. *UCLA Working Papers in Phonetics*, *79*.

Dave, R. (1976). Retroflex and dental consonants in Gujarati: A palatographic and acoustic study. *Annual Report of the Institute of Phonetics, University of Copenhagen (ARIPUC)*, *11*, 27–155.

Dench, A. (1995). *A grammar of Martuthunira*. *Pacific linguistics*, Series C, No. 125.

Fleischhacker, H. (2000). *The location of epenthetic vowels with respect to consonant clusters: An auditory similarity account*. Unpublished master's thesis, University of California, Los Angeles.

Flemming, E. (1995). *Perceptual features in phonology*. Unpublished doctoral disssertation, University of California, Los Angeles.

Frisch, S., Broe, M., & Pierrehumbert, J. (1997). Similarity and phonotactics in Arabic. *Rutgers Optimality Archive*, *223*.

Fujimura, O., Macchi, M., & Streeter, L. A. (1978). Perception of stop consonants with conflicting transitional cues: A cross-linguistic study. *Language and Speech*, *21*, 337–346.

Glasgow, K. (1981). Burarra phonemes. In B. Waters (Ed.), *Australian phonologies: Collected papers* (pp. 63–90). Darwin: Summer Institute of Linguistics.

Grammont, M. (1933). *Traité de phonétique*. Paris: Librairie Delagrave.

Hamilton, P. (1996). *Constraints and markedness in the phonotactics of Australian Aboriginal languages*. Unpublished doctoral disssertation, University of Toronto.

Harkema, H. (1999). *Dutch schwa is not a long vowel*. Unpublished manuscript, University of California, Los Angeles.

Harnsberger, J. (1999). The effect of linguistic experience on perceptual similarity among nasal consonants. *Research Report on Spoken Language Processing*, Progress Report 23, Indiana University.

Henderson, J. (1997). *Topics in eastern and central Arrernte grammar*. Unpublished doctoral disssertation, The University of Western Australia.

Hume, E. (1998). The role of perceptibility in consonant/consonant metathesis. In S. Blakem E.-S. Kim, & K. Shahin (Eds.), *WCCFL XVII Proceedings* (pp. 293–307). Stanford: CSLI.

Hume, E., Johnson, K., Seo, M., & Tserdanelis, G. (1999). A cross-linguistic study of stop place perception. *Proceedings of the 14th International Congress of Phonetic Sciences*, pp. 2069–2072.

Hura, S., Lindblom, B., & Diehl, R. (1992). On the role of perception in shaping phonological assimilation rules. *Language and Speech*, *35*, 59–72.

Jun, J. (1995). *A constraint-based analysis of place assimilation typology*. Unpublished doctoral disssertation, University of California, Los Angeles.

Keen, S. (1983). Yukulta. In R. M. W. Dixon & B. Blake (Eds.), *Handbook of Australian languages*.

Kohler, K. (1990). Segmental reduction in connected speech in German: Phonological facts and phonetic explanation. In W. J. Hardcastle & A. Marchal, A. (Eds.), *Speech production and speech modeling* (pp. 69–92). Dordrecht: Kluwer, Dordrecht.

Kostič, D., Mitter, A., & Krishnamurti, B. (1977). *A short outline of Telugu phonetics*. Calcutta.

Kothandaraman, P. (1997). *A grammar of literary Tamil*. Chennai, India: International Institute of Tamil Studies.

Ladefoged, P., & Maddieson, I. (1986). Some of the sounds of the world's languages. *Working Papers in Phonetics*, *64*.

Lal, S. M. (1991). *A descriptive analysis of Urali: Speech of a Dravidian hill tribe Mysore*. Mysore: Central Institute of Indian Languages.

LaRiviere, C., Winitz, H., & Herriman, E. (1975). The distribution of perceptual cues in English prevocalic fricatives. *Journal of Speech and Hearing Research*, *18*, 613–622.

Lindblom, B. (1990). Explaining phonetic variation: A sketch of the H&H theory. In W. J. Hardcastle & A. Marchal (Eds.), *Speech production and speech modeling* (pp. 403–439). Dordrecht: Kluwer.

Lindblom, B., Guion, S., Hura, S., Moon, S.-J., & Willerman, R. (1995). Is sound change adaptive? *Rivista di Linguistica*, *7*, 5–37.

Lombardi, L. (1999). Restrictions on the direction of voicing assimilation, direction in assimilation. *Rutgers Optimality Archive*, No. 246.

Malik, A. N. (1995). *The phonology and morphology of Panjabi*. New Delhi: Munshiram Manoharlal Publishers.

McCarthy, J. J., & Prince, A. (1995). Faithfulness and reduplicative identity. *University of Massachusetts Occasional Papers in Phonology*, Vol. 5.

McGregor, W. (1990). *A functional grammar of Gooniyandi*. Philadelphia: John Benjamins.

Mojumder, A. (1972). *Bengali language: Historical grammar*. Calcutta: K. L. Mukhopadhyay.

Nayar, V. R. P. (1973). *Malayalam: A linguistic description*. Trivandrum, India: National Research Publishing.

Nordlinger, R. (1998). *A grammar of Wambaya. Pacific linguistics*, Series C, No. 140.

Ohala, J. (1981). The listener as a source of sound change. In C. Masek, R. A. Hendrick, & M. F. Miller (Eds.), *Papers from the parasession on language and behavior* (pp. 251–274). Chicago: Chicago Linguistics Society.

Ohala, J. (1990). The phonetics and phonology of aspects of assimilation. In J. Kingston & M. Beckman (Eds.), *Papers in laboratory phonology, I: Between the grammar and the physics of speech* (pp. 258–275). Cambridge: Cambridge University Press.

Ohala, M., & Ohala, J. (1998). *Correlations between Consonantal VC transitions and degree of perceptual confusion of place contrast in Hindi. Proceedings of the 5th International Conference on Spoken Language Processing*, Sydney, pp. 2795–2798.

Peterson, G., & Barney, H. (1951). Control methods used in the study of vowels. *Journal of the Acoustical Society of America*, *44*(2), 401–407.

Poser, W. (1982). Phonological representations and action at a distance. In H. van der Hulst & N. Smith (Eds.), *Features, segmental structure and harmony processes*, Part II (pp. 121–158). Dordrecht: Foris.

Prince, A., & Smolensky, P. (1993). *Optimality theory*. Publication RuCCS TR-2, Rutgers University, New Brunswick, NJ.

Rajapurohit, B. B. (1982). *Acoustic characteristics of Kannada*. Mysore: Central Institute of Indian Languages.

Reddy, J. (1979). *Kuvi grammar*. Mysore: Central Institute of Indian Languages.

Shepard, R. (1972). Psychological representation of speech sounds. In E. E. David & P. B. Denes (Eds.), *Human communication: A unified view*. New York, McGraw-Hill.

Silverman, D. (1992). Multiple scansions in loanword phonology: Evidence from Cantonese. *Phonology*, *9*, 289–328.

Sridhar, S. N. (1990). *Kannada*. London: Routledge.

Steriade, D. (1995). *Positional neutralization*. Unpublished manuscript, University of California, Los Angeles.

Steriade, D. (1999a). Alternatives to the syllabic analysis of consonantal phonotactics. In O. Fujimura, B. Joseph, & B. Palek (Eds.), *Proceedings of linguistics and phonetics 1998* (pp. 205–245). Prague: Charles University Press.

Steriade, D. (1999b). Lexical conservatism in French adjectival liaison. In B. Bullock, M. Authier, & L. Reed (Eds.), *Formal perspectives in Romance linguistics* (pp. 243–270). Philadelphia: John Benjamins.

Steriade, D. (2000). P-map effects on constraint organization. Unpublished manuscript, University of California, Los Angeles.

Stevens, K., & Blumstein, S. (1975). Quantal aspects of consonant production and perception. *Journal of Phonetics*, *3*, 215–233.

Street, C. S., & Mollinjin, G. P. (1981). The phonology of Murinbata. In B. Waters (Ed.), *Australian phonologies: Collected papers* (pp. 183–244). Darwin: Summer Institute of Linguistics.

Stroop, J. (1981). Metathesis von s en p. *Spektator*, *11*, 224–248.

Wackernagel, J. (1896). *Altindische grammatik*. Göttingen, Vandenhoeck und Rupricht.

Waters, B. (1979). *A distinctive features approach to Djinang phonology and verb morphology*. Darwin: Summer Institute of Linguistics, Australian Aboriginal Branch.

Whitney, W. D. (1889). *Sanskrit grammar*. Cambridge: Harvard University Press.

Wingstedt, M., & Schulman, R. (1988). Listener's judgments of simplifications of consonant clusters. *Linguistics*, *26*, 105–123

Zwicky, A. (1976). Well, this rock and roll has got to stop, Junior's head is hard as a rock. In S. Mufwene, C. Walker, & S. Steever (Eds.), *Proceedings of the Chicago Linguistics Society, 12* (pp. 676–697). Chicago: Chicago Linguistics Society.

CHAPTER

Perceptual Cues in Contrast Maintenance

Richard Wright

Department of Linguistics
University of Washington
Seattle, Washington 98195-4340

I. Introduction
II. Defining *Cue* and *Contrast*
III. Degradation and Robustness
IV. Contrast Maintenance
V. Experiment 1
   A. Methods
   B. Results
   C. Discussion
VI. Experiment 2
   A. Methods
   B. Results
   C. Discussion
VII. Conclusions
   Appendix A: Confusion Matrices for Experiment 1
   Appendix B: Confusion Matrices for Experiment 2
   Acknowledgments
   References

I. INTRODUCTION

Constraint-based phonologies, especially Optimality Theory and its offshoots, have revived interest in the role of perception in a variety of phonological phenomena. Particularly fertile ground for this area of phonological research is in the interaction of formal structural constraints with constraints based on economy of effort and with constraints related to contrast maintenance. Indeed, several recent works have investigated the role of perception in contrast maintenance including the perceptual basis of contrasts and features (Flemming, 1995; Gordon, 1999; Kirchner, 1997), perceptual and positional licensing (Steriade, 1995), and the interaction between articulatory and perceptual demands (Byrd, 1996; Jun, 1995; Silverman, 1997; Wright, 1996). As phonologists turn to the perceptual literature in search of the underpinnings of perceptually motivated constraints, they find volumes of perceptual research on speech cues but few experiments designed with phonology and phonological phenomena in mind. This leaves them with two choices: (1) piecing together evidence from a panoply of experiments from different languages using a variety of perceptual tasks, or (2) designing experiments to test phonological hypotheses themselves. With a few exceptions such as Cutler & Clifton (1983), Ohala (1990), or Pierrehumbert (1979), phonologists are often not equipped with the training or facilities to conduct their own perceptual research and opt for the first choice. However, piecing together evidence in this manner results in generalizations that may not be valid because the differences in the questions being asked and experimental methodologies may result in nonapplicable findings. The purpose of this study is to test two hypotheses that are relevant to phonological theory using experiments with a uniform set of stimuli, tasks, and subjects. The first hypothesis is that formant transitions in syllable onset are a more reliable cue to consonant place than offset transitions. This hypothesis is key to understanding the potential role of perception in positional licensing (Beckman, 1997; Steriade, 1995), the more general NO CODA constraint (Prince & Smolensky, 1993), or the role of perception in sonority sequencing as proposed for example in Kawasaki (1982) and Wright (1996). The second hypothesis is that manner of articulation largely determines the recoverability of consonant cues that are not based on formants: fricative noise, consonant release transients, and nasal murmur. The second hypothesis is crucial to understanding the relationship between sonority violations and perception.

II. DEFINING *CUE* AND *CONTRAST*

A chapter about perceptual cues and contrast maintenance should be explicit about what is meant by the terms *contrast* and *cue*. A commonly used though fairly limited definition for *contrast* is *a distinction that minimally differentiates one word or morpheme from another in the same language*. Phonological contrasts then are those *speech sounds* that minimally distinguish any two morphemes in a language. While this use of contrast has its foundation in distinctive feature theory (Jakobson *et al.*, 1951) and may need refining for use in constraint-based grammars, it is a good starting point for the purposes of this chapter. Implicit in this definition is the perceptual nature of contrast; when we say "to distinguish" we mean to distinguish perceptually, that is, while a phonological contrast might in principle be based on a distinction that did not depend on perceptual *recoverability*, it would in practice be a rather poor contrast and it would be unlikely to be passed on to future generations of language learners. It is also worth noting that phonological contrast is both syntagmatic and paradigmatic — a particular speech sound must be distinguished both from existing neighboring sounds within forms, and also from that pool of all potential sounds in a position that make up a language's sound inventory. Moreover, one word may be distinguished from another by the presence or absence of a particular speech sound — for example, the listener distinguishes "lap" and "lapse" by the presence of /s/ frication noise

In this chapter, the term "cue" is used to mean information in the acoustic signal that allows the listener to apprehend the existence of a phonological contrast. This is a relatively limited definition of *cue*, since much of the information in the signal does not directly concern phonological contrasts. For example, there is information in the spoken signal that identifies the speaker and the rate of speech. However, though this information can affect what cues are salient to a listener by changing the listener's attention and though it has been shown to affect word identification, it is not being investigated in the current set of experiments (Nygaard & Pisoni, 1995). At first blush, these definitions may lead to the mistaken assumption that "cue" and "contrast" may be used interchangeably. However, on closer inspection it should be apparent that phonological contrasts are built on cues; there may be a one-to-one relationship, a many-to-one relationship, or a one-to-many relationship between cues and a phonological contrast, that is, the same aspect of the signal that provides the listener with information about one contrast may simultaneously provide the listener with information about a neighboring contrast. For example, while the second formant transition out of a stop consonant's closure is a cue to the place of articulation of a consonant, it is also a cue to the vowel quality of the vowel following the consonant.

Thinking about cues in the abstract without reference to their role in the transmission of information may lead to some dubious assumptions. One unsupported assumption is that the amount of information that a cue may carry is proportional to its importance to a contrast in phonological processes. This type of assumption has led to a search for a single invariant "primary cue" without regard for robustness in noise or variability across prosodies or syllable positions

(Blumstein & Stevens, 1981). This type of research has also led to the assumption that the perceptual representation of contrasts and the morphemes they distinguish should be underspecified. There are a variety of reasons that have to do with signal transmission for questioning these sorts of assumptions. Some of the relevant points will be discussed below. There is also empirical evidence that listeners depend on an array of cues in the signal, choosing information that is readily available rather than relying on a single cue (see Neary, 1997, for a discussion).

III. Degradation and Robustness

Under optimal laboratory listening circumstances, any one of an array of cues may be sufficient for a listener to recover a phonological contrast. However, while any one cue may in principle suffice, not all cues will be equally effective in conveying their information to the listener in all environments. The inequality of cues comes from the fact that spoken language must rely on transmission through an acoustic medium and on reception of the signal by the listener. Under these conditions, opportunities abound for the introduction of noise into the process. Any event that shapes or distorts the acoustic signal or the signal reception process and bears a random relationship to the information content of the signal may be considered noise. Note that this definition excludes individual speaker variation and variation due to coarticulation, while environmental masking, hearing loss, and listener distractions are included. Perhaps the most ubiquitous type of noise is *environmental masking*. Environmental masking occurs when an event in the environment generates a signal that overwhelms portions of the speech signal. It is rare for speech to occur in the absence of at least some form of environmental masking but the type of masking may vary from moment to moment. What this means for speech is that a robustly encoded phonological contrast is more likely to survive signal degradation or interference in reception. A robust encoding involves cue redundancy, resistance of cues to environmental masking, the ability of cues to survive momentary distractions on the part of the listener, and the auditory impact of cues. These are not mutually exclusive conditions, but rather are largely overlapping.

As has been frequently noted, as more information is brought to bear on the lexical decision, the probability of decision error decreases and the ability of the system to recover from an error increases (Miller *et al.*, 1951). Information redundancy can be equated with a signal-to-noise ratio (e.g., Miller *et al.*, 1951; Sumby & Pollack, 1954), and can occur at a variety of linguistic levels in an utterance: semantic, syntactic, and phonological. At the phonological level, certain syllable structures permit a much greater degree of redundancy than others. It is probably no accident that the typologically most common syllables are those that ensure a robust encoding of information through informational redundancy (see Wright, 1996, for a discussion). As noted by Mattingly (1981), speech gestures that can overlap without destruction of information result in greater speed of signal transmission and an increase in cue redundancy, that is, a preferred syllable structure will allow greater gestural compression resulting in shorter and more information rich syllables. If coarticulation results in changes to the signal that are audible and nondestructive, there is an increase in redundant look-ahead, look-back, and concurrent information about the phonological content of an utterance. The greatest benefit is achieved if constrictions are released in decreasing degree of stricture, and constrictions are made in increasing degree of stricture. The similarity of Mattingly's preferred syllable structure and the Sonority Sequencing Principle should be obvious (e.g., Bell & Hooper, 1978; Selkirk, 1982). Because formants provide the most reliable type of coarticulatory information, phonological forms with alternating consonants and vowels are the optimal organization. The importance of segmental ordering to the information redundancy is illustrated in Figure 10.1, a spectrogram of a VCV sequence and a VCCV sequence. Figure 10.1A illustrates the increased redundancy when closure is made from lesser to greater stricture *and* when aperture is made from greater to lesser stricture; Figure 10.1B illustrates the loss of information when two peak strictures abut.

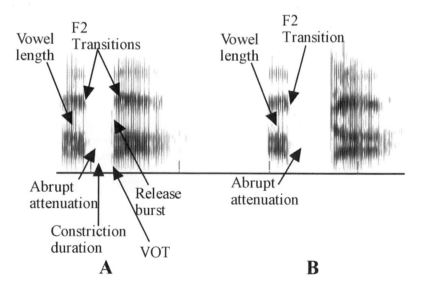

Figure 10.1. Spectrograms of the two nonsense words /aba/ and /abda/ illustrating increased redundancy in V+stop+V (**A**) as opposed to V+stop+stop+V (**B**) sequences. The acoustic cues for the bilabial stop are indicated by the arrows.

A second element of *robustness* of encoding comes from the resistance of cues to environmental masking and other forms of interference. The likelihood that a cue will be lost in transmission and reception is determined in part by its physical characteristics. It is obvious that signals with lower intensity are more likely to be lost to environmental masking (ex: weak /f/ frication vs. strong /s/ frication). Perhaps equally as obvious but less frequently acknowledged is that signals that are transient are more likely to be missed due to listener distraction (ex: release bursts). Moreover, even if a cue is not wholly lost to distraction, the relative importance of cues shift as attentional demands on the listener changes (Gordon *et al.*, 1993). Aperiodic signals are more easily masked by periodic or aperiodic noise than periodic signals are, and this has a direct impact on the type of cues that are most easily masked (Miller & Nicely, 1955). Aperiodic cues such as those contained in isolated release bursts or fricative noise are susceptible to loss or confusion in noise unless they have sufficient intensity to overcome most masking noise (i.e., unless they are sibilant fricatives), whereas periodic cues such as formant transitions are less susceptible to loss or confusion due to noise. Moreover, the more transient a signal, the more likely it is to be masked by abrupt changes in environmental sounds.

The third element of a robust encoding is the *auditory impact* of the signal containing the cue. The importance of auditory factors has been noted for some time (Bladon, 1986; Lindblom, 1990; Greenberg, 1995), but it still remains relatively unaddressed in phonological theories of syllable structure, and, with the exception of Silverman (1997), diachronic and synchronic phonological processes. This section will reiterate and expand on the points of the previous work.

The predominance of onsets over codas in the phonotactics of the world's languages has been frequently noted (Jakobson, 1962). Part of this predominance may be due to the greater inherent cue redundancy for some sounds in onset: while coda stops may be optionally audibly released, onset stops must have a release. Because of the mandatory release, onset stops may have a greater number of cues to place, manner, and voicing contrasts than codas. While redundancy alone may account for the predominance of onsets over codas for stops, other manners with little or no release burst such as nasals, fricatives, affricates, and glides would not gain the same redundancy benefit. A second benefit that onsets have over codas can be found in the way in which our auditory system processes speech sounds and complex sounds in general. Auditory nerve fibers' responses exhibit a dynamic nonlinear response that depends on the environmental context and on the rise-time characteristics of the stimulus signal itself (Kiang *et al.*, 1965; Smith, 1979). An abrupt onset of stimulation (sharp rise-time) in a frequency region that previously had little or no stimulation results in a burst of activity in the firing pattern of the nerve fibers. The initial peak response rate is followed by a very rapid attenuation during the initial 5 ms of the stimulus (rapid adaptation). Rapid adaptation is followed by a slower attenuation in response rate over the next 50 ms (short-term adaptation), settling thereafter into a steady low level of activity as the auditory nerve response becomes saturated (for stimuli at intensity levels typical of speech). After saturation takes place, the nerve fiber becomes much less sensitive to changes in intensity and frequency until after a resting period of approximately 40–50 ms. In the absence of saturation, auditory nerve response rate is equated with signal intensity; thus, the transient boost of activity before rapid adaptation and the elevated level of activity over the next 50 ms is seen as amplifying the onset portion of the stimulus (Delgutte & Kiang, 1984b; Greenberg, 1995). The magnitude of the onset response depends on three factors: (1) the intensity of the stimulus, (2) the abruptness of the onset, and (3) the amount of activity in the frequency region of the nerve fiber immediately preceding the stimulus onset. The greater the intensity and the more abrupt the onset, the greater the response. The less activity in the frequency region of the nerve fiber and the longer the period of inactivity (up to approximately 50 ms), the greater the initial response. There is no equivalent increase in response for signal offsets. This onset asymmetry in the auditory nerve response is mirrored throughout the auditory pathway as high up as the auditory cortex (Greenberg, 1995).

The auditory nerve fiber encoding of a variety of manners of consonants has been studied for both CV (Delgutte & Kiang, 1984a,b; Sinex & Geisler, 1983) and for VC word-final consonants (Sinex, 1995). Overall, the results from such experiments indicate that the onset peak is present for complex speech signals. There is no equivalent boost associated with transitions into a coda closure. Thus, one of the reasons onsets are typologically preferred in the world's languages may be due to low-level auditory processing. Figure 10.2 is a schematic illustration of the onset–offset asymmetry in response to a speech signal.

IV. CONTRAST MAINTENANCE

There may be a variety of ways that contrasts can be maintained. Changes of suboptimal syllables are among the most commonly cited types of phonological repair strategies. One of these is a limitation on the degree of gestural overlap in consonant sequences (see Browman & Goldstein, 1992; Byrd, 1996; Wright, 1999, for discussions). If gestural overlap results in a loss of information in the signal, then a restriction on overlap can preserve critical information about a linguistic contrast that might otherwise be lost. For example, in word-initial stop+stop onsets the release burst may contain the only available cues to the C1 stop; therefore, a limitation on the degree of overlap is the only way of preserving cues to the C1 in the acoustic signal. On the other hand, a word-initial fricative+stop onset, although not as optimal as an alternating CV syllable, may not need the same limitation on

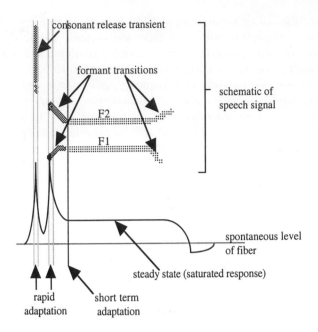

consonant release transient

formant transitions

F2

F1

schematic of
speech signal

spontaneous level
of fiber

steady state (saturated response)

rapid
adaptation

short term
adaptation

Figure 10.2. Schematic illustration of the onset–offset response asymmetry showing rapid and short-term adaptation. The portions of the signal that benefit from the boost (release transient, onset transitions) are darkened. After Wright (1996).

gestural overlap because the fricative's cues are at the peak of stricture rather than in the release. This type of pattern has been documented in acoustic detail in Tsou, an Austronesian language with a wide array of clusters (Wright, 1999). A related and more commonly cited repair strategy is the insertion of epenthetic vowels between consonants. The epenthetic vowel guarantees not only the release burst for stops, but formant transitions for all consonant types. The insertion of epenthetic consonants to break up sequences of vowels has the effect of increasing the redundancy of cues to vowel contrasts. Hume (1998) analyzes metathesis as a type of repair strategy that is motivated by perceptual considerations as well. Last, a common "repair" strategy is to abandon contrast maintenance altogether and simplify the syllable structure. It is worth noting that cluster simplification favors preserving the consonant with the stronger perceptual cues such as the C2 in word-initial stop+stop clusters (Steriade, 1982).

While repair strategies may be motivated by contrast maintenance, a more fundamental contrast maintenance strategy is for a language to maintain more optimal syllable structure in underlying forms. While there are undoubtedly articulatory factors to consider in defining an optimal syllable, the main proposal of this study is that perceptual factors play a significant role in determining the optimal syllable. The following two experiments test two of the most important claims made in the introduction of this chapter. Experiment 1 tests the claim that formant transitions in the onset provide cues that are more robust than formant transitions in the coda. Experiment 2 tests the claim that periodicity and transience affect the robustness of cues in noise.

V. EXPERIMENT 1

There have been several experiments that have probed the onset advantage using a variety of methodologies in a variety of languages (e.g., Fujimura *et al.*, 1978; Ohala, 1990); however, most of these works have compared the relative strength of codas with following onsets. Other studies have examined confusions in onsets or in codas alone without directly comparing onsets to codas (e.g., Miller & Nicely, 1955; Ohala & Ohala, 1998). Few have made a direct comparison between onsets and codas, and even fewer have looked at the interaction of syllable position with noise. The goal of this experiment is to directly compare the relative strength of cues in onsets and codas under a variety of noise conditions. Generally speaking, place cues are the most vulnerable (Miller & Nicely, 1955); therefore, this experiment will focus on identification of place. The general prediction is that listeners will be more accurate in identifying the place of articulation in onsets than they are in codas. A second prediction is that there will be an interaction of syllable position (onset, coda) with noise conditions such that coda cues will be more affected by masking noise than onset cues.

A. Methods

1. Subjects

Twenty-one unpaid volunteers participated in Experiment 1: 11 male and 10 female. All subjects were graduate and undergraduate students at the University of Washington in Seattle. Some were linguistics majors, but all lacked phonetic training and all were naive to the object of the study. All of the subjects had self reported normal hearing, and all were native speakers of American English.

2. Stimulus Choice

Natural speech tokens were used instead of synthetic tokens to ensure stimulus naturalness and to remove any confounds that might be introduced by synthesis methods. Synthetic stimuli give the experimenter more control over the stimulus attributes and have their place in experiments that require delicate and controlled manipulations (such as manipulating the slope of F2 by equal increments across stimuli). It might be argued that synthesizing a coda that is identical to the mirror image of the onset should ensure that the only variable in the experiment is the syllable position. However, it has been common knowledge for decades that synthetic stimuli are highly impoverished in relation to natural speech (Pisoni, 1981). Moreover, a quick glance at even a small number of spectrograms of the target of investigation reveals that onsets do not have the same dynamic characteristics as codas. If there is a difference in the degree to which the stimuli approximate the target of inquiry, then asymmetry in similarity to the target of the study is confounded with syllable position. If the stimulus is modeled closely after a natural production, the control of variables is lost, but an equivalent gain in naturalness is not achieved. Thus, natural speech was chosen to be sure that the responses to the stimuli were not due to the asymmetrically impoverished nature of synthetic stimuli. This does open up debate as to whether or not any results that show a positional advantage may be due to some difference in the signal dynamics between onsets and coda transitions.

3. Stimulus Recordings

Stimuli were constructed from the nonsense syllables /ba, da, ga, ab, ad, ag/ and read by a male speaker of American English. Prior to the recording session, syllable types were subjected to three randomizations and printed out as three lists for the speaker to read. In the list, each syllable type was printed five times on a separate line. During the recording session, the speaker was instructed to read each line at a moderate rate with a flat intonation on all but the last token of each line. The speaker paused for a breath between each line. The speaker took a 1-minute break between each list. The third repetition of each syllable type from the initial list was used to create stimuli. The same position from the same list for all stimuli was used to ensure the greatest similarity in intonation and original signal-to-noise ratio for all the syllable types. The speaker wore a close-talking head-mounted microphone with a flat response between 50 and 15,000 Hz (Sure SM10A) with a specially modified pickup to increase signal-to-noise ratio without changing frequency response. The recordings were digitized direct to disk at 22.05 kHz (16 bit) using Kay's Computerized Speech Laboratory 4300B.

4. Stimulus Editing

The files were leveled so that they all had the same average rms intensity as measured in the 100 ms surrounding the vowel's midpoint. This was done to ensure that the effect of noise was equivalent across places of articulation and across syllable position. The onset and offset bursts were digitally excised because the experiment was designed to concentrate on the relative impact of the information carried in the formant transitions in onset and coda. To ensure that no transient was introduced in the editing, the beginning and end of the cut-point for the excision was made at a zero crossing. The files were visually examined and played out to three trained phoneticians to ensure that no transient had been introduced. After the burst had been excised, a 50-ms period of silence was appended to the beginning and end of each file. Two levels of white noise were then mixed with copies of the stimuli. One noise level was set to be 2 dB below the rms average of the stimuli, and the other level was set at 2 dB above the rms average of the stimuli. There were six base stimuli with three "noise" conditions (no noise, –2 dB noise, +2 dB noise), resulting in 18 stimuli total.

5. Task

Experiment 1 was a self-paced three-way forced-choice task in which the listeners responded to stimuli by pressing one of three keys labeled "B," "D," and "G." The listeners were told that they would hear syllables that contained one of three consonant sounds — "b," "d," or "g" — occurring either at the beginning or at the end of the syllable. They were instructed to listen carefully to the syllables being played by the computer and to respond as quickly as possible by pressing the key that corresponded to the consonant in each syllable. They were to guess at a response if they were uncertain. There were 10 randomizations of each stimulus set resulting in 180 responses per subject. All listeners heard 10 randomizations, but a different randomization was used for each listener. The stimuli played out binaurally over headphones at a comfortable listening level that was fixed across listeners. Psyscope running on a Macintosh PowerBook G3 was used for randomization play-out and response collection.

B. Results

Perceptual salience of cues to place in onset and coda formant transitions was measured using a non-parametric measure of sensitivity, A' (Grier, 1972). A' varies from 0 (least sensitivity) to 1 (most accurate). A sensitivity measure was used because it takes into account potential biases in the listeners' responses (place in this case) by calibrating the proportion of correct responses (hits) with the proportion of incorrect uses of a particular response (false alarms). See the appendices for the overall confusion matrices used in Experiments 1 and 2.

The sensitivity data were submitted to a repeated-measures analysis of variance with *sensitivity* as the dependent variable and *consonant type*, *syllable position*, and *noise condition* as independent variables. The results are shown in Table 10.1. With an alpha level of 0.01, the analysis revealed a significant main

TABLE 10.1

Repeated Measures ANOVA Results for Sensitivity (A′) for Experiment 1

	df	F value	p	Power
Position	1	7.025	0.009	0.759
Consonant	2	13.846	<0.0001	0.999
Noise condition	2	58.189	<0.0001	1.000
Position * consonant	2	2.901	0.0588	0.548
Noise * position	2	7.742	0.0006	0.961
Noise * consonant	4	5.886	0.0020	0.989
Noise * pos * con	4	3.989	0.0037	0.914

effect for syllable position (coda, onset), consonant type (b, d, g), and noise condition (clear, noise at −2 dB below syllable rms, noise at +2 dB above syllable rms). There was a significant interaction between noise condition and consonant type, and between syllable position and noise condition. The three-way interaction between syllable position, noise condition, and consonant type was also significant. The greatest effect was for noise condition, and consonant type had a greater effect than syllable position.

The effect of syllable position on sensitivity is illustrated in Figure 10.3, a bar chart with sensitivity plotted on the *y*-axis and syllable position plotted on the *x*-axis. The *y*-axis shows a range from 0 to 1 (100% accuracy). The clear and reliable syllable position effect bears out the main hypothesis that place is more

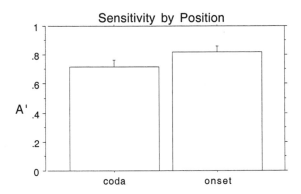

Figure 10.3. Bar chart illustrating the effect of syllable position on sensitivity. Sensitivity is plotted on the *y*-axis, and syllable position on the *x*-axis. The error bars show a 95% confidence interval.

reliably recovered from cues in the onset transitions than cues in the coda transitions. Because the release burst was removed, this result is not due to redundancy alone, but rather indicates a more general perceptual onset advantage.

Figure 10.4 illustrates the effect of noise condition across syllable position: sensitivity is plotted on the *y*-axis, and syllable position and noise level are plotted on the *x*-axis.

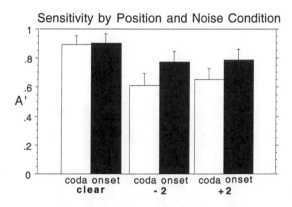

Figure 10.4.   Bar chart illustrating the interaction of syllable position and noise level. Sensitivity is plotted on the *y*-axis, and syllable position and noise level on the *x*-axis.

In comparing the clear condition to the two noise conditions, the difference between the onset and the coda increases with the addition of noise in a way that indicates that the coda is more affected by noise than the onset is. However, while there is a noticeable difference between the clear condition and each of the noise conditions, there is very little difference between the two noise conditions. This pattern may indicate that the position-by-noise interaction is an artefact of the test conditions: the lack of difference between the onset and coda in the clear condition may be the result of a ceiling effect that artificially narrows the onset–coda disparity. A further experiment with larger step sizes or more steps in the noise conditions is needed to be sure that the syllable position-by-noise condition interaction is real. Thus, while the position-by-noise interaction appears to bear out the secondary hypothesis that coda transitions are more detrimentally affected by noise than onset transitions are, any conclusions must be tentative.

The reliable effect for consonant type and the reliable interactions between consonant type and noise conditions is also of interest. Although not significant, the trend in consonant type-by-syllable position interactions should also be considered. It bears directly on assumptions, such as those in Jun (1995), that certain places of articulation are less reliably recovered than others. In Figure 10.5, which illustrates these interactions, sensitivity is plotted on the y-axis, and place of articulation, syllable position, and noise condition on the x-axis. In general, the labial place of articulation is the most reliably recovered across syllable positions and noise conditions. In general, there is little difference between /d/ and /g/ across conditions. The results were submitted to Fisher's PLSD and Scheffé post-hoc tests with an alpha level of 0.01. While the differences between /b/ and /d/, and /b/ and /g/, were significant, the difference between /d/ and /g/ didn't reach significance.

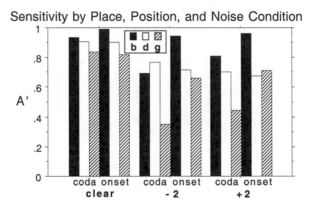

Figure 10.5.   Bar chart illustrating the interaction of consonant type, syllable position, and noise level. Sensitivity is plotted on the y-axis, and consonant type, syllable position, and noise level on the x-axis.

Figure 10.5 illustrates an asymmetry across places of articulation in the noise conditions. Both /b/ and /g/ showed an onset advantage in the noise conditions, but /d/ either showed no onset advantage or an apparent coda advantage. The reason for the asymmetry may be an inherent place of articulation difference. However, it may be that listeners rely more on the release burst cues for alveolar stops in the onset and that the removal of the burst degraded the naturalness of the /d/ stimuli more than the others. If listeners are more reliant on /d/ release bursts, it may be due to their greater intensity and lower variability across vowels than /b/ or /g/ releases (Ohala, 1990). Because syllable final stops are often unreleased, the asymmetry across place of the relative contribution of the release burst may be absent. Further experiments that compare stimuli with and without release bursts are needed to determine the source of the asymmetrical /d/ behavior.

C. Discussion

The results of Experiment 1 are of interest for several reasons. First of all, they show a clear syllable position advantage even in a language that maintains place contrasts in the coda. If this sort of result were found for a language that maintained no coda contrasts, or even a reduced set of contrasts, the results might be interpreted as a language specific attentional factor. For example, speakers of a language such as Japanese might be expected to perform worse on this task than English speakers, because Japanese contains no place contrasts for the coda that are not part of an intervocalic geminate (which would per force have an onset portion). This sort of language-specific attentional factor has been reported for Japanese versus Dutch speakers in response to voicing contrasts in the coda (van Wieringen, 1995). The assumption here is that, because English has stop place contrasts in the coda, English speakers are trained to pay attention to information in the coda transitions, yet they still perform more poorly on place identification in the coda. The difference in salience of onset and coda transitions may be a factor that contributes to the crosslinguistic preference for onsets over codas. It may also be seen as motivating phonological constraints that govern such synchronic processes as resyllabification (MAX ONSET), coda deletion (NO CODA), loss of contrasts in the coda (see, e.g., Steriade, 1995), and metathesis (see, e.g., Hume, 1998).

The place of articulation effect is also of interest. First of all, it is interesting that the results of this experiment contradict both the assumptions in Jun (1995) and the findings of Hume *et al.* (1999). In this study, labial place appeared to be the most reliably recovered. If the findings of this study prove replicable, the interaction between place of articulation, syllable position, and noise condition indicates that we should be cautious in concluding too much about the salience of any particular place of articulation without taking into account syllable position and noise effects.

VI. EXPERIMENT 2

As discussed above, periodicity and transience are factors in a signal's ability to resist masking. The implications of this for phonotactics are obvious: in general, syllables that permit all consonants to have formant transitions in adjacent vowels should be crosslinguistically preferred, while those that strand consonants without formant transitions should be dispreferred. There are further predictions about the types of consonants that are more likely to be recoverable in the absence of vowel formant transitions: the less transient and the more intense a signal, the better internal cues it will have. Thus, fricatives, and especially the sibilants, can still be recovered in the absence of a flanking vowel, whereas a stop will be more likely to be lost. It is also important to remember that one of the choices that a listener is faced with in making lexical choices based on an incoming signal is not only about place, manner, and voicing, but also about whether or not a speech sound occurred at all. Thus, although nasal place information is poorly encoded in the signal, the presence of a nasal is well encoded because of the nasal's periodicity and relatively long duration (relative to release transients). In examining the types of syllable onsets that regularly violate the Sonority Sequencing Principle (and, by extension, Mattingly's preferred syllable types), fricative+stop clusters are the most common, nasal+stop are second most common, and stop+stop are the rarest (Greenberg, 1978). Experiment 2 examines the robustness of what can be called *internal cues*, cues that are found at the peak of stricture and at the onset of release of stricture. The prediction is that fricatives will be more reliably recovered than nasals or stops because they contain the most robust place cues. A second prediction is that there will be an interaction between noise levels and identification such that nasals, while poorly distinguished from each other over all, will be more resistant to masking noise than fricatives or stops, and that stops will be the most affected by noise.

A. Methods

1. Subjects

Experiment 2 had the same 21 unpaid volunteers who had participated in Experiment 1.

2. Stimulus Choice

Natural speech tokens were used: release burst noise, fricative noise, and nasal murmur excised from nonsense VC syllables produced in isolation.

3. Stimulus Recordings

Stimuli were constructed from the nonsense syllables /af, as, at, ap, am, an/ read by a male speaker of American English. "Word-final" consonants were used to ensure that the release bursts were unaccompanied by vowel formants or voicing. The recording methods were identical to those in Experiment 1, except that the speaker was instructed to use slow and careful pronunciation. Careful pronunciation was used to ensure that the word-final stops would be released.

4. Stimulus Editing

For each of the chosen syllables, the vowel portion was digitally removed, leaving behind only the release transient /p, t/, fricative noise /f, s/, or nasal murmur /m, n/. After isolating the stimuli, each pair was leveled. For the fricative pair and the nasal pair, stimuli were leveled to a common rms average intensity. The stop transients were leveled so that their peak intensity was equal to the rms average of the other stimuli. The stimuli were leveled so that the addition of noise was equivalent across stimuli. Because the hypothesis being tested has to do with between-manner and not within-manner differences, this was seen as the only way of being able to test the hypothesis while minimizing the effect of other correlated but untested variables. It must be noted here that leveling potentially decreases the naturalness of the stimuli, and it may degrade within-manner differences that listeners may use in perceiving place of articulation. The most dramatic effect of leveling is in the fricative case, where the amplitude of /s/ was dropped to match the rms value for /f/. The leveling may also artificially increase the sensitivity scores for the stop release bursts, especially /p/, because they become equivalent to the intensity of /s/. After leveling, 50 ms of silence was appended to the beginning and end of stimuli. The stimuli were mixed with the same noise levels as in Experiment 1 (clear, +2 dB, −2 dB).

5. Task

For consonants that are stranded without any flanking vowels (for nasals and obstruents), a listener must distinguish not only one speech sound from another but also whether a speech sound has occurred at all. Therefore, in this task the listeners were presented with three stimulus types: one type for each stimulus pair, and one file that contained no information (only silence or masker noise). Experiment 2 was a self-paced three-way forced-choice task that was blocked for stimulus pairs. For the stop block there were nine stimulus files total: /p/ transient at three noise conditions (no noise, −2 dB of noise, +2 dB of noise), /t/ transient at three noise conditions, and an empty file of the same length at three noise levels (silence, masking for the −2 dB condition, and the masking noise for the +2 dB condition). Similarly, there were nine stimuli for the fricative block, and nine stimuli for the nasal block. The listeners responded to stimuli by pressing one of three keys labeled "P,T,None," "F,S,None," or "M,N,None." In between blocks, the listeners took a break while they received a new set of instructions. The listeners were told at the beginning of the stop block that they would hear syllables that contained one of three types of sounds: "p," "t," or "nothing." Similar instructions were given at the beginning of the other two blocks. They were instructed to listen carefully to the sounds being played by the computer and to respond as quickly as possible by pressing the key that corresponded to the appropriate sound. They were instructed to guess at a response if they were uncertain. There were 10 randomizations of each stimulus block in 90 responses per block and 270 responses over all. All listeners heard 10 randomizations and 3 blocks, but a different randomization and a randomly generated block order was used for each listener. The same playout and button press collection was used as in Experiment 1.

B. Results

Perceptual salience of cues to place in onset and coda formant transitions was measured using the same non-parametric measure of sensitivity, with the empty stimulus treated as a "place." The sensitivity data were submitted to a repeated-measures analysis of variance with *sensitivity* as the dependent variable and *manner* and *noise condition* as independent variables. The results are shown in Table 10.2. With an alpha level of 0.01, the analysis revealed a significant main effect for manner (fricative, stop, nasal), and for noise condition (clear, noise at -2 dB below syllable rms, noise at $+2$ dB above syllable rms). There was also a significant interaction between noise condition and manner. The greatest effect was for noise condition.

TABLE 10.2

Repeated Measures ANOVA Results for Sensitivity (A′) for Experiment 2

	df	F-value	p	Power
Manner	2	70.669	<0.0001	1.000
Noise condition	2	60.093	<0.0001	1.000
Manner * noise	4	19.041	<0.0001	1.000

The results were also submitted to Fisher's PLSD and Scheffé post-hoc tests with an alpha level set at 0.01. Across manner, the differences between 0 and -2 dB was significant, as was the difference between the -2 dB and $+2$ dB conditions. The differences between nasal and stop, and between nasal and fricative, were significant; however, the difference between stop and fricative were not. Figure 10.6 illustrates the effect of noise condition across manner: sensitivity is plotted on the y-axis, and manner and noise level are plotted on the x-axis.

One unsurprising aspect of the results is the overall poor identification of nasals. Nasals are in general hard to distinguish from each other in the absence of formant transitions. On the other hand, as predicted, nasals were much less

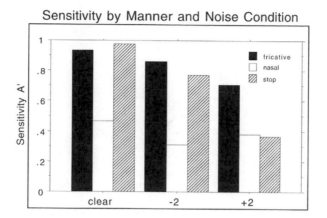

Figure 10.6. Bar chart illustrating the interaction of consonant manner and noise level. Sensitivity is plotted on the *y*-axis, and manner and noise level on the *x*-axis.

affected by noise than the stops. Somewhat surprisingly, when there is no masking noise, listeners were able to identify the stop place of articulation with more accuracy than the fricative stimuli. Although the stop release advantage may be due to stimulus leveling, it is more likely due to the information-rich nature of stop releases (Blumstein & Stevens, 1981). When the transients are heard without masking noise and when the listener's attention is fully on the task of identification, there is little penalty for transience. However, there is a sharp drop off in identification accuracy with the addition of noise, which supports the prediction that transient signals will be more affected by noise than signals with longer durations. At the highest noise level, listener accuracy for stop place identification drops below even the nasal place identification level. The lack of significance between stop and fricative manners in the post-hoc tests may be due to the dramatic effect of noise on the stop release; they range from the highest sensitivity score in the 0 noise condition, to a level equivalent to the stops in the –2 dB noise condition, to having a lower score than the nasals in the +2 dB noise condition.

To examine the change in sensitivity across noise conditions of the individual manners, a second measure was used: the difference between the clear condition and the noisiest condition (+2 dB). Figure 10.7 is a box plot illustrating the effect of noise on the three manner types; the difference in sensitivity is plotted on the *y*-axis against consonant manner on the *x*-axis.

From the plot, two aspects of the data are evident. The first is that the difference in sensitivity between the clear condition and the noise condition is greatest for stops. Moreover, there is a slight difference between the means of the fricatives and the nasals. The second is that there is more variability, seen as the height of the box, in the data for both the fricatives and the nasals than there is for

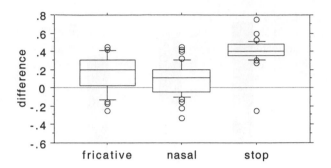

Figure 10.7. Box plot of the difference in sensitivity between the "clear" condition and the "noise" (+2 dB) condition. Difference in sensitivity (**A**′) is plotted on the *y*-axis against consonant manner on the *x*-axis.

the stops. The differences were submitted to an unpaired *t*-test with an alpha of 0.01. As might be expected from the plot in Figure 10.7, there is a reliable difference in the stop–fricative comparison and in the stop–nasal comparison, but the fricative–nasal difference is not reliable.

C. Discussion

The results of Experiment 2 are of interest because they point to the importance of considering the asymmetrical degradation of information across manners of articulation. Both nasal murmur and frication are signals with relatively long durations, giving them an inherent advantage over stop releases when a listener is not devoting all of her attentional resources to the task and when there is low-level background noise, as is the normal case for spoken language. It should be noted that even the "high-noise" condition is not greater than is frequently observed for a wide variety of speaking conditions. It is interesting that, despite being aperiodic, the fricatives still resisted the noise condition as well as the nasals. This may be an indication that at moderate noise levels the periodicity of the signal is of less importance than transience in determining the robustness of information. Without further tests such as phoneme monitoring or other detection tasks, the relative weighting of transience over periodicity remains a speculation and not a real finding.

The differences across manner should be of particular interest to those considering phonetic motivation for constraints on segmental ordering within the syllable or word. This type of finding can motivate a revision of the Sonority

Sequencing Principle: instead of segments being ordered from greatest stricture to least stricture going from the onset to the syllable nucleus, and from least stricture to greatest stricture from the nucleus to the coda, segmental ordering can refer to the relative recoverability of information, or to cue robustness. With this type of perceptually motivated sequencing, the most common sonority "violation" patterns are expected to occur. For example, fricative+stop clusters, the most common sonority reversal, are by far more common than stop+stop clusters. One nice side effect of recasting the Sonority Sequencing Principle as perceptually motivated is that this unifies several phonotactic constraints into a single perceptual sequencing constraint: segments should be ordered so that transitions from one into the next provide sufficient information for the lexical item to be recovered under normal listening conditions (see Wright, 1996, for discussion).

VII. CONCLUSIONS

The results from both experiments illustrate the importance of taking into account environmental factors when considering the role that perception may play in phonological processes and in typological patterns. Experiment 1 demonstrates an onset advantage that may be one of the factors in determining the typological preference for onsets over codas, and may be the foundation for the NO CODA constraint in OT. It is worth noting that the effect was not symmetric across places of articulation; while listeners responses to bilabial stops showed a clear advantage for onsets over codas, and a less extreme but similar pattern for velar stops, responses to alveolar stops show no clear advantage for onsets or codas. Also of interest was the difference across place: on the whole, bilabial place was identified with more accuracy than either alveolar or velar place. It may be that with more vowel conditions the velar–alveolar difference would tease apart, or that the accuracy ranking would change altogether (see Hume et al., 1999). This set of findings should sound a note of caution for those phonologists who use the findings of previous experiments to motivate phonological constraints: not all cues can be treated as equivalent. A cue that was established through work on CV syllables with no noise conditions may not have the same perceptual strength when it occurs in different syllable positions or in noise. The interaction of noise with syllable position in Experiment 1 and with consonant manner in Experiment 2 clearly indicates that cues should not be considered abstract entities; rather, they should be considered under conditions that are more like those of spoken language: with noise and distractions. Although enticing, this set of experiments is but a first step in that direction. Other variables (such as distractions or cognitive loads) should be considered before we can make categorical statements about the role of a cue or cues in a phonological process.

APPENDIX A:
CONFUSION MATRICES FOR EXPERIMENT 1

Onsets

Confusion matrix for onsets no noise

	b	d	g
b	203	3	4
d	1	180	29
g	1	44	165

Confusion matrix for onsets -2 dB noise

	b	d	g
b	167	30	13
d	4	127	79
g	2	122	86

Confusion matrix for onsets +2 dB noise

	b	d	g
b	180	16	14
d	2	90	118
g	11	189	10

Codas

Confusion matrix for codas no noise

	b	d	g
b	193	14	3
d	7	194	9
g	12	53	145

Confusion matrix for codas -2 dB noise

	b	d	g
b	123	47	40
d	9	192	9
g	86	83	41

Confusion matrix for codas +2 dB noise

	b	d	g
b	151	31	28
d	143	39	28
g	46	105	59

APPENDIX B:
CONFUSION MATRICES FOR EXPERIMENT 2

Frication noise

Confusion matrix for fricatives with no noise

	f	s	none
f	182	3	25
s	7	169	34

Confusion matrix for fricatives with -2 dB noise

	f	s	none
f	142	17	51
s	25	146	39

Confusion matrix for fricatives with +2 dB noise

	f	s	none
f	106	39	65
s	30	120	60

Nasal murmur

Confusion matrix for nasals with no noise

	m	n	none
m	139	71	0
n	133	77	0

Confusion matrix for nasals with -2 dB noise

	m	n	none
m	100	87	23
n	126	68	16

Confusion matrix for nasals with +2 dB noise

	m	n	none
m	113	86	11
n	132	65	13

Stop release

Confusion matrix for stops with no noise

	p	t	none
p	189	18	3
t	0	208	2

Confusion matrix for stops with -2 dB noise

	p	t	none
p	104	71	35
t	14	177	19

Confusion matrix for stops with +2 dB noise

	p	t	none
p	66	60	84
t	80	58	72

ACKNOWLEDGMENTS

The author would like to thank Susie Levi for assistance in data collection and tabulation, the organizers of the satellite meeting, and the reviewers and members of the audience for helpful comments.

REFERENCES

Bell, A., & Hooper, J. B. (Eds.) (1978). *Syllables and segments*. Amsterdam: North-Holland.

Bladon, R. A. W. (1986). Phonetics for hearers. In G. McGregor (Ed.), *Language for hearers* (pp. 1–24). Oxford: Pergamon.

Beckman, J. (1997). *Positional faithfulness*. Unpublished doctoral dissertation, University of Massachusetts, Amherst.

Blumstein, S. A., & Stevens, K. N. (1981). Phonetic features and acoustic invariance in speech. *Cognition*, *10*, 25–32.

Browman, C. P., & Goldstein, L. (1992). Articulatory phonology: An overview. *Phonetica*, *49*, 155–180.

Byrd, D. (1996). Influences on articulatory timing in consonant sequences. *Journal of Phonetics*, *24*, 263–282.

Cutler, A., & Clifton, C. (1983). The use of prosodic information in word recognition. In H. Bouma & D. Bouwhuis (Eds.), *Attention and performances, X: Control of language processes* (pp. 183–196). New York: Lawrence Erlbaum.

Delgutte, B., & Kiang, N. Y. S. (1984a). Speech coding in the auditory nerve, III: Voiceless fricative consonants. *Journal of the Acoustical Society of America*, *75*, 887–896.

Delgutte, B., & Kiang, N. Y. S. (1984b). Speech coding in the auditory nerve, IV: Sounds with consonant-like dynamic characteristics. *Journal of the Acoustical Society of America*, *75*(3), 897–907.

Flemming, E. (1995). *Auditory representations in phonology*. Unpublished doctoral dissertation, University of California, Los Angeles.

Fujimura, O., Macchi, M. J., & Streeter, L. A. (1978). Perception of stop consonants with conflicting transitional cues: A cross-linguistic study. *Language and Speech*, *21*, 337–346.

Gordon, M. (1999). *Syllable weight: Phonetics, phonology and typology*. Unpublished doctoral dissertation, University of California, Los Angeles.

Gordon, P. C., Eberhardt, J. L., & Rueckl, J. G. (1993). Attentional modulation of the phonetic significance of acoustic cues. *Cognitive Psychology*, *25*, 1–42.

Greenberg, J. H. (1978). Some generalizations concerning initial and final consonant clusters. In J. H. Greenberg (Ed.), *Universals of human language* (Vol. 2, pp. 243–379). Stanford: Stanford University Press.

Greenberg, S. (1995). Auditory processing of speech. In N. J. Lass (Ed.), *Principles of experimental phonetics*. St. Louis: Mosby.

Grier, J. B. (1972). Nonparametric indexes for sensitivity and bias: Computing formulas. *Psychological Bulletin, 75*, 424–429.

Jakobson, R. (1962). *Selected writings, I: Phonological studies*. The Hague: Mouton.

Jakobson, R., Fant, G., & Halle, M. (1951). *Preliminaries to speech analysis*. Cambridge: MIT Press.

Jun, J. (1995). *Perceptual and articulatory factors in place assimilation: An optimality theoretic approach*. Unpublished doctoral dissertation, University of California, Los Angeles.

Hume, E. (1998). The role of perceptibility in consonant/consonant metathesis. In S. Blake, E.-S. Kim, & K. Shahin (Eds.), *WCCFL XVII Proceedings* (pp. 293–307). Stanford: CSLI.

Hume, E., Johnson, K., Seo, M., & Tserdanelis, G. (1999). A cross-linguistic study of stop place perception. *Proceedings of the 14th International Congress of Phonetic Sciences*, pp. 2069–2072.

Kawasaki, H. (1982). *An acoustic basis for universal constraints on sound sequences*. Unpublished doctoral dissertation, University of California, Berkeley.

Kiang, N. Y. S., Watanabe, T., Thomas, E. C., & Clark, L. F. (1965). *Discharge patterns of single fibers in the cat's auditory nerve*. MIT Research Monograph No. 35. Cambridge: MIT Press.

Kirchner, R. (1997). Contrastiveness and faithfulness. *Phonology, 14*, 83–111.

Lindblom, B. (1990). Explaining phonetic variation: A sketch of the H and H theory. In W. Hardcastle & A. Marchal (Eds.), *Speech production and speech modeling* (pp. 403–439). Dordrecht: Kluwer.

Mattingly, I. G. (1981). Phonetic representations and speech synthesis by rule. In T. Myers, J. Laver, & J. Anderson (Eds.), *The cognitive representations of speech* (pp. 415–420). Amsterdam: North Holland.

Miller, G. A., & Nicely, P. (1955). An analysis of perceptual confusions among English consonants. *Journal of the Acoustical Society of America, 27*, 338–352.

Miller, G. A., Heise, G. A., & Lichten, W. (1951). The Intelligibility of speech as a function of the context of test materials. *Journal of Experimental Psychology, 41*(5), 329–335.

Neary, T. M. (1997). Speech perception as pattern recognition. *Journal of the Acoustical Society of America, 101*(6), 3241–3254.

Nygaard, L. C., & Pisoni, D. B. (1995). Speech Perception: New directions in research and theory. In J. L. Miller & P. D. Eimas (Eds.), *Speech, language, and communication* (pp. 63–96). San Diego: Academic Press.

Ohala, J. J. (1990). Phonetics and phonology of aspects of assimilation. In J. Kingston & M. E. Beckman (Eds.), *Papers in laboratory phonology, I: Between the grammar and the physics of speech* (pp. 258–275). Cambridge: Cambridge University Press.

Ohala, M., & Ohala, J. (1998). *Correlations between Consonantal VC transitions and degree of perceptual confusion of place contrast in Hindi. Proceedings of the 5th International Conference on Spoken Language Processing, Sydney*, pp. 2795–2798.

Pierrehumbert, J. B. (1979). The perception of fundamental frequency declination. *Journal of the Acoustical Society of America, 66*, 363–369.

Pisoni, D. B. (1981). Speeded classification of natural and synthetic speech in a lexical decision task. *Journal of the Acoustical Society of America, 70*, S98.

Prince, A., & Smolensky, P. (1993). *Optimality theory: Constraint interaction in generative grammar.* Unpublished manuscript, Rutgers University, New Brunswick, NJ, and the University of Colorado, Boulder.

Selkirk, E. O. (1982). The syllable. In H. van der Hulst & N. Smith (Eds.), *Features, segmental structure and harmony processes*, Part II (pp. 337–383). Dordrecht: Foris.

Silverman, D. (1997). *Phasing and recoverability.* New York: Garland.

Sinex, D. G. (1995). Auditory nerve fiber representation of cues to voicing in syllable-final stop contexts. *Journal of the Acoustical Society of America, 90*, 2441–2449.

Sinex, D. G., & Geisler, C. D. (1983). Responses of auditory-nerve fibers to consonant–vowel syllables. *Journal of the Acoustical Society of America, 73*(2), 602–615.

Smith, R. L. (1979). Adaptation, saturation and physiological masking in single auditory-nerve fibers. *Journal of the Acoustical Society of America, 65*(1), 166–178.

Steriade, D. (1982). *Greek prosodies and the nature of syllabification.* Unpublished doctoral dissertation, Massachusetts Institute of Technology, Cambridge.

Steriade, D. (1995). *Neutralization and the expression of contrast.* Unpublished manuscript, University of California, Los Angeles.

Sumby, W. H., & Pollack, I. (1954). Visual contribution to speech intelligibility in noise. *Journal of the Acoustical Society of America, 26*(2), 212–215.

van Wierengen, A. (1995). *Perceiving dynamic speechlike sounds.* Unpublished doctoral dissertation, University of Amsterdam.

Wright, R. (1996). *Consonant clusters and cue preservation in Tsou.* Unpublished doctoral dissertation, University of California, Los Angeles.

Wright, R. (1999). Tsou consonant clusters and auditory cue preservation. In E. Zeitoun & P. Li (Eds.), *Selected papers from the eighth international conference on Austronesian linguistics* (Vol. 1, pp. 227–312). Taipei: Academia Sinica, Institute of Linguistics."

Index

A

Acoustic segment duration, inverse covariation
of, 126
Afar, 176
Anti-gemination phenomenon, 176, 177
Apical assimilation, 224–228, 230–231,
240, 245–246
Assimilation
apical assimilation, 224–228, 230–231,
240, 245–246
defined, 220
innocent misapprehension theory of,
232–235
in Korean, 9
likelihood of, 228–230
major place assimilation, 222–224, 241
progressive assimilation, 220
regressive assimilation, 220
Auditory enhancement hypothesis, 124–135
Auditory Scene Analysis, 31–34
Australian languages, 228

B

Backness harmony systems, 63
Bantu languages
labial palatalization in, 148
nasal + obstruent interactions in, 153–165
phonetic naturalness of, 150–152
postnasal de-affrication in, 170
postnasal devoicing in, 143, 157–165, 177
postnasal processes and "counter-processes"
in, 169–170
postnasal voicing in, 154–157, 177
synchronic process in, 175

Basaá, 155–156, 177
Bilabial consonants, phonological
palatalization and, 116–117
Bubi, 166, 179
Bukusu, 155
Burarra, 246

C

Cantonese, 238, 239
Category boundaries, among vowel categories,
130–135
Coarticulatory variation
nasal coarticulation, 65–70, 71
vowel-to-vowel coarticulation, 58–65
Coarticulatory vowel nasalization, perception
of, 65–70, 71
Codas
perceptual cues in contrast maintenance,
259–274
predominance of onsets over codas,
256–257, 258
Consonant confusion asymmetries, 80–82,
95–100
Consonant place identification, vowel
context and, 108–119
Constraints, 104–106, 142, 252
Contrast dispersion, Russian palatalization
and, 188–210
Contrast maintenance, 257–258
perceptual cues in, 259–274
Contrast optimization, 8
Contrasts
defined, 253
as qualitative distinctions, 126–130
of weak perceptibility 7–8

Coronalization, 7
Cues, 254
    defined, 253–254
    perceptual cues in contrast maintenance,
        259–274

D

Degradation, 254
Devoicing. *See* Postnasal devoicing
Diachronic phonology, 143, 147–153, 175
Direct Realist Theory, 135
Dissimilation, in Greek, 8

E

Eastern Arrernte, 246
Environmental masking, 254
Epenthesis, in Maltese, 8
Epenthetic vowel, 8, 258
External forces, phonology and, 11–20

F

Familiarity, role in multimodal perceptual
        organization, 45–48
Faroese, 8–9
First-language acquisition, 6

G

Ganda, 171
German, 131, 179
Gestural covariation, 125
Gestural overlap, in consonant sequences, 257
Gokana, 69
Greek, 8
Gujarati, 224, 225, 243

H

Hayu, 176
Hindi, 225
Hungarian, 63–64

I

Indic languages, 245–246
Indonesian languages, 167
Innocent misapprehension theory, 232–235
Inter-apical assimilation, 227
Inverse durational patterning, 126–130
Irish, 192–195, 198–210
Italian dialects, 168–169, 179

K

Kabardian, 196
Kalkatungu, 246
Kannada, 245
Kikuyu, 155, 177
Kongo, 170
Korean, 6–7, 9
Kuvi, 245
Kwa languages, 69

L

Labial palatalization, in Bantu, 148
Language specificity, 17–20
Lawful specification, 45
Loan adaptation, P-map and, 238–239

M

Major place assimilation, 222–224, 241
Makua, 166
Malay, 142, 245
Maltese, 8
Mandarin Chinese, 10–11
Marathi, 245
Markedness, 80, 82–94
    defined, 82–83
    studies, 83–94
Meinhof's Rule, 171, 180
Metathesis, in Faroese, 8–9
Middle Indic, 245
Morpheme internal phonotactics, 228
Motor Theory, 135
Multimodel perceptual organization (of
        speech), 40–48
    role of familiarity in, 45–48
    temporal discrepancy, 42–44
Murinbata, 246

N

Nande, 155, 177
Nasal + obstruent interactions, in Bantu
        languages, 153–165
Nasal coarticulation, 65–70, 71
Ndebele, 176
Nguni languages, 170, 176
Noise, 110–112, 254
Non-assimilatory neutralization, 221

O

Onset
    perceptual cues in contrast maintenance,
        259–274
    predominance of onsets over codas,
        256–257, 258
Optimality Theory, 104, 142, 209, 238, 252
Oral–nasal vowel distinctions, 69–70
Oral stops, contextual effects on place
        identification in, 107–119

P

Palatalization, 7
    bilabial consonants and, 116–117
    of labial consonants in Bantu languages, 148
    in Russian, 189–192
Palatalization contrast, in Irish, 192–195
Perceptual compensation, 56–73
    nasal coarticulation, 65–70, 71
    vowel-to-vowel coarticulation, 58–65
Perceptual organization (of speech), 29–30
    Auditory Scene Analysis, 31–34
    unimodal auditory, 30–40
Phonetic constraints, 104–106, 142
Phonetic factors, in phonology, 104, 143–153
Phonetic naturalness, of Bantu languages,
        150–152
Phonological systems, speech perception
        and, 5–21, 28–49
Phonology
    constraint-based approaches to, 104–105
    diachronic phonology, 143, 147–153, 175
    external forces and, 11–20
    Optimality Theory, 104, 142, 209, 238, 252
    perceptual compensation and, 56–73
    phonetic factors in, 104, 143–153
    synchronic phonology, 143, 147–153, 169,
        175
Place assimilation, 220–221, 232, 239–243
P-map
    defined, 235–237
    loan adaptation and, 238–239
    place assimilation and, 239–243
    poetic equivalence and, 237–238
Postnasal affrication, 170, 173, 179
Postnasal aspiration, 170
Postnasal de-affrication, 170
Postnasal de-aspiration, 170
Postnasal denasalization, 171

Postnasal devoicing
    in Bantu languages, 143, 157–165, 177
    historical stages in, 163
    in Sotho-Tswana, 162–163, 165
Postnasal voicing, in Bantu languages, 154–157
Progressive assimilation, 220
Proto-Bantu, 162–163
Punu, 166–167

Q

Quantized noise-band signals, 37–39

R

Regressive assimilation, 220
Repair strategy, 258
Robustness, 254–257
Romanesco, 169
Russian, 131, 189–192, 195–210

S

Sanskrit, 231, 246
Scots, 168
Second-language learning, 6
Segment deletion, in Turkish, 9
Shona, 170
Similarity
    cumulative, 237
    poetic uses of, 237–238
Sinewave replication, 34–37
Sotho-Tswana, 162–163, 165, 178
Speech
    multimodel perceptual organization
        of, 40–48
    perceptual organization of, 29–30
    unimodal auditory perceptual organization
        of, 30–34, 39–40
Speech perception
    auditory enhancement hypothesis, 124–135
    Direct Realist Theory, 135
    influence of phonological systems on, 6–7
    Motor Theory, 135
    nasal coarticulation, 65–70, 71
    perceptual compensation and, 56–73
    perceptual organization and, 29–30
    vowel-to-vowel coarticulation, 58–65
Swedish, vowel category boundaries in, 131
Synchronic phonology, 143, 147–153, 169, 175

T

Tamil, 245
Telugu, 245
Temporal discrepancy, 42–44
Tiwi, 225
Tone-Accent Attraction Principle, 175
Tone analogs, 35
Tone sandhi, in Mandarin Chinese, 10–11
Tsou, 258
Tswana, 173
    consonant system of, 157
    postnasal devoicing in, 157–160
    unaspirated stops, 178
    voiced stops in, 163
Tulu, 245
Turkish, 9

U

Unimodal auditory perceptual organization
        (of speech), 30–34, 39–40
    quantized noise-band signals, 37–39
    sinewave replication of utterances, 34–37
Urali, 245

V

Velarization, in Russian, 195–210
Voiced stops, in Tswana, 163

Voiceless stops, in Malay, 142
Vowel context, consonant place identification
        and, 108–119
Vowel harmony
    in Hungarian, 63–64
    vowel-to-vowel coarticulation and, 62–65
Vowel nasalization, 65–70, 71
Vowels
    phonological category boundaries, 130–135
    production of, 124–125
Vowel-to-vowel coarticulation, 58–65, 71

W

Wambaya, 246
Western Arrernte, 225

X

Xhosa, 176

Y

Yaka, 171
Yao, 155, 177
Yawelmani, 177
Yukulta, 246